D1707527

LORD OF THE SACRED CITY

STUDIES
IN MEDIEVAL AND
REFORMATION THOUGHT

EDITED BY

HEIKO A. OBERMAN, Tucson, Arizona

VOLUME LXXII

J. JEFFERY TYLER

LORD OF THE SACRED CITY

LORD OF THE SACRED CITY

THE *EPISCOPUS EXCLUSUS* IN LATE MEDIEVAL AND EARLY MODERN GERMANY

BY

J. JEFFERY TYLER

BRILL
LEIDEN · BOSTON · KÖLN
1999

This book is printed on acid-free paper.

Library of Congress Cataloging-in-Publication Data

Tyler, J. Jeffery.
    Lord of the sacred city : the episcopus exclusus in late medieval
and early modern Germany / by J. Jeffery Tyler.
        p.   cm. — (Studies in medieval and Reformation thought, ISSN
0585-6914 ; v. 72)
    Includes bibliographical references and index.
    ISBN 9004111204 (alk. paper)
    1. Bishops—Germany—Augsburg—History.   2. Augsburg (Germany)–
–Church history.   3. Bishops—Germany—Konstanz—History.
4. Konstanz (Germany)—Church history.   I. Title.   2. Series.
BR854.T95   1998
262'.12243375—dc21   98–41127
                                                                                      CIP

Die Deutsche Bibliothek - CIP-Einheitsaufnahme

Tyler, J. Jeffery:
Lord of the sacred city : the episcopus exclusus in late medieval and
early modern Germany / by J. Jeffery Tyler. – Leiden ; Boston ; Köln
: Brill, 1998
    (Studies in medieval and reformation thought ; Vol. 72)
    ISBN 90–04–11120–4

                              ISSN 0585-6914
                              ISBN 90 04 11120 4

              © Copyright 1999 by Koninklijke Brill NV, Leiden, The Netherlands

PRINTED IN THE NETHERLANDS

For Beth
My Companion in Love and Labor,
Loss and Laughter

TABLE OF CONTENTS

Acknowledgements   ix

Introduction   1

Chapter One   The Scope of the *Episcopus Exclusus* in
Medieval and Early Modern Germany   11
   1. The Dimensions of the 'Episcopus exclusus'   13
   2. The Bishop's 'Real Presence'   19
   3. The Refugees of the Reformation   30

Chapter Two   Confrontation, Expulsion, and Cohabitation
in Late-Medieval Constance   39
   1. Pedigree and Power   45
   2. From Pervasive Presence to Periodic Withdrawal   52
   3. From Sovereignty to Stubborn Survival   60
   4. The Early Reign of Hugo of Hohenlandenberg
     (1496-1511)   72

Chapter Three   Civic Encroachment and Episcopal
Withdrawal in Late-Medieval Augsburg   77
   1. From 'Stadtherr' to 'Stadtbuch'   79
   2. From Warfare to Withdrawal   89

Chapter Four   The Sacred City: The Theater of
Episcopal Ritual   103
   1. The Ritual of the Bishop   108
   2. The Sanctuary of the Bishop: The Holy Cathedral . . .   113
   3. The 'Adventus' of the Bishop: Entry, Procession, and
     Installation   123
   4. The Bishop's Sacred City: Rituals of Life and Death . .   150

Chapter Five   The 'Last Rites' of a Bishop: Reformation
in Constance and Augsburg   172
   1. Confrontation and Conservation   174
   2. Surviving the 'Episcopus exclusus' in Exile   184

Conclusion   The Sacred City after Exile   196

Appendix A   Ecclesiastical Territories   203
Appendix B   The Bishops of Constance   205
Appendix C   The Bishops of Augsburg   208
Appendix D   Residency Patterns – The Bishops of
      Constance (1322-1480)   211

Bibliography   223

Indices   241
  Index of Subjects   241
  Index of Persons and Places   247

ACKNOWLEDGEMENTS

This book owes its inception and completion to generous support, small gestures, patient inspiration, and unyielding strength. A Goethe Institue Scholarship and the staff of the institute in Mannheim gave me enthusiastic and invaluable language instruction and initiated my exploration of German culture. This project is particularly dependent on a Fulbright Grant (1991-92), which provided the essential financial means to study bishops and cities in southern Germany. My dreams of living and pursuing research overseas were fulfilled by the kindness and generosity of these organizations and donors. My experience of German academia is well-represented by Professor Hans-Christoph Rublack of the History Faculty at the University of Tübingen, who prepared me during his visiting professorship at the University of Arizona, introduced me to the archives, guided my work in Germany, and shared with me the wealth of his knowledge, good humor, and friendship. The Sixteenth Century Studies Conference provided a forum for my discoveries on three occasions (1993, 1994, 1996). Professor Thomas A. Brady, Jr. represents the highest expression of this formidable community of scholars; I am thankful for our individual conversations and debate in conference sessions.

I am grateful to the archival staffs at the Stadtarchiv Konstanz, the Badisches Generallandesarchiv in Karlsruhe, the Staatsarchiv and Stadtarchiv Augsburg, who shared their marvelous collections and resources with me. They came through for me time and again, despite wondering what a desert dweller from the United States with Calvinist sympathies could possibly want to know about medieval bishops, their travails and scattered paper trail. Dr. Wolfram Baer, Director of the Stadtarchiv in Augsburg, provided me with helpful suggestions and literature. Professor Helmut Maurer, Director of the Stadtarchiv in Constance, was especially generous and encouraging; he helped me to articulate my project and to find primary sources and secondary literature. I still remember the moments that he, the prolific and industrious director, took time to seek me out in order to check on the progress of my work.

At so many crucial turns in the road, small kindnesses helped me to continue on and find new determination. During my work at the

X ACKNOWLEDGEMENTS

University of Tübingen Suse Rau offered a home away from home at the Institut für Spätmittelalter und Reformation. Hans Müller of the Badisches Generallandesarchiv was always unseasonably warm and smiling at the desk, giving me light and hope before long evenings in silent hotel rooms. Karlfried and Ricarda Froehlich rented their apartment to us and then became inviting and kind neighbors, discussing life, faith, and research. Michael and Ursula Pfeiffer as well as Diana and Peter Rayz made research trips possible by opening their homes so graciously to me. For ten weeks Oliver Endrikat shared his apartment and conversation with me in Markdorf am Bodensee without charge, asking only that I tell him about my findings in the archives. Colleagues and friends at Hope College have given me the encouragement and comfortable environment to finish my work. A summer faculty development grant from Hope in 1995 allowed me to make one last research trip to southern Germany. Dr. Steven Bouma-Prediger, collegial and hardworking colleague in the Religion Department, has listened and encouraged me at critical moments in the depths of the night on third floor Lubbers. Cathleen Jaworowski exemplifies undergraduate passion at Hope with her interest in my research and willingness to read the entire manuscript.

This project was born and nurtured first as a dissertation in the Division for Late Medieval and Reformation Studies at the University of Arizona. Fellow graduate students listened to my research and accompanied me on the journey from the Thursday night seminars to our homes in Europe and Tübingen. On this project I am especially grateful to Dr. Peter Dykema, who accompanied me in the graduate school experience and shared his many findings about late medieval clergy and bishops. Luise Betterton, administrative assistant, was a support at every stage with lively good cheer, organizational mastery, and firm direction. Professor Alan Bernstein helped me to rework many stages of the dissertation; I will always be grateful for his humane and compassionate guidance. Professor Donald Weinstein contributed to this project with hours of taxing and sometimes sudden editing and advising.

To Professor Heiko A. Oberman I am deeply thankful. Beyond his mastery of late medieval and early modern history, beyond his hour upon hour spent guiding our reading, writing, and communal seminar, Heiko Oberman shared his energy and fascination with us. Teacher, mentor, friend – Doktorvater – when my zeal waned and my pen faltered, you brought me through every stage of research and writing with gentle chiding, fierce encouragement, and astounding sensitivity.

Finally, this book would not be possible without the unyielding strength and steady love of my wife, Beth. She has endured my long nights, dark silences, and obnoxious preoccupations with firm commitment and a renewing spirit. Where there are hints of joy, steadfastness, and compassion in this book, she is present.

J.J.T.
April 10, 1998
Hope College
Holland, Michigan

INTRODUCTION

This is a book about the banished and the disenfranchised, about refugees who at one time had given refuge themselves. This work does not explore the tragic histories of marginal groups and pariah peoples. Rather, front and center are the lords and shepherds of the medieval church, bishops who might be deemed holy, whose fragmented bones became relics, or primates who could ride roughshod over diocese, church, and city, whose liturgical vestments cloaked a frame wrapped in armor.[1] Men of wealth, political importance, and noble blood entered the episcopate; they processed into their cities with royal fanfare, resided in lavish palaces, and erected cathedral churches that dwarfed the civic landscape. At times truly ascetic men wielded the shepherd's crook; and they fill the pages of the liturgical calendar: Athanasius, Cyprian, Ambrose, Augustine, Martin of Tours, Boniface, Thomas Becket, and Albert the Great—all were sainted and all held the office of bishop.[2] During the early Middle Ages these holy bishops appeared to embody another kind of charisma, for the spiritual power of the bishop was enhanced by his magic, his ability to declare truth, to bless, heal, and save.[3]

Whether saint or sinner the bishop ruled and pastored a specific region. At the figurative heart of a German diocese stood the bishop's cathedral city, the seignorial court of his secular domain (*Hochstift*) and the sacred center of his ecclesiastical territory (*Bistum*). In the early Middle Ages many a cathedral or 'episcopal' city drew its identity, prosperity, and survival from the bishop.[4] He was lord

---

[1] Bishops are central here, but those superior to bishops—archbishops—are also assumed in this study. The latter not only ruled over bishops but they themselves served as bishops over territories that answered directly to their archiepiscopal court.

[2] 107 bishops are among the early Christian and medieval saints catalogued in H. L. Keller's *Reclams Lexikon der Heiligen und der biblischen Gestalten. Legende und Darstellung in der bildenden Kunst* (Stuttgart: Reclam, 1991 [1968]).

[3] Valerie J. Flint, *The Rise of Magic in Early Modern Europe* (Princeton: Princeton University Press, 1991), pp. 386-392. This magic of the high clergy served to counter the magical power of the king, which was transmitted by bloodlines. On the healing power of monarchs in the Middle Ages, see Marc Bloch, *The Royal Touch. Monarchy and Miracles in France and England* (New York: Dorset, 1989 [1961]).

[4] The association of bishop and city can even be measured in the legend of a far-off Atlantic island, 'Antilla: the isle of seven cities', which was supposedly inhabited by an archbishop and six bishops who fled there from Spain sometime between 507

(*Stadtherr*) over every sphere of urban life: spiritual and cultural, political and judicial, economic and military. The bishop was the architect
and patron of a sacred city. The cathedral stood as a monument to
his spiritual power, as the sanctuary of holy relics, endowed altars,
and episcopal graves. To this church the repentant sinner came for
absolution and the priest for service and synod. Around this church
the residences of canons, chaplains, priests, and ministerials as well as
the palace of the bishop formed a quarter of clergy and episcopal
servants. Monasteries and charitable foundations, collegiate and parish churches, completed the grid of holy sites that comprised the
spiritual topography of an episcopal city. The bishop was lord of a
political and spiritual capital; he ruled subjects and souls. It is precisely the combination or even interpenetration of the secular and
sacred that made this city essential and indispensable to the bishop—
as a sovereign of state and church.

Despite the lofty archetype of their predecessors and the divine
designs of their cities, bishops of the Holy Roman Empire did not
always receive the type of veneration reserved for future saints. In
fact, from the early Middle Ages through the sixteenth century
bishops were repeatedly denied entry to their episcopal cities or
driven into exile by militant residents. Sometimes they withdrew vol-
untarily to escape danger or protest civic policy.[5] The invented neo-
Latin phrase *Episcopus exclusus* encompasses all the dimensions of this
predicament of the German episcopacy. The bishop, the *episcopus*,
could be banished in a number of ways and *excludere* has appropriate

and 734; each bishop founded a city; Donald S. Johnson, *Phantom Islands of the Atlantic. The Legends of Seven Lands that Never Were* (New York: Walker and Company, 1994),
pp. 91-112.

[5] This development could even be extended to the nineteenth century when
church lands were secularized and dioceses such as Constance were dissolved; see
Xaver Bischof, "Das Ende des Hochstifts und Bistums," in *Die Bischöfe von Konstanz.*
Geschichte und Kultur, vol. I, eds. E. Kuhn, E. Moser, R. Reinhardt, and P. Sachs
(Friedrichshafen: Robert Gessler, 1988), pp. 45-55; hereafter cited as *BK* I.

While the practice of *Verbannung* in Germany has received little attention and the
clergy in exile has not been well-studied, critical research on exile as punishment can
be found on the practice of secular banishment in Italian communes; see Susannah
Foster Baxendale, "Exile in Practice: The Alberti Family in and out of Florence
1401-1428," *RQ* 44 (1991) 720-756; Randolph Starn, *Contrary Commonwealth. The
Theme of Exile in Medieval and Renaissance Italy* (Berkeley: University of California Press,
1982); and Peter Pazzaglini, *The Criminal Ban of the Siena Commune 1225-1310* (Milan:
Dott. A. Giuffrè Editore, 1979).

meanings to reflect this variety: 'to shut out, remove, separate, and exclude' or 'to drive out, take out, thrust out'.

Behind these highly public and documented migrations is a gradual, persistent wearing down of the bishop's rights and privileges, first as city lord (*Stadtherr*) and second as shepherd of the church (*Oberhirt*). Slowly, sometimes imperceptibly, and in some cases beginning as early as the tenth century, the civic domain of the episcopal lord dwindled as the bishop was increasingly 'excluded' from the life and space of his city. Indeed, in each bishop's city there was a distinctive 'exfoliation' of episcopal power.[6] Behind the sudden and severe eviction of a bishop were gradual erosive and corrosive forces comprised of elements unique to each city and diocese. In some cases nearly all remnants of the bishop's political power had been worn away. In others his authority remained in odd formations, continuing to slice through, arch over, or tower above civic life.

Bishops as well as cities could expel and exile. When the individual violated episcopal law, the bishop could excommunicate. When a city infringed on the bishop's prerogatives, he could decree interdict. In both cases those 'exiled' could anticipate a banishment encompassing two lifetimes; in the first the sacraments of grace for temporal life were excluded; in the second exile was eternal, a banishment from the heavenly Jerusalem. Likewise excommunication and interdict interfered on the societal plane. The sinner could be shunned or the interdicted city might find no market for its wares.

Until the sixteenth century most German bishops maintained control, residence, or at least some form of influence in their episcopal cities. They held on to the vestiges of their political, economic, and legal lordship whenever possible. They protected their churches and clerical properties as sources of vital income. But given the decline of their authority and the perpetual threat of exile, why did bishops cling so tenaciously to their old episcopal cities, especially when other residences could be founded or were already established in which

---

[6] 'Exfoliation' is a more nuanced synonym for the geological term 'erosion'. It refers to the "peeling off of thin concentric rock layers from the bare outer surface of rock;" geologists use the term exfoliation to describe how different types of rock erode at varied rates, leaving thin high walls, towering buttes, and majestic or oddly shaped arches—all of these formations surrounded by rubble strewn, somewhat level desert; see Halka Chronic, *Roadside Geology of Arizona* (Missoula, Montana: Mountain Press Publishing, 1983), p. 311.

bishops could exercise unchallenged lordship? Given the bishop's seignorial past and his continued threat to magisterial authority, why did civic residents continue to tolerate episcopal presence and influence in the city? In short, why did bishops want to return to the city and why did civic residents let them come back? What accounts for this odd and sometimes destructive relationship, which we in our terms might describe as 'co-dependent'?

Many factors may serve to explain this uneasy cohabitation: the obligations of city and bishop to the Holy Roman Empire, the revenues that civic merchants and the episcopal court generated, the prestige of a bishop's church for clergy and laity. This book turns to the interrelationship of lordship, city, and hallowed ground to pursue the nature and durability of this unwieldy collaboration. Even as the bishop suffered losses on every front, his rule of the church continued to embrace the spiritual and sacred, his care of souls and his reliance on holy places. As long as the bishop's spiritual authority remained intact, as long as he had a primary claim on holy places in the city, he could continue to influence and shape civic life. Through ritual performances late medieval bishops exercised their rule of sacred spaces and might extend that rule to the streets and alleys between and beyond them. This presence, afforded by ritual and sacred space, allowed them periodically to contest and attempt to roll back civic encroachment on old episcopal rights and privileges. Because of the sacred city, embodied in the cathedral, the bishop could not simply abandon this place and start over elsewhere. Even when a second city had become de facto the residence of the bishop, he still returned to his episcopal city for rites of entry, burial, and memorial. These rituals were meant for the ceremonial stage of the sacred city.

Civic residents on the other hand relied on the bishop for his mediation between heaven and earth. Despite their mastery of city government, markets, foreign policy, and even their administration of some ecclesiastical foundations, the bishop remained the 'high priest' of the civic and regional church; the bishop ruled over a web of parishes and priests that saw to the baptism of the newborn, the last rites and holy burial of the dead, and all the sacramental ministrations in between. The bishop relied on the sacred city as a basis for his ecclesiastical reign and the sanctuary of his cathedral as a repository of spiritual power. As long as the inhabitants of the old episcopal city required the bishop's church and intercession, they would have to tolerate a bishop's return, endure his regal pretensions, and his attempts to regain complete political rule, to become again "Lord of the Sacred City."

It is precisely urban movements of religious reform in the sixteenth century that offered a tantalizing escape. Citizens could deny the spiritual power of the bishop, instituting a civic church that denounced all the exclusive, ecclesiastical rights of this medieval shepherd. As a city council exiled the bishop and established a magisterial church, it simultaneously declared that the power of the bishop to punish with excommunication and interdict was now impotent and obsolete, that the sacramental mediation of his clergy was no longer required. This rejection of the bishop's spiritual power was at the same time a re-formation of civic topography, a redefinition of the sacred city, and an unequivocal end to the bishop's lordship—the ultimate form of the *Episcopus exclusus*.

*   *   *

Historians of this long-standing conflict have often sided with the city in sentiment and scholarly focus. Their preference is understandable. They have described the glorious march of civic independence and proto-democracy over against decadent lordship. They have carefully chronicled the growth of 'City Reformation' over against the hierarchical medieval church. But as a result the bishop has been expelled and marginalized yet again, driven to the edge of the story as an irritant to progress or as a minion of papal repression. But as long as the bishop remains in the shadows, the narrative of the later Middle Ages and the Reformation lies broken on a subtle confessionalism wherein even constitutional, Marxist, and social historians have often preferred the cause of lay Protestant groups to that of the high clergy. More generally historians have tended to bypass the episcopal story. Civic residents acted otherwise; they either upheld and defended 'their' bishop or were moved to oppose him in a five-hundred year struggle to eliminate episcopal rule.

In this multi-faceted study of the *Episcopus exclusus* I not only intend to explore the sacred city and the expulsions of German bishops but also address a more enduring form of banishment, the exile of bishops from the historical landscape. For too long episcopal history has been the step-child of medieval and early modern scholarship, the specialty of regional and ecclesiastical historians. Bishops have appeared in historical narratives as the corrupt, absentee, and simoniac adversaries of medieval citizens and Protestant movements, as the ineffective, dispassionate, and slothful defenders of the one church, and as another segment of the pampered aristocracy that oppressed the common man and resisted the flowering of urban democracy. As will be seen in the coming chapters, there are episcopal examples to the contrary.

This book examines these bishops both as lords and exiles; it considers evidence ranging from contracts, chronicles, and correspondence in the archives to published sources and secondary literature. Moreover, this work assumes that while bishops usually came from the landed nobility, they became an essential and inseparable part of civic life. They founded cities, nursed them through seasons of invasion and imperial intrigue, and when enemies laid siege, bishops sheltered urban residents beneath their sacred spires and the broad shoulders of cathedral fortifications. Furthermore, bishops created institutions and markets which in turn spawned a distinctively lay civic world. In many cases German bishops became refugees from the cities they themselves had founded and nurtured. The bishop plays a crucial role in German urban history during the fourteenth and fifteenth centuries, for cities grew and prospered in a fractured, episcopal body. 'Reformation' often flourished in the carcass of the bishop's old city.

There were over sixty cities in the Holy Roman Empire and lands related to the German church that fit the description 'episcopal' at some point in the Middle Ages.[7] Each deserves its own exhaustive history. This study is comparative in scope, drawing on available evidence from many episcopal cities. But two pivotal cases, Constance and Augsburg, lay bare the fierce and violent struggle between bishop and city. On the one hand these two south German cities and their bishops were strikingly different and on the other hand they shared a considerable degree of similarity and continuity. Both cities had broken episcopal lordship during the twelfth and thirteenth centuries. But by the fifteenth century the configuration of bishop and city varied greatly in Constance and Augsburg. The bishops of Constance maintained a viable residence in their old episcopal city, retained the right to appoint a key judicial officer, and as late as 1511 survived a critical standoff with civic magistrates. In contrast, the bishops of Augsburg had been excluded from most judicial, po-

---

[7] See Appendix A: Ecclesiastical Territories.

litical, and economic spheres of civic life and had shifted their chief residence to Dillingen on the Danube; they ruled the church through the resident clergy, especially the cathedral chapter; the bishops were most visible in Augsburg when they received installation, consecration, and burial, or led memorial processions and celebrated feast days. The bishop of Constance lived and died in his old episcopal city. The bishop of Augsburg lived elsewhere but returned to his ancestral home on a permanent basis at death; he 'resided' in his cathedral only after his earthly life no longer posed a threat to the city.

During the sixteenth century Reformation movements were catastrophic for these two south German bishops. By 1537 the bishops of Constance and Augsburg had lost all access to their episcopal cities; they were neither city lords nor bishops of the urban church. Their property had been confiscated, their clergy expelled or converted, and their cathedrals made fit for Protestant worship. The fourth decade of the sixteenth century marked the culmination of the *Episcopus exclusus* in Constance and Augsburg.

Other factors as well make these two cases a natural starting point for a study of banished bishops. First, the dioceses of Constance and Augsburg were neighbors; they shared a common north-south border. Therefore this study has a certain regional coherence which allows for attention to the relationship between adjacent bishops. Second, both cities and bishops had common territorial politics. While the House of Habsburg and the Swiss Confederacy promoted a 'foreign policy' that shaped and challenged episcopal rule in southern Germany, the Swabian Circle (*Kreis*), a key regional, representative, and military organization of the empire, encircled and defended the dioceses of Constance and Augsburg; bishops of both sees had prominent roles in the Swabian Circle.

Third, Constance and Augsburg were often on the razor's edge between controversy and cooperation in the later Middle Ages and Reformation. They provided a venue for critical congresses in the life of the church and the empire. From 1414-18 Constance housed the council that bears its name; here the papacy was reunited, John Hus was burned, and the conciliar movement reached its apogee at a council called by an emperor; for four years the bishops of many sees and cities walked the streets of Constance. During the sixteenth century Augsburg served as host for a series of critical imperial congresses, including the momentous diets of 1530 (Augsburg Confes-

sion) and 1555 (Peace of Augsburg); here representatives began to
resolve controversies of the Reformation as princes and bishops from
throughout the empire attempted to negotiate settlements both
creedal and territorial. Last but not least, collections of printed and
archival sources give incomplete, but intriguing accounts of the con-
flict-laden relationship of bishop and city. The fate of the bishops as
frequent losers, however, has led to a mangled set of sources, a collection of documents that does not allow for a continuous narrative.[8]
Fortunately the records of fierce confrontation and ritual engage-
ment survive. When combined with civic records the perilous and
persevering position of the bishops in Constance and Augsburg takes
shape.

For the most part these bishops have been studied from either a
legal or ecclesiastical standpoint. Here the political, economic, judicial, and ecclesiastical roles are taken up as part of a consolidated
and coherent 'episcopal person'. Four chapters chronicle the decline
and survival of the bishops in these two south German cities, focusing on the period 1300-1548 and when pertinent extending back to
the eleventh century. Chapter one sets the scene and describes the
frequency and nature of episcopal exile throughout the Holy Roman
Empire from the early Middle Ages through the sixteenth century. It
also provides a composite portrait of the medieval German bishop
prior to the erosion of episcopal rights and institutions. This background allows the reader to place the following chapters in a broader
context, to perceive how developments in Constance and Augsburg
compare to trends in the empire. Chapters two and three turn directly to Constance and Augsburg wherein the nature of episcopal
power, the patterns of residence and expulsion, and the tactics of
bishop and city in the Middle Ages are investigated. Chapters four
and five flesh out two as yet unobserved dimensions of the bishop's
sacred city and the *Episcopus exclusus*. In chapter four the issues of
ritual and civic space are explored, focusing on the bishop's cathedral, entries, processions, and burial rites. Finally, chapter five

---

[8] The effort to reconstruct this narrative is further complicated by the lack of an
episcopal archive for the now defunct diocese of Constance. Documents are scattered across southern Germany and Switzerland in over twenty-eight state, civic, and
private collections; see Werner Kundert, "Archive," *Helvetia Sacra*, Das Bistum
Konstanz, Das Erzbistum Mainz, Das Bistum St. Gallen, ed. F. X. Bischof, et al.
(Basel, Frankfurt am Main: Helbing und Lichtenhahn, 1993) I, 2.1, pp. 164-178;
hereafter cited as *H.S.*; Bernd Ottnad, "Die Archive der Bischöfe von Konstanz,"
FDA 94 (1974), 270-516.

chronicles the cataclysmic expulsion of the bishops of Constance and Augsburg in the sixteenth century and the remarkable account of episcopal survival in exile.

The phrase *Episcopus exclusus* encapsulates the decline of episcopal power in the city whether through the seizure of episcopal rights and privileges or the act of violent expulsion and the agony of lengthy exile. These episodes of civic marginalization and banishment reveal not only the unresolved issues that characterize the relationship between bishop and city but they are also crucial turning points in episcopal history—late medieval and early modern. In the confrontations between bishop and city we open a window on the contested legitimacy and periodic instability of episcopal rule; through these confrontations a bishop's waning power and his remarkable resiliency can be measured.

CHAPTER ONE

THE SCOPE OF THE *EPISCOPUS EXCLUSUS*
IN MEDIEVAL AND EARLY MODERN GERMANY

Shortly after his death in February 1513 Pope Julius II (1503-13) came to life a second time as the object of heavenly scorn in "Julius Excluded From Heaven."[1] This dialogue opens with a belligerent, boastful, and bellicose Pope Julius ascending to heaven, storming the ramparts of the eternal Jerusalem, eagerly expecting a grand reception. With the wrong key in hand he fails to open the city gate. Julius then reprimands St. Peter, the retiring doorman: "I demand that you open these gates. Get to it. If you intended to do your job, you would already be out here meeting me and an impressive procession of angels would accompany you."[2] But for the hesitant St. Peter the papal majesty of Julius has been obscured by the visage of a monster, the odor of sewage, and the absurdity of his costume; Julius appears as a "wrecker of cities."[3] As he impatiently awaits his regal entrance Julius demonstrates his own exclusive tendencies. He wields the power of excommunication with reckless abandon. Though himself banned from the heavenly Jerusalem Julius threatens even St. Peter with eternal damnation. As he was willing to exile his apostolic superior, likewise Julius insults his episcopal predecessors. He mocks the ancient church where sincere bishops faced "hard work, vigils, fast-

---

[1] "Dialogus, iulius exclusus e coelis," Desiderius Erasmus, *Erasmi Opuscula. A Supplement to the Opera Omnia*, ed. W. K. Ferguson (The Hague: Martinus Nijhof, 1933), pp. 65-124; hereafter cited as *EO*. For a lively and accurate translation see "Julius Excluded From Heaven: A Dialogue," in *Collected Works of Erasmus*, trans. M. J. Heath (Toronto: University of Toronto Press, 1986), vol. 5, pp. 168-197 and vol. 6, pp. 494-508. A useful translation with critical notes is *The 'Julius exclusus' of Erasmus*, trans. P. Pascal (Bloomington: Indiana University Press, 1968).
[2] "Quin tu fores aperis, quantum potes; quem, si tuo fungi voluisses officio, obviam oportuit venisse, vel universa coelitum pompa;" *EO*, p. 65, 20-23.
[3] "... vrbium eversorem ..." *EO*, p. 65, 16; this phrase alludes to Julius' campaign to restore control over rebellious cities of the Papal States. On the policies of Julius in the Papal States, see Peter Partner, *Renaissance Rome 1500-1559: A Portrait of a Society* (Berkeley: University of California Press, 1976), p. 12.
This conflict between pope and city echoes the larger church/state conflict wherein bishops in Germany were a perpetual threat to cities that had previously gained independence from their episcopal overlords.

ing, study, and all too often, death."[4] Julius rejects this ascetic fool-
ishness and instead savors the lucrative benefits of political conquest.[5] As Julius flaunts his papal and militaristic credentials in the
remainder of the dialogue, St. Peter's initial impressions are confirmed and his resolution hardens:

> Julius: Then you won't let me in?
> Peter: The last person I'd let in is a thug like you. For to you we are all
> excommunicate.[6]

This satire may well reveal a great deal about the elusive author,
Erasmus of Rotterdam (1466?-1536), and about anti-papal sentiment
on the eve of the Reformation.[7] But the exclusion of Julius finds its
historic counterpart in the relationship of bishops and cities in medieval and early modern Germany. The *Julius exclusus* echoes the gen-

---

[4] "... labores, vigiliae, ieiunia, doctrina, saepenumero mors;" *EO*, p. 83, 332-333.

[5] In fact, Julius was less than scrupulous with his episcopal subordinates. He was a
shrewd manipulator of the conciliar impulses of his own Fifth Lateran Council
(1512-17). By announcing, cancelling, and rescheduling sessions Julius had befuddled
clerics attempting to plan a long journey to Rome for the council and eventually
eliminated a great multitude of bishops and abbots, especially those coming from
northern Europe.
   Nelson H. Minnich counters the assertion that a paltry number of non-Italian
bishops were in attendance at Fifth Lateran, a claim fostered by the author of the
dialogue and repeated by subsequent scholarship; Minnich notes that thirty-seven
non-Italian archbishops and 209 non-Italian bishops attended. However, he does not
indicate how poorly the Holy Roman Empire was represented; only ten out of approximately forty-seven bishops and archbishops were present at the council, most
from northern and southeastern regions of the Empire (Gurk, Halberstadt, Havelberg, Lübeck, Magdeburg, Mainz, Meissen, Ratzeburg, Salzburg, and Utrecht).
   A movement to establish an episcopal college in Rome in the early sixteenth
century further underscores the plight of the episcopacy at the highest levels of
church government and administration. Bishops sought to create an institution that
would represent their interests over against the College of Cardinals. This movement
failed, adding yet another chapter to the chronicle of faltering episcopal initiatives at
local, national, and international levels on the eve of the Reformation. See Nelson
H. Minnich, "The Participants at the Fifth Lateran Council" and "The Proposals for
an Episcopal College at Lateran V," in *The Fifth Lateran Council (1512-1517): Studies
on its Membership, Diplomacy, and Proposals for Reform* (Brookfield, Vermont: Variorum,
1993), pp. 157-206, 214-232.

[6] "Iulius: Non aperis igitur?
Petrus: Cuius potius quam tali pesti. Nam tibi quidem omnes excommunicati
sumus;" *EO*, p. 123, 1203-1205.

[7] For a discussion of the probable authorship of Erasmus, see the introduction by
Michael J. Heath in *Collected Works of Erasmus*, vol. 5, pp. 156-160; in addition to the
issue of authorship James K. McConica places this dialogue in the context of Erasmus' humanist and conciliar thought; "Erasmus and the 'Julius': A Humanist Reflects on the Church," in *The Pursuit of Holiness in Late Medieval and Renaissance Religion*,
eds. C. Trinkaus and H. A. Oberman (Leiden: E. J. Brill, 1974), pp. 444-471.

eral plight of the episcopacy, what is described in this study as the *Episcopus exclusus*. As Julius II was denied entrance to the heavenly Jerusalem, so German bishops were periodically excluded from their episcopal cities. Indeed, bishops sometimes received a reception similar to Julius in the imaginative dialogue of Erasmus. Magistrates increasingly challenged the bishop's political, moral, and ecclesiastical authority as well as episcopal ritual and residence in the city. To civic inhabitants bishops brought the twin threats of spiritual censure and military force, the ability to excommunicate and bear arms. Within twenty-five years of the Fifth Lateran Council eight German and Swiss bishops would lose all access to their venerable episcopal seats and the aged cathedrals, which housed their relics and symbolized their sacral power.

This exile of bishops was not limited to the mid-sixteenth century. Rather, this sort of episcopal duress is characteristic of both the medieval and early modern periods. Three issues will serve to underscore the precarious position and resilient power of the German episcopacy: the Dimensions of the *Episcopus exclusus*, the Bishop's 'Real Presence', and the Refugees of the Reformation.

1. *The Dimensions of the 'Episcopus exclusus'*

Although the expulsion of German bishops has received no substantial treatment in scholarship, the conciliar fathers of the church dealt directly with the issue. Two hundred years before the reign of Pope Julius II and his church council the dilemma of exiled bishops had already received ecumenical definition. While the Council of Vienne (1311-12) is known for the condemnation of the Templars and the Free Spirits, the seventh decree deals explicitly with expelled bishops:[8]

> "Although the sacred canons usually do not permit a bishop to exercise his jurisdiction in a diocese other than his own, we exempt bishops who have been driven from their sees by the brazenness of the ungodly. As they fear persecution they do not dare to reside in their own cities or dioceses or any part of them, nor do they themselves exercise jurisdic-

---

[8] The most thorough study of the council remains Ewald Müller, *Das Konzil von Vienne 1311-1312. Seine Quellen und seine Geschichte* (Münster: Aschendorff, 1934). On the Council of Vienne in the larger context of ecumenical councils, see Joseph von Hefele, *Conciliengeschichte* (Freiburg: Herder, 1890), vol. 6, pp. 515-574.

tion directly or through intermediaries. Since the damage done to the churches in the violence of the expulsions might go unpunished, we grant that these bishops may seek out locations where they may reside freely and exercise their jurisdiction—in other dioceses, cities, or prominent places near their own churches. In keeping with legal procedure they may then freely pursue those who expelled them along with their advisors and supporters (these cities and places must be beyond the reach of the expellers, their councilors and supporters. If it can be done safely, they are to be cited personally, or at the bishop's house. Otherwise, they are to be cited in public either in the cathedral church of that place or at their residence)."[9]

The decree further stipulates how the adversaries of the bishop are to be censured—on Sundays or feast days, before a large gathering of the faithful, and in a church in close proximity to the temporary residence of the bishop. When sought out for assistance neighboring bishops should see to the dissemination of episcopal condemnations. Because the bishop is unable to rule in his own diocese, he is permitted to exercise jurisdiction over his subjects from the diocese in which he temporarily resides. Although this exiled bishop should first seek permission from prospective hosts, the Council of Vienne now overrides local reservations, allowing the refugee bishop to take up residence despite regional resistance.

Although this decree refers specifically to a regional dispute in northern Italy, it serves to highlight the plight of the exiled bishop generally.[10] Cut off (*exclusus*) from his episcopal city, diocesan re-

---

[9] "Quamvis sacris canonibus sit generaliter interdictum, ne quis episcopus iurisdictionem in dioecesi exerceat aliena, <u>nos tamen episcopis qui, a suis sedibus protervia impiorum expulsi</u>, non audent propter metum persequentium in suis civitatibus vel dioecesibus aut earum parte aliqua residere, nec iurisdictionem ad se spectantem per se vel per alium inibi exercere, ne iniuria, in eorum expulsione ipsorum irrogata ecclesiis, hoc praetextu remaneat impunita, duximus indulgendum, ut in dioecesibus alienis, in civitatibus videlicet vel locis insignibus suis ecclesiis vicinioribus, in quibus poterunt secure morari et iurisdictionem suam libere exercere, possint contra suos expulsores et eorum in hac parte consiliarios et fautores (dummodo civitates vel loca huiusmodi eisdem expulsoribus, consiliariis et fautoribus sint secura, et ipsi personaliter vel ad domum, si hoc tute fieri valeat, alioquin publice in ecclesia cathedrali loci vel domicilii eorundem citati fuerint), libere procedere, prout iustitia suadebit;" (my emphasis) *Decrees of the Ecumenical Councils*, vol. 1, ed. N. P. Tanner (Washington, D.C.: Georgetown University Press, 1990 [1972]), p. 363, 27-42.
[10] The Archbishop of Milan and the Bishop of Vicenza were under particular duress and made their predicament known to the council. They had been imprisoned, expelled, and hindered from returning to their territories; Müller, *Das Konzil von Vienne*, pp. 479-482; in this case territorial rulers had forced the clerics to flee. This circumstance does not discount the civic role, for cities caught in a conflict between secular or sacred rulers were often compelled to choose sides between them.

sources, and cathedral precincts, the bishop relied on other clergy for residence, promulgation of episcopal censure, and recognition of his ecclesiastical powers. The underlying vulnerability of the exiled bishop surfaces in the repeated use of *audere*, 'to dare'. What powers can the bishop 'dare' to exercise, where does the bishop 'dare' to appear physically to confront his adversaries or to condemn their crime and pronounce judgement without jeopardizing his reign and life? Moreover, the centrality of the bishop's cathedral city is clear. Without the locus of his authority a bishop is thrown upon the largess of neighboring cities and territories both for lodging and a suitable place from which to reign and pronounce punishment.

These measures may appear extreme, as stipulations to be executed under rare and dire circumstances. However, the interaction between bishop and episcopal city sometimes led to violent confrontation. Reinhold Kaiser in his ground-breaking essay, "Mord im Dom" ("Murder in the Cathedral"), has investigated a more sinister and decisive form of episcopal expulsion—the murder of bishops.[11] This 'tradition' actually reaches back to the dawn of the Christian church and includes venerated victims. Martyrs such as Peter the Apostle and Irenaeus, bishop of Lyons (d. 200), are complemented by frequently exiled bishops, including Hilary of Poitiers (d. 367/368) and the five time fugitive Athanasius of Alexandria (d. 373). His harassment by Arian heretics is followed by the frequent murder of missionary bishops at the hands of northern European 'heathens'. Civil war among the Franks and the ninth century invasions of Normans, Huns, Saracens, and Slavs were to claim the lives of many bishops. By the end of the tenth century violent and yet exemplary death in the line of duty had become a likely part of the episcopal expectancy.[12]

Although individual expulsions and murders could be exception-

---

[11] In addition to the *vitae* of bishops and saints Kaiser relies on a few spectacular cases of unrest. As he points out, secondary literature does not yet permit a thorough statistical analysis of episcopal murder and expulsion. However, the geographical breadth of his examples suggest a phenomenon that is not only German, but also generally European (e.g. Cambrai, Cologne, Cremona, Le Mans, Mainz, Milan, Trier, Worms); "'Mord im Dom.' Von der Vertreibung zur Ermordung des Bischofs im frühen und hohen Mittelalter," *ZSR*, KA 110 (1993), 95-134.

The murder of churchmen has been put in a broader historical perspective by Franklin Ford, *Political Murder. From Tyrannicide to Terrorism* (Cambridge: Harvard University Press, 1985), pp. 111-120.

[12] Residents of Metz blinded, castrated, and drove Bishop Benno from his city in 929. Bishop Johannes of Mecklenburg was murdered in 1066; his corpse was muti-

ally brutal, the eleventh-century Investiture Controversy undermined
the legal foundation of episcopal rule. In the dominions of German
Emperor Henry IV (1056-1106) twenty-three of forty-five bishoprics
were rent by schism and thirty-eight bishops were either expelled,
replaced, or resigned; thirty of these bishops were loyal to the crown;
five bishops were murdered. Kaiser identifies a decisive shift; the
aggressors were no longer non-Christian invaders but rival lords and
preeminently residents of episcopal cities.[13] Under these unstable
conditions episcopal chroniclers continued to portray battered bishops in the role of martyr and saint. In reality the office of bishop had
been severely 'desacralized'; his person and body were now vulnerable to increasing acts of violence and the fermenting hostility of
urban residents within Christendom.[14]

Even as homicides decline in the high and later Middle Ages episcopal expulsions continue unabated, often in the wake of imperial
and papal intrigue, but more frequently as a result of open conflict
between a bishop and residents of his cathedral city.[15] The Investi-

---

lated and his head was sacrificed to the god Redigost; Kaiser, "'Mord im Dom',"
103-104.
    Heinrich Fichtenau has emphasized the role of 'public dying' for bishops in the
tenth century. The final days and hours of a bishop's life, as recorded in his *vita*,
might include knowledge of his impending death, drafting of his will, reception of the
eucharist and edifying conversation with fellow clerics. Shortly after a bishop's passing thieves might break into churches and episcopal warehouses. After the death of
its absent bishop, Cambrai was taken by a castellan who oppressed the citizens and
plundered the episcopal palace and stables; *Living in the Tenth Century. Mentalities and
Social Orders*, trans. P. J. Geary (Chicago: Chicago University Press, 1991 [1984]), pp.
213-216.
    [13] Kaiser, "'Mord im Dom'," 104-108. The assassination of Archbishop Thomas
Becket is the most celebrated case of episcopal murder, an example which Kaiser
uses to open his article; indeed his title is drawn from T. S. Eliot's *Murder in the
Cathedral* (New York: Harcourt, Brace, and Jovanovich, 1963 [1935]); the drama of
Becket's personal conflict with Henry II has perhaps overshadowed the far-reaching
dimensions of king vs. bishop and laity vs. clergy, a dimension which draws the
English example closer to that of the German bishops; on Becket's 'final' expulsion
see Frank Barlow, *Thomas Becket* (Berkeley: University of California Press, 1986), pp.
198-250.
    [14] Kaiser is reluctant to posit a communal movement or the incipient formation
of civic institutions as the driving force behind early anticlericalism. Rather, he proposes that cycles of violence, not conspiratorial planning, ignited urban unrest
against the episcopacy; Kaiser, "'Mord in Dom'," 119, 132-134.
    [15] The first significant recorded civic resistance to episcopal rule, including some
expulsions, had already occurred prior to the Investiture Controversy in Mainz (939),
Milan (c. 948-53), and Cambrai (967); David Nicholas, *The Growth of the Medieval City.
From Late Antiquity to the Early Fourteenth Century* (London and New York: Longman,
1997), p. 80.

ture Controversy is merely the first installment of a long-standing struggle wherein bishop and city end up in opposite political camps or two rival bishops battle for control of diocese and city. In addition to rival claimants to the German throne and continuing friction between empire and papacy the papal schism of the late-fourteenth and early fifteenth centuries invariably tended to undermine cooperative relations between bishop and city.[16]

What little is known in detail regarding episcopal exile in the Holy Roman Empire has emerged from research on the capital or cathedral city of the bishop.[17] In 1913 Bruno Dauch published an invaluable study of the bishop's city as residence of the ecclesiastical prince based on his broad reading of charters and chronicles. Though short on conclusions Dauch still offers the best summation of the expulsion and exile of bishops in the Holy Roman Empire from 900-1600.[18] His examination of thirty-three episcopal cities reveals just how often bishops chose to leave or were driven out of their cities, thus abandoning cathedral, palace, and vulnerable clergy.[19] Dauch mentions over sixty-five incidents in which a bishop either flees from his city, departs in protest, or is denied entry. Bishops in exile are cited in over twenty cases, while the frequent founding of alternative episcopal residences suggests that many others were cut off from their cathedral cities without leaving records of negotiation, transfer, or violent confrontation.

Indeed, the transfer of residence is the centerpiece of Dauch's research. Only the bishops of Freising appear to have ruled throughout the medieval and early modern period without suffering a single

---

[16] See pp. 52-54 on developments in Constance from the Investiture Controversy through the schism of the late fourteenth century.

[17] Friedrich Merzbacher set the agenda for recent discussions of the bishop's city in *Die Bischofsstadt* (Köln: Westdeutscher Verlag, 1961).

[18] *Die Bischofsstadt als Residenz der geistlichen Fürsten* (Vaduz: Kraus, 1965 [1913]).

[19] Dauch leaves out the episcopal cities in the north-eastern reaches of the Empire, which from the outset were under regional and territorial control. While focusing on the Middle Ages he occasionally extends his range into the sixteenth and seventeenth centuries. Invaluable is his analysis of the 'French' episcopal cities included in this work (Cambrai, Liège, Metz, Verdun, Toul), offering a perspective in both German and French speaking lands; these cities appear since they are listed as members of the empire in the decrees of the Imperial Diet of Worms in 1521; Dauch, *Die Bischofsstadt*, pp. 163-201.

See Appendix A for the diocesan structure of the 'German Church', which includes not only members of the *Reichskirche*, but also those related to the emperor or imperial princes.

expulsion.[20] Many other bishops gradually began to establish permanent residences outside their cathedral cities as early as the twelfth
(Metz) and thirteenth centuries (Cambrai, Speyer, Strasbourg, Trier,
Verden). During the fourteenth century eight residences were relo-
cated (Augsburg, Basel, Bremen, Mainz, Minden, Paderborn, Toul,
Verdun) as opposed to two in the fifteenth (Chur, Utrecht) and one
in the sixteenth (Magdeburg). Four bishops established new residences in close proximity to their old episcopal cities (Eichstätt,
Hildesheim, Salzburg, Würzburg), while five others maintained and
used domiciles within and outside the episcopal city (Bamberg,
Brixen, Liège, Passau, Regensburg).[21]

Although Dauch's work must be tested afresh against new civic
histories and a broader range of sources, a number of preliminary
conclusions can be drawn regarding the *Episcopus exclusus*. Clearly
most bishops reestablished permanent residence outside of their
original cathedral cities or at least maintained a second co-residence.
In line with the state of later scholarship Dauch proposes the rise of
civic institutions and communal autonomy as the motivating factor
behind expulsion and transfer of residence.[22] However, this view,
which animates the history of civic development, tends to ignore the
critical episcopal perspective. In his dissertation on the German episcopal city of the Middle Ages Norbert Leudemann chronicles how
the old cathedral compound, encompassing the cathedral, episcopal

---

[20] Dauch, *Die Bischofsstadt*, p. 272. The weakness of this work is precisely Dauch's
narrow focus on the issue of residency. The absence of a bishop, however, did not
necessarily indicate a curtailment of his influence or oversight via institutions and
decrees; see below, pp. 103-113.

[21] In regard to Cologne, Constance, Münster, Osnabrück and Worms, Dauch
does not have sufficient information to pinpoint approximate time of transfer or a
dominant residence in the Middle Ages.

[22] Dauch, *Die Bischofsstadt*, p. 272. On the growth of the medieval city and the rise
of civic independence with particular attention to the German context, see Edith
Ennen, *The Medieval Town* (Amsterdam: North-Holland, 1979 [1972]), pp. 95-126;
Hans Planitz, *Die Deutsche Stadt im Mittelalter. Von der Römerzeit bis zu den Zunftkämpfen*
(Wien: Hermann Böhlaus, 1975), pp. 295-344; and Fritz Rörig, *The Medieval Town*
(Berkeley: University of California Press, 1967 [1955]). On broader European devel-
opments in the city and the place of the bishop, see Nicholas, *The Growth of the
Medieval City*, especially pp. 3-168, 202-245, 275-307.

In addition to Kaiser's suggestion that violence toward the clergy cannot always
be taken as a sign of nascent communal self-identity and self-government (note 14
above), Susan Reynolds argues that the rise of civic rights and institutions must be
tied to earlier developments in the countryside; *Kingdoms and Communities in Western
Europe, 900-1300* (Oxford: Clarendon Press, 1984), pp. 155-218. Her position is intriguing since the bishop himself represents not only the city but also the interests of
the larger rural diocese.

palace, and later the domiciles of the canons, became crowded and often unworkable. Bishops shifted their residences to available locations outside the cathedral precinct and in many cases outside the city altogether.[23] This transfer, based on the internal policy of the bishop and his cathedral chapter, points to a fundamental question regarding episcopal influence. To what degree did bishops continue to wield episcopal authority in cities where they no longer held a primary residence and what role exactly did lay citizens play in that transfer? The decrees of councils, the murder and expulsion of bishops, and the role of residence—all dimensions of the *Episcopus exclusus*—can only be understood in terms of actual episcopal power and authority.

2. *The Bishop's 'Real Presence'*

On October 27-28, 1462 the free city of Mainz suffered a decisive and shocking defeat. Archbishop Adolf of Nassau punctured civic defenses and conquered the old episcopal city as the Metropolitan of Mainz. The victory was unprecedented, for no other medieval commune had enjoyed over two hundred years of independence and then had its freedoms crushed by its ancient city-lord (*Stadtherr*).[24] The residents of Mainz had fought a ten hour battle and suffered heavy casualties only to see 150 homes go up in flames. The next day the archbishop ordered all the citizens along with the city council and the members of the guilds to assemble in the Dietmarkt; a large occupation force, including five hundred Swiss soldiers poised for

---

[23] Norbert Leudemann, *Deutsche Bischofsstädte im Mittelalter. Zur topographischen Entwicklung der deutschen Bischofsstadt im Heiligen Römischen Reich* (München: Holler, 1980), pp. 164-165.

[24] In 1244 Mainz had received archiepiscopal recognition of its lay city council after a stormy rise to partial independence which included the murder of Archbishop Arnold of Selenhofen in 1160; Anton P. Brück, *Mainz vom Verlust der Stadtfreiheit bis zum Ende des Dreissigjährigen Krieges (1462-1648)* (Düsseldorf: Walter Rau, 1972), pp. 1-2. Dieter Demandt has investigated the relationship of clergy and citizens as the critical backdrop for understanding conflict in Mainz and the eventual failure of civic freedom: *Stadtherrschaft und Stadtfreiheit im Spannungsfeld von Geistlichkeit und Bürgerschaft in Mainz (11.—15. Jahrhundert)* (Wiesbaden: Franz Steiner Verlag, 1977).
On the role of printing and the conflict in Mainz in the 1460s, see Konrad Repgen, "Antimanifest und Kriegsmanifest. Die Benutzung der neuen Drucktechnik bei der Mainzer Stiftsfehde 1461/63 durch Erzbischöfe Adolf von Nassau und Diether von Isenburg," in *Studien zum 15. Jahrhundert. Festschrift für Erich Meuthen*, vol. 2, eds. J. Helmrath and H. Müller (München: R. Oldenbourg, 1994), pp. 781-804.

battle, surrounded the defenseless crowd of 800. Those guilty of sedition would be banished, the Archbishop declared. Even as the 'guilty' fell to their knees crying 'Vergebens!' (forgive us!), Adolf of Nassau commanded 'Steht auf!' (get up!). Perhaps in mockery of episcopal expulsion, the victorious metropolitan drove the condemned citizens through a gauntlet of ridiculing mercenaries and then cast them out of the city. The archbishop permitted only women and children, bakers, and a few day laborers to remain. In April 1465 the inhabitants of Mainz formally surrendered their status as citizens and submitted to the archiepiscopal regime as 'servants'.[25] With the city now firmly in his grasp Adolf of Nassau and his successors retained Aschaffenburg, not Mainz, as their chief residence.[26] Even a triumphant and restored city lord did not deem it necessary to reside in his old episcopal city. Primary residence does not always indicate the civic power of a bishop.

The defeat of Mainz remained a haunting display of episcopal power and a reminder of the vulnerability of civic independence. In a grim and impressive display of military force Adolf of Nassau had exercised the formidable powers at the disposal of a German bishop. Well over forty years later this example still inspired dread. In 1506 Wilhelm of Honstein, Bishop of Strasbourg, was elected to the post of Vicar General in the Archdiocese of Mainz. Bishop Wilhelm's adversaries in Strasbourg feared that he would emulate the tradition of Mainz and the militant Adolf of Nassau.[27] While scholars have chronicled the remarkable rise of civic independence and lay autonomy, they have not captured the specter of the episcopal overlord and his perpetual threat to reverse centuries of urban liberty. In addition to military prowess what resources did Adolf of Nassau and his colleagues have at their disposal?

Place of residence serves as one possible indicator of a bishop's

---

[25] *Chroniken der deutschen Städte vom 14. bis ins 16. Jahrhundert*, vol. 18, Die Chroniken der mittelrheinischen Städte, vol. 2, Mainz (Göttingen: Vandenhoeck und Ruprecht, 1965 [1881-1882]), pp. 176-183; henceforth cited as *CDS*.

[26] Volker Press, "Bischöfe, Bischofsstädte und Bischofsresidenzen. Zur Einleitung," in *Südwestdeutsche Bischofsresidenzen ausserhalb der Kathedralstädte*, ed. V. Press (Stuttgart: W. Kohlhammer, 1992), p. 24; for a broader exploration of the nature of 'residence', see *Residenzen des Rechts*, eds. B. Kirchgässner and H.-P. Becht (Sigmaringen: Jan Thorbecke, 1993).

[27] Francis Rapp, "Straßburg, Hochstift und freie Reichsstadt," in *Die Territorien des Reichs im Zeitalter der Reformation und Konfessionalisierung. Land und Konfession 1500-1650*, vol. 5 Der Südwesten, eds. A. Schindling and W. Ziegler (Münster: Aschendorff, 1993), p. 76.

relative influence. But as the example of Mainz shows, even bishops with substantial control in their cathedral cities could choose to reside elsewhere most of the time.[28] Physical access or entry to the episcopal city can also serve to reveal a bishop's relative standing vis-á-vis the urban world nestled behind walls manned by 'patriotic' citizens. In every case it is important to inquire, did bishops have unlimited access to the city or was episcopal entry negotiated on each occasion?[29] How often did bishops appear and how long did they remain within the city walls? Moreover, rights and privileges could manifest the bishop's authority and could sometimes serve his ends more profoundly than bodily entry or residence. To use the language of the Eucharist, to what degree did the bishop continue to have a 'real presence' in the city? What offices and institutions continued to ensure the 'remembrance' of the bishop's claims or indeed directly incarnated his wishes?[30]

The medieval German bishop had a vast arsenal of powers, privileges, and pontifical functions: he was lord of the city, prince of the empire, and shepherd of the church. His rule could extend from the individual to the corporate, from the local to the national, from the confessional to the marriage bed, from the neighborhood parish to the market place, the election of town councilors, the formulation of civic foreign policy, and the negotiations of the imperial diet. Whether in residence or in absentia the bishop could guide or meddle in practically every aspect of city life. He was usually not a

---

[28] Volker Press has described this development and its variations for northern and southern Germany in "Bischöfe, Bischofsstädte und Bischofsresidenzen," in *Südwestdeutsche Bischofsresidenzen ausserhalb der Kathedralstädte*, pp. 19-26.

[29] Bishop Wilhelm, Count of Honstein, came to Strasbourg in 1507 and found a populace armed to the teeth; he was the first bishop to enter to say mass and to be consecrated since the mid-fourteenth century; Thomas A. Brady, "Rites of Autonomy and Dependence: South German Civic Culture in the Age of Renaissance and Reformation, in *Religion and Culture in the Renaissance and Reformation*, ed. S. Ozment (Kirksville, Missouri: Sixteenth Century Journal Publishers, 1989), pp. 15-16.

[30] Portrayals of the bishop have tended to favor either his status as secular prince (*Fürst*) or as Bishop (*Oberhirt*). A thorough and comprehensive description of the bishop's person and work does not yet exist, although Robert L. Benson has explored the process of election for an earlier period in his *The Bishop-Elect. A Study in Medieval Ecclesiastical Office* (Princeton: Princeton University Press, 1968). In this section the bishop's position and powers will be described in terms of his role as city-lord and resident as well as his larger ecclesiastical and princely functions.

The concept of the 'real presence' of the bishop encompasses not only the bishop's identity but also resonates with the corporeal imagery of Ernst H. Kantorowicz's *The Kings Two Bodies. A Study in Medieval Political Theology* (Princeton: Princeton University Press, 1957).

burgher, a citizen of the city; rather his political and cultural ties could be found among the landed nobility.[31] In an age when cities strove to become islands of self-regulated trade and self-rule, bishops were ever present reminders of the legacy of territorial lordship within their walls and the persistent threat of the landed nobility without.

The phrase 'episcopal city' (*Bischofsstadt*) or 'cathedral city' (*Kathedralstadt*) suggests a period when the bishop not only ruled a smaller cathedral-palace complex but also when he held sway throughout the streets and alleys of an entire city; 'episcopal city' describes a community that once drew its identity from the bishop's church and its civic structures from political institutions ruled by the bishop.[32] Long after magistrates and citizens had eliminated full episcopal lordship, bishops continued to refer to their cathedral cities with the same possessive pronoun they applied to their dioceses.[33] Three roles

---

[31] The aristocratic character of the German episcopacy is emphasized by Aloys Schulte in *Der Adel und die deutsche Kirche im Mittelalter. Studien zur Sozial-, Rechts-, und Kirchengeschichte* (Amsterdam: P. Schippers, 1966 [1910]), pp. 61-73; Leo Santifaller has reached a similar conclusion regarding the period from the seventh through the fifteenth century, noting that of the 2,074 German Bishops (excluding Prague), 1,527 ranged from the rank of ministerials or knights to that of the high nobility as compared to only 115 who are identified as civic residents or *Bauer*, *Zur Geschichte des ottonisch-salischen Reichskirchensystems* (Wien: Hermann Böhlaus, 1964), p. 132.

[32] The role of the bishop is considerable in the survival and growth of cities during the decline and fall of the Roman Empire. In some cities in Italy and Gaul bishops moved from participation in civic government in the fourth century to unchallenged leadership in the fifth century. Capitals of bishoprics often stood a better chance of survival than other cities in the succeeding centuries of the tumultuous early Middle Ages. The bishop's church, court, and political leadership shaped the city. The cathedral replaced the forum as the center of civic life. The needs of the episcopal household, clergy, and ministerials provided the basis of a local service economy. Bishops supported the city by appointing civic officials, maintaining defenses, occasionally making loans to the populace, securing food supplies, collecting tolls, and minting coinage. The earliest lay political bodies sometimes convened in the square before the cathedral or within the bishop's church. Many of the earliest lay civic leaders came from the ranks of the episcopal ministerials; Nicholas, *The Growth of the Medieval City*, pp. 17-19, 21, 26-30, 32, 38, 45, 47-48, 55-56, 105; David Nicholas, *The Later Medieval City 1300-1500* (London and New York: Longman, 1997), pp. 3-4; G. H. Martin, "New Beginnings in North-Western Europe," in *European Towns. Their Archaeology and Early History*, ed. M. W. Barley (London: Academic Press, 1977), p. 407; Edith M. Wightman, "The Towns of Gaul with Special Reference to the North-East," in *European Towns*, p. 309.

[33] The bishops of Constance regularly promulgated decrees naming the city of Constance as their own. Since the twelfth century they had been steadily losing ground in the city and were especially vulnerable to civic encroachment at the turn of the sixteenth century. In 1497 the newly elected Bishop, Hugo of Hohenlandenberg, addressed the members of his church and territory with the phrase "... per

typify the powers vested in the bishop: city lord , imperial prince, and shepherd of the church.[34]

City-Lord (Stadtherr). Civic lordship could be tied to the land or based on the power of jurisdiction; rule could rest on possession of property or on the receipt of rights and privileges.[35] A bishop might actually possess the ground on which the city stood, holding it as part of his feudal lordship.[36] More commonly episcopal authority was based on privileges granted by the emperor, imperial rights that shaped economic, judicial, and political life in the bishop's city. Under Ottonian

---

nostram ciuitatem et diocesum Constantiensis ..." (my emphasis), indicating that he still held particular rights in that single city in his bishopric that the bishops of Constance once ruled as lords and citizens now proclaimed as free and imperial; *Constitutiones synodales ecclesie Constantiensis 1497*, GLA 65/291: p. 74v.

In 1522-23 when Reformation movements were surfacing in the diocese and major cities such as Zürich, Ulm, and Constance, Bishop Hugo appears to have softened episcopal claims regarding 'his' episcopal city by removing the possessive pronoun: "vnsers Bistumbs vnd der statt Costantz ..." in "Ernstliche Ermahnung Hugo von Landenbergs Bischofs zu Konstanz, zu Frieden und christlicher Einigkeit, mit schöner Auslegung und Erklärung," in *Flugschriften aus den ersten Jahren der Reformation*, vol. 4, ed. O. Clemen (Nieuwkoop: B. De Graaf, 1967), p. 287.

[34] It is important to note that no one bishop held every right and privilege here depicted. But the range of possibilities will be portrayed as an idealized portrait of episcopal authority.

Historians of legal and constitutional history have usually described episcopal rights as part of the dramatic story of civic independence. The bishop only appears in some stage of political, judicial, economic, and religious decline over against the city. In this section the bishop's rights, powers, and position will be sketched without emphasizing the demise of episcopal influence. This approach will instead highlight the episcopal profile, assessing the position of the bishop at the height of his powers.

[35] Several works inform this section and should be consulted on the issue of *Stadtherrschaft* as well as the rise of civic institutions. For the overarching issue of lordship and city, see *Stadt und Stadtherr im 14. Jahrhundert. Entwicklungen und Funktionen*, ed. W. Rausch, (Linz, Donau: Österreichischer Arbeitskreises für Stadtgeschichtsforschung, 1972) and *Bischofs- und Kathedralstädte des Mittelalters und der frühen Neuzeit*, ed. F. Petri (Köln: Böhlau, 1976). Several important works have a south German focus: Klaus Hefele, *Studien zum Hochmittelalterlichen Stadttypus der Bischofsstadt in Oberdeutschland (Augsburg, Freising, Konstanz, Regensburg)* (Augsburg: Werner Blasaditsch, 1970); Gisela Möncke, *Bischofsstadt und Reichsstadt. Ein Beitrag zur mittelalterlichen Stadtverfassung von Augsburg, Konstanz, und Basel* (Berlin: Freie Universität, 1971); and E. Rütimeyer, *Stadtherr und Stadtbürgerschaft in den rheinischen Bischofsstädten. Ihr Kampf um die Hoheitsrechte im Hochmittelalter* (Stuttgart: W. Kohlhammer, 1928).

[36] The best example of enduring, overarching lordship is the Bavarian episcopal city of Freising, where only slight civic agitation or organization threatened the bishop; see Hefele, *Studien zum hochmittelalterlichen Stadttypus*, pp. 97, 102, 110-111, 120, 126-127; Leudemann, *Deutsche Bischofsstädte*, pp. 180-183; and Dauch, *Bischofsstadt*, pp. 21-24.

rule, bishops, like secular princes, ruled in the emperor's stead.[37] They received three privileges fundamental to their civic overlordship: the right to mint coins, oversee market transactions, and collect tolls.[38] In the twelfth and thirteenth centuries bishops served as imperial tax-collectors. Periodically gathering imperial assessments from their cities they would sometimes be granted half of the revenues collected. Beyond the market-place and imperial coffers the bishop safeguarded public peace.[39] He appointed officials to oversee maintenance of civic fortifications and administer higher and lower justice in the city.[40] Finally, as the complexities of civic administration and government multiplied, lay committees were established, the forerunners of the later city council elected by the residents of the city. But in the earliest manifestation of lay representation the bishop selected the chairman if not all members of this advisory body.[41]

Imperial Prince (Fürst). Unlike their colleagues in France, England, Italy, and Spain, German bishops are cited in the records of the Vatican by a singular appellation—'princes' *(principi)*.[42] Imperial

---

[37] These rights include the 'Verwaltung der Regalien'; in similarity to secular princes the rights of the bishop here can be termed 'eine grafenähnlichene Stellung'; Hefele, *Studien zum hochmittelalterlichen Stadttypus*, p. 45; the meaning of the term *Regalien* remains amorphous, although it signifies that the medieval king grants the ecclesiastical property of the empire *(Reichskirchengut)* to church officials, W. Wegener, "Regalien," *HRG* 4, pp. 471-479.

[38] The three rights are typically identified as *Münzrecht, Marktrecht* and *Zollrecht*. Thus the bishop controlled trade—the valid currency used, monitoring of weights and measures, and charging of tolls at major points of entry to the city (gates and bridges).

[39] By the twelfth and thirteenth centuries, bishops were viewed as a hindrance to economic growth in the cities. However, in the tenth century episcopal cities provided vital venues for trade. As religious and cultural centers, they attracted clerics and led to the establishing of markets advantageous to merchants; Hefele, *Studien zum hochmittelalterlichen Stadttypus*, pp. 29-30.

[40] Although bishops were responsible for civic peace and protection, they usually hindered efforts to enclose cities with fortifications. Walls could thwart the siege of the enemy but could be used to deny a bishop access to his city; Leudemann, *Deutsche Bischofsstädte*, pp. 100-101.

[41] For a pan-European introduction to the variety of offices and titles created by the city lords and their role in rise of lay city governments, see Nicholas, *The Growth of the Medieval City*, pp. 141-145.

[42] Hans Jürgen Brand, "Fürstbischof und Weihbischof im Spätmittelalter. Zur Darstellung der sacri ministerii summa des reichskirchlichen Episkopats," in *Ecclesia Militans. Studien zur Konzilien- und Reformationsgeschichte*, vol. 2, eds. W Brandmüller, H. Immenkötter, and E. Iserloh (Paderborn: Ferdinand Schöningh, 1988), p. 1.
   On the relationship of bishops as princes to the empire, see Benjamin Arnold, *Princes and Territories in Medieval Germany* (Cambridge: Cambridge University Press,

bishops were vassals of the German king; they received the scepter of political rule, participated in diets of the empire, and formed a valuable pool of talent for the emperor; clerical leaders offered experience and education that made them exceptional prospects for high office at the imperial court.[43] Two dimensions of princely rule proved especially threatening to urban communities. First, as princes and lords bishops carried both the secular and the spiritual swords. They could be called upon to mobilize forces for imperial campaigns and could turn those same soldiers on recalcitrant and rebellious cities.[44] Second, the bishop was a territorial lord with towns and lands held as his feudal possessions. In fact, the entire cathedral city might be considered part of this episcopal territory, part of the consolidated lordship of the bishop.[45] This political territory provided the bishop with financial resources—the so-called 'bishop's table' or *mensa episcopalis*. As the cathedral chapter solidified into a corporation created to assist the bishop, certain lands, including the cathedral, came under the control of the chapter canons, the so-called *Hochstift* and in particular the *mensa capitularis*. When civic residents attempted to break free from rural lordships, they were continually confronted by a prince and a chapter that had one foot in the city and one foot on the land, an institutional and personal bridge between the urban opportunities lay civic residents sought to protect and the countryside where lords held sway.

1991), 79-81; Albert Werminghoff, *Geschichte der Kirchenverfassung Deutschlands im Mittelalter*, vol. 1 (Darmstadt: Wissenschaftliche Buchgesellschaft, 1969), pp. 206-218.

[43] Not all bishops in the empire claimed princely status; for the specific members of the *Reichskirche*, including the imperial abbots, see Appendix A.

[44] For a helpful overview of this military function, see Benjamin Arnold, "German Bishops and their Military Retinues in the Medieval Empire," *German History* 7 (1989), 161-183. For the broader context of clerics and conflict, see *Warriors and Churchmen in the High Middle Ages. Essays Presented to Karl Leyser*, ed. T. Reuter (London: Hambledon Press, 1992).

The anonymous author of the 'Reformatio Sigismundi' devotes a substantial section to the betterment (die Besserung) of the episcopacy, which includes the elimination of this military function and the return to a spiritual priesthood of bishops; "Reformation Sigmund" or "Reformatio Sigismundi" in *Monumenta Germaniae Historica: Staatsschriften des späteren Mittelalters*, vol. 4, ed. H. Koller (Stuttgart: Anton Hiersemann, 1964), pp. 116-122.

[45] Bishopric or *Bistum* identifies the ecclesiastical territory or see of the bishop; *Hochstift* signifies his temporal possessions, including land, castles, and towns; Benjamin Arnold, *Count and Bishop in Medieval Germany. A Study in Regional Power 1100-1350* (Philadelphia: University of Pennsylvania Press, 1991), p. 173.

Shepherd of the Church (Oberhirt).[46] Sublime appellations characterized the sacral authority of the medieval bishop: 'successor to the apostles', 'mediator of salvation', heir to a venerable line of episcopal saints. The iconography of his vestments and adornments signified his sovereignty and holiness; the ring on his finger, the miter gracing his head, the pallium across his shoulder, on his breast a cross often enclosing a sacred relic, all displayed his sacred continuity with Metropolitan superiors (Archbishop and Pope—who bore similar signs of dignity). With the crosier (shepherd's crook) at his side, symbol of his pastoral role and spiritual jurisdiction, the bishop blessed churches and led processions.[47]

Similar to the papacy the bishop stood at the pinnacle of his clerical hierarchy as the head of sacred, administrative, and disciplinary power. Churches, altars, and holy vestments awaited his holy consecration. With his own hands the bishop ordained his priests; on Easter and Pentecost he baptized the faithful. Under his overarching jurisdiction poor relief and care for the sick were administered. However, the sheer number of duties and the dimensions of a diocese usually proved too demanding for one bishop. Absenteeism as well led to the establishment of offices and institutions that extended the bishop's authority and power. While the cathedral chapter managed the property of the *Hochstift* and held worship services in the central

---

[46] The title 'shepherd', symbolized by the episcopal hooked staff or crosier, embraces the roles of the bishop as overseer of the church and pastor of souls. In the classical world the term ἐπίσκοπου denoted an overseer, watcher or scout. The title was applied to government officials, managers of temples and cultic societies as well as to the gods. In the Septuagint God 'oversees' the cosmos and the human heart.

In the New Testament oversight and shepherding are yoked in meaning. In 1 Peter 2:25 the faithful are described as 'sheep' and Christ himself as "the Shepherd and Guardian of your souls" (τον ποιμένα και ἐπίσκοπου των ψυχῶν ὑμῶν). This connection is made to the leaders of the church when the Apostle Paul exhorts the Ephesians to care for the flock as overseers (Acts 20:28). The church office of bishop appears initially as a synonym or of equal rank with the position of elder (πρεσβύτερος) and takes on more specific definition in the Pastoral Epistles (1 Timothy 3:1; Titus 1:5-9). During the second century the monarchial episcopate emerged as the dominant office of the early church; H. W. Beyer, "ἐπίσκοπου," *TDNT* 2, ed. G. Kittel, trans. G. W. Bromiley (Grand Rapids: William B. Eerdmans, 1964), pp. 608-620 and L. Coenen, "ἐπίσκοπου," in *The New International Dictionary of New Testament Theology*, vol. 1, ed. C. Brown (Grand Rapids: Zondervan, 1967), pp. 188-192.

[47] The ecclesiastical significance of the episcopal regalia is clear at the end of the Investiture Controversy. At the Concordat of Worms in July of 1122 Emperor Henry V conceded to the church the right to invest a bishop with ring and crosier; Uta-Renate Blümenthal, *The Investiture Controversy. Church and Monarchy from the Ninth to the Twelfth Century*, trans. U. Blümenthal, (Philadelphia: University of Pennsylvania Press, 1988 [1982]), p.173.

church of the diocese, the 'consecrating bishop' (*Weihbischof*) substituted for the diocesan bishop, especially by blessing holy objects and ordaining the clergy.[48] The Archdeacon (*Archidiakon*) and later the Official (*Offizial*) pursued the discipline of laity and clergy alike. The rural chapters (*Dekanate*) and deans (*Dekane*) extended episcopal authority to the far corners of the ecclesiastical territory—the diocese or bishopric. The bishop gathered his curia and clergy at diocesan synods where he governed as chief administrator and legislator of his church. He announced papal and conciliar mandates, reshaped institutions and procedures, and decreed statutes designed to reform the worship and pastoral care of the church as well as to improve the morality of clergy and laity alike.[49]

Legislation and jurisdiction relied on enforcement. Not only did episcopal courts deal with the unrepentant sinner, the testaments of

---

A brief description of the bishop's vestments and regalia can be found in Johannes Neumann, "Bischof," *TRE* 6, pp. 667-669. For a full description of episcopal and clerical iconography see Pierre Salmon, *Mitra und Stab. Die Pontifikalsignien im römischen Ritus* (Mainz: Matthias-Grünewald, 1960); Philipp Hofmeister, *Mitra und Stab der wirklichen Prälaten ohne bischöflichen Charakter* (Stuttgart: Ferdinand Enke, 1928); and Klemens Honselmann, *Das Rationale der Bischöfe* (Paderborn: Verein für Geschichte und Altertumskunde Westfalens, 1975).

[48] I have given a literal translation of *Weihbischof* to underscore how this office assisted the diocesan bishop (*Episcopus ordinarius*) in his overwhelming charge. When the residing bishop is in ill health or unable to manage the responsibilities of the diocese a Consecrating or "Auxiliary" Bishop is appointed. The sacramental role of this bishop is of primary importance. The Consecrating Bishop is assigned a symbolic titular diocese, derived from an episcopate no longer a part of the present church such as an ancient ecclesiastical center in the Near and Middle East; S. E. Donlon, "Bishop, Auxiliary," *New Catholic Encyclopedia*, vol. 2 (New York: McGraw-Hill, 1967), pp. 591-592.

The rise of the assisting and consecrating bishop (*Hilfsbischof, Chorepiscopus*) is described by Theodor Gottlieb, *Das abendländische Chorepiskopat* (Bonn: Kurt Schroeder, 1928).

[49] The structures and offices of dioceses vary. The above description is based on the model of the diocese in Constance. On the specific offices (such as *Offizial, Generalvikar, Weihbischof*) see Brigitte Degler-Spengler, "Das Bistum vom 13. bis zum 15. Jahrhundert," in *Helvetia Sacra.* I, 2.1, Das Bistum Konstanz, Das Erzbistum Mainz, Das Bistum St. Gallen, ed. F. X. Bischof, et al. (Basel, Frankfurt am Main: Helbing und Lichtenhahn, 1993), pp. 97-99; henceforth cited as *HS*. The most informative discussion of the ecclesiastical duties and rights of the German bishops as well as the episcopal curia remains Hans Erich Feine, *Kirchliche Rechtsgeschichte*, vol. 1 (Weimar: Hermann Böhlaus, 1955), pp. 180-225, 322-389; an earlier and still critical overview is Paul Hinschius, *Das Kirchenrecht der Katholiken und Protestanten in Deutschland*, vol. 2: System des katholischen Kirchenrechts mit besonderer Rücksicht auf Deutschland (Graz: Akademische Druck- und Verlagsanstalt, 1959 [1878]), pp. 38-348.

For a substantial summary of the development of the bishop from the early church to the present, see Neumann, "Bischof," *TRE* 6, pp. 653-661.

the dead, the broken marriage, and the wayward cleric but these
courts also had the weapon of episcopal censure, the ability to excommunicate—to deny the sacraments and require the communi-
cant to shun the sinner.[50] Entire communities could fall under the
daunting shadow of episcopal disdain as the decree of interdict suspended the sacraments, including baptism of the newborn, extreme
unction for the dying, and Christian burial of the deceased.[51]

In addition to his roles as lord, prince, and shepherd the bishop
enjoyed privileges that combined the secular and sacred—namely the
hotly contested clerical immunities. Two rights set the clergy apart
from lay society. First, fiscal immunity, the *privilegium immunitatis*, exempted the clergy from lay taxation and civic service such as guard
duty. Second, juridical immunity, the *privilegium fori*, insured that the
clergy would only be prosecuted in ecclesiastical courts. Because
these privileges usually extended to the *familia* of the clergy and their
servants as well as to the bishop's ministerials, a sizable part of the
urban population could be exempt from lay taxation and jurisdiction.[52] These exceptional privileges ignited intense lay violence and
anticlerical protest throughout the later Middle Ages. To critics it
seemed that the clergy enjoyed immunity from prosecution and the
economic advantages of civic life without defending or paying for
them. Clerics accused of crimes could count on the ministrations and
sometimes the sympathetic rulings of church courts.[53]

'Immunity' had a spatial dimension as well. The chief royal privi-

---

[50] E. Kaufmann and H. Lentze, "Bann," *HRG* 1, pp. 306-310.
   Brian A. Pavlac explores how excommunication as defined by Canon Law was
put into practice on an archiepiscopal level in "Excommunication and Territorial
Politics in High Medieval Trier," *CH* 60 (1991), 20-36; George W. Dameron reveals
how the practice of excommunication is tied to civic and rural politics in *Episcopal
Power and Florentine Society 1000-1320* (Cambridge: Harvard University Press, 1991),
pp. 96, 99-100, 115-116, 139, 165.
   [51] For an intriguing and well researched case study at the papal level, see Richard
C. Trexler, *The Spiritual Power: Republican Florence under Interdict* (Leiden: E. J. Brill,
1974).
   [52] Clergy and clerical personnel made up 10% of the population in medieval
Augsburg; 5-7% in Cologne and 7-7.5% in Würzburg; for further information regarding clergy and city as well as clerical privileges, see Eberhard Isenmann, *Die
deutsche Stadt im Spätmittelalter. Stadtgestalt, Recht, Stadtregiment, Kirche, Gesellschaft,
Wirtschaft* (Stuttgart: Eugen Ulmer, 1988), pp. 211-216.
   [53] This anticlerical violence, typified by assault and battery as well as destruction
of clerical property, was especially apparent in the episcopal cities studied by D. A.
Eltis, "Tensions between Clergy and Laity in some Western German Cities in the
Later Middle Ages," *JEH* 43 (1992), 231-248; Robert Scribner contends that anticlerical attacks were similar in intensity during the later Middle Ages and the Refor-

lege granted to the bishop pertained to his 'cathedral city'.[54] While this phrase can be used to describe all civic space, it is technically limited to the cathedral compound or to the original bishop's residence around which the lay city formed and expanded.[55] Even as this lay commune 'expelled' the bishop's overarching claims from the market place and city hall, the precinct of the bishop's church and palace remained immune to lay encroachment. Thus, while the bishop had once relied on a web of privileges and a cadre of officers to monitor, guide, and invade every facet of lay activity, he still maintained a physical and legal island of immunity. Long after citizens had claimed the city as their own, the bishop retained a base for his fading ties to civic lordship, a stubborn remnant and spatial reminder of his former sovereignty.

Given the number and complexity of episcopal rights and prerogatives, the growth of civic independence appears all the more

---

mation; he also reveals how conflict between bishop and city occurred in diocesan cities outside the cathedral city; "Anticlericalism and the Cities," in *Anticlericalism in Late Medieval and Early Modern Europe*, eds. P. A. Dykema and H. A. Oberman (Leiden: E. J. Brill, 1993), pp. 147-166, esp. 150-151.

For a helpful overview see Kaspar Elm, "Antiklerikalismus im deutschen Mittelalter," in *Anticlelricalism in Late Medieval and Early Modern Europe*, pp. 4-18; a regional study of this fierce 'war' between laity and clergy is Bernd-Ulrich Hergemöller's *'Pfaffenkriege' im spätmittelalterlichen Hanseraum. Quellen und Studien zu Braunschweig, Osnabrück, Lüneburg und Rostock*, 2 vols, (Köln: Hermann Böhlau, 1988).

[54] The division of rights and privileges into the categories of city lord, prince, and bishop is somewhat artificial. The immunity from civic burdens and taxes originates from earlier privileges that ensured immunity from other secular lords. The king granted this privilege in order to ensure that the bishop had a basis for his lordship and jurisdiction. The king also guaranteed the freedoms of the church, including royal protection of episcopal buildings inside the city. The bishop enjoyed the *Bannimmunität* in his episcopal cities; this right was the foundation of his civic lordship. The bishop exercised the *Marktrecht* as well, denoting a specific public space in which a particular lord ruled and monitored economic activity; D. Willoweit, "Immunität," *HRG* 2, pp. 315-325.

[55] The bishop's civic lordship originally protected the cathedral, the episcopal palace, other adjoining chapels and warehouses as well as the dwellings of the cathedral canons. The appellation *Bischofsburg* suggests the military purpose of the complex, usually an elevated place in the city fortified against outside aggression and serving as a refuge for a fleeing populace. This kernel of episcopal property was immune to civic taxation and jurisdiction. Other clerical foundations in the city gained immunity from city and bishop; this right often included clerical houses and gardens. Therefore, from the lay perspective, the ecclesiastical immunity, both episcopal and more generally clerical, withdrew a substantial amount of urban real estate from civic demands and burdens. Leudemann shows that this development is especially characteristic of episcopal cities founded from the 8th to the 10th century; *Deutsche Bischofsstädte*, pp. 9-100; see B. Diestelkamp's brief but helpful discussion of "Bischofsstadt," *HRG* 1, 446-447.

unexpected. Each community on the road from episcopal rule to the
status of 'free' or 'imperial' city had varied success against its former
lord. Even when the episcopal residence had been transferred outside
the city on a temporary or permanent basis, the bishop could continue to exercise a 'real presence' in the city. This presence manifested itself in a net of episcopal influence—courts, clergy, cathedral
canons, synods—that continued to contest civic policy, censure lay
morality, and claim property beholden to the church and immune to
the city fathers. Episcopal influence was not merely tied to an individual or residence but was manifest in the rights and privileges,
sacred and secular, handed down from one bishop to the next. During the sixteenth century this real presence was contested afresh and
in some cases eliminated. In number and extent bishops were exiled
as never before.

3. *The Refugees of the Reformation*[56]

It is tempting to create a grand narrative for the ongoing relationship
of bishop to city or a single thesis that would complement and perhaps even compete with the dramatic story of civic independence
and City Reformation. But neither the collapse nor survival of episcopal rule was a unified process. Myriad factors—civic, ecclesiastical,
constitutional, juridical, religious, economic, political—gave the
struggle of each bishop and city its own distinctive shape in the sixteenth century. By 1500 many former episcopal cities had reached
the status of 'free' (*freie Stadt*), 'imperial city' (*Reichsstadt*), or 'free imperial city' (*freie Reichsstadt*) and now controlled the political and judicial

---

[56] The predicament of the German bishops during the Reformation has yet to be
fully described. Volker Press has written a programmatic introduction to the issue in
"Bischof und Stadt in der Neuzeit," in *Stadt und Bischof*, eds. B. Kirchgässner and W.
Baer (Sigmaringen: Jan Thorbecke, 1988), pp. 137-155. For a survey which provides
biographical sketches of all the German bishops of the sixteenth century and their
responses to the Protestant Reformation, see Georg May's *Die deutschen Bischöfe
angesichts der Glaubensspaltung des 16. Jahrhunderts* (Wien: Mediatrix-Verlag, 1983). The
best study of a single bishopric remains Francis Rapp's *Réformes et Réformation a Strasbourg: Église et Société dans le Diocèse de Strasbourg (1450-1525)* (Paris: Edition Ophrys,
1974). Two monographs provide a contrast to the German episcopacy: Frederick J.
Baumgartner, *Change and Continuity in the French Episcopate: the Bishops and the Wars of
Religion 1547-1610* (Durham: Duke University Press, 1986) and Felicity Heal, *Of Prelates and Princes: A Study of the Economic and Social Position of the Tudor Episcopate* (London:
Cambridge University Press, 1980).

institutions of their former lords.[57] But as long as the clergy of the medieval church continued to live and minister in the city, the bishop maintained a tenuous grasp on many spheres of urban life.[58] As Reformation movements took hold in many of these cities and were eventually sanctioned by the city council, every vestige of episcopal authority—the bishop's clergy, institutions, and property—could be expelled or liquidated. Protestant magistrates often came to oversee every aspect of religious life; they renounced the bishop's sacred charge. This elimination of the bishop's ecclesiastical headship was the culmination of the *Episcopus exclusus*. The bishop became a refugee from a city he had in some cases founded, protected, and ruled.

Just as the bishop's surviving rights and privileges varied from city to city by the sixteenth century, the nature of expulsion and exile was distinctive from place to place. In at least three cases the bishop's flight was brief but violent: Salzburg (1523), Würzburg (1525), and Münster (1534-35); after a short period of lay rule episcopal authority was quickly restored.[59] In many cities Protestant movements made significant inroads, usually gaining an aggressive following and dominating civic and church government (Bremen, Breslau, Liège, Osnabrück, Paderborn, Regensburg, Reval, Riga, Speyer, Strasbourg,

[57] For a precise discussion of '*freie Stadt*' and '*Reichsstadt*', and "*freie Reichsstadt*" in the context of regional and imperial politics, see Georg Schmidt, *Der Städtetag in der Reichsverfassung. Eine Untersuchung zur korporativen Politik der freien und Reichsstädte in der ersten Hälfte des 16. Jahrhunderts* (Stuttgart: Franz Steiner, 1984), pp. 80-86. For the late medieval relationship of the crown to these cities, see Paul-Joachim Heinig, *Reichsstädte, Freie Städte und Königtum 1389-1450. Ein Beitrag zur deutschen Verfassungsgeschichte* (Stuttgart: Franz Steiner, 1983), pp. 10-54, 353-366.

[58] This investigation focuses on those cities which were originally the main residence under the lordship of the bishop. However, this study could also be extended to every commune, large and small, where the bishop exercised pastoral oversight of worship, clergy, and morality. For example, in addition to the former episcopal city and imperial city of Constance, the cities of the diocese could be examined, including prominent and eventually Protestant locations such as Esslingen, Reutlingen, Stuttgart, Ulm, and Zürich. These cities denied episcopal authority and oversight as well.

[59] All three bishops fled in the face of violent upheavals: the 'Latin War' in Salzburg, the Peasants' Revolt in Würzburg, and the Anabaptist Kingdom of Münster; for conditions in Würzburg, see Hans-Christoph Rublack, "Die Stadt Würzburg im Bauernkrieg," *ARG* 67 (1976), 76-100; on Münster see the survey article by R. Po-Chia Hsia, "Münster and the Anabaptists," in *The German People and the Reformation*, ed. R. Po-Chia Hsia (Ithaca: Cornell University Press, 1988), pp. 50-69; for the predicament of episcopal lands and cities during the Peasants' Revolt and the Anabaptist kingdom: Volker Press, "Bischof und Stadt in der Neuzeit," in *Stadt und Bischof*, pp. 141-142.

Utrecht, Verden, Worms). Here the bishop maintained some influence in the city. Though often barred from entering a city bishops were able to preserve their symbolic ties and clerical institutions. In Bremen and Riga, Speyer, and Strasbourg, the cathedral chapters weathered civic hostility and provided the bishops with a critical toehold, a basis for later advantageous arbitration during the Augsburg Interim (1548).[60]

Despite aggressive protest and negotiation some bishops still fell victim to bold territorial and civic initiatives: their presence and their

---

[60] On the success of the city and the stubborn survival of the cathedral chapter in Bremen, see Herbert Schwarzwalder, *Geschichte der freien Hansestadt Bremen: Von den Anfängen bis zur Franzosenzeit (1810)*, vol. 1 (Bremen: Friedrich Röver, 1975), pp. 172-231. The cathedral chapter also survived in Riga until 1566; see E. O'Rourke, "Riga," *LTK* 8, p. 1309. Although the city became formally Lutheran in 1555, Speyer still tolerated the Roman Catholic Stifte; Willi Alter, "Von der Konradischen Rachtung bis zum letzten Reichstag in Speyer (1420/22-1570)," in *Geschichte der Stadt Speyer*, vol. 1, ed. W. Eiger (Stuttgart: W. Kohlhammer, 1982), pp. 493-544. In Strasbourg the chapters survived even after their worship services were taken over by ministers sanctioned by the city council; the canons were under civic jurisdiction but the institutions did not perish; Miriam Usher Chrisman, *Strasbourg and the Reform. A Study in the Process of Change* (New Haven: Yale University Press, 1967), pp. 241-242. Francis Rapp has studied in detail the relationship of bishop and city during the Reformation in Strasbourg; in "Straßburg, Hochstift and Freie Reichsstadt," *Die Territorien des Reichs*, vol. 5, pp. 83-88.

For the other episcopal cities the following secondary literature offers critical background. Breslau was a volatile example of civic hostility and episcopal survival; see Alfred Sabisch, *Die Bischöfe von Breslau und die Reformation in Schlesien* (Münster: Aschendorff, 1975), pp. 62-99. Liège was eventually won to Roman Catholicism by Bishop Gerhard of Groesbeeck (1564-80); see M. Dierickx, "Lüttich," *LTK* 6, p. 1243; Dauch, *Die Bischofsstadt*, p. 201. Osnabrück experienced several confessional reversals well into the seventeenth century; see Christine van den Heuvel, "Städtisch-bürgerliche Freiheit und fürstlicher Absolutismus. Verfassung und Verwaltung der Stadt Osnabrück in der frühen Neuzeit," in *Recht, Verfassung und Verwaltung in der frühneuzeitlichen Stadt*, ed. M. Solleis (Köln: Hermann Böhlau, 1991), pp. 159-171; and L. Niehus, "Osnabrück," *LTK* 7, p. 1266. On Paderborn see Heinrich Schoppmeyer, *Der Bischof von Paderborn und seine Städte. Zugleich ein Beitrag zum Problem Landesherr und Stadt* (Paderborn: Verein für Geschichte und Altertumskunde Westfalens, 1968). In Regensburg the bishop had always divided his sovereignty with the emperor, the Dukes of Bavaria, and later with the city council; the support of the latter may well have insured the bishop's survival; as late as the reign of Pankraz of Sinzenhofen (1538-48), the bishop still had access to the city for consecration; see Karl Hausberger, *Geschichte des Bistums Regensburg*, vol. 1 (Regensburg: Friedrich Pustet, 1989), pp. 312-319. On Reval, see E. O'Rouke, "Reval," *LTK* 8, p. 1268. Utrecht was changed from a bishopric to an archbishopric to a Calvinist church government in 1580; see A. G. Weiler, "Utrecht," *LTK* 10, p. 587. Verden had equally volatile reversals of confession until the end of the Thirty Years' War; see E. Weise, "Verden," *LTK* 10, pp. 674-675. In Worms the developing legal autonomy of the lay city government provided the foundation for the institution of Reformation in the 1520s; Friedrich Battenberg, "Gerichtsbarkeit und Recht im spätmittelalterlichen und frühneuzeitlichen Worms," in *Residenzen des Rechts*, p. 76.

powers were meticulously eliminated. On the regional level bishops
surrendered to the larger designs of territorial lords, especially in the
northeastern corner of the empire (Brandenburg, Halberstadt,
Havelberg, Kammin, Lebus, Meissen, Merseburg, Minden, Naumburg, Ösel, Pomesanien, Ratzeburg, Samland, Schleswig, Schwerin);
in most cases a Protestant bishop and church government eventually
replaced the medieval church.[61] But city councils could act alone,
often without territorial support; they eradicated the bishop's presence from every nook and cranny inside the ramparts. With the
exception of three northern cities (Hildesheim: 1542-43, Lübeck:
1530-31, Magdeburg: 1546) this development was southwest German and Swiss in character (Augsburg: 1537, Basel: 1529, Constance: 1526-27, Geneva: 1536, Lausanne: 1536).[62]

The career of one prominent cleric spanned many of the fault

---

[61] Developments in this region have not usually been included in the narrative of
bishop and city in the German Empire, in part because some of the bishops were not
imperial princes and thus answered to territorial lords in the area or the bishops
would soon be subsumed in territorial states in the sixteenth century. The bishop of
Brandenburg answered to the Markgraf of the same name in the Later Middle Ages;
in 1571 administration of the diocese was taken over by the Markgraf; it had been
Protestant since 1557; see B. Stasiewski, "Brandenburg," *LTK* 2, pp. 646-647. For
the late-medieval rule of the Markgraf in episcopal matters generally see Karl-Heinz
Ahrens, "Die Verfassungsrechtliche Stellung und politische Bedeutung der märkischen Bistümer im späten Mittelalter," in *Mitteldeutsche Bistümer im Spätmittelalter*, ed.
R. Schmidt (Lüneburg: Nordostdeutsches Kulturwerk, 1988), pp. 19-52. Roman Catholicism was abolished in Halberstadt in 1576; see J. Klapper, "Halberstadt," *LTK*
4, p. 1329. Havelberg was incorporated into the Protestant Markgrafschaft in
1571—Gottfried Wentz, *Das Bistum Havelberg* (Berlin: Walter de Gruyter, 1933), pp.
27-28. The last Roman Catholic Bishop in Kammin died in 1544; see B. Stasiewski,
"Kammin," *LTK* 5, p. 1272. In the mid-1550s Lebus became Protestant under the
influence of the Markgraf of Brandenburg; see B. Stasiewski, "Lebus," *LTK* 6, p.
870. Under August, Electoral Duke of Saxony (1553-1586), the bishoprics of
Saxony—Meissen, Merseburg, and Naumburg—were dissolved (1581); see Willi
Rittenbach and Siegfried Seifert, *Geschichte der Bischöfe von Meissen, 968-1581* (Leipzig:
St. Benno-Verlag, 1965), pp. 378-384. Ösel, Pomesanien, Samland, Schleswig and
Schwerin came under the control of Protestant princes; see M, Hellmann, "Ösel,"
LTK 7, p. 1261; H. Schmauch, "Pomesanien," *LTK* 8, p. 601; H. Schmauch,
"Samland, *LTK* 9, p. 297; W. Göebel, *LTK* 9, "Schleswig," p. 418; H.-D. Kahl,
"Schwerin," *LTK* 9, p. 547. Bodo Nischan has provided a thorough study of Refor-
mation movements and stages in northwestern Germany in *Prince, People, and Confes-
sion. The Second Reformation in Brandenburg* (Philadelphia: University of Pennsylvania
Press, 1994).

[62] The cathedral canons departed from Basel in 1529 and took up residence in
nearby Freiburg im Breisgau, a city in the diocese of another bishop who himself was
exiled from his episcopal city—the bishop of Constance; see Hans R. Guggisberg,
*Basel in the Sixteenth Century. Aspects of the City Republic before, during, and after the Reforma-
tion* (St. Louis: Center for Reformation Research, 1982). Hans Berner has investigated the complex relationship between city, bishop, and bishopric during and after

lines emanating from the conflict of bishop and city and was vulnerable to fissures both geographical and confessional. A glaring example of the vice of pluralism—holding multiple church offices—Cardinal Albert of Brandenburg was Archbishop of Mainz (1514-45),
Archbishop of Magdeburg (1513-45), and Bishop of Halberstadt
(1513-45). Not only did Albert receive a copy of Martin Luther's *95
Theses* and the brunt of Luther's attack in the *Resolutiones* but the
archbishop also lost a number of crucial cities to the Protestant
cause, including the episcopal cities of Halberstadt and Magdeburg
as well as the archiepiscopal residence in Halle. Even Erfurt, the
second city and former eastern residence of the Archdiocese of
Mainz, tolerated a Lutheran Reformation.[63] Given all of these cases

---

the recognition of Reformation in Basel; *"die gute correspondenz."* *Die Politik der Stadt
Basel gegenüber dem Fürstbistum Basel in den Jahren 1525-1585* (Basel and Frankfurt am
Main: Helbing und Lichtenhahn, 1989). As late as the 1530s Geneva was still ruled
by an episcopal *Stadtherr* under the control of the house of Savoy; the expulsion of the
bishop was the result of the fusion of movements for lay self-rule and reformation; on
the importance of the very late development of independence and its implications for
Calvin's church in Geneva, see William J. Bouwsma, "The Peculiarity of the Reformation in Geneva," in *Religion and Culture in the Renaissance and Reformation*, pp. 65-77.
In Hildesheim the festivities of Fastnacht provided the context for the take-over of
the urban church; see J. Gebauer, *Geschichte der Stadt Hildesheim*, vol. 1 (Hildesheim:
August Lax, 1922), pp. 327-348. The ministrations of Bern stand behind not only
the expulsion of the bishop of Geneva but also Lausanne; see H. Marmier,
"Lausanne," *LTK* 6, p. 835. The city council took over the role of the bishop of
Lübeck; on this development see Wolf-Dieter Hauschild, *Kirchengeschichte Lübecks.
Christentum und Bürgertum in neun Jahrhunderten* (Lübeck: Max Schmidt Römhild, 1981),
pp. 183-193. The bishop of Chur, Henry of Hewen (1491-1505), had already fled his
episcopal city during his reign, leaving a lay and canonical regency that weakened
resistance to the spread of Zwinglianism and Lutheranism on the eve of the Reformation; see Oskar Vasella, "Die Ursachen der Reformation in der deutschen
Schweiz," *Zeitschrift für schweizerische Geschichte* 27 (1947), 404.
   [63] On Albert's stormy career see Franz Schrader, "Kardinal Albrecht von
Brandenburg, Erzbischof von Magdeburg, im Spannungsfeld zwischen alter und
neuer Kirche," in *Von Konstanz nach Trient*, ed. R. Bäumer (München: Ferdinand
Schöningh, 1972), pp. 419-445. These civic difficulties also extended to the church
territories formerly under Albert's reign as researched by Schrader in two volumes:
*Ringen, Untergang und Überleben der Katholischen Klöster in den Hochstiften Magdeburg und
Halberstadt von der Reformation bis zum Westfälischen Frieden* (Münster und Leipzig:
Aschendorff, 1977) and *Die Visitationen der Katholischen Klöster im Erzbistum Magdeburg
durch die evangelischen Landesherren 1561-1651* (Leipzig: St. Benno Verlag, 1978). On the
Reformation of Erfurt and the bi-confessional outcome in the city, see Robert
Scribner, "Civic Unity and the Reformation in Erfurt," in *Popular Culture and Popular
Movements in Reformation Germany* (London: Hambledon Press, 1987), pp. 185-216.
   It is ironic that the house of Brandenburg also produced princes that dissolved
dioceses in the northeast, showing that the princes of Albert's homeland were as
disastrous for the territories of the old church as his precarious position proved un-
fortunate for his episcopal cities.

Albert of Brandenburg might be deemed the 'poster child' of the *Episcopus exclusus*.

Urban centers have long been celebrated as the ideal context for the coalescing of dissenting religious groups, the spread of evangelical theologies and church discipline, as the incubators of Reformation.[64] A number of examples counter this model. Cologne was an imperial city that resisted its archiepiscopal overlord and yet remained faithful to its ancestral church even as Hermann of Wied, Archbishop of Cologne (1515-47) turned Protestant.[65] Moreover, in episcopal cities Reformation movements could be resisted, repressed, and made impotent by an efficient and aggressive bishop. Hans-Christoph Rublack identified this pattern in his study of the 'Failed Reformation' in the episcopal cities of Bamberg, Eichstätt, Freising, Mainz, Passau, Salzburg, Trier, and Würzburg.[66] In each case the bishop or archbishop had maintained his civic lordship in the later Middle Ages, thus distinguishing these cities from the free and imperial cities: "When the Prince-bishop possessed and wielded all of his spiritual and secular power [the power of a lord], the resistance of a Protestant minority had no chance."[67]

Other factors may help to explain the relative success or failure of attempts to drive the bishop out of town and assure his permanent

---

[64] See Bernd Moeller, *Imperial Cities and the Reformation. Three Essays*, trans. H. C. E. Midelfort and M. U. Edwards Jr. (Durham: Labyrinth Press, 1982), pp. 41-115; this work has been revised in German with an extensive afterword: *Reichsstadt und Reformation* (Berlin: Evangelische Verlagsanstalt, 1987). For a more nuanced discussion of free cities and Reformation in an European context, see Euan Cameron, *The European Reformation* (Oxford: Clarendon Press, 1991), pp. 211-266 and Heinz Schilling, *Die Stadt in der frühen Neuzeit* (München: R. Oldenbourg, 1993), pp. 94-112.

[65] On the peculiar case of Cologne, see Robert Scribner, "Why was there no Reformation in Cologne?," in *Popular Culture and Popular Movements in Reformation Germany*, pp. 217-242. On the case of Hermann of Wied, see August Franzen, *Bischof und Reformation. Erzbischof Hermann von Wied in Köln vor der Entscheidung zwischen Reform und Reformation* (Münster: Aschendorff, 1971).

For a thorough study of an imperial city that remained faithful to the Roman Catholic Church, see Wilfried Enderle, *Konfessionsbildung und Ratsregiment in der katholischen Reichsstadt Überlingen (1500-1618) im Kontext der Reformationsgeschichte der oberschwäbischen Reichsstädte* (Stuttgart: Kohlhammer, 1990). Überlingen was an invaluable ally of the expelled bishop of Constance, who transferred the cathedral chapter there in 1527.

[66] Hans-Christoph Rublack, *Gescheiterte Reformation. Frühreformatorische und protestantische Bewegungen in südwestdeutschen geistlichen Residenzen* (Stuttgart: Klett-Cota, 1976).

[67] Rublack, *Gescheiterte Reformation*, p. 126; other cities might be added to Rublack's list, including Brixen, Münster, Seckau, and Trent; their bishops did not permanently loose their episcopal status in the city.

exile. Volker Press has restated the old description of the connection between lordship and reformation, noting that two volatile impulses fused and overwhelmed episcopal resources. Evangelical preachers harnessed latent anticlericalism; they combined this hostility with a long-standing movement to break free from episcopal lordship. In addition to the internal civic politics of the bishop described by Rublack, Press has emphasized how territorial context played a considerable role in the resiliency and longevity of civic autonomy or episcopal rule. In the northeast of Germany expelled bishops were replaced by Protestants who formed new evangelical church governments. In the southeast the Wittelsbach/Habsburg axis served to shore up weak ecclesiastical lords and ensure the survival of the 'episcopal city'.[68] This tendency is also evident in far northeastern bishoprics loosely associated with the empire; their ties to solidly Roman Catholic Poland may have ensured episcopal survival (Ermland, Kulm, Laibach).[69]

The social and religious turmoil of the sixteenth century proved catastrophic for many German bishops. At the very least this disaster led to a fierce assault on episcopal lordship and ecclesiastical oversight. Protestant growth could also result in the dissolution of nearly all episcopal institutions, the outright expulsion of the bishop's clergy, confiscation of church property, and the establishment of an overarching civic church order. Bishops not only retreated into physical exile but they also lost the manpower and sacred space that had until then allowed them to identify a certain city as the ancient capital of their diocese, a place where the bishop had symbolically ruled *ex cathedra* from his throne in the cathedral. Now he faced the loss of an ancient sort of citizenship, not borne of a communal oath or the shouldering of civic burdens but rather rooted in his role as founder and protector of the city, shepherd of his city's churches, and apostolic descendant of bishops buried beneath the vaults of his cathedral.

---

[68] Press, "Bischof und Stadt in der Neuzeit," in *Stadt und Bischof,* pp. 137-144.

Benjamin Arnold has studied how the medieval bishops of Eichstätt regained land and authority from their lay advocates, thus creating a stable territory on which to enlarge and solidify their regional power. Perhaps this provides yet another explanation for the resilience of the city of Eichstätt as an episcopal capital throughout the sixteenth century; *Count and Bishop in Medieval Germany.* On advocates as a threat to diocesan peace and episcopal rule, see Arnold, *Princes and Territories in Medieval Germany,* pp. 83-87.

[69] See M. Hellmann and E. M. Wermter, "Ermland," *LTK* 3, pp. 1032-1034; M. Hellmann, "Kulm," *LTK* 5, p. 658; and J. Ploner, "Laibach," *LTK* 6, p. 732.

The Reformation produced a wave of clerical refugees, including some clerics of the highest standing—the bishops who once ruled as city lords, imperial princes, and shepherds of their civic churches.

*   *   *

This chapter has focused on the 'experience' of those who knelt for consecration from hallowed hands, who received a ring on the finger and seized the shepherd's crook, the symbols of their pastoral and juridical authority. Ascendance to the episcopal throne in late-medieval and early modern Germany did not merely signify the high point of a career in the church hierarchy. In cities deemed 'episcopal' a new bishop took on the continuing struggle against expulsion—physical, political, economic, legal, ecclesiastical, and pastoral. In fact, there is an irregular rhythm to episcopal life as bishops came and went, withdrew and returned, forsook and forgave, fled and retaliated, reassessed and rebuilt their base of power and authority, a rhythm that ties the travails of early medieval bishops to their sixteenth-century counterparts. The German episcopacy rode out the storms of early medieval 'episcopicide', the controversies of pope and emperor, the rise of civic independence, and the cataclysm of the Reformation. Indeed, sometimes it was exile from the start as citizens bolted their gates, manned the ramparts, and demanded concessions from a new bishop seeking entry to his cathedral and altar of consecration.[70]

This chapter has marginalized one traditional dimension of the narrative of bishops and cities—the theme of civic rights and institutions. Usually the episcopal experience is subsumed under or completely overlooked in accounts of the strident march to urban 'democracy'. However, this brief description of episcopal office, rights, privileges, and institutions is likewise a catalogue of many of the benefits citizens gained as they wrested control from their lord, prince, and bishop. While political and economic gains might be attributed to a shift in governmental rule, a change which does not directly undercut the apostolic mission of the bishop, the slow erosion of

---

[70] A pivotal moment in the independence of Augsburg occurred when residents refused entry to newly elected Bishop Hartmann, Count of Dillingen (1248-86) in 1249; Friedrich Zoepfl, *Das Bistum Augsburg und seine Bischöfe im Mittelalter*. Geschichte des Bistums und seine Bischöfe, vol. I (München: Schnell und Steiner, 1969), pp. 197-199; hereafter cited as Zoepfl I.

ecclesiastical oversight alienated the bishop from his institution—the church. Part of this disassociation was internal. The cathedral chapter gained limited autonomy, held its own property, and at times forged alliances with the city against the bishop.[71] Collegiate churches and their canons were institutionally independent of the bishop. Mendicants held their own immunities vis-à-vis the bishop, answering to Rome alone.[72] Long before the sixteenth century cities acquired custodial rights over parish property and donations of the faithful; in some cases they came to control the appointment of clergy. Charitable foundations and schools were absorbed into the matrix of civic institutions.[73] The Protestant Reformation, the culmination of the story of the *Episcopus exclusus*, appears as the full extension of episcopal exile, wherein the lay city council took full responsibility for the oversight of the faithful and the maintenance of the church and its clergy. Until the sixteenth century the bishop was still accepted as part of the divinely ordained order of church and civic life. I have yet to discover a medieval vision of civic church and society which conceived of this divinely sanctioned order without the ministrations of a bishop. The remarkable development spawned by religious dissent was not the expulsion of the bishop. For centuries that exclusion had been part and parcel of the cohabitation and cooperation, competition and conflict of bishop and city. New was the idea that the bishop was no longer necessary, that the city council would govern the city *and* shepherd the civic church. This claim transcended expulsion and exile. By definition the bishop no longer belonged to the city once deemed his own. This ultimate form of exclusion occurred in the southwest German cities of Constance and Augsburg.

[71] For a thorough study of this development, see Lawrence G. Duggan's *Bishop and Chapter: The Governance of the Bishopric of Speyer to 1552* (New Brunswick: Rutgers University Press, 1978).
[72] See Norbert Hecker, *Bettelorden und Bürgertum. Konflikt und Kooperation in deutschen Städten des Spätmittelalters* (Frankfurt am Main: Peter D. Lang, 1981) and *Stellung und Wirksamkeit der Bettelorden in der städtischen Gesellschaft* (Berlin: Duncker und Humboldt, 1981).
[73] See *History of the Church*, vol. 4, eds. H. Jedin and J. Dolan (New York: Crossroad, 1980), pp. 566-570. The right of patronage provided the laity with the best opportunity to take control of church lands and institutions; see Jörn Sieglerschmidt, *Territorialstaat und Kirchenregiment. Studien zur Rechtsdogmatik des Kirchenpatronatsrechts im 15. und 16. Jahrhundert* (Köln: Böhlau, 1987).

CHAPTER TWO

CONFLICT, EXPULSION, AND COHABITATION IN
LATE MEDIEVAL CONSTANCE

In May of 1496 the cathedral canons of Constance met to elect a
new bishop. They chose a youthful, rising star in the diocesan clergy,
a candidate who appeared ideally suited for the times. Hugo of
Hohenlandenberg (1496-1530, 1530-31) was about to inherit a community shaped and fractured by its regional importance, episcopal
heritage, and civic freedoms. To the Celts and Romans first, then
bishops and burghers, emperors and envoys, Constance was especially fit for command, communication, and commerce. Lake Constance (*Bodensee*), which today borders Germany, Switzerland, and
Austria, laps the eastern edge of Constance, while the Rhine flows
west out of the great lake, marking the northern extent of the old
city. From the turn of the sixth to the seventh century the fortunes of
the city rose and fell with its prince-bishop, who ruled the streets and
markets of Constance, hosted kings and emperors in the episcopal
palace, and sculpted the city as the sacred capital of a far-flung diocese. But by the twelfth century residents had made significant inroads into episcopal authority, winning imperial exemption from direct episcopal taxation. In the mid-thirteenth century Constance was
listed among the imperial cities of the Holy Roman Empire, replac-
ing the bishop's primary lordship with the rule of the emperor. By
the inauguration of Bishop Hugo Constance was both an imperial
city and a bishop's residence, a community of about 5,000 ruled by a
lay city council and yet serving as an episcopal capital. During the
first years of Hugo's reign Constance shifted from a significant regional capital in the Swabian/Swiss region of the empire to a city
teetering on a fiercely contested border. While to the north and east
river and lake shaped Constance, to the south and west the victorious
Swiss Confederacy ruled, fresh from its crushing defeat of imperial
forces in the Swabian War (1498-99).[1]

A shrewd politician who could resist and roll back civic encroach-

---

[1] Helmut Maurer, "Das Bistum bis zum 12. Jahrhundert," *HS* I, 2.1, pp. 85-92,
152-156; Brigitte Degler-Spengler, "Das Bistum von 13. bis zum 15. Jahrhundert,"

ment on bishop and cathedral chapter, Hugo of Hohenlandenberg was a Swiss noble who could play the emerging confederacy against the envoys and armies of the Holy Roman Empire. The new bishop had the appropriate aristocratic background for high church office.[2] He augmented the prestige of his ancestry with university training and reforming zeal.[3]

The promising career of Hugo of Hohenlandenberg was celebrated and memorialized by the influential humanist Sebastian

---

HS I, 2.1, pp. 85-122, 156-160; Rudolf Reinhardt, "Das Bistum in der Neuzeit," *HS* I, 2.1, pp. 122-126, 160-161; Helmut Maurer, *Konstanz im Mittelalter*, vol. I, (Konstanz: Stadler Verlagsgesellschaft, 1989), pp. 11-24, 101-102, 112-113, 115; henceforth cited as Maurer I; Helmut Maurer, *Konstanz im Mittelalter*, vol. II (Konstanz: Stadler Verlagsgesellschaft, 1989), pp. 90-91, 108-109; henceforth cited as Maurer II.

[2] Because the *Regesta Episcoporum Constantiensium* ends in the middle of the reign of Bishop Otto of Sonnenberg (1474-1491), it is difficult to trace the precise activities of Bishop Hugo of Hohenlandenberg. However, the *Protokolle des Konstanzer Domkapitels* compensate to some degree, revealing episcopal collaboration and disagreement with the cathedral canons. The range of the *Protokolle* (1487-1526) covers the reign of Hugo's predecessor, Thomas Berlower (1491-1496), and all but five years of Hugo's tenure; *Regesta Episcoporum Constantiensis. Regesten zur Geschichte der Bischöfe von Constanz von Bubulcus bis Thomas Berlower 517-1496*, ed. Badische Historische Commission (Innsbruck: Universitäts-Verlag, 1905-1941); henceforth cited as *REC;* "Die Protokolle des Konstanzer Domkapitels," ed. M. Krebs. *ZGO* 61 (1952); 62 (1953); 63 (1954), Beiheft; 64 (1955), Beiheft; 65 (1956), Beiheft; 67 (1958), Beiheft; 68 (1959), Beiheft; henceforth cited as *DKP.*

A recent and remarkably detailed account of Hugo's career has been provided by Rudolf Reinhardt, "Hugo von Hohenlandenberg, 1496-1530; 1531-1532," *HS* I, 2.1, pp. 376-385. The most complete biographical study of the pre-Reformation career of Hugo remains Alfred Vögeli's "Bischof Hugo von Hohenlandenberg: Von den Anfängen bis zum Beginn der Reformation (1460-1518)," in Jörg Vögeli, *Schriften zur Reformation in Konstanz*, vol. II.1, ed. A. Vögeli (Tübingen: Osiandersche Buchhandlung, 1973), pp. 589-625; Rudolf Reinhardt provides a short sketch in "Hugo von Hohenlandenberg," in *BK* I, pp. 392-395. Two articles are representative of nineteenth century approaches to Hugo: C. J. Glatz, "Zur Geschichte Hugos von Landenbergs, Bischof zu Konstanz," *FDA* 9 (1875), 101-140; and Emil Egli, "Hugo von Landenberg, Bischof von Konstanz," *Zwingliana* 1 (1901), 184-191.

[3] Hugo studied at the University of Basel in the 1470s. He received papal funding for his education in the early 1480s in Erfurt. Hugo supported his early career with a multitude of benefices and offices; he received his first benefice from the parish of Ehingen on the Danube (1468). Numerous positions followed: canon and dean around 1480 of the foundation of St. Bartholomäus in Friesach, canon of the cathedral church in Chur (1481), canon of the cathedral church of Basel (1481), dean in Erfurt (before 1481), provost of the *Marienkirche* in Erfurt (1483), cathedral provost in Trent (1482), beneficed positions in St. Peter in Reichenberg and Hinwil (1482), canon of the cathedral church in Constance (before 1487), and an expectancy from the Großmünster in Zürich. He was also appointed as provisional diocesan administrator (*Bistumsverweser*) in Constance (1480). As a prelude to his episcopal election, Hugo was promoted to Dean in the cathedral church in Constance in 1492.

During the early 1480s Hugo established his career at the papal court in Rome,

Brant (1458-1521), the author of *The Ship of Fools*.[4] Hugo may have first met Brant as a student at the University of Basel in the 1470s and maintained contact during his episcopal career.[5] In fact, this relationship hints at Hugo's clerical and humanist network, all part of an education and career that culminated in Constance.[6] Brant penned a Latin elegy to commemorate the inauguration of Hugo's ambitious diocesan synod in 1497 and adorn the printed edition of Hugo's episcopal statute:

> In the name of God, a solemn regent;
>   sovereign of a holy see.
> Rising up to shield your people:
> Regent, Ruler, Guardian, Bishop;
>   you are called shepherd as much as
>   father of your people.
> From the inception of your office, Hugo,
>   illustrious regent,
>   you stand prepared with greatest vigilance.
> This synod you convene,
>   to correct vice and error;
> Your own you command to walk
>   the path of virtue.

---

receiving the titles "familiaris" and "continuus commensalis" and the honorable office of "parafrenarius Papae." In 1482 Pope Sixtus IV sent Hugo to the Swiss Confederacy and to Basel to arrest and discipline the wayward Archbishop of Krain, Andrea Zamometić; Reinhardt, "Hugo von Hohenlandenberg," *HS* I, 2.1, pp. 376-377; Vögeli, *Schriften zur Reformation in Konstanz*, II.1, pp. 591-596.

[4] On the career of Sebastian Brant, see Edwin H. Zeydel, *Sebastian Brant* (New York: Twayne, 1967) and William Gilbert, "Sebastian Brant, Conservative Humanist," *ARG* (1955), 145-167.

[5] Vögeli, *Schriften zur Reformation in Konstanz*, II.1, p. 592.

[6] While a complete reconstruction of Bishop Hugo's humanist network is not possible, his reign does allude to a world of wider contacts. A circle of enthusiastic Erasmians met in Constance in the early sixteenth century, including cathedral canon Johann of Botzheim, Generalvikar of the diocese Johannes Fabri (d. 1541), and future Augsburg preacher and Protestant Urbanus Rhegius (d. 1541). Erasmus of Rotterdam sojourned briefly in Constance (September, 1522). During his stay Erasmus received hand delivery of a partridge dinner from the episcopal table and shared breakfast with Hugo in the bishop's palace. Thereafter, Erasmus would describe the Bishop of Constance as a churchman characterized by *humanitas* and *liberalitas*; see Vögeli, *Schriften zur Reformation in Konstanz*, II.1, p. 591; and Karl Hartfelder, "Der humanistische Freundeskreis des Desiderius in Konstanz," *ZGO* 47 (1893), 1-33. This clerical circle was complemented by a wider network of humanists in Constance and in upper Swabia; see Maurer II, pp. 156-166; Reinhardt, "Hugo von Hohenlandenberg," *HS* I, 2.1, p. 380; and Heribert Smolinsky, "Die Kirche am Oberrhein im Spannungsverhältnis von humanistischer Reform und Reformation," *FDA* 110 (1990), 23-38.

> New statutes you decree
> to be carefully observed,
> so that life might be improved.
> May the almighty protector of this
> most tender life
> grant you, gracious lord, times in keeping
> with your first sacred steps.[7]

This elegy not only celebrates Hugo's elevation to the ranks of ambitious reforming clerics but also gives an idealized portrait of a late-medieval churchman. Hugo possessed the distinguished titles of political authority (regent, sovereign, ruler) and ecclesiastical oversight (guardian, bishop, shepherd, father). Through his own remarkable virtue and his stern episcopal statutes he would set out to renew the church and revive the bishop's rule in Constance.

Young Bishop Hugo was quickly to discover the limitations of poetic praise; he lacked political and ecclesiastical power to fulfill the vision of Brant's grandiose elegy. In his education and humanist ties Hugo of Hohenlandenberg did appear to be a new episcopal prototype for the diocese of Constance, a cleric who would restore the luster of high church office and the authority of bishops, if he had the means at his disposal.[8] Indeed, as an avid supporter of the arts Hugo would sponsor painting, sculpture, and architectural modification of churches and episcopal residences: a polishing of the episcopal im-

---

[7] "Numine divino presul celeberrime sacre
Prefectus sedi: stas populum ante tuum.
Presul et antistes, speculator, episcopus: inde
Diceris, ut pastor sis populi atque pater.
Id quod in officii monstras Hugo inclyte presul,
Principio, vigili cuncta labore parans.
Nam synodum celebras, vitia atque errata reformas,
Virtutumque iubes semitam adire tuos.
Hec nova et imprimis servari rite statuta
Precipis ad mores condita proficuos.
Det tibi cunctipotens vite, mitissime presul,
    Tempora tam sanctis consona principiis."

Constitutiones synodales ecclesie Constantiensis 1497, GLA 65/291: 74v; another copy can be found in the library of the Wilhelmsstift in Tübingen. Brant's prologue to his dedication reads: "Ad reverendissimum dominum Hugonem de Landenberg ecclesie Constantiensis episcopum. Elogium Sebastiani Brant," GLA 65/291, 74v.

[8] Such training and experience could not always be assumed. Hermann of Wied, Archbishop of Cologne (1515-47), could not read latin. His affinity for Protestantism led Roman Catholics to ascribe his heresy to illiteracy in the language of the church; August Franzen, *Bischof und Reformation. Erzbischof Hermann von Wied in Köln vor der Entscheidung zwischen Reform und Reformation* (Münster: Aschendorff, 1971), pp. 14-15.

age.[9] In other respects he was typical of his predecessors. As a noble he was well-connected in regional politics. As a bishop he was economically impoverished and politically vulnerable. Hugo of Hohenlandenberg would undergird his episcopal reforms with the twin pillars of diocesan administration and civic immunity. He would quickly discover the precarious condition of these critical supports.

The diocese of Constance, the first pillar of Hugo's episcopal power, encircled the landscape of southwest Germany. This enormous territory appears more than sufficient to have supported the aspirations—religious and remunerative—of the most ambitious of bishops. But cartography can be deceptive. To be sure, among all the dioceses in Germany Constance was the largest, reaching from the heartland of the Neckar in the north to the outskirts of Bern in Switzerland to the south, from the Rhine and the Aare in the west to the Iller in the east. This diocese embraced the Black Forest, the Swabian Alb, and the Alpine foothills of the Thurgau. Seven dioceses bordered the single bishopric of Constance. But the diocese was administratively impossible to control. Thorough episcopal visitations of all ecclesiastical institutions would take years to complete. Fiscal oversight and monitoring of deanships, monasteries, and parishes was spotty at best. By the mid-fifteenth century the bishop's administration was overwhelmed by 17,000 priests, 1,760 parishes, and thirty-five cloisters.[10] The diocese included numerous secular jurisdictions, each a potential threat to episcopal dominion over the

---

[9] Five portraits of Hugo survive, attesting to his patronage of the late-medieval *Bodensee* school. Most noteworthy is the 'Landenberg Altar', which Hugo commissioned shortly after 1496; Hugo is portrayed on the wings of the altar with the two patron saints of the diocese of Constance—Konrad and Pelagius. He supported architectural and musical endeavors, remodeled four castles, had his own crypt constructed in the cathedral, and added arches, windows, and towers to the bishop's church. He commissioned the construction of a new organ, supported local composition of organ music, and founded a boys choir in the cathedral; Bernd Konrad, "Die Malerei im Umkreis von Hugo von Hohenlandenberg," in *BK* II, pp. 134-142; Karl Osber, "Der Hohenlandenbergeraltar in der Kunsthalle zu Karlsruhe," *ZGO* 75 (1921), 192-201; *Katalog: Alte Meister bis 1800*, ed. J. Lauts (Karlsruhe, 1966), pp. 21-23, 54; Manfred Schuler, "Die Bischöfe und Musik," in *Die Bischöfe von Konstanz*, vol. II. Kultur, eds. E. L. Kuhn, E. Moser, R. Reinhard, and P. Sachs. (Friedrichshafen: Robert Gessler, 1988), p. 239; henceforth cited as *BK* II; and Vögeli, *Schriften zur Reformation in Konstanz*, II.1, pp. 593-594.

[10] Franz Hundsnurscher, "Die Kathedrale des Bistums," in *Glanz der Kathedrale. 900 Jahre Konstanzer Münster* (Konstanz: Städtische Museen Konstanz, 1989), p. 37. On the original borders of the diocese, see Helmut Maurer, "Die Anfänge," in *BK* I, pp. 7-14. On the administration of the diocese, see the exhaustive set of articles in *HS* I, 2.2, pp. 503-923; and the section, "Das Bistum," in *BK* I, pp. 64-158.

clergy and church lands. In addition to a myriad of minor lordships bishops had to contend with the larger competing jurisdictions of the growing Swiss Confederacy, the Duchy of Württemberg, and the emerging Habsburg territory of Upper Austria (Vorderösterreich). The diocese embraced eighteen imperial cities, bastions of civic free-dom; nearly all of these cities would eventually reject episcopal au-thority and create urban churches guided by magistrates.

Oversight of the clergy and negotiation with secular counterparts was only part of this complex puzzle for the bishop of Constance. The size of the *Hochstift*, the lands belonging directly to the bishop and the cathedral canons of Constance, was a further liability. The diocese was impossible to manage. In contrast, the *Hochstift* was too small to support adequately the episcopal court and administra-tion.[11] During the later Middle Ages the *Hochstift* had been steadily shrinking as bishops sold or pawned property to counter a rising deficit. Such a one-time sale or lengthy period of pawning did not make up for lost annual revenues in goods, rents, and other fees.[12] By the end of the fifteenth century Bishop Hugo inherited a debt of 50,000 Florins.[13]

The instability of this precarious diocesan pillar prompted bishops to guard jealously their real estate, revenues, and trades within the city of Constance. Rents, properties, and court fees in the city added

---

[11] Werner Kundert has provided a history of the *Hochstift* (*Herrschaftsgebiet*) and an exhaustive list of every known location and office that was once a part of bishop's secular lands; "Weltliches Gebiet," *HS* I, 2.1, pp. 54-84.

[12] The poverty of the diocese could scare away a newly elected bishop. Frederick of Nellenburg served as bishop for only eleven days in 1398 and then resigned. Not that he was intimidated by his new found sacral authority or by the moral imperative of his office; rather, he had checked the books and found the diocese in wretched financial condition; *REC* 3:7558-7559.

[13] Matthias Becher, "Mittelalter," in *BK* I, p. 24. On the financial situation in the *Hochstift* of Constance and the efforts of bishops in the later Middle Ages to improve fiscal conditions, see Degler-Spengler, "Das Bistum vom 13. bis zum 15. Jahrhun-dert," *HS* I, 2.1, pp. 105-107, 117-121; Franz Keller, "Die Verschuldung des Hochstifts Konstanz im 14. und 15. Jahrhundert," *FDA* 30 (1902), pp. 1-104. The financial status of the diocese has been studied by Karl Rieder, "Beitrag zu den wirtschaftlichen und kirchlichen Zuständen in der Diöcese Konstanz in der zweiten Hälfte des 14. Jahrhunderts," *FDA* 29 (1901), pp. 245-254; and Walther Dann, "Die Besetzung des Bistums Konstanz vom Wormser Kondordat zur Reformation," *ZGO* 61 (1952), 3-96.

Perhaps the most compelling visual example of the economic plight of the bishops of Constance may be found by examining a map in *BK* I, p. 504, where the tiny *Hochstift* of the massive diocese of Constance can be compared to the extensive *Hochstifte* of wealthy and smaller dioceses such as Münster and Würzburg or even neighboring Augsburg, Basel, and Chur.

essential funds to episcopal coffers. In fact, Hugo like his predecessors inherited a critical charge—to maintain Constance as a city of the bishops, the capital of the diocese and *Hochstift*, an episcopal residence at the crossroad of lucrative trade routes and a thriving administrative hub for an extensive ecclesiastical territory. Without this city the bishops of Constance might be paralyzed fiscally and administratively, cut off from their sacred city, their ancient church and relics, from the ground that had nourished nearly 1000 years of episcopal rule.[14]

Hugo and his colleagues were charged not only with the reform of the church but also with the maintenance of episcopal residence and jurisdiction in the city of Constance. During the later Middle Ages they had suffered significant political and legal losses in the city. Hugo soon faced this dilemma, learning that partisan politics and imperial patronage were more effective than university training, multiple benefices, and elegiac praise.

In Constance bishops had discovered how to maintain an official and active presence despite periodic expulsion, loss of civic lordship, and erosion of church oversight. To grasp Hugo's predicament and promise, it is critical to understand the pedigree and power of his predecessors, the nature and rhythm of episcopal expulsion (*Episcopus exclusus*), and the sources of survival in the city. From the mid-fourteenth to the late fifteenth century bishop and city repeated and re-enacted a struggle for civic control. In the process episcopal rule had been weakened, but the bishop's presence and vital role in the city endured.

1. *Pedigree and Power*[15]

In 1491 the newly elected Bishop Thomas Berlower (1491-96), Hugo's predecessor, provoked the magistrates of Constance by nail-

---

[14] See above, pp. 115-119.

[15] Brief and detailed biographies of every bishop of Constance can be found in Franz Xaver Bischof, Brigitte Degler-Spengler, Helmut Maurer, and Rudolf Reinhardt, "Die Bischöfe," in *HS* I, 2.1, pp. 229-494. Two studies provide critical background on the high-medieval bishops of Constance: Ursula-Renate Weiss, *Die Konstanzer Bischöfe im 12. Jahrhundert. Ein Beitrag zur Untersuchung der reichsbischöflichen Stellung im Kräftefeld kaiserlicher, päpstlicher und regional-diözesaner Politik* (Sigmaringen: Jan Thorbecke, 1975); and Detlov Zimpel, *Die Bischöfe von Konstanz im 13. Jahrhundert (1206-1274)* (Frankfurt am Main: Peter Lang, 1990).

ing a charter on the cathedral door; it invoked a single, offensive name—Henry of Brandis (1357-83).[16] Six years later Hugo of Hohenlandenberg followed the lead of Bishop Thomas, citing their infamous predecessor.[17] The very mention of Henry of Brandis spoke volumes about the agenda of a bishop-elect, proclaiming an aggressive pursuit of lost episcopal rights and the restoration of Constance as the bishop's city first and foremost. The career and cunning of Bishop Henry provides the beginning of a logical periodization for the late medieval bishops of Constance, as Bishop Thomas Berlower himself recognized when he recalled the image and agenda of Henry of Brandis. From the middle of the fourteenth to the end of the fifteenth century, bishops followed a similar policy toward the city; they pressed for the restoration of episcopal rights and rule and they clung to legitimate episcopal presence in the city.

In the mid-fourteenth century Bishop Henry of Brandis had won the support of the empire for his ancient claims on the city of Constance, a critical concession because the city relied on imperial recognition for its independence from the bishop.[18] In a charter branded by the city council as the '*falsche Carolina*', Emperor Charles IV (1347-78) rolled back civic rights and restored the lordship of the bishop.[19] But within a decade this initiative failed and the city had retained its hard-won freedoms. A regional feud followed this strategic battle over imperial politics, a war aimed directly at the city. Marshalling the forces of feud was none other than the clan of Brandis, led not by Bishop Henry, but by his nephew Mangold, the

---

[16] "Anno 1491 uff suntag vor unser frowen tag ze mitten Augsten habend bischoff Thoma und das capittel im thumb iere freyhaiten, so sy von bäpsten, kaysern und kunigen haben, offenlich an die kirchen türen angeschlagen und denen ist ouch die Carolina aine gwesen, die Carolus 4s bischoff <u>Hainrichen von Brandis</u> geben hat ..." (my emphasis), Christoph Schulthaiß, "Constanzer Bisthums-Chronik," ed. J. Marmor, *FDA* 8 (1874), p. 74, 19-23; henceforth cited as Schulthaiß-*Chronik*. Even after the bishop and the cathedral canons renounced the above document, Thomas Berlower continued to cite the name of Henry of Brandis in his confirmation of civic rights (*Verschreibung*); no previous bishop had listed the name in this fashion; StAK A II 30, p. 70r, 13; GLA 5/ 7208, line 12.

[17] StAK A II 30, p. 76r, 12; GLA 5, 7210-7212, line 11.

[18] On the career and reign of Henry of Brandis, see Degler-Spengler, "Heinrich of Brandis, 1357-1383," in *HS*, I, 2.1, pp. 316-321; and Rüdiger Schell, "Die Regierung des Konstanzer Bischofs Heinrich III. von Brandis (1357-1383) unter besonderer Berücksichtigung seiner Beziehungen zur Stadt Konstanz," *FDA* 88 (1968), 102-204.

[19] Degler-Spengler, "Das Bistum Vom 13. bis zum 15. Jahrhundert," *HS* I, 2.1, p. 104. An original copy of this charter can be found in GLA D/ 317.

Kellermeister on the nearby Benedictine island of Reichenau.[20] In short, Henry of Brandis had personified an episcopal agenda which drew on imperial connections and familial force in order to make Constance a full-fledged city of bishops once more.

What pedigree did Henry, as well as his predecessors and successors, claim as a basis for their ambitious vision of the city of Constance? Henry of Brandis, like nearly all bishops of Constance, came from the nobility. He represented not only the tradition of episcopal lordship but also the designs of the landed aristocracy on this island of civic freedoms.

Before turning to the episcopal narrative of Henry to Hugo (1357-1530), it is critical to understand how broader political alliances in the first half of the fourteenth century raised the stakes and fractured the civic and religious community. The reign of Henry was symptomatic of the turmoil that pitched church against city in fourteenth century Constance. The travails of the Great Schism (1378-1415) generally divided and ravaged western Europe. Germany had suffered a painful, half-century prelude in destructive rounds of papal and imperial confrontation. Papal interdict, both threatened and promulgated, interrupted the worship of the citizenry, ministrations of the clergy, sacred burial of the dead, and regular presence of the bishops of Constance for most of the fourteenth century. The vicious clash between Pope John XXII (1316-34) and Emperor Lewis of Bavaria (1324-47) led to nearly a quarter century of strife between bishop and city.[21] Constance was a loyal supporter of the emperor, earning the censure of the Avignon popes and alienation from the bishop. Lewis was a personal actor on the civic and episcopal stage of Constance in 1344, attempting to expel clergy unresponsive to his

---

[20] *REC* 2:5916; Maurer II, pp. 214-216.

[21] Brigitte Degler-Spengler summarizes the impact of this struggle between church and state: "Der Kampf zwischen den Päpsten zu Avignon und Ludwig dem Bayern beherrschte die Politik bis zur Jarhundertmitte. In der Diözese äußerte er sich in zwiespältigen Bischofswahlen, im Unfrieden des Interdikts und in Streitigkeiten mit der Stadt. In dieser zerissenen Situation konnten auch tüchtige Bischöfe nicht 'glücklich' regieren;" "Das Bistum vom 13. bis zum 15. Jahrhundert," *HS* I, 2.1, p. 100. On the stages of this conflict, see Joachim Leuschner, *Germany in the Late Middle Ages* (Amsterdam: North-Holland Publishing Company, 1980), pp. 107-115. Pope John XXII excommunicated King Lewis in 1324; papal interdict fell over the city of Constance as punishment for supporting the king in 1326; in April of 1330 Lewis ordered the arrest of clerics who refused to hold services and the confiscation of their property; *REC* 2:3992-3994, 4001, 4065, 4212.

demands and besieging Bishop Nicholas of Frauenfeld (1334-44) in his episcopal residence of Meersburg.[22]

After the death of Lewis of Bavaria in 1347 the citizens of Constance anxiously awaited a declaration of episcopal absolution; their imperial impediment to sacred acceptance had been removed. The bishop remained silent. The residents of Constance would await their release from interdict for another two years—until the election of Emperor Charles IV. This delay was all the more galling because the bishop possessed an unusual and intimate pedigree: Ulrich Pfefferhart (1345-51) was the first home-grown bishop of Constance, the son of a burgher-family and the first elected bishop, who did not stem from the nobility. Not until April 1349 did this bishop lift the interdict.[23] In 1352 the cathedral canons elected another son of the city, John III Windlock (1351-56), who again antagonized his fellow citizens by proclaiming interdict in 1355, leaving Constance bereft of clerical services once more.[24] One year later Bishop John suffered the ultimate form of what we have called the *Episcopus exclusus*; he was murdered in his palace in Constance and his considerable episcopal legacy disappeared. The case was never solved.[25]

Finally, after the fourth double-election of the century, decades of papal, imperial, episcopal, and civic strife, Henry of Brandis was consecrated as bishop.[26] It is likely that citizens hoped for a coopera-

---

[22] *REC* 2:4435-4439. Imperial troops besieged Bishop Nicholas in his episcopal castle for fourteen weeks. Those who assisted in the defense were granted a papal dispensation from interdict and ban. The continuing interdict even had an impact on the funeral and burial of Bishop Nicholas. At his death in July, 1344 Nicholas received his wish to be buried in the grave of a former bishop, Henry of Klingenberg (1293-1306); due to the interdict, Nicholas received a 'silent burial' (*stilles Begräbnis*); Degler-Spengler, "Nikolaus of Frauenfeld, 1334-1344," *HS* I, 2.1, pp. 302, 304.
[23] *REC* 2:4863, 2:4865, 2:4904. Maurer I, pp. 194-196; 203-205; Degler-Spengler, "Ulrich Pfefferhart, 1344-1451," *HS* I, 2.1, pp. 306-307.
[24] Bishop John Windlock censured the city since it continued to permit the residence of an episcopal enemy—Diethelm of Steinegg, the cathedral dean of Constance; *REC* 2:5175; Degler-Spengler, "Johann Windlock, 1351-1356," *HS* I, 2.1, pp. 311-312.
[25] *REC* 2:5210; for an overview of the case see Degler-Spengler, "Johann Windlock, 1351-1356," *HS* I, 2.1, pp. 312-313; K. H. Roth von Schreckenstein, "Die Ermordung des Bischofs Johann III. von Konstanz," in *ZGO* 25 (1873), 1-24; on the alleged complicity of the house of Brandis in this murder, see P. Schubiger, "Über die angebliche Mitschuld der Gebrüder von Brandis am Mord des Bischofs Johannes Windlock von Constanz," *FDA* 10 (1876), 3-48. On civic participation in the attack, see Maurer I, p. 213. August Karg explored the reign of this unfortunate bishop in "Bischof Johann IV. von Konstanz (1351-1356)," *FDA* 3 (1868), 103-121.
[26] The four double elections, which divided the clergy and civic loyalties, occurred in 1306, 1318, 1334, and 1356.

tive bishop. Instead of healing the painful relationship between laity and clergy, acquiescing to the claims of the city fathers, supporting conciliation and cooperation, Henry demanded complete submission to his episcopal lordship.[27] To the citizens of Constance Bishop Henry would come to symbolize the volatile interlude between the clash of papacy and empire in the first half and the Great Schism of the later half of the fourteenth century. To his episcopal heirs Henry represented the ongoing struggle to reassert their rightful claims to the old episcopal city.

Bishop Henry was typical of many late-medieval bishops of Constance in background and career. From 1357 to 1530 fourteen bishops ruled the diocese.[28] The average episcopal tenure was thirteen years, although four bishops ruled for over twenty, including Henry of Hewen (1436-62), who dominated the middle of the fourteenth-century and Hugo of Hohenlandenberg, who resigned in his thirty-fourth year of episcopal service.[29] Only Albert Blarer (1407-10) followed in the footsteps of Ulrich Pfefferhart and John Windlock

---

[27] After decades of episcopal alienation from the emperor, Bishop Henry had the opportunity to combine papal and imperial support for his plan to reestablish Constance as a city under the lordship of the bishop; apparently Emperor Charles IV initially agreed.

The alliance of Henry of Brandis and Emperor Charles IV was most likely solidified during the emperor's visit to Einsiedeln in 1354, where Henry was abbot; Degler-Spengler, "Heinrich von Brandis, 1357-1383," *HS* I, 2.1, p. 316.

Unfortunately Henry quickly alienated the curia in Avignon by refusing to restore the legacy of the murdered Bishop John Windlock. Felix Stucki received the papal appointment of *Dompropst* in Constance to work against Bishop Henry and resolve the legacy issue. But Stucki was murdered by relatives of Henry of Brandis, most likely with Henry's knowledge. The bishop was temporarily excommunicated in 1369 and removed from office for three years; Degler-Spengler, "Das Bistum vom 13. bis zum 15. Jahrhundert," *HS* I, 2.1, p. 104.

[28] In addition to the line of 'legitimate' bishops two clerics were appointed as bishops by Avignon Popes during the Great Schism—Mangold of Brandis (1384-85) and Henry Baylor (1387-88). Lewis of Freiberg (1474-80) is the third candidate during the later Middle Ages to fail in his bid to become the legitimate bishop of Constance.

[29] I have not computed the ten day tenure of Frederick III of Nellenberg (1398) in this average.

Yet to be studied is the relationship of tenure to episcopal policy and city/bishop relations. Bishops Henry of Brandis, Otto III of Hachberg, Henry IV of Hewen, and Hugo of Hohenlandenberg sponsored bold initiatives to regain episcopal privileges and, in the case of the latter two bishops, to reform the clergy. Otto III published a treatise on the conception of the virgin Mary; see U. Janson, "Otto von Hachberg (1410-1434), Bischof von Konstanz und sein Traktat, 'De conceptione beatae virginis,'" in *FDA* 88 (1968), 205-358; see Degler-Spengler, "Otto von Hachberg, 1410-1434," *HS* I, 2.1, pp. 343-348. On Henry of Hewen see, Degler-Spengler,

as a son of the citizenry turned bishop.[30] Ten successors of Henry of
Brandis stemmed from south German or Swiss nobility, thus adding
the assets of nearby familial lands to episcopal resources while rein-
forcing civic concern about the designs of the rural nobility.[31] Two
bishops came with a more distant pedigree; Nicholas of Riesenburg
hailed from West Prussia and by 1388 was bishop of Olmütz;[32] Thomas Berlower came north to take up his episcopal see in Constance;
he had contributed to the establishment of the bishopric of Vienna in
1480.[33] With the exception of these two clerics the cathedral canons
of Constance selected candidates familiar with the intricacies of south
German and Swiss politics, another characteristic typical of most
bishops from Henry of Brandis to Hugo of Hohenlandenberg.

Nearly all of the late-medieval bishops of Constance took the route
of monk, cleric, or canon to the episcopal throne. Two candidates,
Henry and Mangold of Brandis, were elected as bishops after ruling
as abbots in Einsiedeln and Reichenau respectively.[34] Seven bishops
were selected from the ecclesiastical administration of other dioceses
and collegiate churches. Five of those bishops had formerly served in
the nearby dioceses of Augsburg, Basel, Chur, and Strasbourg, attesting to the regional ties of Constance to neighboring church territories.[35] The cathedral chapter of Constance produced six bishops,

---

"Heinrich of Hewen, 1436-1462," *HS* I, 2.1, pp. 351-356; and Peter Kramml,
"Heinrich IV. von Hewen," in *BK* I, pp. 384-392.

[30] On the civic pedigree of the Blarer clan, see *REC* 3:7995, Degler-Spengler,
"Albrecht Blarer, 1407-1410," *HS* I, 2.1, pp. 349-351.

[31] Mangold of Brandis (*REC* 3:6738), Burkhard of Hewen (*REC* 2:7132), Frederick of Nellenburg (*REC* 3:7551), Marquard of Randeck (*REC* 3:7569), Otto of
Hachberg (*REC* 3:8210), Henry of Hewen (*REC* 4:8210), Burkhard of Randegg (*REC*
4:12612), Hermann of Breitenlandenberg (*REC* 4:13105), Otto of Sonnenberg (*REC*
5:14208), and Hugo of Hohenlandenberg (Vögeli, *Schriften zur Reformation in Konstanz*,
II.1, pp. 559-560).

[32] Bishop Nicholas held benefices and offices in the dioceses of Pomesanien,
Magdeburg, and Breslau; he was also the Dean of St. Kassius in Bonn (*REC* 4:6940,
6943); Degler-Spengler, "Nikolaus von Riesenburg, 1384-1387," *HS* I, 2.1, p. 323;
REC identifies his birthplace as Bohemia: 3:6939, 7121.

[33] Degler-Spengler, "Thomas Berlower, von Cilli, 1491-1496," *HS* I, 2.1, p. 372.
Berlower's place of origin is identified as Croatia or Steiermark; Schulthaiß-*Chronik*,
p. 72.

[34] *REC* 2:5264-5265; 6739-6740.

[35] In addition to Nicholas of Riesenburg and Thomas Berlower, Marquard of
Randeck was a cathedral canon in Eichstätt and Augsburg; he held benefices from
Passau, Breslau, and Salzburg; Marquard was bishop of Minden prior to his transfer
to Constance (*REC* 3:7571, 7573, 7577, Degler-Spengler, "Marquard von Randeck
(Randegg), 1398-1406," *HS* I, 2.1, p. 337). Otto of Hachberg received canonships in

revealing how often the canons elected a candidate they knew well.[36]

In addition to local and regional service in the church, many of the fourteen late medieval bishops pursued higher education and served secular rulers, including king and emperor, prior to taking episcopal office. Eleven bishops matriculated at European universities.[37] Two bishops had distinguished records at secular courts. Nicholas of Riesenburg served as pronotary and secretary at the court of Rudolf II of Saxony-Wittenberg before entering the chancellery and eventually the post of pronotary in the court of Emperor Charles IV. Thomas Berlower became imperial secretary, pronotary, and diplomat for Emperor Frederick III (1440-93).[38]

The bishops of Constance of the late fourteenth and fifteenth cen-

---

Mainz, Speyer, Cologne, and Basel (*REC* 3:8213, Degler-Spengler, "Otto von Hachberg, 1410-1434," *HS* I, 2.1, p. 343). Both Frederick of Zollern and Henry of Hewen came to Constance after rising to the office of cathedral canon in Strasbourg (*REC* 3:9597, 9790). Hugo of Hohenlandenberg held various offices in Chur, Erfurt, Salzburg, and Zürich (Vögeli, *Schriften zur Reformation in Konstanz*, pp. 594-595).

[36] Burkhard of Hewen (*REC* 3:7133), Albert Blarer (*REC* 3:7997), and Otto of Sonnenberg (*REC* 4:14120) were cathedral canons in Constance. Burkhard of Randegg rose to the rank of *Domkustus* in Constance (*REC* 4:12614), while Hermann of Breitenlandenberg and Hugo of Hohenlandenberg received cathedral canonships and later were elected to the rank of *Domdekan* in the cathedral chapter; *REC*: 4:13106; Degler-Spengler, "Hermann of Breitenlandenberg, 1466-74," *HS* I, 2.1, p. 358; Vögeli, *Schriften zur Reformation in Konstanz*, p. 592.

[37] Burkhard of Hewen studied in Bologna and Padua in 1350. The education of Marquard of Randeck is revealed in his stature at the University of Vienna: as "lector ordinarius in iure canonico" (1382) and as Rector of the University (1392). Albert Blarer earned a bachelor of arts in Prague with the support of his cathedral canonship (1385). Otto of Hachberg studied at Heidelberg (1404). Henry of Hewen was a student in Vienna (1415), Rome (1424), Padua (1426), and perhaps Bologna (1427). Hermann of Breitenlandenberg matriculated at Heidelberg (1424) and Bologna (1436). Otto of Sonnenberg studied in Pavia (1454). Thomas Berlower entered the University of Vienna in 1446; he rose to Master of the Arts Faculty (1451) and chancellor (1480); he served as tutor for the young Austrian prince, Maximilian, the future emperor of Germany. Hugo of Hohenlandenberg entered the University of Basel in 1470. Lewis of Freiberg, although never officially installed as bishop of Constance, held an impressive academic pedigree, including study at Pavia, Heidelberg, and Basel as well as a doctorate in canon and civil law. *REC* 3:7136; 3:7571; 3:9792; 4:13106; Degler-Spengler, "Marquard von Randeck (Randegg), 1398-1406," *HS* I, 2.1, p. 337, "Albrecht (Albert) Blarer (I.), 1407-1410," *HS* I, 2.1, p. 340; "Otto von Hachberg, 1410-1434," *HS* I, 2.1, p. 343, "Heinrich von Hewen, 1436-1462," *HS* I, 2.1, p. 351, "Otto von Sonnenberg, 1474-1480, Electus; 1480-1491," *HS* I, 2.1, p. 366, "Bistumsstreit. Ludwig von Freiberg, 1474-1480," *HS* I, 2.1, p. 361, "Thomas Berlower, von Cilli, 1491-1496," *HS* I, 2.1, p. 372, "Hugo von Hohenlandenberg, 1496-1530; 1531-1532," *HS* I, 2.1, p. 376 .

[38] Degler-Spengler, "Nikolaus von Riesenburg, 1384-1387 (1388)," *HS* I, 2.1, p. 323; "Thomas Berlower, von Cilli, 1491-1496," *HS* I, 2.1, p. 372.

turies brought a common vision to episcopal service, a vision tied to the politics of the south-German nobility, clarified in ecclesiastical service, and, in most cases, sharpened by university education. These bishops never regained the status of civic lords but they marshalled all of their resources in order to maintain a viable and effective episcopal presence in the city of Constance. In 1357 Henry of Brandis set out to reclaim Constance. Hugo of Hohenlandenberg continued to pursue the dream of Brandis in 1496.

2. *From Pervasive Presence to Periodic Withdrawal*

The relationship between bishop and city in Constance did not change in one year or decade; citizens did not lay claim to their civic freedoms after a single, local, and conclusive military confrontation. In fact, the first recorded expulsion of a bishop was not the outcome of conflict *within* Constance. Episcopal exile resulted from the interplay of empire and papacy in the eleventh century. From the dawn of the bishopric in the late sixth century to the tenure of Karlmann (1069-71) the bishops of Constance appear to have ruled their episcopal city without any noticeable or at least recorded lay resistance. But when Emperor Henry IV (1056-1106) and Pope Gregory VII (1073-85) vied for supremacy over the German episcopacy, the lay populace in Constance participated decisively in the city's political fate. Residents could not always rely on the bishop's presence and protection. Therefore, they took matters into their own hands, monitoring civic fortifications in self-defense. They also clashed with their episcopal lord for the first time on record. In 1077 Bishop Otto I (1071-86), a supporter of Henry IV, fled Constance before the approach of, Rudolf of Swabia, a Gregorian candidate for the German throne; the bishop resided elsewhere for one year.[39] Civic initiative filled the void left by episcopal departure. In 1092 residents refused entry to Arnold of Heiligenberg, the imperial candidate for the episcopal

---

Provisional bishop Lewis of Freiberg was a diplomat in the service of Duke Sigismund of Austria; Degler-Spengler, "Bistumsstreit. Ludwig von Freiberg, 1474-1480. Provisius," *HS* I, 2.1, p. 361.

[39] *REC* 1:511; Maurer I, p. 87.

see.[40] They also closed the gates to the arrival of Gebhard III (1084-1110) in 1095.[41]

These acts of defiance did not lead to further expulsions in the twelfth and thirteenth centuries. But during the fourteenth century civic residents were again moved by the machinations of distant powers as the feud between the Avignon popes, especially John XXII (1316-34), and Emperor Lewis of Bavaria (1314-47) divided the episcopacy and disrupted church services across Germany. From May to August 1334 Lewis pursued and besieged the papal candidate to the see of Constance, Nicholas of Frauenfeld (1334-44). The old fortress in Meersburg sheltered Nicholas during his exclusion from Constance and withstood the imperial siege.[42]

Less than a decade later the clash between papacy and empire led to a new round of communal division and expulsion. In 1343 the cathedral canons upheld papal decrees of interdict against Constance and suspended the mass. The magistrates ordered the canons to leave the city while persuading the clergy of two parishes, St. Stephan's and St. John's, to defy the pope and continue to hold services.[43] In April 1346, nearly five months after his election, Bishop Ulrich Pfefferhart (1346-51) made his first formal appearance in the divided city of Constance. Dominican friars followed in his train. The citizens of Constance had expelled them seven years earlier in retaliation for their order's loyalty to the papacy and the strictures of interdict.[44] In April 1348 Ulrich himself fled to the small residence of Klingnau, avoiding both civic unrest in Constance and marauding knights in the hinterlands of the city.[45]

The antagonism between bishop and city continued unabated after the 1340s, fueled by local factionalism and international politics. Bishop John III of Windlock (1352-56) was murdered in his palace in Constance. Henry of Brandis (1357-83) left Constance periodically,

---

[40] Maurer I, pp. 89-90.
[41] Schulthaiß-*Chronik*, pp. 27-28.
[42] Emperor Lewis was active around the western edge of Lake Constance, especially in Constance and Überlingen from May 19-August 26, 1344; *REC* 2:4435-4436. In 1318, Lewis' early clash with the papacy had disrupted services in Constance; priests who continued to observe the papal ban were driven from the city; Schulthaiß-*Chronik*, p. 38.
[43] *REC* 2:4654; Maurer I, p. 198.
[44] *REC.* 2:4757-4762; 4779.
[45] Maurer I, p. 204.

perhaps recognizing the lack of security in his episcopal quarters.[46]
In February 1366, as relations between city and bishop began to
deteriorate, Henry made a formal withdrawal. Over the objections of
citizens he transferred his household, administrative staff, and clerical
court (*geistliches Gericht*) to Zürich.[47] Thus, the bishops of Constance
not only departed the city under duress but they also withdrew as a
tactical ploy.

The Great Schism (1378-1415) entailed exclusion and acceptance
of certain episcopal candidates. The bishops promoted by the Avignon papacy never set foot in Constance; some clerics loyal to the
northern pontiff departed in protest after the election of 1384.[48] In
contrast, two bishops loyal to Rome, Nicholas of Riesenburg (1384-
87) and Burkhard of Hewen (1388-98), were grateful for communal
support and pledged their loyalty to the city by swearing the citizen's
oath.[49] For the most part Constance was spared further conflict during the later fourteenth century. Although the papal schism disrupted
diocesan government, it proved beneficial to the city and its unusu-
ally docile episcopal residents. One set of bishops was excluded. Two
bishops submitted to the city council and accepted the responsibilities
of citizenship.

When the Council of Constance opened in 1414, twenty-two year
old Otto of Hachberg (1410-34) may well have suffered another form
of exclusion. Although he was bishop of Constance and shepherd of

---

[46] Bishop John was murdered on January 21, 1356; *REC* 2:5210-5213.
On the residency patterns of Henry of Brandis, see Appendix D. Henry appears
often in Constance in episcopal records from 1357-1365. However, he was seldom in
the city in 1366 and 1368; he appears to be absent altogether in 1370, 1371, and
perhaps in 1369. Constance was most likely not his primary residence for eleven
years.
[47] *REC* 2:5937; Degler-Spengler, *HS* I, 2.1, "Heinrich von Brandis, 1357-1383,"
p. 318.
[48] Maurer I, p. 225. Pope Clement VII supported the candidacy of Mangold of
Brandis (1384-85), the newly elected abbot of Reichenau, and Henry Baylor (1387-
1409).
[49] The city council at first supported the Avignon candidate, Mangold of Brandis,
despite his central role in the Brandis feud with Constance fifteen years before and
the legacy of his uncle, Bishop Henry. In fact, Bishop-elect Mangold even held the
Bürgerrecht before his opponent, Nicholas of Riesenburg (*REC* 3:6757). Similar to
his predecessor, John Windlock, Bishop Mangold may well have been assassinated,
this time by a potent elixir which took lethal effect as he was mounting his horse
(*REC* 3:6785).
In addition to the oath of Bishop Nicholas (*REC* 3:6955), the cathedral canons
who supported his candidacy swore allegiance to the city, including the successor to
Nicholas, Burkhard of Hewen (*REC* 3:6740).

civic churches, he does not appear in civic negotiations regarding the imminent ecumenical council. Yet during the four years of ecclesiastical deliberation in Constance the episcopal residence housed a succession of papal and imperial guests.[50] In the late 1420s Bishop Otto became embroiled more directly in civic politics. Patricians and guildsmen clashed violently over the composition of the city council. In October 1429 many patrician families departed from Constance. They had lost their seats in the small council; now they moved to Schaffhausen with Bishop Otto and his clerical court (*Geistliches Gericht*).[51] The clash of bishop and city was not the only grounds for episcopal withdrawal. Bishop Otto moved to Schaffhausen again in 1431 but this time due to a long-standing disagreement with the cathedral canons.[52] Finally, weary of conflict within and outside his own administration, Otto of Hachberg stepped down from the episcopal throne in 1434.

For the remainder of the century the bishops and city of Constance shared an uneasy cohabitation. The diocesan schism of 1474-80 compelled Bishop Otto IV of Sonnenberg (1474-91) to garner the support of the city and brought about the exclusion of the

---

[50] Apart from the cathedral and other ecclesiastical facilities the episcopal dimension in Constance appears to have played no major role in the selection of the city for the ecumenical council. Rather, the long-standing use of Constance as a site for regional and imperial congresses as well as the critical contribution of Constance to the successful imperial campaign in the Appenzell War were deciding factors in the selection of Constance; see Maurer I, p. 100; Maurer II, p. 9.

Pope John XXIII lived in the episcopal palace at the outset of deliberations; *REC* 3:8430. On the activities of the episcopal administration in the midst of the Council of Constance, see *REC* 3:8431-8645.

[51] *REC* 3:9286; Ruppert, p. 155, Schulthaiß-*Chronik*, pp. 53-54. On the nature of the politically active classes in Constance, see Klaus D. Bechtold, *Zunftbürgerschaft und Patriziat. Studien zur Sozialgeschichte der Stadt Konstanz im 14. und 15. Jahrhundert* (Sigmaringen: Jan Thorbecke, 1981).

[52] Schulthaiß-*Chronik*, p. 56; *REC* 3:9400. The relationship between bishop and chapter is yet another important dimension of episcopal rule and power in Constance. The cathedral chapter only appears here as it intersects or surfaces in specific events and episcopal deliberations. Konstantin Maier in his *Das Domkapitel von Konstanz und seine Wahlkapitulation. Ein Beitrag zur Geschichte von Hochstift und Diözese in der Neuzeit* (Stuttgart: Franz Steiner, 1990) has explored the agreements which defined the rights of chapter and bishop before the final confirmation of an episcopal candidate. The best comprehensive study of a similar location remains Lawrence Duggan's *Bishop and Chapter*, a careful reading of the archival sources in the diocese of Speyer. On the development of the Cathedral Chapter as an institution, see Philipp Schneider, *Die bischöflichen Domkapitel, ihre Entwicklung und rechtliche Stellung* (Mainz: Franz Kirchheim, 1892) and Hofmeister, *Bischof und Domkapitel nach altem und nach neuem Recht*.

papal candidate, Lewis of Freiberg.[53] The vulnerability of both bishops parallels the schisms of the fourteenth century. Disputed episcopal elections not only disrupted diocesan administration they also left
the episcopal seat in question and offered the city yet another opportunity to prey on a candidate's lack of *stabilitas loci*.

   Although the sources for the history of Constance reveal a variety
of causes of episcopal expulsion, it is conceivable that many other
episodes of exile and withdrawal were not recorded in surviving
sources. Still it is possible to identify approximate patterns of residency and ascertain when bishops were absent for unusual periods
and how often they appeared in civic space. Although records of
episcopal activity do not identify every place in which the bishop
slept or enjoyed aristocratic leisure, they do indicate where he functioned as bishop, lord, or prince of the empire. These figures do not
offer a complete and exhaustive account of the bishop's itinerary in a
given year but the relative pattern of episcopal residency can be
delineated across a century and a half. In some cases what appears to
be episcopal absence may simply be due to the loss of documentation, especially when chronicles as well as civic and episcopal records
indicate no reason for a bishop's departure. Ecclesiastical and imperial service sometimes accounted for prolonged residence elsewhere.
Bishop Henry of Hewen (1436-62) served as administrator for the
nearby bishopric of Chur from 1441-56, a position which took him
far afield from his episcopal city.[54] Appendix D lists patterns from

---

[53] Otto of Sonnenberg confirmed the rights of the city on December 22, 1475
(StAK A II 30, 64r-68r; GLA 5:7206; *REC* 5:14585). Usually the bishop's consecration, formal entry, and first mass coincided with this ceremony (see above, pp. 124-
136). But Bishop Otto did not receive consecration or chant his first mass until
November 6, 1480, nearly six years after his recognition of civic rights.
   Lewis of Freiberg did make one attempt to take the episcopal throne by force,
entering Constance and breaking into the cathedral and bishop's palace on the eve
of the *corpus Christi* feast in 1475. Otto of Sonnenberg excommunicated Lewis and his
relatives; Lewis departed from Constance after staying a few days with a sympathetic
cathedral canon; *REC* 5:14361-14366; Maurer II, pp. 138-141.
   A comprehensive study of this last contested episcopal election is yet to be written.
A set of twenty-five pieces of correspondence between the cathedral chapter, *Dekan*,
and Bishop Otto traces the issues of rule and administration at stake in the schism
during the years 1475-76; GLA 82/962. On the broader geographical implications
of the conflict, see Peter Haußmann, "Die Politik der Grafen von Württemberg im
Konstanzer Schisma der Jahre 1474-1480," in *Mittel und Wege früher Verfassungspolitik*
(Stuttgart: Klett-Cotta, 1979), pp. 320-355; and Johannes Gisler, *Die Stellung der Acht
Orte zum Konstanzer Bistumsstreit 1474-1480* (Freiburg: Universitäts Verlag, 1956).
[54] *REC* 4:10417.

1322-1480 for sixteen bishops, who held residence in Constance.[55] In three critical instances patterns of a bishop's absence conform to historical data about civic conflict and episcopal withdrawal, suggesting that information based on surviving sources offers tantalizing evidence about the relationship between bishop and city.[56] Bishops resided primarily in Constance 131 out of 158 years.[57] In only nine years is the bishop absent from his episcopal city altogether.[58]

A number of provisional conclusions about the relationship of

---

[55] In Appendix D I have enumerated all the surviving instances of episcopal residence from 1322-1480. This sample is limited to a particular sort of habitation— specific cases of official episcopal activity: the drafting of charters, the transfer of property, the promulgation of reform decrees, the founding of a new church, the acceptance of a bequest, the reception of local and international envoys.

The patterns of three episcopal candidates (Mangold of Brandis, Henry Baylor, and Lewis of Freiberg), who never ascend to the episcopal seat *in* Constance, are presented in Appendix D, but are not included in the following analysis.

[56] The reign of Nicholas of Frauenfeld opened with civic alienation and imperial siege of the episcopal fortress in Meersburg. Given the bishop's volatile relations to city and empire, it is not surprising that he was virtually absent from Constance in 1335 and 1336.

Henry of Brandis held primary residence outside of Constance in approximately two periods: 1366, 1368, 1370, 1371, and 1377, 1378, 1379, 1381, 1383. During the former period Henry's conflict with the city escalated to open warfare. Although Henry of Brandis continued to be active in Constance in the latter period, it is clear that, after his failed civic policy, excommunication, and restoration, he resided predominantly in Klingnau. He died there in November, 1383, but was buried in Constance.

Otto of Hachberg's controversies with the city of Constance and the cathedral chapter, which culminated in his resignation, are clearly evident in his residency patterns for 1430, 1432, and 1434.

[57] Years in which other episcopal residences or itinerant locations predominate are as follows: 1322, 1330, 1334, 1335, 1336, 1338, 1366, 1368, 1370, 1371, 1372, 1377, 1378, 1379, 1381, 1383, 1399, 1400, 1411, 1412, 1416, 1430, 1432, 1434, 1435, 1436, 1439, 1440. There are no records of episcopal residence for 1369. In 1383 a succession of bishops occurred in which neither the predecessor or the successor resided primarily in Constance. Only Frederick II of Zollern, who reigned briefly from 1434-1436, failed to reside predominantly in Constance during his reign.

In seven out of twenty-nine years in which bishops were absent a majority of the time, bishops and bishops-elect were either entering or leaving office, accounting for lower residency rates in Constance: 1322, 1334, 1383, 1399, 1411, 1434, 1436. In only thirteen years was a bishop's residency in all other locations combined considerably greater than his presence in Constance (at a rate of 5 or more incidents of residency than in Constance: 1334, 1336, 1368, 1371, 1378, 1379, 1381, 1383, 1411, 1412, 1430, 1435, 1440).

[58] The records for only four of the nine years appear truly reliable: 1335, 1370, 1371, 1412. In five cases records on residency in general are either sparse or completely lacking: 1322, 1345, 1352, 1353, and 1369. It is possible to argue that Henry was most likely not in Constance in 1369, given his feud with the city.

bishop and city emerge from the indicated residency patterns recorded in Appendix D. First, from 1322-1470 the city of Constance
remained the primary residence of the bishops. The variety of alternative sites for episcopal habitation, listed in Appendix D, reflect a
bishop's personal preference as well as the changing fortunes of a
bishop's aristocratic network and the sale or purchase of properties
for the episcopal patrimony—the *mensa episcopalis*. Meersburg on
Lake Constance was the leading private episcopal residence after
Constance in the later Middle Ages. But as Appendix D makes clear
at least until 1470 Meersburg did not often serve as an alternative
capital for the bishop and his administration, as a city from which
the bishop ruled. The clerical court was transferred to Zürich,
Schaffhausen, or later to Radolfszell under emergency conditions,
not to Meersburg.[59] Gottlieben, an episcopal residence just west of
Constance on the Rhine, often served as an alternative location to
the palace in the city.[60]

Even during periods of heightened controversy and conflict the
bishop continued to seek and gain access to Constance. Throughout
the lengthy interdict of the first half of the fourteenth century, with
the exception of 1335, the bishops were active in Constance every
year. Even as they excluded the populace from divine grace, they
gained access to the city. During the later fifteenth century bishops
such as Burkhard of Randegg (1452-66), Hermann of Breitenlandenberg (1466-74), and Otto of Sonnenberg (1474-91) continued
to rule the diocese from the capital city and appear there during
some years with remarkable regularity. Henry of Brandis is some-

---

[59] See Appendix D. The bishops of Constance ruled over Meersburg and its envi-
rons beginning in 1210. They drafted charters regarding property and policy in the
small town; see sections A (*Urkunden*) and B (*Akten*) in the Stadtsarchiv of Meersburg
(*StAM*). However, the registers of *REC* for the period 1322-1480 record less than
twenty instances of a bishop's activity on behalf of the diocese (see Appendix D) as
compared to Gottlieben, the episcopal castle-residence a short distance from
Constance where the bishop was present on episcopal business in at least 124 instances. Meersburg was important as an episcopal fortress of refuge for Nicholas of
Frauenfeld in 1344 (see pp. 47-48, 53) and for Hugo of Hohenlandenberg, especially
in 1526 (see pp. 178-179).

On the history of the city, see Steven R. Fischer, *Meersburg im Mittelalter. Aus der
Geschichte einer Bodenseestadt und ihrer nächsten Umgebung* (Meersburg: List und Franck,
1988) and Franz Götz, "Meersburg, Stadt des Bischofs von Konstanz und
bischöfliche Residenzstadt," in *Südwestdeutsche Bischofsresidenzen außerhalb der
Kathedralstädte*, pp. 27-33.

[60] See Appendix D and the residency patterns of John III Windlock, Henry of
Brandis, Marquard of Randeck, and Henry of Hewen.

what exceptional. He can be found frequently in Constance during the first eight years of his reign, the period of his campaign to restore episcopal lordship. But beginning in 1366 his presence in Constance became less regular and this trend continued to the end of his tenure. At the same time Klingau was the predominant residence in this later period, taking the place of Constance as the official habitation of Henry in 1377-79, 1381, and 1383. Henry's successors did not continue this trend, returning to Constance as the main venue for episcopal administration.[61]

On the basis of accounts of episodic expulsions and records of residency it is clear that bishops continued to be a present and active force within the walls of their original episcopal city throughout the fourteenth and fifteenth centuries. They encountered civic resistance, expulsion, and exclusion. But the departure of bishops from Constance could be a forceful act of protest, shifting the episcopal household and administration to other cities around the diocese— cities perhaps in keen economic and political competition with Constance.[62] After expulsion and withdrawal the episcopal regime always returned to Constance, the capital of the diocese and from the bishop's vantage point still primarily an episcopal city.

The imperial city of Constance had grown and prospered around the old cathedral compound.[63] Lay magistrates came increasingly to control the city but could not exclude the bishop on a permanent basis. Beyond the cycles of periodic expulsion and withdrawal the city council sought increasingly to exclude the old episcopal lord from all facets of urban life by making the cathedral compound a quarantine island in a sea of lay power. During the Middle Ages magistrates never attempted to expel the bishops of Constance per-

---

[61] It is likely that records of episcopal residence outside of Constance have not survived. But the diligent chroniclers of *REC* cataloged documents from throughout the diocese of Constance; therefore even when a record of the original was not preserved in the episcopal archive in Constance, the editors uncovered the document at the point of reception.

[62] Zürich and Schaffhausen were two of the largest cities in the vicinity of Constance and could offer the sort of resources that a bishop had come to rely on in his original episcopal city.

[63] On the remarkable expansion of the Bürgerstadt around the old cathedral compound, see Helmut Maurer, "Stadterweiterung und Vorstadtbildung im mittelalterlichen Konstanz," in *Stadterweiterung und Vorstadt*, eds. E. Maschke and J. Sydow (Stuttgart: W. Kohlhammer, 1969), pp. 21-38; and Frank Meier, *Konstanzer Stadterweiterungen im Mittelalter. Grundstücksbezogene Untersuchungen zur Erschließungsgeschichte und Sozialtopographie* (Konstanz: Hartung-Gorre, 1989).

manently; rather they tightened their grip on the political, legal, economic, and ecclesiastical spheres of urban life—the *Episcopus exclusus*
on the level of government, law, market and church. Thus, the
bishop became increasingly alien to the life of the community

3. *From Sovereignty to Stubborn Survival*[64]

When Henry of Brandis revealed his intent to restore ecclesiastical
sovereignty in 1357, he hearkened back to a golden age of episcopal
rule. Bishop Henry rested his claims on the broad shoulders of Emperor Charles IV, who decreed restoration of episcopal control of all
secular courts, assured full economic immunity for all clerical persons
and properties, and finally stipulated that the mayor, city council,
and residents had to swear homage to their bishop as lord.[65]

Royal and imperial confirmation had always played a role in the
growth and maintenance of episcopal and civic power in Constance,

---

[64] Drawing in part on the conclusions of the last twenty-five years of scholarship
we will explore the demise of episcopal lordship as a critical facet of the *Episcopus
exclusus*. The rise of lay, proto-democratic institutions and the resulting exfoliation of
the bishop's political, legal, and economic rights are two of the most carefully re-
searched facets of the history of Constance, based on a long tradition of
Rechtsgeschichte in the region of Lake Constance; see Hans-Wolfgang Strätz, "Der
Bodensee als Rechtsobjekt in Gegenwart und Geschichte," in *Der Bodensee: Landschaft,
Geschichte, Kultur*, ed. H. Maurer (Sigmaringen: Jan Thorbecke, 1982), pp. 597-617;
Hefele, *Studien zum Hochmittelalterlichen Stadttypus*; and Möncke, *Bischofsstadt und
Reichsstadt*; these works laid the groundwork for this field, focusing on south German
episcopal cities, including Constance and Augsburg. Two shorter yet excellent stud-
ies address the position of the bishops of Constance in the Middle Ages: Peter F.
Kramml, "Konstanz: Das Verhältnis zwischen Bischof und Stadt," in *BK* I, pp. 288-
300 and Peter-Johann Schuler, "Bischof und Stadt vor Beginn der Reformation in
Konstanz," in *Kontinuität und Umbruch. Theologie und Frömmigkeit in Flugschriften und
Kleinliteratur an der Wende vom 15. zum 16. Jahrhundert*, ed. J. Nolte (Stuttgart: Klett-
Cotta, 1978), pp. 300-315. Helmut Maurer has integrated the findings of both civic
and episcopal research in his two volumes on the history of Constance in the Middle
Ages. His careful analysis shows how Constance remained not only a *Bürgerstadt* and
Reichsstadt, but also a *Bischofsstadt* until the Protestant Reformation. The best explora-
tion of imperial politics in Constance during the fourteenth century is Peter Kramml,
*Kaiser Friedrich III. und die Reichsstadt Konstanz (1440-1493). Die Bodenseemetropole am
Ausgang des Mittelalters* (Sigmaringen: Jan Thorbecke, 1985).

[65] A Latin copy of the 'Carolina' (or the 'falsche Carolina', as it was called by the
residents of Constance) can be found in GLA D-317 (11 October 1357). A German
translation in the civic archival holdings of Constance, offers the title "Die so genant
schädliche Carolina," (A II 24, 85r, line 1; note the second copy in A II 29 132v-
135v); therefore, from the civic perspective, this charter of Charles IV was both
incorrect (*falsch*) and injurious (*schädlich*).

especially under the Hohenstaufen in the twelfth and thirteenth centuries.[66] In fact, a secular power had given birth to the bishopric in the seventh century, when an Alemanni duke or perhaps the Merovingian Dagobert I (623-39) made Constance an episcopal seat and donated lands south of the settlement—the so-called *Bischofshöri*—to finance the episcopal household.[67] The bishops of Constance built on this secular foundation, turning a small settlement on the ruins of a Roman site into a thriving town dedicated to supporting the episcopal residence. Bishop Salomo III (890-919) completed this transformation, creating a regional capital and minting coins in the bishop's name—currency which circulated as far afield as Poland and Finland.[68] The citadel of the cathedral formed the heart of the city, defining a space which would remain immune to the claims of civic and foreign powers until the sixteenth century.[69] This stronghold embraced the bishop's church, administrative quarters, and palace as well as the dwellings of the cathedral canons.[70] As the bishop shaped a city of stone and mortar, he drew craftsmen and ministerials to his service, forming the rudiments of a civic population.[71] This lay community lived under the lordship of the bishop who possessed the

---

[66] Maurer I, pp.100-106, 112-115; Möncke, *Bischofsstadt und Reichsstadt*, pp. 37-41.

[67] Helmut Maurer, "Das Bistum bis zum 12. Jahrhundert," *HS* I, 2.1, pp. 88-89; "Die Anfänge," Maurer I, pp. 27-30.

[68] Maurer I, pp. 53-55, 58-62.

[69] It is often difficult to trace the legal developments of episcopal cities of the sixth and seventh centuries, since critical records are missing. Thus Norbert Leudemann focuses on cities founded by bishops from the eighth to the eleventh century, where episcopal, royal, and imperial initiatives can be carefully documented (e.g. Bamberg, Eichstätt, Freising, Münster, and Würzburg); *Deutsche Bischofsstädte im Mittelalter*, pp. 9-10.

The original charters specifying episcopal immunities and rights in Constance have not survived. Emperor Frederick I (1152-90) granted the bishop a charter in 1155 which lays out many of the bishop's long-held rights over market, toll, and coinage; Möncke, *Bischofsstadt und Reichsstadt*, p. 23.

[70] This ecclesiastical territory enclosed the *oberen Münsterhof* (the episcopal palace, palace-chapel of St. Peter, residences of the secular administrator of the palace, and the court house of the episcopal *Ammann*) and the *unteren Münsterhof* (the dormitory and later separate living quarters of the canons, a guest-house, and the so-called *Stauf*, the *Domkapitelstube*); Peter Kramml, "Konstanz: Das Verhältnis zwischen Bischof und Stadt," p. 288. This fortified settlement functioned as a refuge (*Fluchtburg*) and sheltered the clerical populace when the Huns sacked the suburbs of the city in 926; Hefele, *Studien zum Hochmittelalterlichen Stadttypus*, p. 25.

Markus Bauer has studied the development of this quarter of the city in remarkable detail; *Der Münsterbezirk von Konstanz. Domherrenhöfe und Pfrundhäuser der Münsterkapläne im Mittelalter* (Sigmaringen: Jan Thorbecke, 1995).

[71] For a helpful reconstruction of the social structure of episcopal cities, including Constance, see Hefele, *Studien zum Hochmittelalterlichen Stadttypus*, pp. 152-165. The

imperial right to hold a market in Constance and collect tolls at the
gates and on the Rhine bridge. He ruled the city and enforced law
through his Advocate of High Justice (*Vogt*) and his Officer of Low
Justice (*Ammann*).[72] In the early Middle Ages the bishops of
Constance reigned over every sphere of urban life, ensuring civic
security, holding weekly markets, and executing justice; the city
would not have flourished without episcopal administration and business.

The needs of the bishop's household combined with the conven-
ient location of this city on trade routes and major waterways. The
episcopal seat attracted local merchants and long-distance traders to
take up residence in Constance. This distinctively lay, merchant
quarter of the city would eventually grow into a civic community
which would challenge the sovereignty of the bishop.[73] We must not,
however, read later developments back into the early Middle Ages,
as if merchants could envision a full blown *Bürgerstadt* or as if a bishop
might sense the first signs of his successors' demise. In the ninth and
tenth centuries the bishop fostered economic growth. Long-distance
traders and regional merchants brought added resources and prestige
to this episcopal city.[74] The bishop possessed the right to hold markets and thus assured a legal and regular space for trade. He exercised the right to charge tolls, verify fair weights and measures, and
produce stable currency. He provided a safe environment for commerce by maintaining the defenses of the city and enforcing high and
low justice through the *Vogt* and *Ammann*.[75] The Golden Age of the
episcopal city was at the same time a remarkable opportunity for the
burgeoning merchant community.

The significant period of civic growth occurred between the reign

---

episcopal ministerials would eventually form the lay ruling class of the city; see Klaus
H. Koch, "Bemerkungen zum Anteil der Ministerialität an der städtischen Führungsschicht in Konstanz," in *Stadt und Ministerialität*, eds. E. Maschke and J. Sydow
(Stuttgart: W. Kohlhammer, 1973), pp. 92-97; and Knut Schulz, "Die Ministerialität
in Rheinischen Bischofsstädten," in *Stadt und Ministerialität*, pp. 16-42.

[72] The *Ammann* primarily ruled on disputed cases concerning trade in the market
and property transactions; Hefele, *Studien zum Hochmittelalterlichen Stadttypus*, pp. 94f.

[73] The lay quarter grew around the *second* church of the city of Constance—St.
Stephan's. This parish and later collegiate church lay outside the cathedral citadel,
and originally served the lands of the episcopal patrimony (*Bischofshöri*); Maurer I, pp.
42-44; and Helmut Maurer, *Das Stift St. Stephan in Konstanz.* (Berlin: Walter de
Gruyter, 1981), pp. 39-42.

[74] Hefele, *Studien zum Hochmittelalterlichen Stadttypus*, p. 27.

[75] Hefele provides a crisp and cogent description of these rights, *Studien zum Hochmittelalterlichen Stadttypus*, pp. 94-137.

of Salomo III and ended after the aggressive regime of Henry of Brandis. In the early twelfth century merchants began to assist in the administration of market regulations.[76] Cells of civic self-representation began to appear in records as attachments to the episcopal court.[77] This practice of temporal and spiritual cooperation was shattered by the Investiture Controversy in the late eleventh and early twelfth centuries. The absence of the bishop or the warring of rival candidates spurred on by emperor and pope threw the residents of Constance back on their own resources. During these volatile years the laity acquired the right to defend the city. The inhabitants of Constance further developed urban policy as they chose to embrace one episcopal candidate and exclude another.[78]

Over the next two centuries episcopal lordship declined as citizens gained freedom from episcopal taxation while forming a city government. A lay advisory committee increasingly displaced the bishop's administration by drafting civic laws, devising its own seal, employing a civic secretary (*Stadtschreiber*), recording city council minutes, and electing magistrates and a mayor.[79] Two developments indicate the demise of the bishop's political lordship. In 1249 King William of Holland decreed that the Advocate of High Justice (*Vogt*) was an office of the empire and could not be pawned to another potentate.

---

[76] This cooperation was supported by the bishop; it was further accelerated by the creation of a market distant from the cathedral citadel, the *Obermarkt*; Hefele, *Studien zum Hochmittelalterlichen Stadttypus*, pp. 51-53. Kramml sees this cooperation occurring already in the tenth century with a Marktregal administered by episcopal officials and merchants; "Konstanz: Das Verhältnis zwischen Bischof und Stadt," *BK* I, p. 289.

[77] Lay witnesses appear in the bishop's *civic court (Chorgericht)*; Möncke, *Bischofsstadt und Reichsstadt*, pp. 88-89.

[78] See Maurer I, pp. 90-99.

[79] The precise coordinates of civic political development are not always clear, especially when attempting to pinpoint the exact moment the lay city council appeared, when the office of mayor was created, or when all of the above were elected by the populace at large. In any case the city council is in evidence as of 1255; the first city seal was used in 1246; the first *Stadtschreiber* appears in 1256. In the late thirteenth century the magistrates drafted their first city regulations, a clear infringement on episcopal legal jurisdiction; Konrad Beyerle, "Die Entwicklung der Konstanzer Stadtrechts," in *Das Rote Buch*, vol. 1, pp. 1-28. Peter Meisel has explored the final shape of the late medieval city government in *Die Verfassung und Verwaltung der Stadt Konstanz im 16. Jahrhundert* (Konstanz: Jan Thorbecke, 1957). *Das Rote Buch*, vol. I., ed. O. Fegger (Konstanz: Merk, 1949) contains the first regulations or *Satzungen* of the city council. On the further development of civic laws during the later Middle Ages, see the collection compiled by the sixteenth century city secretary, Jörg Vögeli, in *Die Statutensammlung des Stadtschreibers Jörg Vögeli*, ed. O. Fegger (Konstanz: Merk, 1951).

This royal initiative eliminated the bishop's role in appointing the *Vogt* and ensured that capital crimes henceforth fell under imperial and not episcopal rule. The city now possessed the first important qualification needed to reach the status of *Reichsstadt*.[80] Next in 1312 the city council not only sought to control the streets of Constance but also signed a treaty with neighboring cities, thus pursuing a civic foreign policy independent of episcopal direction or approval.[81]

The bishop's political losses were in turn compounded by a weakening of his status as the benefactor and high priest of the city. During the thirteenth century the city council replaced the bishop as the chief patron of the poor, taking over the direction of a new hospital (*Heiliggeistsspital*) in 1225, coordinating a system of alms distribution (the *Raiten*), and building a house for lepers (*Siechenhaus*).[82] Although magistrates did not attempt to seize control of the bishop's cathedral, they did begin to reshape ecclesiastical life in the city. The fabric of the Collegiate Church of St. Stephan came increasingly under the direction of the city council.[83] In addition to assisting the needy and supporting churches the city council created its own sacred space. The *Ratskapelle* of St. Laurentius was the center-piece of lay, political piety. The magistrates saw to its construction on the *Obermarkt*, a location beyond the reach of the bishop's cathedral immunity. They furnished the chapel with altars, appointed priests to their service, and installed a bell to call magistrates to meetings. Before gathering for business they heard mass in the St. Laurentius chapel.[84] By the fourteenth century the cathedral compound of the bishop stood over against the self-supporting city, symbolized by the lay city hall and

---

[80] Gisela Möncke characterizes this development as the decisive shift from *Bischofsstadt* to *Reichsstadt* in Constance, *Bischofsstadt und Reichsstadt*, esp. pp. 69-73.

[81] Maurer I, pp. 166-177. This development comes after the rule of the last true *Stadtherr* of Constance, Bishop Henry of Klingenberg (1293-1306), who used his patronage of the arts in the city, his position as administrator of the Benedictine island, Reichenau, and service as vice-chancellor in the Empire to solidify episcopal rule in Constance.

[82] Maurer I, pp. 127-130. Civic initiative is especially obvious in the *Oath Book* (*Aydbuch*) of the civic hospital where every facet of the institution was regulated by lay authorities; a 1470 copy is extant in the civic archive of Constance (StAK A IV, fol. 2). On the development of this charitable institution, see Wolfgang Schürle, *Das Hospital zum Heiligen Geist in Konstanz. Ein Beitrag zur Rechtsgeschichte des Hospitals im Mittelalter* (Konstanz: Jan Thorbecke, 1970).

[83] Maurer, *Das Stift St. Stephan in Konstanz*, pp. 53-58.

[84] Helmut Maurer, "Die Ratskapelle. Beobachtungen am Beispiel von St. Lorenz in Konstanz," *Festschrift für Hermann Heimpel zum 70. Geburtstag* (Göttingen: Vandenhoeck und Ruprecht, 1972), pp. 225-236.

the spire of the magistrates' chapel. The singing of mass and the ringing of bells might be heard in the choir stalls of the cathedral canons or in the worship services of the city council in St Laurentius.

The decline of episcopal power continued throughout the later Middle Ages. In fact, the efforts of Bishop Henry of Brandis to fore-stall civic encroachment backfired. In the aftermath of his campaign to restore lordship Bishop Henry not only surrendered control of the episcopal mint but also suffered a severe curtailment of his political and judicial power.[85] The officer of low justice, the *Ammann*, had always represented the bishop in the city council; but now the magistrates demanded that the *Ammann* be chosen from a list of citizens. Then in the late fourteenth century the city fathers took further measures against the bishop's officers in the city, demanding that the *Ammann* depart from council proceedings whenever ecclesiastical matters were on the docket. Moreover, after 1375 a magistrate of Constance usually held the office of *Vogt*, ensuring that imperial high justice was oriented towards the interests of the city council.[86]   By the end of the fourteenth century the tables had turned. The bishops of Constance were no longer on the offensive; now they had to defend their clergy, properties, and assets from civic confiscation and taxation.[87]

During the fifteenth century magistrates continued to undermine

---

[85] See the settlement between Bishop Henry and the city in 1372 (GLA 209/469; StAK A II 24, pp. 93-98; and A II 29, 136r-139v). By 1384 the city had changed the minting molds for the old episcopal Münze; the coins now displayed the bust of St. Konrad, bishop and patron of the city; they no longer placed the profile of the reigning bishop on the coin; Möncke, *Bischofsstadt und Reichsstadt*, pp. 171-172.

[86] Hefele, *Studien zum Hochmittelalterlichen Stadttypus*, pp. 135-137; Möncke, *Bischofs-stadt und Reichsstadt*, pp. 74, 139-140.

[87] Meersburg is intriguing as an example of episcopal lordship during the Middle Ages and as a contrast to conditions in Constance. Here the bishops controlled markets and properties, installed key public officials, and determined foreign policy with limited consultation from the community. Bishops ruled Meersburg as they wished to dominate Constance. Meersburg never rose to the status of a free city. On April 23, 1233 the bishops of Constance received the royal privilege to hold weekly markets in Meersburg (*REC* 1:1450). In 1299 Emperor Albert bestowed immunity from all foreign jurisdictions with the exception of royal and imperial courts (*REC* 2:3234). This privilege was renewed by Emperor Lewis in 1333 (StAM, U-2; c.f. U-30, U-186). While the city magistrates of Constance compelled bishops to confirm civic rights in the initial *Verschreibung*, in Meersburg the bishops continued to exercise lordship, receiving an oath of submission (*Huldigung*) from the residents of Meersburg (StAM, U-19).

In Meersburg the bishops of Constance appointed the civic *Ammann* and *Vogt* while controlling elections to the city council and having free reign to dispose of property;

episcopal rule. In 1442 Emperor Frederick III granted them the right
to create two new courts dealing with matters of lower justice, cutting
directly into the jurisdiction of the episcopal *Ammann*.[88] This imperial
bequest followed a crowning moment in the history of the city. From
1414-18 the city was the capital of Christendom, as the Council of
Constance resolved the Great Schism, burned the condemned John
Hus, and sought to reform the church in head and members. In
recognition of civic service to the empire and church during the
council Emperor Sigismund (1410-37) granted jurisdiction over the
territory south of the city—the Thurgau. This bequest provided the
opportunity for a city bordered on two sides by bodies of water to
create a city-state, a metropolis with rich hinterlands and subjects.
The city council would now administer justice over many residents
near the old *Bischofshöri*, the original lands of the episcopal patrimony
as well as the more distant acreage of the Thurgau.[89] Thus, magistrates were reaching beyond the walls of the city to grasp yet more of
the bishop's real estate and rights.

In the late fourteenth century the city council of Constance made
a critical, legal demand on the bishop by requiring that he acknowledge civic rights in writing. When Bishop-elect Nicholas of
Riesenburg entered Constance in 1384, he produced a document
called a *Verschreibung*, confirming his good intentions toward the
city.[90] This statement was a concession to the magistrates meant to
insure that Nicholas would not adopt the tactics of his predecessor,
Henry of Brandis. Moreover, a divided episcopal election, a militant
counter-candidate (Mangold of Brandis), and the larger specter of a
Christendom divided between Rome and Avignon did not leave
Bishop Nicholas with many alternatives; a civic oath was necessary to
secure the support of the citizens of Constance.

After the reign of Bishop Nicholas magistrates continued to de-

---

Otto of Sonnenberg gave full expression to these rights in his decrees for Meersburg
in November of 1480 (StAM, U-146; GLA 67/499, 54r-60v; for other examples of
episcopal lordship in Meersburg, see StAK A II 15, 18v-19r; GLA 67/499, 113r-
115v; and GLA 67/499, 1r-4r). Moreover, the bishops oversaw the securing of the
gates and keys of the city (StAM, U-330)

The residents of Meersburg turned to the bishop as arbitrator of disputed cases;
see the episcopal decisions and decrees in StAM U-47, U-173, U-205.

[88] Maurer II, pp. 85. On the lengthy reign of Emperor Frederick III and his
impact on the development of the city of Constance, see Peter F. Kramml, *Kaiser
Friedrich III. und die Reichsstadt Konstanz (1440-1493)*.

[89] Maurer II, pp. 71-73.

[90] StAK A II 30, 30r-33r.

mand that each new bishop draft a *Verschreibung* confirming civic rights and privileges. Until this document reached the city council a newly elected bishop might not be allowed to make formal entry into the city of Constance. As a result the bishop-elect might wait as long as a year or more before civic acceptance of his reign. This type of exile would prove all the more practical, because even a hostile episcopal candidate, such as Henry of Brandis, would be more likely to recognize civic lordship in exchange for civic approval of his residency. Once a bishop had sworn to uphold the rights and privileges of the city, magistrates could monitor, affirm, or reprimand episcopal policy and practice on the basis of the *Verschreibung*.[91] Between 1384 and 1498 each bishop of Constance swore the oath that would serve as the basis for episcopal and civic cohabitation. Bishop Thomas Berlower (1491-96) provides the best example of the development of the *Verschreibung* in part because he intentionally revived the specter of Henry of Brandis and posted the *falsche Carolina*, the old charter that had soured relations between bishop and city a century before. After the failure of his scheme to revive the grand vision of Brandis, Bishop Thomas settled down to draft a *Verschreibung* that represented the last episcopal revision of the document in the later Middle Ages.[92]

Over the century between Nicholas of Riesenburg and Thomas Berlower this charter shaped the discussion and limited conflict between bishop and city. A basic set of articles can be found in all the *Verschreibungen*, giving cogency to the late-medieval discussion of episcopal and civic rights. An episcopal salutation opened every *Verschreibung*, affirming the bishop's spiritual status in a brief blessing, followed by the name of the bishop and a greeting to those present at the moment of promulgation or at a later reading.[93] Then on behalf of the *Hochstift* the bishop confirmed his peaceful intentions toward

---

[91] On the ritual implications of the *Verschreibungen*, see above, pp. 136-139.

[92] In fact, Hugo of Hohenlandenberg produced the last *Verschreibung* in 1498 but his decree is in part a reproduction of Thomas Berlower's document and in part a return to the earlier form produced by Bishop Otto of Sonnenberg (1474-91); for Bishop Otto's *Verschreibung*, see StAK A II 30, 64r-68r or GLA 5-7207; for Bishop Hugo, see StAK A II 30, 75r-79v or GLA 5-7210-12.

[93] "In Namen der Hayligen vnzerthailichen drivaltigkhait sägclich. Amen. Wir Thomas von Gottes gnaden bestätter Bischoff zu Costennz Thund kund vnd veriehenn offentlich mit disem gegenwürtigen brief gegen allen denen die in ansehen oder hören lesen;" StAK A II 30, 68r, 5-12. The decree of Thomas Berlower will be cited here as an example of continuity and change in the drafting of *Verschreibungen*.

the city, including the mayor, city council, guildmaster, and general citizenry.[94] After formal greetings and assurances of good will the bishop made the critical concessions of the decree: the confirmation of all the rights and traditions of the city in their individual articles and points to the date of the *Verschreibung*. This stipulation made special mention of those privileges granted by king and emperor, the basis of civic claims to the status of *Reichsstadt*.[95]

Once the bishop recognized the fundamental freedom of the city as recorded in charters and contracts, he addressed matters requiring episcopal and civic cooperation. First, the bishop promised to recognize all contracts regarding land loaned to residents; these property rights would be extended to the children and relatives of the original lessee.[96] Second, the office of *Ammann*, an episcopal appointment, would always be filled by a citizen.[97] The bishop would not be able to install a foreigner—lay or cleric—in the court of low justice. Third, if the clerical court (*geistliches Gericht*) remained in Constance, the clients, judge, jurors of the court, and their relatives would submit themselves to civic oversight as well as to the laws and customs of the city.[98] The city council could directly influence the *Ammanngericht* through the *Ammann* who sat on the council. But magistrates had

---

[94] "Wann wir von den obgenanten gnaden Gottes vnnd von seiner göttlichen verhengde zuo dem stifft vnnd bistumb zu Costannz ze Bischoff genomen seyen zimpt vns nun vol vnd seyen darzuo genaigt das auch die die zu vns vnnd dem selben vnsernn stifft gehören by ruewen frid vnnd gemach beleiben als verr das an vns ligen mag, darvmb vnd auch vmb das Wann Wir die Ersamen vnser besunder lieben vnnd getrewen den Burgermaister den Rathe Zunfftmaister vnnd alle burgere gemainlich der Statt Costannz bißher so freündtlich willig vnnd guetmüetig an vnns vnnd an der egenanten vnser Stift erfunden habenn vnnd sy ab Gott will hinfüro finden vnnd ersehen sollen;" StAK A II 30, 68v, 12—69v, 2.

[95] "... bey allen den freyhaiten rechten vnd guten gewonhaiten by allen Iren brieffen vnd gnaden die sy von Rhomischen Kaysern vnd Königen bisher vff den Heütig tag als diser brief geben ist; Herbracht erlanngt vnnd erworben Hand. Vnnd auch bey allen den puncten artigkheln vnd begreiffungen;" StAK A II 30, 69v, 19-26.

[96] "Was auch dehain burger oder burgerin zuo Costannz von ainem Bischoff zu Costannz zu Lehen hannd geen, dem oder denen sollen Wir gutmüetig willig vnnd gnädig sein. Dieselben lehen zeleihen Inen vnd Iren khinden khnaben vnnd tochtern frowen vnnd mannen vnnd Iren erbenn vnnd Iren damit gestatten kauffent vnnd verkauffens;" StAK A II 30, 70r, 16-25.

[97] "Auch sollen Wir vnser vnd vnserss Stiffts Aman Ampt zu Costannz niemandts andern leihen dann ainem der ain Ingessesner burger daselbs zu Costennz ist;" StAK A II 30, 70r, 27-30.

[98] "... auch vnser gaistlich gericht Wenn wir das ze Costennz haltend vnd beleiben lassend vnnd auch die Richter vnnd die personen, so den gerichten verwandt seyen schirmind vnnd haltind by Iren guten vnnd loblichen gwonhaiten gerechtigkhaiten vnnd rechten als das von Alterherkhomen is one geverd;" StAK A II 30, 70v, 34-41.

little control over the judge, lawyers, notaries, foreign and clerical clients who came to the bishop's ecclesiastical court. This stipulation ensured that those entering the city on episcopal business would abide by civic laws and customs. Fourth, the episcopal mint, now operated by the city, would remain in Constance.[99] Fifth, the process of adjudication in cases between the clergy and laity was carefully laid out. In fact, this section comprises over half of the *Verschreibung*, detailing the steps of appellation and mediation when routine negotiation failed to resolve a dispute or claim.[100] Sixth, the bishop offered assurances that he would honor the *Verschreibung* in each section and article.[101] Finally, the promulgation of this decree was authenticated by a series of episcopal witnesses.[102]

Although these articles and concessions form the bulk of the

---

[99] "Wir sollen auch vnnser vnnd vnsers Stiffts münz ze Costennz daselbst zuo Costennź lassen beleiben als sy von Alterher besetzt ist;" StAK A II 30, 70v, 40-43.

[100] This section (StAK A II 30, 69v, 28—73v, 13) includes a variety of scenarios and stages of negotiation which would guarantee due process in all matters of dispute between bishop and city. For example, a committee comprised of lay and clerical jurors would be formed; they would choose someone to oversee the case and his identity would depend in part on whether the case regarded a lay or clerical matter: "... Wir zu der selben sach geben sollen drey vnnser Thumbherren zuo Costanz ob an Iren han mügen das sy das thun wellen, wöllten sy aber das nit thun, So mögen Wir drey annder biderman dar zu setzen vnd geben die In vnserm bistumb wonhafft sind vnnd auch die Statt Costennz drey erbar man dieselben sechs sollen vns dann zuo baiderseyth verhören. Mögen sy vnns dann nach vnser baiderthail red vnnd widerred verrichten mit lieb vnd mit freündtschafft wol vnd gut möcht aber das nit gesein. So sollen dieselben sechs, mit wissen vnnd willen der parthayen, nach ainem biderman zu Inen nemen zu ainem gemainen der ain lay seye. Es wäre dan das die sach gannz lauter gaistliche genant in Latein mere Spiritualis were, Dann so sollen die Sechs mit wissen der Partheyen ainem Obman nemen der ain gaistliche Person seye. Vnnd wäs sich dann dieselben ainmüetiglich oder der merthail vnnder Inen vmb ain Iegclich sach nach red vnnd nach widerred vff Ir aide vnnd ehre erkhennen vnd darumb zum rechten sprechen, dabey soll es dann beleiben vnnd bestan. Wär aber sach das ain Statt von vmb lauter Leyisch sachen In Latein genant mere Civilis zuspruch vermaintend zehaben, so sollend die von Costannz sollichs zum ersten an vns bringen vnnd langen lassen, ob wir freündtlich mitaindern veraint werden möchten vnd ob die güetlichehait nicht verfieng ..." StAK A II 30, 71v, 10—72r, 14. In these matters the bishop also demands that all documents brought into judicial matters have the appropriate ecclesiastical seal, "... ains Bischoffs vnnd ains Capittels Insigeln ..." StAK A II 30, 72v, 9-10; the seal is attached so as to avoid the submission of forged documents asserting previous clerical bequests or concessions. Documents without proper seals would not admissible in judicial proceedings (StAK A II 39, 72v, 14-23).

[101] "Dise vorgenanten stukh vnnd Artigkhel alle gemainlich vnd Irgelich Insunders Haben wir vorbenempter Thoma Bischoffe zuo Costanntz gelobt vnnd verhaissen bey vnserm fürstlichen treüwen Inn Aides weis zehalten vnnd dabey zebleiben ..." StAK A II 30, 73r, 13-19.

[102] "Darzuo haben wir gebetten die Erwürdigen Edlen Vesten vnd hochgelerten

Verschreibung, the bishops of Constance continued to alter the document throughout the fifteenth century, focusing on individual phrases and crucial issues. Bishop Otto of Hachberg (1410-34) replaced the very first words of the decree, "In dem Namen Gottes," with a fuller appellation in Latin—"In nomine patris et individual trinitatis."[103] Otto also eliminated a more affective affirmation of episcopal intentions toward the city.[104] In 1399 Marquard of Randeck (1398-1406) addressed the due process for disputes between bishop and city, revising the list of possible mediators provided by Bishop Nicholas. He replaced the former list of cities (Überlingen, Ravensburg, Lindau, and St. Gall) with a committee system comprised of civic and clerical representatives. This alteration ensured that confrontations would be dealt with by city and bishop and not by external judicatories and arbitrators in the vicinity of Lake Constance.[105]

Under Thomas Berlower two crucial additions significantly altered the last *Verschreibung* of the fifteenth century. First, the name of Bishop Henry of Brandis appears in the text, though in this case the allusion is a reference to previous documents with the name of Henry as a marker.[106] Second, Bishop Thomas won an important concession

---

vnser lieben Andächtigen vnd getreüwen Herrn Johansen von Randegg, maister Iergen Wintterstetter baider rechten Licentiaten Connraden gremlich von Memingen vnsers obgemelten Stiffts Thumbherren vnnd Balthassarn von Randegg Hoffmaister das die Ir Insigel zuo mehrer gezeügkhnus. Aller vorgeschribner ding doch In selbs vnnd Iren erben on schaden heiran zuo vnserm Insigel thun henkhen;" StAK A II 30, 72v, 24—73r, 5.

[103] The latter Latin phrase was translated into German twenty-six years later by Bishop Henry of Hewen (1436-62)—"In Namen der Hailigen vnzerthailichen trivaltigkhait." This appellation became the standard opening in successive *Verschreibungen*. The phrase certainly indicates greater theological sophistication; it may have also served to enhance the pedigree of the bishop as a high churchman. For examples of these phrases and the places where the new expressions are introduced, see the *Verschreibungen* of Nicholas of Riesenburg (StAK A II 30, 30r, 4), Otto of Hachberg (StAK A II 30, 43r, 5-6), and Henry of Hewen (StAK A II 30, 50r, 5-6).

[104] Nicholas of Riesenburg included the following in the initial section of the first *Verschreibung*: "... das Wir mit dem Hilff Gottes mit begirigen Herzen betrachten vnd bedencken ..." StAK A II 30, r, 14-15. As with the greeting this reference to inner integrity may have been removed, since it weakened the bearing of the bishop in his decree.

[105] On the original process proposed by Bishop Nicholas, see StAK A II 30, 31v, 18f. Marquard's alternative, on which all successive *Verschreibungen* were based, can be found in A II 30, 36r, 6—36v, 7. These instructions were in turn expanded and reached their most complex form in the *Verschreibung* of Thomas Berlower; see note 94 above.

[106] "... deßglichen diselben von Constannz wider vns vnnd vnnser Stifft sydt da-

from the city. For the first time in civic records, so far as we can determine, the city council and mayor swore to uphold the *Verschreibung*. Now the bishop's declaration could be used not only to ensure episcopal recognition of civic rights but also to bind the magistrates of the city to certain conditions of cohabitation with this very same episcopal decree.[107] This civic concession most likely reveals the vulnerable position of Constance on the border between the Holy Roman Empire and the emerging Swiss Confederacy. The bishop was a prince of the empire and spiritual overseer of lands in Swiss territory. The magistrates may well have needed episcopal assistance to support trade in the Thurgau to the south of the city.

In 1384 Bishop Nicholas of Riesenburg submitted the first *Verschreibung*, a telling sign of episcopal weakness at the end of the fourteenth century. No longer lords of the city the bishops submitted a statement of their intentions before taking up formal residence while the magistrates deliberated on *episcopal* promises to uphold *civic* rights. The bishops bound themselves to uphold all civic charters and rights, recognize all previous land-tenures with the civic populace, appoint a citizen as *Ammann*, leave the episcopal mint in Constance, and compel all members of the clerical courts to acknowledge civic jurisdiction. In disputed cases the bishop's palace was no longer the final court of appeal; a joint panel comprised of lay and clerical representatives would decide the case.

Although the bishops were clearly at a disadvantage in this arrangement, the *Verschreibung* worked both ways since it legitimated the bishop's continuing presence in the city. In fact, by the reign of Otto of Hachberg (1410-34) the decree had taken on a permanent form,

---

tum diß richtumbs brieff Bischofs Heirnichs von Brandis erwarben hetten oder furo erwurben;" StAK A II 30, 70r, 10-14.

[107] The content of the civic declaration does not include new articles or demands but it does offer civic recognition of the new bishop and his regime: "Wir der Burgermaiser vnnd Rathe der Statt Constannz Thund khundt alle vnmenigclichem mit disem brieff, das vns der hochwürdig Fürst vnnd herr, Herr Thomas Bischof zu Costannz, vnnser gnediger herr, disen nachgeschribnen brieff besigelt geben hat. Allso lautendt in namen den Hailigen. Vff das so Bekhennen Wir das wir sollichen vorgeschribnen brieff Inn allen puncten vnnd Artigkheln wo der vff vns vnd die vnsern thut weisen getrewlich halten vnd dem nachkhomen wellen, Als Wir das bei vnnsern wahren guten treüwen an rechter Aidesstatt gelobt vnnd versprachen haben. Vnnd versprechen Inn crafft diß Briefs alle gefard hindan gesetzt ..." StAK A II 30,74r, 4-20.

Brigitte Degler-Spengler rightly describes this oath as a *Gegenverschreibung*; "Das Bistum vom 13. bis zum 15. Jahrhundert," *HS* I, 2.1, p. 117.

confining not only episcopal schemes but also civic efforts to infringe on the bishop and his administration. Thomas Berlower managed a significant victory for the episcopal front; the reading of the *Verschreibung* would be a two-sided event in which both parties swore to observe the stipulations of the decree. Once again the bishops, though impoverished and politically weakened, had tied the city to its former lord in a ceremony of mutual trust and affiliation. In the late 1490s the young and ambitious Hugo of Hohenlandenberg would press forward with a renewed episcopal offensive, challenging a city council severely weakened by political misfortune and deeply troubled by the continuing menace of the residing bishops of Constance.

4. *The Early Reign of Hugo of Hohenlandenberg (1496-1511)*

During the later Middle Ages the bishops of Constance waged a continuous battle to maintain their rights and residency in their old episcopal city. Since the early fourteenth century they had endured the long struggle between empire and papacy, the civic hostility generated by the enforcement of interdict, the dissension of the Great Schism, the ravages of seven contested episcopal elections, and the rise of the lay city to the heights of imperial and international prestige. As Constance became affluent and ambitious and as the city council dissolved episcopal lordship and encroached on the church itself, bishops relied more and more on their spiritual powers and the immunity of the cathedral compound to stabilize a shrinking episcopal jurisdiction.

Despite considerable legal, political, and economic decline, the indignity of the public *Verschreibung*, and the fact that the efforts of the aging Thomas Berlower had not resulted in a clear cut episcopal victory, Hugo of Hohenlandenberg continued to press for the restoration of episcopal rights and privileges, the century-old aspirations of Bishop Henry of Brandis. Unlike most of his predecessors Bishop Hugo had some grounds for being optimistic in the pursuit of the long-faltering episcopal agenda. After the precipitous rise of the city in the early 1400s, culminating in the prestige of hosting the ecumenical council (1414-18), Constance had suffered a steady economic and political decline. In 1460 Swiss troops seized the Thurgau, the territory on which much of the local prosperity of Constance depended. The city retained legal jurisdiction over the region but an expansion of civic territory now appeared impossible; the rural holdings of patrician families in the Thurgau now lay in a foreign domain. As conflict increased along the Swiss-German border the empire pressed Constance to join the Swabian League of cities and princes, while the Swiss repeatedly solicited Constance to unite with the confederacy.[108]

The magistrates of Constance pursued a policy of neutrality but the bishops of Constance took sides. Bishop Hermann of Breitenlandenberg (1466-74), the uncle of the later Bishop Hugo, had already asserted one of his remaining political rights—the conduct of foreign policy—forming an alliance with the confederacy in 1469 and his successors concluded further treaties in 1483 and 1494. In 1497 Bishop Hugo signed yet another pact. Two years later the Holy Roman Empire and the confederacy went to war; both city and bishop were compelled to join the side of the empire. In 1499 the Swiss crushed imperial forces in the Swabian War with dire consequences for the lay government of Constance. Bishop Hugo and his successors could no longer oversee and expand their secular domain in the Thurgau as independent lords, but they continued to rule on both sides of the border as shepherds of the church and as holder of certain episcopal estates. Constance, however, lost legal jurisdiction as well as easy access to markets and trade routes in the Thurgau. The city of Constance was surrounded: to the north and the east water confined the growth of the city; to the south and the west, the walls of Constance looked out on the territories of the confederacy.[109]

In the early years of the sixteenth century Hugo of Hohenlandenberg sought to tighten this territorial noose around the city, negotiating with Emperor Maximilian (1483-1519) for the transfer of the island of Reichenau as well as the Abbey Petershausen and the Augustinian canonry of Kreuzlingen to the patrimony of the bishops of Constance. Acquisition of these cloisters, especially the wealthy Benedictine island of Reichenau, would not only fill the empty coffers of the bishop, it would also complete an episcopal ring

---

[108] On renewed Swiss appeals during the Protestant period in Constance, see Thomas A. Brady, Jr., *Turning Swiss. Cities and Empire, 1450-1550* (Cambridge: Cambridge University Press, 1985), pp. 163-166, 200-206.

[109] On the relationship of the bishop to the growing Swiss Confederacy, see Degler-Spengler, "Das Bistum vom 13. bis zum 15. Jahrhundert," *HS* I, 2.1, pp. 110-116; on the city of Constance and the confederacy, see Maurer II, pp. 196-272.

around the city of Constance with the castle Gottlieben to the west,
Petershausen and Reichenau to the north, Meersburg and Markdorf
over Lake Constance to the northeast, and Kreuzlingen and the episcopal towns of Arbon and Bischofszell to the south in the
Thurgau.[110]

Hugo's foreign policy and territorial initiatives were certainly not
acceptable to the magistrates of Constance. Although Hugo of
Hohenlandenberg took up his reign with the effusive elegy of Sebastian Brant as a "regent, ruler, guardian, and bishop," he did not
receive such civic acclaim and submission in the old episcopal city.
Only one year after the diocesan synod in Constance (1497) Hugo
attempted to reassert episcopal rights of coinage which had been lost
to the city over a century before.[111] In 1504 he conferred with the
cathedral canons, seeking specifically to strengthen the jurisdiction of
the *Ammanngericht*, condemn the use of St. Stephan's for civic ceremonies on New Years Eve, and protect clerical rights to sell wine in the
city.[112]

In 1506 Hugo could take exact measure of civic hostility. His relative, Beringer of Landenberg, had travelled in the bishop's train
through Constance in route to the Thurgau to the south. Beringer
was a wanted man in Constance, charged with violently assaulting a
citizen. In anticipation of Hugo's return with Beringer in tow, offi-

[110] Rudolf Reinhardt, "Das Bistum in der Neuzeit," *HS* I, 2.1, pp. 123-124;
Wolfgang Dobras, "Konstanz zur Zeit der Reformation," in *Konstanz in der frühen
Neuzeit* (Konstanz: Verlag Stadler, 1991), pp. 29-32.
[111] Maurer II, pp. 217-218; on Hugo's initiative to mint coins across the lake
from Constance, see C. Maillard-Zechlin, "Die Meersburger Münze des
Fürstbischofs Hugo von Hohenlandenberg," *FDA* 72 (1952), 213-219.
[112] *DKP*, August 16, 1504, sec. 3, pp. 5-6. The bishop's continuing appointment
of the *Ammann* allowed him to claim a last vestige of judicial lordship in the city; for
documentation of oaths, cases, and disputes, see StAK A II 28; A II 29, 64r-68v;
GLA 65/288. The right of the clergy to sell wine and other goods was also a perpetual irritant in Constance; the city had made only minimal progress against this
practice. On the clerical economy in Constance and its relationship to the city, see
the documents in A II 28, especially fol. 1-3v, fol. 52-57; and GLA 209-353, 1r-2v.
The most devastating critique of clerical immunities in the economic sphere came
from Ulrich Molitoris, a notary and a procurator of the episcopal court. Molitoris
took the oath of citizenship in Constance; in 1485 he took the side of the city in a
dispute regarding the right of the clergy to sell wine in their homes; he even represented the city before the imperial *Hofgericht*. On the controversy regarding Molitoris,
see StAK A II 28, sec. 6, fol. 38-50, 107-114. On the Molitoris case in the larger
context of clerical impact on the economy of Constance, see Peter-Johann Schuler,
"Bischof und Stadt vor Beginn der Reformation in Konstanz," in *Kontinuität und
Umbruch*, pp. 305-310.

cials monitored the city gates. As expected Beringer arrived in the bishop's entourage. But at the last moment Beringer bid farewell to Hugo, broke from the episcopal train, and rode off without entering the city. Once inside the walls Hugo faced a gauntlet of armed and angry citizens. When he reached the northern edge of the city Hugo decided to leave but he found the Rhine Gate closed. For an hour and a half the citizens of Constance harangued their bishop with all manner of insults.[113] The 'Beringer incident' illustrates not only the personal animosity between city and bishop but also the underlying conflict over jurisdiction and civic space. Did the bishop have the right to harbor a fugitive in his entourage in the city? Did residents have the right to harass, insult, and detain the bishop of Constance?[114] Given the deteriorating conditions in the city it is not surprising that Hugo of Hohenlandenberg considered a permanent solution, a final and irrevocable withdrawal from Constance. In fact, he discussed such an option with the cathedral chapter as early as February 1, 1498 and in 1505-1506 he temporarily moved his household and servants to Meersburg.[115] In an even more drastic step he sought to purchase the town of Diessenhofen in the Thurgau. This town would be squarely under the bishop's thumb and would provide a peaceful residence for the episcopal administration and the cathedral chapter. Hugo was not able to purchase the city.[116]

As of 1510 the bishop and city had failed to resolve the dilemma of episcopal residence and cooperative cohabitation. The magistrates of Constance renewed clandestine negotiations with the confederacy.[117] But this plan was scrapped when Emperor Maximilian arrived in Constance with imperial troops and coerced the city council to display its loyalty; his efforts culminated in submission to a treaty with Habsburg Austria in April 1511. In May imperial envoys arbitrated a contract between city and cathedral chapter; in October

---

[113] Beatus Widmer, *Cosmographia*, Württembergische Landesbibliothek Stuttgart, HB. V., 117r-117v; Peter-Johann Schuler, "Bischof und Stadt vor Beginn der Reformation in Konstanz," p. 312; Maurer II, p. 260.

[114] Bishop Hugo himself earned the animosity of magistrates of Constance through his lengthy and scandalous affair with Barbara of Hof, the wife of the mayor of Constance. She was awarded the name 'Jezebel' by her detractors and was accused of dominating an effeminate Hugo; Vögeli, *Schriften zur Reformation in Konstanz*, II.1, p. 590.

[115] *DKP*, sec. 1, 835, p. 240.

[116] Maurer II, pp. 259-260.

[117] See note 108, above.

bishop and city signed a negotiated settlement. The stipulations largely favored the city, granting greater civic control of clergy and clerical staff. Bishop Hugo retained the immunities of his cathedral compound and maintained vague assurances that clerics could sell wine. Most importantly episcopal appointments to the *Ammanngericht* remained intact, giving the bishop a claim to participation in the judicial machinery of the city and the execution of lower justice.[118]

Bishop Hugo of Hohenlandenberg had held the line against civic advances. The settlement of 1511 addressed many of the confrontations of the fifteenth century between bishop and city. This agreement represented a hardening of relations. Imperial envoys secured a peace of sorts but did not resolve underlying conflicts and assumptions about civic rights and clerical freedoms. In 1511 Hugo of Hohenlandenberg had maintained the vestiges of episcopal power in Constance while successfully pursuing a multi-faceted foreign policy. The empire had confirmed episcopal claims to the city. While civic emissaries had failed to forge an alliance with the confederacy, Hugo of Hohenlandenberg continued under treaty. Cut off from territorial expansion Constance was surrounded on all sides by natural and political barriers. Bishop Hugo continued to pursue the Benedictine cloister-island of Reichenau. For the first time in nearly two-hundred years it may have seemed that the bishops of Constance could actually gain ground and begin to reverse the steady erosion of episcopal rights and privileges. But as an international incident, the Swabian War, had opened new possibilities for the bishops of Constance, so another European development would soon justify the eradication of every last vestige of episcopal power, presence, and protocol. The Protestant Reformation would legitimate the decisive expulsion of the bishop.

---

[118] A full text of the *Vertrag* between Bishop and city can be found in Vögeli, *Schriften zur Konstanzer Reformation*, II.1, pp. 626-628. The key points of the contract are discussed in Maurer II, pp. 271-272 and Dobras, "Konstanz zur Zeit der Reformation," in *Konstanz in der frühen Neuzeit*, pp. 26-29.

CHAPTER THREE

CIVIC ENCROACHMENT AND EPISCOPAL
WITHDRAWAL IN LATE MEDIEVAL AUGSBURG

Along the eastern border of the unwieldy diocese of Constance a
river born in the Alps makes its way north from the rolling hills of
the Allgäu through the flat lands of lower Swabia to the Danube. In
the Middle Ages the Iller river cleaved the dioceses of Constance and
Augsburg. On the west side of the Iller Konrad, Bishop of Constance
(934-75), founded new churches across his diocese while directing a
meticulous building plan in his cathedral city. The profile of
Konrad's Constance reflected tenth century Rome with its churches
of St. Mary, St. Stephen, St. John, St. Lawrence, and St. Paul. In
addition to his topographical genius Konrad displayed episcopal
sanctity in his pilgrimages to the Holy Land and his avid collection of
relics. Along with his predecessor, Salomo III (890-919), Konrad
made the sleepy town of clerics and farmers into a regional capital, a
city known for its bountiful relics and episcopal administration, a city
of powerful and holy bishops.[1]

Across the Iller a contemporary bishop matched Konrad in longevity, ambition, and sanctity. Ulrich of Dillingen ascended the episcopal throne of Augsburg in 923, eleven years before the onset of
Konrad's reign. He died two years before Konrad. The two bishops
had met often on ecclesiastical and imperial business. During
Ulrich's last days a presbyter questioned the frail bishop, 'who would
he prefer to join him in his last hour?' Ulrich replied, "... my bishop
Konrad."[2] Both Konrad and Ulrich came to symbolize the legitimacy and sanctity of episcopal lordship over diocese and cathedral
city. Konrad was canonized in 1123 and would be elevated to patron
saint of the city along with St. Pelagius; in the later Middle Ages
Konrad's bust still adorned civic coins minted in Constance.[3] Ulrich

---

[1] Maurer I, pp. 53-57, 66-79; Klaus Hefele, *Studien zum Hochmittelalterlichen Stadttypus*, pp. 28-30; Maurer, "Konrad (I.), 934-975," *HS* I, 2.1, pp. 255-258; Maurer,
"Der Heilige Konrad," *BK* I, pp. 368-369.
[2] "... meus Konradus episcopus;" *REC* 1:378; see *REC* 1:376.
[3] The Virgin Mary was the first patron of the cathedral; Konrad and Pelagius

was canonized shortly after his death at the Lateran Synod of 993. His providential lordship ensured the survival and growth of Augsburg during the tenth century; city chroniclers continued to celebrate his rule in the later Middle Ages.[4] Konrad and Ulrich represented not only the holiness of the bishop's office but also the historical birthright and benevolence of episcopal rule. To expel their bishops the residents of Constance and Augsburg had to wrest their cities from the successors of saints.[5]

As Konrad left his stamp on the topography of Constance, so Ulrich rebuilt and remodeled his episcopal city. Medieval Augsburg rose from the rubble of a Roman city and from the shrines of late-antique Christianity. From the late first to the early fifth century Augsburg was the capital of the Roman province Raetia II. As imperial forces withdrew and late-antique Augsburg withered, a new community formed around a martyr's grave; the bones of St. Afra gave Augsburg a sacred reputation long before the arrival of bishops. Ulrich built on this holy heritage through military prowess and episcopal leadership. He received praise and prestige by resisting the enemies of the Holy Roman Empire. In August 955 the Huns swept through Bavaria and besieged Augsburg. Bishop Ulrich gathered the populace of the city and countryside into his cathedral fortress and rallied his forces to hold against the siege. Episcopal resistance bought precious hours for imperial forces in route under Otto I (936-73). On the lowlands of the Lech near Augsburg Emperor Otto crushed the Huns, ensuring the security of his realm and the reputation of Ulrich as the valiant warrior bishop of Augsburg.[6] During the remaining years of his reign Bishop Ulrich orchestrated the recovery

---

were patron saints of the diocese; residents of Constance celebrated Konrad's status as patron saint of the episcopal city on November 26; B. Degler-Spengler, W. Kundert, H. Maurer, R. Reinhardt, "Einleitung," *HS* I, 2.1, p. 41; Maurer I, pp. 93-94; Gisela Möncke, *Bischofsstadt und Reichsstadt*, p. 172.

[4] *CDS* 4 [1], pp. 295-297; Clemens Sender, *CDS* 23 [4], pp. 11-12; on the life and work of Sender, see pp. 107, n. 4.

[5] On the cult of St. Ulrich and Afra, see Franz Xaver Bischof, "Der Kanonisation Bischof Ulrichs auf der Lateransynode des Jahres 993," in *Bischof Ulrich von Augsburg 890-973. Seine Zeit - sein Leben - seine Verehrung. Festschrift aus Anlaß des tausendjährigen Jubiläums seiner Kanonisation im Jahre 993*, ed. M. Weitlauff (Weißenhorn: Anton H. Konrad Verlag, 1993), pp. 197-218; Walter Pötzl, *Bischof Ulrich und seine Zeit* (Augsburg: Winfried Werk, 1973), pp. 55-59.

[6] *CDS* 34 [9], pp. 45-68. Manfred Weitlauff, "Bischof Ulrich von Augsburg (923-73). Leben und Wirken eines Reichsbischof der ottonischen Zeit," in *Bischof Ulrich von Augsburg 890-973*, pp. 121-128; Wolfgang Zorn, *Augsburg. Geschichte einer deutschen Stadt* (München: Hermann Rinn, 1955), pp. 58-60.

of the city, including the foundation of the aristocratic convent of St. Stephen's (969) and the reconstruction of the cloister dedicated to St Afra, a foundation which would eventually include his name—St. Ulrich and Afra.[7]

Bishop Ulrich was revered as a model of episcopal holiness and civic lordship for his successors during the Middle Ages. However, as in Constance, the bishops of Augsburg could not maintain the civic lordship of their patron saint. From the mid-twelfth century to the Reformation the lay populace gained control of nearly every sphere of urban life, compelling their old *Stadtherr* to withdraw to the asylum of ecclesiastical holdings in the city. Lay leaders violently confronted and periodically denied entry to bishops. After a last attempt to reestablish partial lordship in the mid-fifteenth century the bishops transferred their primary residence to Dillingen on the Danube. Yet they clung to their pedigree as bishops of Augsburg, maintaining a 'real presence' in the city in the sanctuary of the cathedral and through the ministrations of their clergy. While the bishops of Constance continued to reside in the city of St. Konrad, the bishops of Augsburg gradually surrendered their rights and privileges to lay magistrates and eventually developed their new and substantial episcopal residence; they maintained their ties to Augsburg through properties in the city and through the chapter that maintained the cathedral immunity.

1. *From 'Stadtherr' to 'Stadtbuch'*[8]

Episcopal lordship was based on imperial largess and·the initiative of Augsburg's bishops. The city's prestige came to rival its former status as a regional Roman capital, flourishing as a periodic royal residence

---

[7] *CDS* 4 [1], p. 297; *Das Benediktiner-Reichsstift Sankt Ulrich und Afra (1012-1802)*, ed. M. Hartig (Augsburg: Dr. Benno Filser, 1923), p. 25. The cloister of St. Afra was the first bishop's church in Augsburg and was eventually superseded by the cathedral after the death of Ulrich; "Die bischoff von Augspurg haben lange zeit iren sitz und wonung in sant Ulrichs und sant Afra closter gehapt. Dieses closter ist auserhalb der stat gelegen und anno domini 1100 ist das closter, als die stat erweittert ist worden, in die stat eingezogen und mit der rinckmaur umfangen ..." Sender, *CDS* 23 [4] p. 9:7-11.

[8] Several works offer a complete overview of the medieval and early modern history of Augsburg. Although historians of Augsburg do not have an exhaustive catalog of episcopal documents such as the *REC*, Friedrich Zoepfl did devote his

and as a diocesan administrative center. Carolingian rulers visited Augsburg at least five times.[9] Subsequent Holy Roman Emperors would frequent Augsburg as a short-term residence and a venue for imperial assemblies; the Salian and Hohenstaufen emperors were particularly fond of this episcopal city. The proximity of Augsburg to alpine passes prompted German emperors such as Henry IV (1056-1106) to muster troops here in preparation for campaigns to Italy. Henry was particularly devoted to the martyr St. Afra; he not only worshiped at her shrine in Augsburg but also built a chapel to St. Afra in Speyer.[10]

Although these imperial visits put a terrific strain on the coffers of the church, the presence of kings and emperors served to legitimate episcopal rule. Beyond legitimacy the bishops of Augsburg used the imperial gift of land on which to build an episcopal residence; around this foundation they encouraged the growth of the local economy. After the defeat of the Huns in 955 Bishop Ulrich and his successors developed Augsburg as a city of churches and the capital of a substantial German diocese. The sacred city expanded around and between the twin poles of St. Afra (later St. Ulrich and Afra) in the south and the cathedral citadel to the north. Bishop Henry II (1047-63) added an episcopal palace to the Cathedral of St. Mary; the citadel was soon complemented by the residences of the cathedral canons.[11] The bishops of Augsburg sponsored new foundations

---

life's work to two biographical volumes on the bishops of Augsburg: *Das Bistum Augsburg und seine Bischöfe im Mittelalter* (cited as Zoepfl I) and *Das Bistum Augsburg und seine Bischöfe im Reformationsjahrhundert*. Geschichte des Bistums und seine Bischöfe, vol. II (München: Schnell and Steiner, 1969); hereafter cited as Zoepfl II. For a succinct overview of the relationship of bishop and city, see Wolfram Baer, "Zum Verhältnis von geistlicher und weltlicher Gewalt in der ehemaligen Reichsstadt Augsburg," in *Aus Archiven und Bibliotheken, Festschrift für Raymond Kottje zum 65. Geburtstag*, ed. H. Mordek (Frankfurt: Peter Lang, 1992), pp. 429-441. The best short treatment of the history of Augsburg remains Wolfgang Zorn, *Augsburg. Geschichte einer deutschen Stadt*; this work has been amplified and updated by the multi-author work *Geschichte der Stadt Augsburg von der Römerzeit bis zur Gegenwart*, ed. G. Gottlieb (Stuttgart: Konrad Theiss Verlag, 1984); hereafter cited as *GSA*.

[9] In 787, 832, 874, 889, and 910 Carolingian Emperors appear in Augsburg; Georg Kreuzer, "Augsburg in fränkischer und ottonischer Zeit (ca. 550-1024)," in *GSA*, p. 120. The original charter of episcopal immunities no longer survives. Sometime after 738 Pippen did provide the bishops of Augsburg with holdings for the financial support of the diocese, a grant renewed by Charlemagne; Hefele, *Studien zum Hochmittelalterlichen Stadttypus*, pp. 15-16.

[10] Kreuzer, "Augsburg als Bischofsstadt unter den Saliern und Lothar III," in *GSA*, pp. 121-127.

[11] Kreuzer, "Das Verhältnis von Stadt und Bischof in Augsburg und Konstanz

such as St. Stephan's (969), St. Maurice's (c. 1020), St. Peter's (1070) and St. Gertrude's (1070). Between 1221 and 1225—shortly after the founding of their orders—Franciscan and Dominican friars arrived. They followed the Augustinian canons (St. George's and Holy Cross) who had built their churches in the twelfth century. The Carmelites arrived in 1270.[12] The churches, foundations, and cloisters of Augsburg formed a complex ecclesiastical organism, providing the bishop with a web of clerical influence in the city.

The various clerical institutions stimulated the civic economy, complementing the market rights garnered by the bishops.[13] The diocesan administration played a crucial role in the growth of Augsburg as a city of bishops and merchants. The bishops of Augsburg ruled over an ecclesiastical territory stretching from the Alps in the south to the cities of Schwäbisch Gmund and Dinkelsbühl beyond the Danube in the north. To the west the diocese hugged the Iller, while to the east the border crossed into the dukedom of Bavaria, winding around the Starnbergersee to Neuburg on the Danube. This eastern section of the diocese would often prove unstable for the bishops of Augsburg, first as a German frontier and then as homelands of the aggressive houses of Welf and Wittelsbach. In total the diocese embraced 250 square miles and by the end of the Middle Ages over one thousand parishes and ninety-six cloisters. At the center of this ecclesiastical territory stood the bishop's citadel in Augsburg; here cathedral canons monitored the property of the church near and far; clerics made their way to the episcopal court (*das Kuriengericht*) to file grievances and answer charges.[14] Ecclesiasti-

---

im 12. und 13 Jahrhundert," in *Stadt und Bischof*, p. 55; Detlev Schröder, *Stadt Augsburg* (München: Kommission für bayerische Landesgeschichte, 1975), pp. 112-114.

[12] Augsburg quickly became a major base for Franciscan writings in Germany, producing the works of the popular preacher David of Augsburg. The male houses oversaw seven women's cloisters—Maria Stern, St. Martin's, St Clara's (Franciscan), and St. Catherine's and St. Margaret's (Dominican); St. Nicholas was a Benedictine abbey first cited in civic records in 1262; Rolf Kießling, *Bürgerliche Gesellschaft und Kirche in Augsburg im 14. und 15. Jahrhundert. Ein Beitrag zur Strukturanalyse der spätmittelalterlichen Stadt* (Augsburg: Hieronymus Mühlberger, 1971), pp. 33-39; Wilhelm Liebhart, "Stifte, Klöster und Konvente in Augsburg," in *GSA*, pp. 193-201.

[13] The earliest surviving *Marktrecht* for Augsburg first appears in 1039; Kreuzer, "Augsburg in fränkischer und ottonischer Zeit," in *GSA*, p. 125. On the early growth of the economy in Augsburg, see Peter Lengle, "Handel und Gewerbe bis zum Ende des 13. Jahrhunderts," in *GSA*, pp. 166-170.

[14] Zoepfl I, pp. 565-590.

cal traffic, imperial visitations, and trade routes—stretching from the Danube in the north to the alpine passes in the south—all served to undergird the episcopal administration and the growing number of merchants who arrived to dwell in the bishop's city.

The primary benefactors of the bishops of Augsburg were the emperors of Germany. But as in Constance imperial foreign policy gave rise to the first measurable signs of lay civic initiative in Augsburg. Loyalty to the imperial house in particular left this bishop's city vulnerable to the arch-enemy of the Salians, the Welf, who periodically ravaged Augsburg. The rivals of Henry IV invaded Augsburg six times during the eleventh century—in 1080, 1081, 1084, 1087, 1091, and 1093. These military confrontations prompted the residents of Augsburg to defend themselves. They drove Welf IV from the city in 1087 and again in 1093. Finally, they denied entry to counter-bishop Wigolt (1077-88)—the first example of the *Episcopus exclusus* in the history of Augsburg.[15]

During the twelfth century the bishops of Augsburg and their subjects in the city sided with the growing power of the Hohenstaufen. In this alliance the emperors not only protected the bishops from the encroachment of the Welf and Wittelsbach they also gave episcopal lordship legal and institutional definition. During the last years of Hohenstaufen reign Augsburg would become an imperial city, free of

---

[15] The city of Augsburg was a geographical and jurisdictional rival to the Bavarian Dukes in southeastern Germany. This hostility increased since Emperor Henry IV had intimate ties with the clergy and bishops of the city. Bishop Henry (1047-63) was an adviser to the young Henry. Even though the cathedral chapter had duly elected Wigolt as bishop in 1077 Emperor Henry replaced him with a member of his own court, Bishop Siegfried II (1077-96). Henry IV installed other Augsburg clerics in various sees and appointed one cathedral canon as Patriarch of Aquileia and another as bishop of Trent. The dean of the cathedral in Augsburg became the bishop of Chur under Henry's direction; Kreuzer, "Augsburg als Bischofsstadt unter den Saliern und Lothar III," *GSA*, pp. 124-126; Kreuzer, "Das Verhältnis von Stadt und Bischof in Augsburg und Konstanz im 12. und 13. Jahrhundert," in *Stadt und Bischof*, p. 44.

The complexity of relations between bishop, king, and city is well illustrated by the arrival of King Lothar III (1125-37) in Augsburg in August of 1132. While he was meeting with Bishop Hermann (1096-1133), attempting to resolve the robbery of a papal nuncio by residents of Augsburg, a fight broke out between shopkeepers and a royal contingent; this scuffle eventually drew in the rest of the citizenry and episcopal forces as well. In the end the bishop fled and the king razed much of Augsburg, including the fortifications of the city. The bishops displayed their lordship once more by rebuilding the city in cooperation with the abbot of St. Ulrich and the city's residents; Kreuzer, "Das Verhältnis von Stadt und Bischof," in *Stadt und Bischof*, pp. 43-44; Pankraz Fried, "Augsburg unter den Staufern (1132-1268)," in *GSA*, p. 128.

the bishop's secular rule. In June 1156 Emperor Frederick I (1152-90), Hohenstaufen, drafted a *Stadtrecht* (civic law) for the city.[16] This decree confirmed that the bishop was to be considered the only lord of the city, the *Stadtherr* of Augsburg. All tolls and interest charges were deposited in his coffers. When the bishop travelled to Rome on ecclesiastical business or departed in service to the German crown, the residents of Augsburg contributed dues (*Abgaben*) toward his expenses. The three main officers of the civic administration—*Münzmeister* (mint-master), *Burggrafen* (officer of lower justice), and *Vogt* (officer of high-justice) all served at the pleasure of the bishop. The jurisdiction of the *Burggrafen* included property transactions as well as oversight of markets, bakeries, butcher shops, and breweries. The bishop had the power to appoint and remove the *Burggrafen* without consultation. The *Vogt* administered high justice under episcopal authority, punishing capital crimes both in city and *Hochstift*. Thus, in the mid-twelfth century the bishop stood at the apex of Augsburg, ruling over all economic, political, legal, and ecclesiastical dimensions of urban life.[17]

Although the decree of 1156 confirmed episcopal rule, at the same time it enhanced imperial power and offers evidence for the sort of lay initiative that first appeared during the Investiture Controversy. This decree foreshadowed the coming breakdown of episcopal rule; it confirmed and legitimated episcopal rule *in detail* concerning each office, toll, tax, and right. Marking the first legal and royal infringement on the bishop's civic domain, the *Stadtrecht* alluded to a non-episcopal political agenda in Augsburg; the bishop, clergy, and populace together requested a precise articulation of civic offices, taxation, and due process in Augsburg. This initiative did not reflect exclusively clerical interests: the residents of Augsburg, though not represented by a consulting body or independent city council, demanded definition of the nature and limits of episcopal government; the *Bevölkerung* of Augsburg now appeared for the first time in a royal

---

[16] *Die Urkunden des Hochstifts Augsburg 769-1420*, ed. W. Vock (Augsburg: Verlag der Schwäbischen Forschungsgemeinschaft, 1959), 30, pp. 13-15; henceforth cited as *UHA*.

[17] The *Stadtrecht* of 1156 has been studied extensively. For two succinct and careful accounts of this civic law, see Wolfram Baer, "Das Stadtrecht von Jahre 1156," in *GSA*, pp. 132-138; and Rolf Kießling, *Bürgerliche Gesellschaft und Kirche in Augsburg*, p. 24.

decree as a recognized segment of the populace over against bishop
and clergy.[18]

The *Stadtrecht* of 1156 foreshadowed later Hohenstaufen activity in
Augsburg. Frederick I would come to the city at least eight times to
hold imperial court, meet with his relatives, and make preparations
for an expedition to Italy. In 1182 he entered the confraternity
(*Gebetsbruderschaft*) of St. Ulrich and Afra. Beginning in 1187 the emperor, his sons, and entourage celebrated Christmas each year at the
Benedictine abbey in the city.[19] This personal connection was part of
the political reorientation by which Frederick and his successors
would increasingly assume the mantle of lordship in Augsburg.

Only eleven years after the *Stadtrecht* the emperor took advantage
of yet another opportunity to establish his rule in Augsburg. The
house of Schwabegg had held the office of *Vogt* at the discretion of
the bishop; in 1167 this aristocratic line died out. The emperor
moved quickly to assert his control over a vacant office (*Heimfallrecht*),
claiming the right to appoint the next officer. The *Vogt* would administer high justice and represent imperial interests in Augsburg.
Henceforth residents owed allegiance to two lords.[20]

During the thirteenth century imperial influence continued to expand in the cities of southwest Germany. In 1231 Augsburg appeared on imperial tax rolls; in 1235 the city was cited in imperial
minutes as "a city of the German Emperor."[21] Undoubtedly the
emperors were interested in Augsburg as a source of political support
and revenue. By the thirteenth century lay quarters of the city
reached from St. Ulrich and Afra on one side of the city to dwellings
well north of the old cathedral complex; a further *suburbium* had developed around the eastern fortifications of Augsburg. Thus, the old
episcopal city was gradually undercut by the claims of kings and
enveloped by the dwellings of the laity.[22]

In 1248 episcopal election provided residents with a remarkable
opportunity to exercise their imperial status and undermine the very

[18] "... auf Bitten des Bischofs Cuonradus, des gesamten Klerus und der Bevölkerung der Stadt ..." *UHA* 30, p. 13, 12-14.
[19] Pankraz Fried, "Augsburg unter den Staufern (1132-1268)," in *GSA*, p. 129.
[20] Wolfram Baer, "Der Weg zur königlichen Bürgerstadt (1156-1276), in *GSA*, pp.
137-138.
[21] "... civitas ... imperatoris in Alemannia ..." cited in Baer, "Zum Verhältnis von
geistlicher und weltlicher Gewalt in der ehemaligen Reichsstadt Augsburg," in *Aus
Archiven und Bibliotheken*, p. 434.
[22] Kießling, *Bürgerliche Gesellschaft und Kirche in Augsburg*, p. 25.

foundation of episcopal lordship. For the first time since the Investiture Controversy they barred the gates and denied entry to a bishop, this time not only in the name of the king but also in the name of the king's city of Augsburg. The exclusion of Bishop Hartmann (1248-86), Count of Dillingen, remains the high point of civic initiative and freedom in medieval Augsburg. When Bishop-elect Hartmann arrived at his episcopal city sometime in 1248-49, he found the gates closed and the populace determined to deny him obedience as city-lord. Hartmann was beholden to Pope Innocent IV (1243-54), the antagonist of the Hohenstaufen emperor Frederick II (1215-50) and thus perceived as an adversary of the city. Denied entry Hartmann withdrew to his rural residences of Mergenthau and Gunzenlee. In 1251 the bishop gathered an episcopal army in order to march on 'his' episcopal city. The residents of Augsburg now turned against the immunities of the church, invaded the cathedral compound, and burned the residences of the canons, thus prompting them to flee from the city. On 9 May 1251 mendicant mediators negotiated a peace without bloodshed.[23] Episcopal representatives signed a contract conceding complete control of civic fortifications to the burghers of Augsburg; the agreement also recognized the right of citizens to raise taxes, though not on the clergy, their households and feudal subjects. A critical and revealing stipulation ensured that the clergy and their servants would be allowed to come and go from the city without restraint. Now the city, and not the bishop, guaranteed access to the churches and clerical households of Augsburg.[24]

Over the next twenty-six years the residents of Augsburg would

---

[23] Wolfgang Zorn, *Augsburg*, pp. 100-102; Zoepfl I, pp. 197-198.

[24] "Qua propter notum fieri cupimus universis presens scriptum intuentibus, quod nos propter bonum pacis et concordiae et ad tollendam omnem dissensionis materiam, que inter nos et cives nostros Augustenses super articulis subscriptis posset in posterum suboriri, ipsis de consilio et bona voluntate capituli nostri et aliorum prudentum virorum libertates et iura subscripta recognoscenda duximus et auctoritate pontificali liberaliter confirmanda, ut videlicet ipsi cives portas urbis seu civitates universas constructas et construendas in sua potestate teneant futurum et de nostra concessione sibi a nobis facta eas pro nobis et se ipsis fideliter custodiant et observent taliter provisuri, ne nobis aut nostris seu clericis quibuslibet et claustralibus nec non et familiae ipsorum per eas intrare et exire volentibus ab ipsis civibus malitiose aliquo tempore precludantur" (my emphasis); *Urkundenbuch der Stadt Augsburg*, ed. C. Meyer, vol. I: 1104-1356 (Augsburg: A. F. Butsch, 1874) I, 9, pp. 9, 20 - 10, 5; henceforth cited as *UBA*. The cathedral chapter signed a similar agreement with the citizens of Augsburg; *Monumenta Boica*, ed. Academia scientiarum Boica (München: Typis Academicis, 1814f), 33.1, 78, pp. 79-80; hereafter cited as *MB*.
While the bishop conceded many of his taxation rights to the city, he did retain

continue to expand lay-dominated institutions. Already in 1234 the first civic seal had appeared; by 1257 documents record city councilors (*consules*) as representatives of the populace; in 1260 a city hall (*domus civium*) was mentioned. Civic officers appear in the 1260s—a mayor (*magister civium*, 1266), custodian of seals, and notaries (1268). These offices and institutions were neither condoned nor resisted by Hartmann. In 1276 Emperor Rudolf (1273-91) mandated the creation of the Augsburger *Stadtbuch*, a document that confirmed the lordship of the empire, the local authority of the city council, and the right of this elected lay body to draft civic law. In a most telling omission the royal mandate failed to mention Bishop Hartmann, Count of Dillingen, the former *Stadtherr* of Augsburg.[25]

In a little over a century the status of the bishops of Augsburg had plummeted from absolute lordship over their cathedral city to disenfranchisement and expulsion. By 1276 they had yielded the keys to the city, surrendered control of civic fortifications, and conceded the right to raise taxes. Through the intercession of the king the city council now replaced the episcopal administration as governing body in the city; statutes regulating markets, guilds, and civic morality would increasingly be drafted by lay magistrates. Augsburg was now a full-fledged imperial city, owing allegiance to the empire and submitting to the imperial *Vogt* in matters of high justice. Bishop Hartmann seems to have had few options. Because episcopal coffers were nearly empty when he entered office, he had no funds to raise a sizeable army. The only solution was to pawn many remaining episcopal properties.[26] Hartmann did form a temporary alliance with the cathedral chapter and city in an attempt to wrest control of the

---

the right to collect tolls. This arrangement received final form in a settlement in 1454; *UBA* I, 12, pp. 12-14. Empty episcopal coffers compelled Bishop Hartmann to further weaken even this remaining financial reserve. He pawned the *Burggrafenamt, Stadtzoll, Münzrecht*, and other incomes to various citizens of Augsburg; Kießling, *Bürgerliche Gesellschaft und Kirche in Augsburg*, p. 26; Kreuzer, "Das Verhältnis von Stadt und Bischof in Augsburg und Konstanz," in *Bischof und Stadt*, p. 53.

[25] *UBA* I, 51, pp. 37-38. The omission of Hartmann's name may be due in part to a charter drafted the same day that settled disputes between bishop, cathedral chapter, and city; *UHA* I, 50, pp. 36-37. However, these two documents only heighten the contrast; in the second charter it is no longer relevant to discuss the bishop or chapter in relation to political rule and legal jurisdiction. For a brief survey of the first *Stadtbuch* see Rolf Schmidt, "Das Stadtbuch von 1276," in *GSA*, pp. 140-144.

[26] Kreuzer, "Das Verhältnis von Stadt und Bischof in Augsburg und Konstanz," in *Stadt und Bischof*, p. 54.

Augsburger *Vogtei* from Duke Lewis of Bavaria.[27] But this agreement neither diminished conflict with the city nor slowed its pursuit of full imperial standing.

In the end the Counts of Dillingen did make a lasting contribution to the diocese of Augsburg. After the deaths of his brothers, all without heirs, Bishop Hartmann added the aristocratic seat of Dillingen to the patrimony of St. Ulrich.[28] During periods of exile bishop and clergy often turned to the generosity of a neighboring city or to their allies among the landed nobility. The small town and castle of Dillingen would serve as a place of refuge. As the city government continued to encroach on episcopal prerogatives, Dillingen became an effective counter-weight to Augsburg, allowing the bishops to continue to pursue a vital presence in their old episcopal city, while creating a new base of power in the countryside.

During the ensuing period of surprisingly tranquil civic life between bishop and city the *Stadtbuch* defined civic life in Augsburg. The institutions of civic government continued to develop under imperial protection and free of episcopal intervention.[29] In 1316 King Lewis (later emperor) bestowed a new privilege on the city; no king could pawn Augsburg to another prince; the city would remain directly under royal control.[30] The tumultuous reign of Lewis during the first half of the fourteenth century undermined the relationship of city and bishop in Constance, leading to expulsion, a long interdict, and eventually murder. Because Augsburg lay so much closer to Lewis' Bavarian homelands, both bishop and city tended to side with the king against papal anathemas. Bishop Frederick Spät of Famingen (1309-31) supported Habsburg and papal interests at first and moved his residence to Dillingen. By 1322 he renounced his support for the papacy and returned to Augsburg; Frederick forged an alliance with Lewis that endured throughout the king's reign.[31] In fact, only two incidents exemplify the chronic friction between bishop and city. In the early 1330s it appeared that Nicholas of Frauenfeld, the favored candidate of Pope John XXII (1316-34)

---

[27] 24 October 1269, *MB* 33.1, 107, pp. 116-118. For the royal pawning to Lewis on 9 March 1270, see *MB* 33.1, 108, pp. 118-121.

[28] 28 June 1286; *MB* 33.1, 159, p. 177.

[29] Wolfram Baer, "Die Entwicklung der Stadtverfassung 1276-1368," in *GSA*, pp. 146-150.

[30] 9 January 1316; *UBA* I, 235, pp. 196-198.

[31] Pankraz Fried, "Augsburg in nachstaufischer Zeit (1276-1368)," in *GSA*, pp. 145-146; Zoepfl I, pp. 253-254.

might become bishop of Augsburg, however the Pope installed him
in Constance in 1334. Shortly thereafter, Lewis forced Bishop
Nicholas to flee Constance and then besieged him in nearby
Meersburg.[32] The clergy and city of Augsburg had avoided the diffi-
culties of a controversial episcopal appointment. In 1339 when
Bishop Henry III (1337-48) was accused of sexually assaulting the
daughter of a house guest, he was immediately driven from the city.
In this case Lewis mediated a settlement allowing Henry to return to
Augsburg.[33]

Notwithstanding such exceptions, by the middle of the fourteenth
century the bishops and city of Augsburg appear to have achieved
some degree of peaceful cooperation. Although the bishop was no
longer *Stadtherr* he continued to reside in Augsburg, maintain his spatial immunities in the city, and rule over the church.[34] The expulsions of the early and high Middle Ages were sporadic and yet their
impact was decisive. During the Investiture Controversy and its aftermath the residents of Augsburg took up defense of their own city.
This civic initiative surfaced again when the people demanded a
thorough description of episcopal government confirmed by the emperor—the *Stadtrecht* of 1176. The second set of expulsions proved
fatal for episcopal lordship. Physical exclusion from the city brought
the surrender of critical rights and privileges, leading to the *Stadtbuch*
of 1276. By 1350 city and bishop had achieved a remarkable level of
cooperation, despite the independence of the magistrates and the
bishop's previous lordship in the city. This century of cooperation
contrasts sharply with all of the animosity in Constance during the
mid-fourteenth century. During the late fourteenth and fifteenth centuries, however, further civic encroachment, regional politics, and

---

[32] See below, pp. 47-48, 53.

[33] Zoepfl I, p. 293.

[34] Unfortunately there is no comprehensive register of the bishops of Augsburg
that would allow the reconstruction of residency patterns. Most *Ukundensammlungen*
focus on major undertakings of the bishops, especially in relation to Augsburg, the
Bavarian nobility and princes, and the empire. But the record of extraordinary interaction between bishop and city does not necessarily indicate patterns of residency;
the large number of charters pertaining to consecrations, property transfers, and
bequests offer the possibility for a far better assessment of the relative importance of
Augsburg and Dillingen as the primary locations of episcopal activity and administration. Until insignificant charter collections in minor archives are checked, it is
impossible to discern *when* one residence became more prominent than another—at
least until the late fifteenth century when offices of the episcopal regime moved to
Dillingen.

the revival of old episcopal claims would reignite the controversy between bishop and city. The bishops of Augsburg would seek to maintain a lively presence in the city, probing civic resources to discern if episcopal lordship might be resurrected and whether it was yet possible to reclaim the city of St. Ulrich.

2. *From Warfare to Withdrawal*

During the later Middle Ages both the bishops and citizens of Augsburg discovered new resources and vied with each other for supremacy on the civic stage. Peter of Schaumberg (1424-69) dominated the diocese during a term of forty-one years. Although this bishop served pope and emperor he also won the approval of his city's clergy and laity as a tireless servant of the church and as a man formed from the cloth of St. Ulrich. Peter would pool all of his resources in order to challenge the magistrates of Augsburg and revive the *Stadtrecht* of 1156. His final settlement with the city council ensured another sixty years of relative cooperation between city and bishop. As a resurgent episcopacy attempted to regain lost rights and privileges the city of Augsburg was entering a "golden age." By 1490 Augsburg had replaced Nuremberg as the political center of southern Germany; the wealthy families and corporations of Augsburg now financed emperors and competed in European markets. Magistrates pursued a foreign policy that often deviated from that of the desperate leagues of neighboring cities.[35] In this atmosphere the bishops of Augsburg would prove no match for the city. Nevertheless Peter of Schaumberg and his colleagues continued to promote an agenda that emphasized free access for clerics to the city; they were able to secure the immunity of clerical privilege, property, and personnel. At the end of the fifteenth century bishops continued to rule the church in a limited way and still pursued policies that outraged civic residents.

With few exceptions the late-medieval bishops of Augsburg brought a similar social pedigree and ecclesiastical career to their church service and their conflict with lay magistrates. Between 1373 and 1517 eight bishops ruled the diocese. Excluding the unusual

---

[35] Karl Schnith, "Die Reichsstadt Augsburg im Spätmittelalter (1368-1493)," in *GSA*, pp. 153-165; Rolf Kießling, "Augsburgs Wirtschaft im 14. und 15. Jahrhundert," in *GSA*, pp. 171-181.

forty-five year tenure of Peter of Schaumberg and the contested election of Frederick of Grafeneck, the remaining six bishops held office
for an average of sixteen years. All of the bishops hailed from a south
German, landed, and aristocratic background.[36] Among all the
bishops only Frederick of Grafeneck came from a monastic career,
having been appointed by Pope John XXIII after serving as Abbot in
the Hungarian cloister of Szerâd.[37] Three bishops rose through the
clerical ranks in other dioceses before episcopal election in
Augsburg.[38] The cathedral chapter itself provided the diocese with
four bishops.[39] Five of the eight bishops had university training.[40]

The social profile of the late-medieval bishops of Constance was
remarkably similar to that of the bishops of Augsburg.[41] Nearly all of
them came from the south-German nobility; a substantial number
had a formal education; most were chosen from clerical institutions
in close proximity to their eventual episcopal city. They differed,
however, in their length of tenure. Although the averages of sixteen
years for Augsburg and thirteen years for Constance appear significantly close, the forty-five year reign of Peter of Schaumberg exceeds
the long reign of Hugo of Hohenlandenberg by eleven years, thus
altering the average in Augsburg to twenty years. This trend suggests
greater stability in the eastern diocese.[42]

The bishops of Augsburg and Constance not only shared similar

---

[36] Zoepfl I, pp. 325-326, 350, 360, 362, 381, 453, 485, 537.

[37] Zoepfl I, pp. 362-363.

[38] Eberhard II (1404-13) was a canon and *Domdekan* in Strasbourg; he also served
as *Generalkollektor* for the Archbishopric of Mainz (Zoepfl I, pp. 350, 353); Peter I of
Schaumberg (1424-69) rose through the ranks in the diocese of Bamberg, filling the
offices of cathedral canon, judge on the clerical court, member of the bishop's council, and *Archidiakon* of the diocese (Zoepfl I, p. 382); Frederick of Zollern (1486-1505)
was a cathedral canon in Strasbourg and Constance (Zoepfl I, p. 485).

[39] Burkhard of Ellerbach (1373-1404) held a canonship (Zoepfl I, p. 325). Anselm
of Nenningen (1414-23) was a canon and *Domkustor* in Augsburg as well as a cathedral canon in the neighboring diocese of Freising (Zoepfl I, p. 361). John of
Werdenberg (1469-86) held cathedral canonships in Constance and Augsburg; he
was elected as Coadjutor for the aging Peter of Schaumberg in 1463 (Zoepfl I, pp.
453-455). Henry of Lichtenau (1505-17) was a cathedral canon in Augsburg prior to
his election (Zoepfl I, p. 558).

[40] Anselm of Nenningen in Prague (Zoepfl I, p. 360); Peter of Schaumberg in
Heidelberg and Bologna (Zoepfl I, p. 381); John of Werdenberg in Heidelberg
(Zoepfl I, p. 453); Frederick of Zollern in Freiburg and Erfurt (Zoepfl I; p. 485);
Henry of Lichthenau in Freiburg (Zoepfl I; p. 539).

[41] See below, pp. 49-50.

[42] The election, confirmation, consecration, and installation of a bishop could
prove lengthy, contentious, and costly. The *servitium commune* required that a new
bishop give one third of his first year's salary to Rome.

backgrounds, they were also embroiled in the feuds of the late four-teenth century in southern Germany.[43] The family of Bishop Henry of Brandis fought with Constance throughout the later 1360s and early 1370s, using the Benedictine cloister-island, Reichenau, as a base from which to harass burghers from the nearby city. In south central and southeast Germany the conflict between Augsburg and Bishop Burkhard of Ellerbach (1373-1404) was part of a broader confrontation between cities and princes, estates and empire, Luxem-bourg, Wittelsbach, and Habsburg.[44] In the late fourteenth century regional and national politics unhinged the Augsburg settlement of 1276. While city magistrates sought greater control of the urban clergy, Burkhard turned to his princely alliances, reminding the burghers of Augsburg that landed resources and imperial favor might compensate for episcopal weakness in the city.

Almost from the start relations between Bishop Burkhard and Augsburg were acrimonious. During the thirteenth century the mag-istrates of Augsburg had won the right to tax residents of the city. A century later the roles were reversed when Burkhard filed a griev-ance with Emperor Charles IV (1347-78), contesting civic attempts to tax the clergy. In December 1377 Charles IV confirmed the immunities of the *Hochstift* and specifically forbade clerical taxation.[45]

Although a comprehensive study of fiscal conditions in the diocese of Augsburg has not been written, the lavish episcopal banquets and funeral-cycles held there during the later fifteenth and early sixteenth centuries suggest that the bishops of Augsburg enjoyed greater financial flexibility and stability than their counterparts in Constance. See below, pp. 44, 157-170.

[43] F. R. H. Du Boulay has pointed out the number of civic associations forming throughout Germany from the Hanseatic league in the north to the Rhenish and Swabian associations in the south. German cities joined leagues to pursue marauding associations of knights and to resist the encroachment of princes and their growing territories; *Germany in the Late Middle Ages* (London: Athelone Press, 1983), pp. 133-136.

[44] See Karl Schnith, "Die Reichsstadt Augsburg im Spätmittelalter (1368-1493)," in *GSA*, pp. 155-160.

[45] "... sprechen wir vnd declarieren mit craffte diez brieues das czu dem male vnser meynung nicht gewesen ist vnd nicht ist das sulche priuilegia vnd brieue dem Bischoue, Capitel, Tumherren vnd der pfafheit zu Ausburg schaden sullen noch sie antreffen in dheyne weis, darumb gebieten wir den egenanten Burgern von Ausburg vnd wollen ernstlichen, das sie von sulcher priuilegien vnd brieue wegen die egenanten pfafheit zu Ausburg vnd ire guter nicht besweren noch betruben sullen in dheyne weis als lip yn sey vnser vnd des Reichs swere vngenade zu vormeyden;" 4 December 1377, *MB* 33.2, 448, p. 503, 18-25. "... gebieten wir euch ernstlichen bi vnsern vnd des Richs hulden vnd wollen, daz ir den egenantvn Tumherren vnd Capitel, was ir in von garten, wisen, husern oder andern iren guten genomen habt, lasset genczlichen wider werden vnd si wider ire pfefflich friheyt nicht besweren noch

This interchange was followed by greater confrontation and violence in the 1380s. After Augsburg joined the Swabian City League in 1379 Bishop Burkhard in turn became a member of the Order of the Lion, the prestigious association of south German knights. In 1381 the cities and noble orders went to war with dire results for the clergy whom the residents of Augsburg had already voted to tax in 1379.[46] When Burkhard joined the Order of the Lion residents of Augsburg vandalized the episcopal and clerical properties adjacent to civic fortifications.[47] Magistrates then compelled the clerics to swear the oath of citizenship.[48] When war ended in favor of the cities, Burkhard and the clergy were forced to accede to the demands of the Augsburg contingent at a meeting of the Swabian City League in Ulm.[49]

The revival of hostilities between the cities and princes in 1387 provided Bishop Burkhard with the opportunity to recoup some of his losses. In 1388 he housed and then confiscated goods borne by Augsburger merchants journeying north from Venice. At first he promised to safeguard the merchandise, but later divided these goods with Duke Stephen of Bavaria as booty of war.[50] The reaction in Augsburg was swift and violent; the residents of the city ransacked the episcopal palace, mint, and warehouse as well as the domicile of

---

betruben sullet in dheyne wis als lieb euch si vnser vnd des Reychs swer vngenade zu vermiden;" 5 December 1377, *MB* 33.2, 449, p. 504, 18-24.

The intervention of Charles IV on behalf of the clergy of Augsburg parallels his early involvement with Henry of Brandis in Constance and his promulgation of the *Carolina*, the charter that restored episcopal lordship in Constance. The emperor had offered similar support to Augsburg Bishop Markward of Randegg (1348-65) in 1364; *UBA* II, 583, p. 124.

[46] "Und darnach auf sant Thomastag vor weihennechten kamen arm und reich auf das rathaus und wurden uberain, daß alle pfaffhait und clöster hie in der stat muesten versteuern alles gut, das sie hetten in der stat ..." Burkhard Zink, *CDS* 5 [2], p. 25:26-28, on Burkhard Zink's chronicle, see pp. 000, note 0 above.

[47] Zink, *CDS* 5 [2], p. 27:18-29.

[48] "Item es ist ze wißen, daß auf das mal alle pfaffen, pröbste und klöster die hie in der stat wolten sein, die muesten burger werden und genant steur geben;" Zink, *CDS* 5 [2], p. 27, 32-33.

[49] *UHA* 533, pp. 258-261; Hektor Mühlich, *CDS* 22 [3], p. 26:3-8; on the chronicle of Hektor Mülich, see pp. 107, n. 4 above.

[50] Hektor Mülich gives his assessment of episcopal character: "... also in dem vergaß der treulos bischof seiner trew und eere und widersagt der stadt Augspurg, wiewol er und sein capitel zuo der stat geschworen hetten ..." *CDS* 22 [3], p. 31:21-23. A similar evaluation appears in an anonymous chronicle: "der bischoff Burkhart von Ellerbach ... was ain rechter böswicht, er ward main aid, triwlos und erlos, wan er hett der statt Augspurg geschworen und sinem capitel;" *CDS* 4 [1], p. 84:5-7.

the cathedral dean.[51] However, the anticlerical tumult in Augsburg was ill-timed. In August of 1387 an army of princes defeated the Swabian League near Döffingen. The victory of the princes strengthened Burkhard's hand in Augsburg. In a series of settlements worked out over the remainder of 1387 the magistrates of Augsburg restored the immunities of the clergy and paid Bishop Burkhard seven thousand gulden in restitution.[52]

The fortunes of regional warfare might benefit bishop as well as city. If the Swabian League had defeated the princes in 1387 the magistrates of Augsburg would have regularized clerical taxation and exercised full jurisdiction over its body of clerical residents. The actual course of the war allowed Burkhard not only to regain clerical privileges and drive back civic encroachment but also to humiliate the city by confiscating the goods of itinerant merchants and demanding financial restitution for damaged property. Although during the late 1370s and 1380s Bishop Burkhard was certainly excluded from Augsburg, and his absence had severe repercussions for the clergy and church property, in the end the city of Augsburg proved to be no match for the bishop's alliances and power in the countryside.

The late-fourteenth century wars between princes and cities in southeast Germany paralleled the feud between the house of Brandis and the city of Constance in the west. But the outcome was not favorable for Henry of Brandis and his successors; their position was decisively weakened by schism in the diocese and in the church at large. While Bishop Burkhard was attempting to reassert his episcopal authority in Augsburg, Bishop Nicholas of Riesenburg was swearing an oath of citizenship and drafting the first *Verschreibung* in Constance. Less than ten years after the death of Burkhard the bishops of Augsburg would suffer a similar setback.

The diocesan clergy of Augsburg had been remarkably fortunate in its unity. Throughout the fourteenth century no major episcopal schism had rent the church, despite the clash of Emperor Lewis and the Avignon Popes and the beginning of the Great Schism. In 1413 when it appeared that the Council of Constance would soon resolve

---

[51] *CDS* 4 [1], p. 84:7-13; p. 314:14-16.
[52] 15 June 1389, *MB* 34.1, 27 and 28, pp. 46-50; 18 July 1389, *MB* 34.1, 30, pp. 52-55; 17 November 1389, *MB* 34.1, 32, pp. 56-60. This agreement was renewed in 1391, 1396, and 1399; Rolf Kießling, *Bürgerliche Gesellschaft und Kirche in Augsburg*, p. 28.

the papal schism and ensure diocesan unity, the cathedral chapter of
Augsburg elected Anselm of Nenningen (1414-23). After receiving
the homage of the second and third cities of his bishopric, Dillingen
and Füssen, Anselm arrived in Rome expecting papal confirmation.
Instead he was renounced by Pope John XXIII (1410-15) who installed Frederick of Grafeneck (1413-14) as bishop.[53] Over the next
decade Anselm and Frederick would contend for the throne of St.
Ulrich, offering the city yet another chance to encroach on clerical
rights and institutions.[54]

Conflict between Avignon and Rome as well as schism in the diocese had left the bishops of Constance vulnerable to civic demands in
the late fourteenth century; some bishops swore the oath of citizenship.[55] Magistrates undercut ecclesiastical rule in the early fifteenth
century by actively intervening in the Augsburg schism. The city
council supported the campaign of Frederick until 1418 and resisted
the claims of Anselm to the bitter end.[56] The first confrontation

---

[53] Zink, *CDS* 5 [2], pp. 58-61; Zoepfl I, pp. 362-363.

[54] The most detailed account of the schism can be found in Zink, *CDS* 5 [2], pp.
339-371. The election and appointment of two bishops in 1413 was merely the first
conflict in a decade of hostility and political reversal. After his papal rejection
Anselm of Nenningen proceeded to Mainz where he received the confirmation of
Archbishop John of Nassau. Shortly thereafter a representative of Frederick of Grafeneck entered Augsburg and received the diocese in his name (April, 1414); cathedral canons who supported Anselm then departed from Augsburg. In July of 1414
Frederick himself came to Augsburg and accepted the support of the city. Emperor
Sigismund then appealed to all parties to await a decision from the upcoming Council of Constance. In a surprising decision Pope John XXIII appointed Anselm, the
candidate he had formerly rejected (17 September 1414), and transferred Frederick
of Grafeneck to the north German diocese of Brandenburg. These papal decrees set
off further appeals by Frederick, who refused to accept the transfer. On 9 March
1418 Martin V confirmed Anselm as bishop of Augsburg and Frederick as bishop of
Brandenburg. Frederick again appealed with the support of the city of Augsburg and
Emperor Sigismund. Finally, in the summer of 1418 Frederick abandoned his episcopal career and returned to his abbey in Hungary; Zoepfl I, pp. 365-368.

[55] See below, p. 54.

[56] The hostility of the Augsburg magistrates has been traced to two possible
sources. First, in 1407 or 1408 residents of Augsburg demolished a small building
and garden near the city wall, a structure belonging to cathedral canon Anselm of
Nenningen. While Anselm proceeded immediately to his allies in the Wittelsbach
court in Munich, stone-masons added a tower to the fortifications of the city, cover-
ing the garden owned by Anselm; Zoepfl I, p. 362. Second, Anselm was the favored
candidate of Dukes Ernst and Wilhelm of Bavaria, Duke Eberhard of Württemberg
and Duke Frederick of Austria, all actual or potential adversaries of the city;
Kießling, *Bürgerliche Gesellschaft und Kirche in Augsburg*, pp. 28-29. After the reign of
Bishop Burkhard of Ellerbach the city council may have been wary of another
bishop with intimate ties to the land. Frederick of Grafeneck was of noble origin but
he was loyal first to Emperor Sigismund and then to Hungary.

occurred in November 1413 when the city council denied Anselm the right of formal entry as bishop-elect. The magistrates threatened to expel any citizen who recognized him as shepherd of the church (*Oberhirt*). When Pope John XXIII finally confirmed Anselm as bishop, the city council appealed to Emperor Sigismund (1410-1437) in order to maintain his support of Frederick.[57] The refusal of Augsburg to recognize the papal ruling led to hostilities in 1415-16 during which episcopal property in nearby Zusmerhausen was damaged and temporarily annexed by the city.[58] In June 1416 the city council harassed clerics who had sought to support Anselm by refusing to hold services and bury the dead. The magistrates of Augsburg reacted swiftly, assembling the clergy before city hall where they read a letter of imperial support for the civic position and threatened immediate expulsion if the clerics did not comply. The clergy of Augsburg submitted to civic demands.[59] Even after a second papal confirmation by Pope Martin V in March 1418, the city continued to appeal for the candidacy of Frederick of Grafeneck. Not until 1421 did Anselm finally celebrate his first mass in Augsburg.[60]

Bishop Anselm remained a stubborn and intractable adversary, employing all of his episcopal resources to counter civic aggression and resistance. Since he was not allowed to enter Augsburg with all the pomp and ceremony of a new bishop in early November 1413, Anselm arrived later in the month, made his way to the cathedral, the center of episcopal topography, and was enthroned there as bishop. This quarter of the city still belonged to the cleric elected by the cathedral chapter.[61] But due to civic hostility Anselm immediately left the city. After his papal confirmation in 1418 Anselm wielded his ultimate ecclesiastical weapon, placing Augsburg under interdict. This time the cathedral canons remained loyal to the bishop and departed from Augsburg.[62] Although the city recruited foreign clerics and relied on the interim support of the mendicants to maintain services, Anselm's interdict could be turned toward the

---

[57] Zoepfl I, p. 363.
[58] Zink, *CDS* 5 [2], pp. 75-76.
[59] Zink, *CDS* 5 [2], pp. 76-77.
[60] Zoepfl I, pp. 364-369.
[61] "Item der Nenninger rait ein zu Augspurg und die korherrn und die pfaffen satzten in auf den altar ..." Zink, *CDS* 5 [2], p. 59, 1-2.
[62] 30 June 1418, *UHA* 765, pp. 378-379; Zoepfl I, p. 368.

economy as well. In support of his action the Dukes of Bavaria out-
lawed trade with Augsburg in their territory.[63]

As his absence from Augsburg continued Anselm awaited his full
consecration in the cathedral. But in 1419 he disregarded this traditional practice, turning to the Bishop of Constance, Otto of Hachberg (1410-34), who consecrated him in Lindau on Lake Constance.[64] In 1420 now a full-fledged bishop, elected, confirmed, and
consecrated, he pursued his case against the city at the court of the
bishop of Würzburg and then in Rome.[65] When in 1420 the city was
beset by plague, Bishop Anselm displayed his power over the living
and the dead. As magistrates attempted to cope with the mounting
number of corpses, Anselm ordered the exhumation of a man named
Bittinger from the graveyard of the Augsburg cathedral. The city
council ignored this demand, refusing to recognize Anselm's authority. But the bishop persisted, forbidding the clergy to hold funeral
services and ordering them to cease burying the dead. In the end the
magistrates surrendered to his demands and ordered the exhumation
of Bittinger's body. Eighty corpses decaying as long as fourteen days
could finally be laid to rest.[66] In the rites of death the magistrates
had little recourse against the clergy, even against a bishop they
openly despised.

Anselm of Nenningen exercised nearly every right available to him
as bishop: he sought the approval of popes and the assistance of both
bishops and archbishops; he laid claim to the cathedral of Augsburg
at his installation; he decreed interdict; he appealed his case to the
regional clergy and to Rome and disrupted the burial of the dead. In
the end Anselm was undone not by the persistence of city magistrates
but by papal-imperial politics. Emperor Sigismund and Pope Martin
V (1417-31) required Augsburg's financial support for a renewed
campaign against the Hussites. On 13 September 1423 Martin V
removed Anselm of Nenningen from office on the grounds that he

---

[63] Zoepfl I, p. 368.
[64] Zink, *CDS* 5 [2], p. 84, 19-21.
[65] Zoepfl I, p. 370.
[66] Zink, *CDS* 5 [2], pp. 68:10-69:30; Mülich, *CDS* 22 [3], pp. 477:12-478:2.
Bittinger had been buried without receiving last rites. He had been a fierce critic of
contemporary eucharistic doctrine; perhaps he was a Hussite. Bittinger is described
as "a sworn enemy of the clergy throughout his life" ("er was auch ain rechter
pfaffenfeind in seinem leben gewesen"; Zink, *CDS* 5 [2], p. 68:24).

had not received legitimate consecration.[67] It appeared that the city council had won a decisive battle with the bishops of Augsburg, a reversal of their defeat at the hands of Burkhard of Ellerbach thirty-five years earlier. On June 2, 1424 a new shepherd of the church rode into Augsburg for his consecration and installation, Peter of Schaumberg, a young cleric hand-picked by Martin V. This bishop would outlive most of his civic adversaries, reigning for forty-five years. He would direct the last episcopal offensive against urban encroachment and reassert an episcopal agenda that echoed the *Stadtrecht* of 1156.

By the first quarter of the fifteenth century the bishops of Augsburg had suffered a new round of losses. Clerical property had been damaged or destroyed, the city had seized episcopal tolls and confiscated excise taxes; civic courts had severely diminished the jurisdiction of the *Burggrafen* over markets and trade. Although the minting of coins remained firmly in episcopal hands, the master of mints now had to swear an oath to the city council.[68] In order to rejuvenate episcopal power in Augsburg Peter of Schaumberg brought to bear expert knowledge of canon law and a far-flung ecclesiastical network. Unlike Anselm of Nenningen, who enjoyed little support from empire and papacy, Peter was a valued servant of a succession of popes and emperors. Sigismund, Albert V (1438-39), and Frederick III (1440-93) employed the services of the Augsburg bishop as a representative to the Council of Basel, advocate at meetings of the Reichstag, and member of the imperial *Hofgericht* (1447-51); he provided troops and leadership in the Hussite wars. Likewise Peter served at the behest of Popes Martin V, Eugenius IV (1431-47), and Nicholas V (1447-55), crowning his ecclesiastical career with an appointment to the General Consistory in Florence in 1439 and his elevation to the Cardinalate in 1450.[69]

In 1449 the bishop and the canons of the cathedral chapter pledged that they would seek to recover clerical control of certain civic tolls and excise taxes.[70] In 1451 Peter returned to Augsburg

---

[67] Zoepfl I, pp. 370-371; Schnith, "Die Reichsstadt Augsburg im Spätmittelalter (1368-1493)," in *GSA*, p. 159.

[68] Möncke, *Bischofsstadt und Reichsstadt*, pp. 170-171.

[69] Anton Uhl, *Peter von Schaumberg. Kardinal und Bischof von Augsburg 1424-1469* (München: Ludwig-Maximilians-Universität, 1940), pp. 17-103; Zoepfl I, pp. 382-410.

[70] 14 January 1449, *MB* 34.1, 165, pp. 419-421; 166, pp. 421-423.

with a new title and an ambitious agenda. In Rome Peter had filed
grievances with the papacy regarding privileges expropriated by the
city. After returning to Augsburg as Cardinal Bishop he attempted to
renew episcopal lordship.[71] Peter issued a list of grievances against
the city, seeking the restoration of tolls and excise taxes as well as
oversight of the *Vogtei* in Augsburg and demanding full observance of
clerical immunities, courts, and rights of asylum. The citizens of
Augsburg, he insisted, must relinquish guardianship of all ecclesiastical institutions.[72] Despite his earlier insistence on an ecclesiastical
court venue, in 1456 Cardinal Peter agreed to submit his case to the
Imperial Chamber Court (*Reichskammergericht*). For the most part,
however, the court ruled in favor of the city. Although the court
preserved the immunity of church properties and restored episcopal
tolls, it also confirmed the city's control over the political, judicial,
and economic institutions in the city as well as lay patronage rights
over ecclesiastical foundations.[73]

The ruling of the Imperial Chamber Court in 1456 made clear
that episcopal lordship could not be even partially recovered. Neither
by legal action nor brute force could the imperial city of Augsburg be
compelled to relinquish all of its gains in civic rights and ecclesiastical
privileges, let alone be reconstituted as an episcopal city. In hindsight
it may appear that the policies of Peter of Schaumberg were fool-
hardy and obtuse. Yet the bishop of Augsburg had several distinct
advantages and may have surprised the city council with his sudden
and aggressive demeanor. For twenty-six years bishop and city had
coexisted in relative calm. During the absence of Bishop Peter in
Rome the magistrates of Augsburg had taken the clergy and diocese
under civic protection apparently without encroaching further on ecclesiastical rights and privileges.[74] Besides Peter had served papacy
and empire with distinction. His elevation to Cardinal crowned an
ambitious career in the church and offered new opportunities in
Rome to press for a restoration of episcopal and clerical rights. In
Germany Peter might expect unusual support for his cause in the

---

[71] *CDS* 4 [1], p. 325:8-17.
[72] The specific grievances are cataloged in Uhl, *Peter of Schaumberg*, pp. 161-168;
for a general overview see Kießling, *Bürgerliche Gesellschaft und Kirche in Augsburg*, pp.
29-30.
[73] 3 June 1456, *MB* 34.1, 189, pp. 478-487; Uhl, *Peter von Schaumberg*, pp. 173-176.
[74] Zoepfl I, p. 421.

imperial administration in recognition of his service to the crown. The city of Augsburg was an anomaly in the German southeast. In the neighboring dioceses of Eichstätt, Freising, Passau, and Salzburg, the episcopal *Stadtherr* yet reigned over his cathedral city. To the north Bamberg and Würzburg remained in the hands of the bishop. In fact, the agenda of Peter of Schaumberg anticipated the campaign of the Archbishop of Mainz, who in 1462 captured the old cathedral city and reestablished episcopal overlordship after centuries of lay rule.[75] But the conflict of the 1450s in Augsburg did not lead to a reversal of the civic status quo. Rather, the failure of the most powerful and gifted bishop of fifteenth century Augsburg underscored the need for new episcopal tactics. At the very least the settlement of 1457 clarified the relationship of bishop and city, providing a foundation for relatively peaceful cooperation over the next eighty years.

*   *   *

In Constance in the 1490s two successive bishops attempted to revive the vision of Henry of Brandis (1356-84). Thomas Berlower (1491-96) and Hugo of Hohenlandenberg (1496-1529; 1530-31) pressed for reinstatement of episcopal rule in a city beset by shrinking markets for civic goods and by the growing prowess of the neighboring Swiss Confederacy. But the bishops of Augsburg no longer attempted to recreate the city of St. Ulrich or to rule as civic lords. Augsburg had reached its peak as a hub of trade and production, a center of liquid capital, and as a city of the emperor. The population of Augsburg was at least four times larger than in Constance. The bishops of Augsburg now sought to protect their remaining rights and immunities in this city dominated by burghers and to maintain a "real presence" in the city through their civic property and oversight of the clergy.[76]

Two issues shaped episcopal policy in the late fifteenth century: transfer of residence and clerical immunity. Since 1268 Dillingen on

---

[75] See below, pp. 19-21.

[76] Population and economic productivity peaked in Constance around 1419; Peter Kramml estimates the population at about five thousand residents; "Konstanz: Das Verhältnis zwischen Bischof und Stadt," in *BK* I, p. 288. While population dropped in the second half of the fifteenth century in Constance, between 1396 and 1492 Augsburg grew from around twelve thousand to nineteen thousand residents; Joachim Jahn, "Die Augsburger Sozialstruktur im 15. Jahrhundert," *GSA*, p. 188.

the Danube had emerged as the second city of the diocese, where unlike Augsburg, the populace, markets, councils, and courts answered to the bishop.[77] As early as 1356 the bishops minted coins in both Augsburg and Dillingen.[78] In 1318 Bishop Frederick Spät of Faimingen (1309-31) strengthened the ties of this second episcopal city to the diocese by incorporating the parish church of St. Peter's in Dillingen as a church of the cathedral chapter in Augsburg.[79]

Under the guidance of Bishop Peter of Schaumberg and his successors Dillingen became the primary episcopal residence in the diocese. Peter erected a new and larger parish church to shelter an expanding schedule of services and to match the new prominence of Dillingen as an ecclesiastical center. He also remodeled and expanded the old castle of the Counts of Dillingen while the episcopal chamber court began to hold sessions alternately in Augsburg and Dillingen. Although it is difficult to establish the residency patterns of the bishops, Peter and many of his followers died in Dillingen and only then were their remains transferred to Augsburg for burial.[80] John of Werdenberg (1469-86) and some of his successors forsook the cathedral in Augsburg, the traditional venue for consecration, and were anointed in Dillingen.[81] After the Augsburg synod of 1452 diocesan convocations were held in Dillingen in 1469, 1486, 1506, and

---

[77] On the history of Dillingen, see Friedrich Zoepfl, *Geschichte der Stadt Dillingen an der Donau* (München: R. Oldenbourg, 1964).
Since 1313 Füssen, an Allgäu commune nestled in the foothills of the Alps, was the southern and third episcopal residence; Rudibert Ettelt, *Geschichte der Stadt Füssen* (Füssen: Verlag der Stadt, 1971), pp. 181-183.

[78] Charter of Charles IV, 18 July 1356, StaatsA MBL 255, C; and a second charter of Charles IV, 23 June 1357, StaatsA MBL 255 D; King Ruprecht renewed this right on 17 August 1401: StaatsA MBL 255, H; the bishop also retained the right to appoint the Master of Minting (Münzmeister) in Augsburg until the 1520s. But this officer also swore an oath of allegiance to the city council; the loyalty of the Master of Minting was unclear; see StaatsA, MBL 255, I and J.

[79] In 1402 Burkhard of Ellerbach (1373-1404) established a foundation with a chapter and dean; Adolf Layer, "Dillingen als zweiter Bischofssitz und Dillingens Pfarrkirche als zweite Kathedralkirche im Bistum Augsburg," *JHVD* 82 (1980), p. 71.

[80] See the burial sites of the bishops of Augsburg in Appendix C.

[81] Adolf Layer, "Dillingen als zweiter Bischofssitz," in *JHVD*, pp. 66-67, 71-72. Peter of Schaumberg left Augsburg in protest in 1451 and took up residence in Dillingen. In 1462 the magistrates of Augsburg sent emissaries to enquire about purchase of the right to collects tolls. The magistrates also sent recently exhumed remains to Dillingen in 1463, asking for an expert opinion; did Bishop Peter believe these bones to be relics? Dauch, *Die Bischofsstadt*, p. 46. At the very least it is clear that the bishop would not be back in Augsburg in the near future: but a longer period of absence cannot be easily determined.

1517.[82] By the sixteenth century the bishops of Augsburg had established a thriving episcopal capital far from their traditional cathedral
city. Dillingen increasingly received the patronage of the bishops and
hosted significant episcopal celebrations and convocations. Here the
bishops of Augsburg could rule without civic encroachment, building
a new clerical city to the glory of St. Ulrich.

Yet in the early sixteenth century Augsburg continued to play a
critical role. There is no evidence that the bishops contemplated a
change of geographic title. They were never cited as the *Bishops of
Dillingen* and they still collected revenue from the mint, various tolls,
and properties of the church in Augsburg.[83] Moreover, Augsburg
remained a city of chapters, churches, and cloisters. In addition to
the cathedral canons and the remaining administrative offices in the
cathedral complex, the city housed seventeen ecclesiastical institutions with a total population of six hundred secular clergy, monks,
mendicants, and nuns.[84] The largest clerical community in the diocese lived in Augsburg, where it was a witness to the bishops who
built the city, established the first clerical foundations, and attracted
other ecclesiastical institutions.

During the later Middle Ages civic encroachment on the bishop's
secular domain went hand in hand with lay infiltration of clerical
foundations. Lay guardianships and patronage rights were supplemented by the sons and daughters of burghers who became priests,
canons, monks, and nuns. Rolf Kießling has explored the creation of
a "citizen's church" (*bürgerliche Kirche*) and the remarkable extent of
lay control of parishes, collegiate chapters, monastic communities,
and charitable foundations.[85] Absent from this list is the most prestigious ecclesiastical institution in the city—the cathedral chapter.

In 1474 the cathedral canons renewed a 1322 statute which pro-
hibited the election of citizens of Augsburg or their sons to chapter
membership. When, in the 1480s, the city council came to understand the implications of this measure, magistrates protested and vig-

---

[82] Zoepfl I, p. 579.
[83] Two painstaking studies have traced patterns of property ownership in and
around Augsburg from earliest written records to the modern period; see Detlov
Schroeder, *Augsburg Stadt*, pp. 159-168 and Joachim Jahn, *Augsburg Land* (München:
Kommission für bayerische Landesgeschichte, 1984), pp. 210-383.
[84] Kießling, *Bürgerliche Gesellschaft und Kirche in Augsburg*, pp. 31, 40.
[85] *Bürgerliche Gesellschaft und Kirche in Augsburg*. For a brief statement of Kießling's
major discoveries, see "Bürgertum und Kirche im Spätmittelalter," in *GSA*, pp. 208-
213.

orously pursued the case in Rome. After seven years a papal ruling
confirmed the ultimate form of clerical immunity—the right to offer
benefices and the right to discriminate against particular groups of
the population.[86] The access of the citizens of Augsburg to every
clerical body was recognized except in the institution that mattered
most. A cathedral canonship was the first step to a distinguished
ecclesiastical career in the administration of a bishop and in service
to the papacy, but the sons of Augsburg who aspired to it had to look
elsewhere. In the meantime the cathedral chapter in Augsburg would
continue to fill its ranks with the sons of the Swabian and Bavarian
nobility; a reminder that this one institution remained firmly in the
hands of the landed clergy and the bishop.

In the old cathedral compound, the ancient kernel of this city,
bishop and chapter reigned supreme; here they excluded the taxes,
laws, and sons of the city; here in the sanctuary of St. Mary's and the
dwellings of the canons, the bishop of Augsburg continued to rule. As
long as this fortress of clerical immunity held, they would continue to
lay claim to this city and call themselves the *Bishops of Augsburg*.

---

[86] 25 February 1474, *MB* 34.2, 43, pp. 118-120; 20 March 1491, *MB* 34.2, 96,
pp. 268-270; Kießling, *Bürgerliche Gesellschaft und Kirche in Augsburg*, pp. 30-31, 323-352.

CHAPTER FOUR

THE SACRED CITY: THE THEATER OF EPISCOPAL RITUAL

By the end of the fifteenth century the bishops of Constance and Augsburg were no longer political lords of their episcopal cities. Lay magistrates now ruled over nearly every aspect of urban life; they drafted laws, formulated foreign policy, monitored markets and trade, and maintained fortifications. Bishop Hugo of Hohen-landenberg (1496-1529, 1530-31) had struggled to preserve his epis-copal residence in Constance; his right to appoint the *Ammann* was a vestige of the secular power once wielded by his predecessors two centuries before. As in Constance Peter of Schaumberg (1424-69) and his successors no longer ruled as sovereigns in Augsburg. They gradually moved episcopal operations to Dillingen on the Danube, the second city of the diocese.

Despite an overall decline in episcopal authority the bishops of Constance and Augsburg did not abandon their original cathedral cities. Rather, they desperately resisted civic encroachment, protested to imperial courts, and guarded their ancient immunities. Although magistrates and citizens were increasingly hostile toward their former lords Constance and Augsburg continued to serve as centers of eccle-siastical authority and primary venues for many of a bishop's sacred ministrations. The Cathedral of Our Dear Lady in Constance stood at the heart of the diocese, housing the holy relics and episcopal graves that validated the bishop's ecclesiastical authority. The bish-ops of Augsburg venerated their 'mother churches', the Cathedral of St. Mary and St. Ulrich's, two centers of episcopal power.

These sanctuaries symbolized the old episcopal claims to civic rule. Cathedral immunities were surviving connections to patron saints and former lords, to St. Konrad in Constance and St. Ulrich in Augsburg. As long as a bishop maintained the independence of his cathedral compound he could demand entrance to the city and as a resident could pursue episcopal policies on the urban stage. As long as a bishop preserved the inviolability of his sanctuary, he was able to give performances that manifested his authority in the city. Through ritual the bishop exercised his power over civic souls. Some of these acts required a larger urban stage upon which the bishop might once more display his contested claims to lordship. Through ritual bishops maintained a viable presence in their old cathedral cities that countered all the exclusive tendencies of the lay city council.

In the later Middle Ages, while the bishops of Constance and Augsburg were losing much of their political, judicial, and economic privilege, they continued to rule through ritual. Whenever citizens drove a bishop into exile they denied him access to the theater that gave meaning to his ritual, therefore crippling his charismatic and sacred power. As shepherd of the church and lord of the cathedral immunity the bishop always regained access to his episcopal city. Even outside the city the bishop could still exclude the populace from sacraments of life and death. In the end there were rituals that only a bishop and his clergy could perform. As long as the bishop ruled the church he was able to retain a 'real presence' in the city. Episcopal ritual was a crucial counterbalance to civic encroachment; through this medium the bishop continued to have an impact on civic life and preserve access to the sanctuaries that were essential to episcopal rule.

In this chapter we will explore how bishops survived and influenced the city through ritual and the extent to which the city sought to control or harness this form of episcopal expression. The citizens of Constance and Augsburg had driven their bishops from the chambers of government, the administration of markets, and the adjudication of high justice; they had taken control of the institutions of secular rule. But they could not so easily claim a monopoly on ritual. It is assumed here that ritual is the 'institutionalization of charisma,' a manifestation and means through which power was transmitted within communities, and between communities and their deities; this institutionalization allowed 'charisma' to be passed on from one generation to the next in literary and behavioral forms.[1] Charisma was institutionalized in specific rituals such as episcopal entries, burial ceremonies, and memorial cycles. Through ritual bishops displayed their claims to authority in the city. Through ritual bishop and city

---

[1] The phrase 'institutionalization of charisma' is drawn from Max Weber, *Wirtschaft und Gesellschaft. Grundriß der verstehenden Soziologie*, vol I (Tübingen: Mohr-Seebeck, 1985 [1922]), pp. 140-148. The expression 'literary and behavioral forms' is used to suggest the ways in which ritual is remembered, repeated, expressed, and justified as having a precedent in the past.

negotiated disputed issues and resolved conflict. When the bishop's charisma took shape in ritual he might threaten the growing lay commune in which he resided.

The magistrates of Constance and Augsburg found justification for their communal incorporation under the auspices of the empire; they possessed imperial privileges that guaranteed their right to hold office and bind the community in an oath of loyalty, service, and financial support. The bishop and his clergy were not bound to this 'sworn' community and its form of 'charisma'. Rather, the bishop relied on previous traditions that combined sacred and secular rule. He turned to rituals that reasserted and illustrated an earlier connection between city and cathedral, tying the oversight of civic life to the episcopal mediation of divine grace. Through this medium of ritual, this institutionalization of episcopal charisma, the bishops of Constance and Augsburg continued to maintain their presence within the city and their intervention on the civic stage. For the sake of this crucial source of ritual power inside civic walls the bishops struggled to preserve a 'real presence' in their sacred cities. When bishops were exiled, they were driven off stage, refused access to the civic theater that gave their ritual meaning and denied the ritual that institutionalized their charismatic power.

In order to grasp the vital importance of this source of authority we must understand the nature of episcopal ritual, the spaces made holy by bishops, and the ceremonial undertones of civic resistance. Critical questions have to be raised about the role of ritual in the relationship between bishop and city. Is ritual merely a cover for devious and clever politics or is ritual itself a medium of power? What is the role of the cathedral as the geographical center of the bishop's diocese and as the 'charismatic center' of the episcopal cult? What is the significance of the episcopal entry, the *adventus*? Does this sort of entry expose the nature of political conflict between bishop and city in the language of ritual? How did other rituals such as clerical synods, imperial visitations, and episcopal burials undergird the bishop's claims to civic space? Finally, what are the implications of ritual for episcopal rule in the later Middle Ages?

My analysis of episcopal ritual relies heavily on the revealing records and suggestive musings of late-medieval chroniclers.[2] Explaining how rituals were remembered and understood, they were

---

[2] Rarely are we in a position to confirm the veracity of a particular chronicler.

among the first authors to describe the ceremonial life of the city and
clergy. The late-medieval chronicle literature of Constance and
Augsburg is substantial in breadth and detail, including authors rep-
resenting a wide range of civic and clerical viewpoints. Two chroniclers of Constance, Gebhard Dacher and Christoph Schulthaiß, were
particularly attentive to episcopal history though themselves laymen
and citizens of the city.[3] The late-medieval chronicle literature of
Augsburg is remarkable, filling more volumes of the German civic
chronicle edition (*Die Chroniken der deutschen Städte*) than any other city.
The particularly rich chronicles of two clerics, the Benedictine monk
Clemens Sender and an anonymous episcopal scribe, are comple-

---

But a test of veracity does not necessarily reveal the significance of such a source. In
fact, the chronicle is an invaluable record of the perceptions of past events and their
meanings even when the *facts* are not cogent; perceptions themselves came to shape
what observers *believed* to be true or to have happened. In many ways these perceptions tell us as much about power and how it was expressed and articulated as
treatises on government and treaties between sovereigns. Fortunately chronicle literature often overlaps in its story of persons and events, allowing for a corrective comparison of records and perceptions.

For a general overview of German chronicle literature and the themes characteristic of these authors, see F. R. H. Du Boulay, "The German Town Chroniclers," in
The Writing of History in the Middle Ages. Essays Presented to Richard William Southern, eds.
R. H. C. Davis and J. M. Wallace-Hadrill (Oxford: Clarendon Press, 1981), pp. 445-
469.

[3] Gebhart Dacher's notations are interspersed throughout the larger collection of
literature edited by P. Ruppert in *Die Chroniken der Stadt Konstanz* (Konstanz: Leop.
Mayr, 1891); henceforth cited as Ruppert. Dacher was a citizen of Constance, a
member of the Fishermen's Guild, and in 1471 sat on the large council. His notes on
Constance focus almost exclusively on the history of the bishops, until his perspective
broadens from the year 1449 onwards. His death date is not known (Ruppert, pp. ix-
xi). He appears to have collected information for his chronicle without adding a
noticeable anticlerical bias. Dacher's chronicle stands behind most of the citations of
Ruppert in the following footnotes.

The life of Christoph Schulthaiß (d. 1584) spans the volatile years of the early to
mid-sixteenth century—the time of the rise and fall of Protestant movements in
Constance. His earliest personal recollection concerns a cathedral fire in 1511.
Schulthaiß had a distinguished record of public service; he was a member of the
large (first in 1530) and small councils (first in 1539); he held the offices of *Steuerherr*,
Stadtvogt (seven terms), civic ambassador, and beginning in 1558, mayor (eight terms
in all). With a remarkable evenness and seeming lack of partisan slant, Schulthaiß
wrote two chronicle collections. His *Bisthums-Chronik* traces the history of the bishops
of Constance from the earliest fragmentary accounts to 1574; see "Constanzer
Bisthums-Chronik von Christoph Schulthaiß," ed. J. Marmor, *FDA* 8 (1874), pp. 3-5;
henceforth cited as Schulthaiß-*Chronik*. His ambitious history of Constance fills eight
hand-written volumes; he devotes six of the volumes to the Reformation period and
its aftermath (StAK A I 8).

An anonymous chronicle also parallels and deviates from the above works, cover-
ing the years 307-1466; *Konstanzer Chronik*, ed. F. T. Mone (Karlsruhe: C. Macklot,
1848); henceforth cited as *KC*.

mented by the earlier writings of two laymen, Burkard Zink and Hektor Mülich.[4] Although the lay and clerical versions of civic history may differ, together they give a vivid picture of the relationship between bishop and city in the late-medieval and Reformation periods.[5]

---

[4] Clemens Sender was born in November of 1475. He entered the Benedictine cloister of *St. Ulrich* in 1496. After service to a sister house in Kaufbeuron, he returned to Augsburg and by 1527 had risen to the rank of Prior. Throughout the 1520s and 1530s Sender remained faithful to his order. His chronicle begins with the history of Augsburg 2,400 years before the birth of Christ; it ends cryptically in 1536, just before the expulsion of the Augsburg clergy. It is likely that Sender did not survive these events; Friedrich Roth, "Einleitung," *CDS* 23 [4], pp. iii-ix.

The anonymous episcopal scribe or scribes wrote detailed accounts of the first months of the reigns of bishops Henry of Lichtenau and Christopher of Stadion. This description of episcopal rituals provides an intriguing contrast to the accounts of Burkard Zink and Hektor Mülich. See StaatsA, MBL 221, 222.

Burkard Zink was born in 1396 in Memmingen and died in 1474 or 75; his chronicle covers the span 1368-1468. After a period of travel and study in various Swabian cities and schools he rejected a priestly career and came into the service of an Augsburg merchant in 1419. From 1420-1450 Zink rose in prominence as an independent merchant of some means and as a civil servant in minor offices. His travels on behalf of his business and his city took him as far as Venice and Trent; *Augsburger Stadtlexikon. Geschichte, Gesellschaft, Kultur, Recht, Wirtschaft*, eds. W. Baer, J. Bellot et al. (Augsburg: Perlach Verlag, 1985), p. 421, II; F. Frensdorff, "Einleitung," *CDS* 5 [2], pp. xi-xiii.

The exact life span of Hektor Mülich is unclear, though his chronicle covers the years 1348-1487. He was born sometime between 1410 and 1420; he is last mentioned in civic records in 1489. He was raised in an aristocratic family that found its fortune in the city. Since the mid-fourteenth century the Mülich clan appears in guild and civic documents, rising to become one of the wealthiest merchant families in the city. While Mülich's business connections gave him a broader perspective on events in Augsburg he had only a moderately successful political career in the city itself, reaching his apex both as a member of the city council and as master of the shopkeeper's guild in 1466. He held numerous civic offices including those of *Steuermeister, Siegler, Einnehmer*, and *Baumeister*; Friedrich Roth, "Einleitung," *CDS* 22 [3], pp. xiii-xvi. For a critical study of Mülich's work in the context of the literature of the period, see Dieter Weber, *Geschichtsschreibung in Augsburg. Hektor Mülich und die reichsstädtische Chronistik des Spätmittelalters* (Augsburg: Hieronymous Mühlberger, 1984).

[5] Winfried Eberhard has investigated how late-medieval German chroniclers viewed ecclesiastical corruption and reform. He contends that in nearly every work chroniclers were critical of individual cases of abuse. But they did not offer a systematic or overarching critique of clergy and church; "Klerus- und Kirchenkritik in der spätmittelalterlichen deutschen Stadtchronik," *HJ* 114 (1994), p. 379. Therefore, while lay and clerical chroniclers had decidedly different interests, it cannot be assumed that their works were at odds. Rather, such chronicles often do not contradict but offer complementary views of the same or similar incident.

1. *The Ritual of the Bishop*

With lay magistrates usurping their rights and privileges, civic residents becoming increasingly anticlerical, and the patronage of churches and ecclesiastical foundations coming into the hands of the laity, why did the bishops of Constance and Augsburg strive to maintain a real presence in their old episcopal cities? Would it have been the best policy to cut their losses, desert their ancestral cities for good, and found new, primary, and sacred episcopal cities in their dioceses? Even when bishops did in fact establish other residences, they continued to maintain the old city at the very least as a symbol of episcopal rule and a periodic venue for public ritual. The bishops of Constance and Augsburg were tethered to their first episcopal cities by ritual, a kind of ritual beyond the ultimate control of city councils and shrewd merchants. Through ritual they continued to lay claim to cathedral compound and civic spaces.

Elaborate entry and sacred burial were two of the central ceremonies that manifested a bishop's spiritual and political authority in the episcopal city. In addition, these performances were the hallmarks of a resplendent church career, two liminal moments wherein bishops, archbishops, and popes first received the chrism of the living pontificate. They ultimately achieved lasting sanctity among the tombs of their episcopal ancestors. But these ceremonies also suggest a public and political characteristic of episcopal practice and power, an attribute usually overlooked in studies of bishop and city. Bishops served and ruled through ritual. They celebrated mass, ordained priests, blessed the married, consecrated altars, and sanctified churches.[6] They granted indulgences, led processions, and translated relics. They devised ceremonial calendars for the diocese, often emphasizing the place of episcopal saints.[7] They excommunicated the

---

[6] By the later Middle Ages the consecrating bishop (*Weihbischof*) shouldered much of the ritual burden for anointing individual churches, altars, and priests. For an introduction to this office in Constance, see Hermann Tüchle, "Die Weihbischöfe," *HS* I, 2.2, pp. 503-534; and Konstantin Maier, "Zum Amt des Weihbischofs," in *BK* I, pp. 76-83.

[7] See above, pp. 117-118. Bishops could influence the ritual of an entire region. Compared to other European territories, medieval Flanders had a remarkably basic ceremonial calendar. David Nicholas attributes this simple calendar to the lack of an episcopal seat in Flanders; "In the Pit of the Burgundian Theater State. Urban Traditions and Princely Ambitions in Ghent, 1360-1420," in *City and Spectacle in Medieval Europe*, eds. B. A. Hanawalt and K. L. Reyerson (Minneapolis: University of Minnesota Press, 1994), p. 272.

sinner and restored the penitent. Metropolitan bishops were essential to the highest levels of royal ritual; they elected and consecrated kings.[8]

Although ritual was central to the traditions of the medieval church, historians have yet to place the bishop's ritual under the scrutiny of the social sciences. Scholars of popular, civic, and royal ritual have been among the first to bring the resources of anthropology and sociology to bear on the religious expression and behavior of peasants and the urban lower classes as well as on burghers, kings, and priests. Edward Muir and Richard C. Trexler have reconstructed the public ritual of two Renaissance cities, Venice and Florence; they explore how religion and politics intertwined to produce a civic ritual calendar, how church and cloister, saint and relic, priest and procession legitimated political control and affirmed social hierarchy. Sydney Anglo, Lawrence Bryant, and Geoffrey Koziol have given flesh to the constitutional and legal discoveries of Ernst Kantorowicz by exploring how religious ritual influenced specific royal entries, rites, festivals, and ceremonies.[9] Janet Nelson has

---

[8] The archbishops of Mainz, Trier, and Cologne played a central role in the royal cult as imperial electors and participants in rites of coronation. The specific tasks of each elector were laid out by Emperor Charles IV in his *Golden Bull* (1356). After the death of a king the Archbishop of Mainz would contact the other electors to arrange a meeting in Frankfurt on the Main. This Archbishop would cast the seventh and often deciding vote in an election. He also counted the votes. At imperial diets the Archbishop of Trier led the procession of king and electors into the opening session; see Joachim Leuschner, *Germany in the Late Middle Ages*, pp. 157-158.

[9] Scholars of popular culture and Carnival have made many of the initial breakthroughs in this comparative approach. See M. Bakhtin, *The World of Rabelais*, trans. Helene Iswolsky (Cambridge: Massachuttes Institute of Technology Press, 1968); Natalie Z. Davis, *Society and Culture in Early Modern France* (Stanford: Stanford University Press, 1975); and Robert Scribner, "Reformation, Carnival, and the World Turned Upside-Down," in *Popular Culture and Popular Movements in Reformation Germany*, pp. 71-102. On urban ritual, see the excellent collection of articles in *City and Spectacle in Medieval Europe*, as well as Richard C. Trexler, *Public Life in Renaissance Florence* (New York: Academic Press, 1980); Edward Muir, *Civic Ritual in Renaissance Venice* (Princeton: Princeton University Press, 1981); and David M. Bergeron, *English Civic Pageantry* (London: Edward Arnold, 1971). The central works on royal liturgy and ceremony remain Ernst Kantorowicz's *The King's Two Bodies. A Study in Medieval Political Theology*; and *Laudes Regiae. A Study in Liturgical Acclamations and Medieval Ruler Worship* (Berekely: University of California Press, 1946). Rituals of royalty have been carefully studied by Sydney Anglo, *Spectacle, Pageantry, and Early Tudor Policy* (Oxford: Clarendon Press, 1969); and Lawrence M. Bryant in *The King and the City in the Parisian Royal Entry Ceremony: Politics, Ritual, and Art in the Renaissance* (Geneva: Librairie Droz, 1986). Geoffrey Koziol has opened up the world of ritual supplication to rulers in the early Middle Ages in *Begging Pardon and Favor. Ritual and Political Order in Early Medieval France* (Ithaca: Cornell University Press, 1992).

shown how religious ritual in general, and the rite of baptismal anointing in particular, shaped royal consecration in the Carolingian period and provided the foundation for subsequent medieval kingly ceremony, especially in France, Germany, and Italy.[10] Yet despite this connection between ecclesiastical practice and secular ceremony the ritual and liturgy of the church have yet to receive a substantial study which draws on the broader family of social sciences. What ritual resources did a priest or bishop possess and how did he bring them to bear on society, how was his charisma institutionalized in church and city? We cannot fully grasp the bishop's position and relative power in the city without measuring his ritual resources and observing his ceremonial potency in action.

Recently scholars have established how formal behavior defines, frames, and shapes religious conviction, political power, and human relations. In his article on the relationship between the Duke of Guelders and his towns, Gerard Nijsten writes, "Forms of culture are not only an expression of power relations, they also play a part in determining those relations."[11] Thomas Bisson makes a similar point in his work on political assemblies: "Up to the fifteenth century and beyond, assemblies of lordly festivity, whatever their immediate pur-

---

[10] Nelson points out that the rudiments of the Carolingian anointing ceremony remained in tact in French royal ritual until 1825. "The Lord's Anointed and the People's Choice: Carolingian Royal Ritual," in *Rituals of Royalty. Power and Ceremonial in Traditional Societies*, eds. D. Cannadine and S. Price (Cambridge: Cambridge University Press, 1987), pp. 137-180, p. 137. On other connections between royal anointing and ecclesiastical rite, see Nelson's "National Synods, Kingship as Office, and Royal Anointing: an Early Medieval Syndrome," in *Politics and Ritual in Early Medieval Europe* (London: Hambledon Press, 1986), pp. 239-258; and "Symbols in Context: Rulers' Inauguration Rituals in Byzantium and the West in the Early Middle Ages," in *Politics and Ritual in Early Medieval Europe*, pp. 259-282.

Lawrence Bryant notes how the rituals of the early medieval church carried the "redeemable aspects" of classical spectacles and how the Christian liturgy overpowered pagan rites and spectacles: "From the point of view of urban spectacles, institutional Christianity appears as a legitimizing veil over the forms and images of spectacle. The church subverted events with the potential for *spectacula* and *ludi scinendi* (such as coronations, receptions, and assemblies), with the solemnity and *gravitas* of Christian ritual;" "Configurations of the Community in Late Medieval Spectacles. Paris and London during the Dual Monarchy," in *City and Spectacle in Medieval Europe*, pp. 3-33, p. 9.,

[11] Gerard Nijsten, "The Duke and his Towns. The Power of Ceremonies, Feasts, and Public Amusement in the Duchy of Guelders (East Netherlands) in the Fourteenth and Fifteenth Centuries;" in *City and Spectacle in Medieval Europe*, p. 236; he also notes how ritual can bind the cosmos together: "Rituals create relations. They connect individuals to groups, and individuals to the holy. Ultimately, they bring about contact between the 'earthly' and the 'heavenly';" Nijsten, p. 238.

pose, functioned as a mode of persuasion in themselves, and were often the scene of a political rhetoric consistent with the ceremony and designed to elicit assent."[12] The medium is an inherent part of the message for prince, assembly, and bishop.

While it would be intriguing to pursue the nature and 'frame' of episcopal ritual on the diocesan, national, and pan-European level, a bishop's prowess can be well measured in a city which serves as base of operations, capital, burial ground, and as the theater and stage for his ceremonial ministrations.[13] The city was a place of exchange in goods and salvation; trade and negotiation were themselves forms of ritual.[14] The bishop could play both markets to his own advantage. He owned property; his clergy produced competitive and usually tax-exempt goods for market. But the bishop was also the supreme merchant of salvation. While the wine and victuals of his clerics undercut the ritual of barter monitored by the city magistrates, the bishop came close to exercising a monopoly over the dealings of the soul. Although the cathedral was the main theater of episcopal performance, a new bishop could redefine the civic landscape as he paraded from a residence in the country to the city, entered the battlements, and processed down the streets to his mother church. Avenues and squares offered multiple stages for the display of episcopal power. In his first mass the bishop-elect asserted his control over the cathedral compound. In public procession the bishop threatened to retake the

---

[12] Thomas N. Bisson, "Celebration and Persuasion: Reflections on the Cultural Evolution of Medieval Consultation," *Legislative Studies Quarterly* 7 (1982), p. 183.

[13] Without this base, bishops could find it difficult to wield their most formidable retributive weapons—excommunication and interdict. See the discussion of the Council of Vienne below, pp. 13-15.

The imagery of theater and performance is more than a metaphor. Spectacles and processions were inherently theatrical as they played to a given audience and displayed certain symbols of power. City streets and squares provided the stage for these performances. As noted by Lawrence Bryant (footnote 10, above), Christian rites may even have carried some elements of classical performance and spectacle.

Studies of royal and aristocratic court culture have used the imagery of theater to expound ritual behavior and spectacle; see Roy Strong, *Splendor at Court. Renaissance Spectacle and the Theater of Power* (Boston: Houghton Mifflin, 1973) and *Art and Power. Renaissance Festivals, 1450-1650* (Suffolk: Boydell Press, 1984); Marie Axton, *The Queen's Two Bodies. Drama and the Elizabethan Succession* (London: Royal Historical Society, 1977). On urban and princely ritual as theater, see David Nicholas, "In the Pit of the Burgundian Theater State," in *City and Spectacle in Medieval Europe*, pp. 271-295. Victor Turner has explored the anthropological dimensions of the issue in *From Ritual to Theater. The Human Seriousness of Play* (New York: Performing Arts Journal Publications, 1982).

[14] Trexler, *Public Life in Renaissance Florence*, p. 7.

civic stage through ritual. This procession intimates another danger always on the civic horizon. In a military confrontation the bishop might seize the city by force.

A number of theoretical models may be invoked here to understand this complex interplay between bishop, city, and ritual. Ritual is polysemic; it is a composite of similar and discordant rites.[15] Episcopal entries on the one hand imitated the majesty of royal or princely processions, a reference that unnerved magistrates fearing the triumph of an episcopal city-lord. On the other hand, episcopal entries resembled and indeed imitated the *adventus* of Christ as he entered Jerusalem—the triumphant liturgy of Palm Sunday. The city provided the theater, frame, and arena in which ritual dramas occurred. As Victor Turner puts it:

> "'Arenas' are the concrete settings in which paradigms become transformed into metaphors and symbols with reference to which political power is mobilized and in which there is a trial of strength between influential paradigm bearers. 'Social dramas' represent the phased process of their contestation."[16]

Hence we turn to the civic stage to observe the conflicting paradigms of bishop and city, and how they are played out in social dramas that have ritual at their center.[17] We will search for what Clifford Geertz calls a 'charismatic center,' "the inherent sacredness of sovereign

---

[15] Geoffrey Koziol offers a clear and useful definition of the meaning of *polysemic*: This term implies that "... every ritual action is capable of conveying several possible meanings, many of them contradictory." Koziol further describes how the act of *confession* could be *polysemic*: "So here confession was not simply confession. It was an act that restored a deferential order. It was an act that allowed the penitent to show he had renounced his pride and returned to humility. It was an act that symbolized his return from madness to reason;" *Begging Pardon and Favor*, pp. 308 and 205 respectively.

[16] Victor Turner. *Dramas, Fields, and Metaphors. Symbolic Action in Human Society* (Ithaca: Cornell University Press, 1974), p. 17.

[17] By 'civic paradigm' I mean the model for urban life espoused by a particular group or governing body. For the bishop the city is a diocesan capital and a residence for his clergy. Civic life should center on the cathedral and be based on the lordship of the bishop. The paradigm of the magistrates includes city hall and the civic markets as foci of urban life.

Compared to the number of works on Italy and England there are few studies of German urban ritual and especially the nexus of religious and civic ritual. The only substantial work on the subject is Karl Schlemmer's *Gottesdienst und Frömmigkeit in der Reichsstadt Nürnberg am Vorabend der Reformation* (Würzburg: Echter Verlag, 1980). A partial beginning has been made by Rolf Kießling in *Bürgerliche Gesellschaft und Kirche in Augsburg im 14. und 15. Jahrhundert*, especially pp. 159-180.

power."[18] Through this sort of 'sacred power' a bishop might continue to exert considerable influence in the city while his legal and institutional control waned. 'Charisma' implies a type of authority which is reflected in the ability of ceremony to move and persuade, and in the power of a bishop to mediate the redemptive presence of God as no other civic resident could. The indispensable theater of episcopal ritual was the cathedral, from this base, the bishop could make ceremonial forays into the surrounding city—his sacred city.

2. *The Sanctuary of the Bishop: The Holy Cathedral*

The cathedral has long served as the prime example of medieval ingenuity and monumental architecture.[19] However, emphasis on the rise of the Romanesque and the grandeur of the Gothic usually overshadows the original function of the cathedral as the bishop's church. Indeed, a bishop's patronage and initiative often spurred construction, renovation, and architectural experimentation. First and foremost, the cathedral church (*ecclesia cathedralis*) was the sanctuary of *the cathedra*, the church of the throne.[20] This exalted chair was the final destination of the bishop-elect, who came to the cathedral with the blessing of papacy and empire; there he would celebrate his first mass and take his place on the episcopal seat. From this elevated platform the bishop surveyed his high altar, cathedral canons, lay and clerical flock, his side chapels and reliquaries. From this regal seat the bishop looked out on his spiritual and secular dominions, to his episcopal city and diocese beyond.

The cathedral church stood at the center of a vast web of parishes and monasteries. From this principal church a bishop sent word out to the far corners of his diocese; the clergy gathered in the episcopal

---

[18] Clifford Geertz. "Centers, Kings, and Charisma: Reflections on the Symoblics of Power," In *Rites of Power, Symbolism, Ritual, and Politics Since the Middle Ages*, ed. S. Wilentz (Philadelphia: University of Pennsylvania Press, 1985), pp. 13-38; p. 14.

[19] Richard Sennett suggests a broader approach. He explores the interconnection of the cathedral and urban life in his work on the human body and the city; he notes the place of the cathedral in the formation of civic unity and the importance of cathedral art in shaping how the populace viewed the human body—the body politic and the body physical; *Flesh and Stone. The Body and the City in Western Civilization* (New York: W. W. Norton and Company, 1994), pp. 157-159, 172-173.

[20] "Cathedra," *Dictionary of the Middle Ages*, vol. 3, ed. J. R. Strayer (New York: Charles Scribner's Sons, 1983), pp. 191-192.

cathedral for holy synods in order to worship, confer, and reform. To
this sacred ground the lay penitent and the wayward cleric came for
trial, judgment, and absolution. Moreover, the bishop's church not
only formed the heart of the diocese but it also stood at the center of
the extended cathedral compound (*Dombezirk*). This clerical complex
usually embraced the palace of the bishop, residences of the cathedral canons, various offices of the episcopal administration, and
workshops of the cathedral's stonemasons. Regardless of civic hostility and growing lay independence in the city beyond, in the cathedral compound the bishop and his canons ruled with impunity, controlling a tightly-knit clerical city as the pope and cardinals would
dominate the Vatican in Rome. Even after they demolished the early
medieval walls enclosing the 'cathedral citadel' (*Domburg*), the bishop
and his church continued to maintain spatial and legal immunity
over against the encroaching city of burghers.[21]

However, the city could displace episcopal ceremony or penetrate
the sacred space of the cathedral through the ministrations of coun-
ter-ritual. Edward Muir has shown how a ducal office came to dominate ritual life in Renaissance Venice. The role of the Doge was
fundamental to all ceremonies that defined both the political and
sacred identity of the Venetian commune. In civic legend the Doge
obtained a series of gifts and symbols that defined and legitimated his
rule. He received the ring of St. Mark, the patron saint of the city.
Pope Alexander III (1159-81) bestowed six symbols of political and
ecclesiastical power, including a white candle that identified the
Doge as protector of the church and a ring that symbolized his ecclesiastical jurisdiction. Even during Holy Week the Doge dominated
rites around and in the Church of San Marco. In this way he seized
the communal and sacred stage, overshadowing the rituals of the
Venetian bishop (later Patriarch in 1451) and his church of San
Pietro di Castello.[22]

Similarly, the lay political elite of late-medieval Siena came to

---

[21] On the *Domburg* as urban space independent of and *immune* to lay jurisdictions—rural and civic—see Leudemann, *Deutsche Bischöfsstädte*, pp. 130-140; for the
cathedral immunity in Constance, see Markus Bauer, *Der Münsterbezirk von Konstanz.
Domherrenhöfe und Pfründhäuser im Mittelalter*, pp. 111-119.

[22] Muir, *Civic Ritual in Renaissance Venice*, pp. 89-90, 103-119, 213-223. Trexler
traces a similar development in Florence where the *Signoria* and urban males came to
control civic ritual and defined the ceremonial calendar in a city devoted to St. John
the Baptist. At least in Trexler's analysis of Florentine ritual the bishop appears
rarely; *Public Life In Renaissance Florence*, pp. 215-278.

dominate the ceremonial rhythm of the city while superseding certain ministrations of the bishop and cathedral canons. In this case civic authorities not only gained control of religious processions in city streets but also reshaped rituals celebrated in the bishop's cathedral, particularly those venerating the images of the Madonna. Here ritual power was re-routed and the bishop's sacred space redefined to accommodate the designs of lay authority.[23]

Unlike Italian cities to the south the bishops and canons of Constance and Augsburg maintained control of the cathedral sanctuary; the rituals, patronage, and renovations of the old church remained firmly in their hands—until the cataclysm of the Protestant Reformation. When the cathedral toppled or burned, bishop and clergy ensured that she stood once more. In both cities the cathedral provided a base from which the clergy could continually revive and reassert clerical demands in the surrounding city. Many ceremonies either emanated from or culminated in the cathedral, the sacrosanct precinct of the bishop.[24] Long after the bishops of Constance and Augsburg had surrendered civic lordship, they continued to navigate tempestuous civic seas with the cathedral as flagship of episcopal sovereignty. Early and high-medieval bishops had nourished the charisma of the cathedral and this sacred power had been handed down to their late-medieval successors.

In Constance the bishop's first church originally formed the heart of a walled fort and a small village; she went on to nurture a thriving market-city. While fragmentary evidence points to her existence already in the seventh century, this church first appears in a charter in the middle of the eighth century.[25] Sometime during this century the

---

[23] Bram Kempers offers two examples that reveal civic initiative in the sacred sphere. First, regarding processions, "New civic ordinances made participation in the festivals of the Virgin, particularly that of the Assumption, compulsory. The religious festivals were seen as a means of cementing the city-state's peace and prosperity. Civic authorities used the cathedral rites to make clear that the merchants and bankers enjoyed a dominant position vis-á-vis the bishop and chapter and the feudal nobility." Second, in times of military crisis, magistrates paraded to the cathedral; they proceeded to the altar of Our Lady of Thanks and gave her the keys to the city in return for her protection. Neither the bishop nor his canons participated in the rite; "Icons, Altarpieces, and Civic Ritual in Siena Cathedral, 1100-1530," in *City and Spectacle in Medieval Europe*, pp. 112 and 123 respectively.

[24] See above, pp. 123-170.

[25] The original bishop's church may well have been built on the ruins of a Roman fort. Sidonius (746-80) is the first bishop mentioned in association with the church; Heribert Reiners, *Das Münster unserer Lieben Frau zu Konstanz* (Konstanz: Jan Thorbecke, 1955), p. 23; Maurer I, p. 41.

cathedral compound received its ecclesiastical immunity from secular lordships and courts.[26] The Cathedral of our Dear Lady (*das Münster unserer Lieben Frau*) was honored by two annual feasts in the civic calendar. On September 8 the clergy and residents of Constance celebrated the birth of Mary, patroness of the cathedral. On September 9 they commemorated the first consecration of the church.[27]

The nave, vaults, and towers of Our Dear Lady rose on the dominant point in the vicinity, a hill that sloped down on the north to the Rhine and on the east to Lake Constance (*Bodensee*). From this vantage point the bishop had easy access to the two waterways, their docks and fishing villages as well as to ships waiting to depart to episcopal estates around the lake. The bishop's proximity to a crucial Rhine crossing led to perpetual disputes over control of ferries and tolls from the Swabian mainland to the north and the city to the south. Between the cathedral compound and the river the oldest quarter of the city grew, housing many of the clergy, ministerials, lay craftsmen and laborers who served the episcopal court and household.[28]

From the ninth to the twelfth century bishops and canons developed the cathedral compound, adding housing and a library for the clergy (*Dombibliothek*), a workshop for stone masons, and a palace for the bishop (*Dompfalz*). To travellers arriving in Constance by ship the cathedral and her compound dominated the profile of the city with her two and later three spires towering over the churches, cloisters, and houses of burghers. The bishop's palace proved especially invaluable as a temporary residence for itinerant kings and as the venue for royal and ecclesiastical assemblies. Under the Hohenstaufen emperors Constance became an imperial capital, sharpening the episcopal profile of the bishops of Constance as German princes of high standing. Frederick I 'Barbarossa' (1152-90) held imperial diets in the city and negotiated in the bishop's palace with Lombard delegations in 1183. From 1414-18 Constance was the capital of Christendom. The Cathedral of Our Dear Lady served as *the* sanctuary of the Western Church, housing major sessions of the Council of

---

[26] Hefele, *Studien zum Hochmittelalterlichen Stadttypus*, p. 14.

[27] Maurer I, pp. 41-42.

[28] Maurer I, pp. 41-45; Markus Bauer has provided a detailed and painstaking analysis of the cathedral quarter in Constance, focusing the properties of the cathedral chaplains: *Der Münsterbezirk von Konstanz. Domherrenhöfe und Pfründhäuser der Münsterkapläne im Mittelalter.*

Constance, while Emperor Sigismund (1410-37) resided in the episcopal palace and welcomed a new pope in the bishop's courtyard.[29]

Fortifications, immunities, buildings, and assemblies alone could
not ensure the continued prominence of Our Dear Lady in the region or in the city. In fact, for her first two centuries two monasteries
wealthy in goods, books, and relics—Reichenau and St. Gall—overshadowed the material and sacral resources of the cathedral in
Constance. Under Bishop Salomo I (838-71) the balance began to
shift.[30] Salomo tied the relic-cults of St. Gall to new altars he bestowed on the cathedral. But Salomo also pursued an aggressive
campaign of acquisition. He contributed a large number of liturgical
objects to the cathedral treasury while enlarging the relic crypt in
preparation for anticipated additions. First, Salomo gained some par-
ticles of the body of St. Constantius. Next he travelled to Rome and
brought back the bones of St. Pelagius, an investment sure to draw
pilgrims to Constance and thus enhance the reputation of Our Dear
Lady. Shortly thereafter, Emperor Otto I (936-73) made a special
visit to honor the saint in 972. By the eleventh century Pelagius had
risen in status and had taken his place next to Mary as the second
patron of the cathedral and as a patron saint of the city of
Constance. Bishop Salomo's successors now possessed the requisite
collection of relics to challenge Reichenau and St. Gall for sacred
dominance in the region.[31]

The successors of Salomo I added to his legacy by increasing the
holy artifacts housed in Constance and contributing their own bodily
remains. Bishop Konrad (934-75), the most revered bishop in the
history of the diocese of Constance, was an avid pilgrim, travelling to
Jerusalem at least three times. He sponsored the construction of the

---

[29] Maurer I, pp. 14, 19, 20. The bishop's palace received added prestige when it
served as a royal venue. On the bishop's palace as a residence of the king, see
Helmut Maurer, "*Palatium Constantiense.* Bischofspfalz und Königspfalz im hochmittelalterlichen Konstanz," in *Adel und Kirche. Gerd Tellenbach zum 65. Geburtstag dargebracht
von Freunden und Schülern*, eds. J. Fleckenstein and K. Schmid (Freiburg: Herder, 1968),
pp. 374-388.

[30] For the coordinates of the reign of Salomo I, see *REC* 1:115-147.

[31] Maurer I, pp. 53-55. The recovery or display of relics served to illustrate the
miraculous power of the saints and underscore the sacred potency of the cathedral
sanctuary. In 1441 the relics of many of the cathedral saints of Constance were
exhumed, including Conrad, Bartholomew, and Pancratius. Saint Pelagius and his
burial gown were unearthed and found to be "as fresh as on the first day" (*als frisch,
als des ersten tags*); Ruppert, p. 210, 3; *KC*, 342, I, 6. This sacred atmosphere of the
cathedral assisted the living to salvation and preserved the last vestiges of the holy
dead.

St. Maurice Rotunda, which was added to the northeast corner of
the choir. This sanctuary not only sheltered a relic from the patron
saint of the empire but also housed a re-creation of the Holy Sepul-
chre Church in Jerusalem. Soon dramas would be performed here,
celebrating the resurrection of Christ and the experience of the first
disciples as they discovered the empty tomb.[32]

To this sanctuary Konrad would contribute his own remains.
Though his episcopal career had long been deemed remarkable,
miracles at the cathedral grave site of Konrad further confirmed his
sanctity. In 1123 Konrad was declared a saint of the church. The
first feast in his honor on November 26, 1123 drew a large multitude
from the countryside as well as distinguished clerics, abbots, and
princes from all of Swabia. After the festivities those travelling home
by ship were caught in a fierce storm on Lake Constance. Yet they
were spared, it was believed, through the mercy of Holy Konrad.[33]

Eleven years later Bishop Gebhard II (979-95) was raised to sainthood. His bones graced the monastery of Petershausen, a community
originally founded by Gebhard on the northern bank of the Rhine
directly across from Constance. Episcopal holiness now reached beyond the cathedral and city of Constance to embrace a neighboring
community. Eventually Petershausen would be incorporated into the
route of holy processions beginning in Our Dear Lady. The bones of
a bishop could serve to expand the reach of the city and religious
procession could bring a new commune within her orbit.[34]

In devotion and in death the sacral significance of Our Dear Lady
would grow. From 900-1600 the bishops and clergy of Constance
endowed nearly all of the 51 altars standing in the cathedral.[35] The
number of altars commissioned and supported is not unusual. However, overwhelming episcopal and clerical patronage suggests how
much she remained the church of bishops and canons, and not first
of all the church of burghers. Moreover, the cathedral served as *the*
cemetery for the bishops of Constance. Beginning with Salomo III in
919 and ending on the eve of the Reformation with the reign of

---

[32] Maurer I, p. 10; Reiners, *Das Münster unserer lieben Frau zu Konstanz*, pp. 499-502.
[33] Maurer I, p. 93.
[34] P. Gebhard Spahr, "Zur Geschichte der Benediktinerabtei Petershausen, 983-
1802," in *1000 Jahre Petershausen. Beiträge zu Kunst und Geschichte der Benediktinerabtei
Petershausen in Konstanz* (Konstanz: Stadler, 1983), pp. 9-10; Maurer I, pp. 94-95.
[35] Reiners, *Das Münster unserer Lieben Frau*, pp. 287-345.

Thomas Berlower (d. 1496), thirty-one bishops would be entombed in Our Dear Lady, some honored with mere epitaphs, others with detailed grave plates or elaborate sarcophagi.[36] Even Robert Hallum (d. 1417), Bishop of Salisbury in England, was honored with a cathedral burial in Our Dear Lady after his death at the Council of Constance. Furthermore, records of nine lost epitaphs attest to the remembrance of cathedral canons and episcopal staff in the cathedral before the Reformation.[37] In her foundation and walls, her chapels and cloistered halls, her reliquaries and sarcophagi, Our Dear Lady incorporated and 'incarnated' the hardened bones and charisma of saints and bishops.[38]

This holy building material proved equally durable in the episcopal city of Augsburg. Unlike Constance, where the Cathedral of Our Dear Lady was from the first the prominent church and sacred site in the early Middle Ages, the episcopal landscape was bi-polar in Augsburg. The Cathedral of St. Mary to the north and the Benedictine Cloister of St. Ulrich to the south framed the city.[39] The size and date of construction for the first bishop's church on the site of the cathedral compound remains unknown; perhaps this church was built as early as the late fourth century. By the late eighth century Bishops Wikterp (d. c. 774) and Sintpert (d. c. 807) oversaw the construction of a new church, which was consecrated in 805 and was known as the Sintpert Cathedral. July 2 marked the festive occasion for honoring St. Mary, the patron of the church, and September 28 marked the consecration of the cathedral.[40]

Although the cathedral site included the episcopal palace and the

---

[36] See Appendix B, p. 206. Bishop John III Windlock, (1352-56) was buried in the cathedral in September of 1357 "as was customary" (*wie üblich*); Ruppert, p. 438, 22-23.

[37] Reiners, *Das Münster unserer Lieben Frau zu Konstanz*, pp. 435-498.

[38] The bishops and cathedral canons of Constance can also be credited with maintaining, expanding, and periodically rebuilding Our Dear Lady. In 1052, 1299, and 1511 the cathedral was severely damaged and each time was restored at the initiative of bishop and chapter; Reiners, *Das Münster unserer lieben Frau zu Konstanz*, pp. 35-61. The fire of 1511, which claimed all three towers of the cathedral, revealed the loyalties of the laity as well. Citizens of Constance and residents on the near shores of the lake rushed to assist in extinguishing the fire; Helmut Maurer, *Konstanz im Mittelalter*, vol II, Vom Konzil bis zum Beginn des 16.Jahrhunderts (Konstanz: Stadler Verlagsgesellschaft, 1989), p. 272; henceforth cited as Maurer II.

[39] The complete title of the cathedral is the *Dom zu Augsburg, Mariens Heimsuchung*. The *Heimsuchung* refers to the visit of Mary, the mother of Jesus, at the home of Elizabeth, the mother of John the Baptist.

[40] *Der Dom zu Augsburg* (München: Schnell und Steiner, 1985 [1934]), p. 2.

residences of the cathedral canons, the earliest and most revered of Augsburg churches was devoted St. Afra, the fourth century martyr. A chapel at her grave site (c. 565) was later replaced by an eighth century foundation of canons. In 1012 the community became a Benedictine monastery and in 1023 came under the direct protection of the emperor (*Reichskloster*).[41] Until the late tenth century at least six bishops were entombed in St. Afra, including the early episcopal saints of Augsburg.[42] The second patron saint of the cloister and preeminent bishop in the history of the diocese, Ulrich or Uldalrich I, was buried there in 973, leading to the new appellation of St. Ulrich's. In fact, Bishop Ulrich had indeed been a savior of episcopal churches; he salvaged and rebuilt the cathedral and the cloister; both nearly destroyed by the Huns in the early tenth century and in 955. On January 31, 993 Pope John XV proclaimed the sainthood of Ulrich. His legacy is best captured by the miracles witnessed at his tomb, the distant celebrations of his saint's day, and churches founded in his name.[43]

As the cloister of St. Ulrich's gradually gained independence from the bishop, the cathedral and her surrounding precincts received added attention and architectural renovation.[44] By 1065 the high medieval cathedral had been completed. In the later Middle Ages the bishops of fourteenth and fifteenth century Augsburg completely

---

[41] *Das Benediktiner-Reichsstift Sankt Ulrich und Afra in Augsburg.* ed. M. Hartig, p. 1; Zoepfl I, pp. 3-5.

[42] Zoepfl I, pp. 37-43.

[43] Churches in Ulrich's name were established in the dioceses of Aquileia, Cologne, Freising, and Regensburg, and in the Swiss Canton of Luzern; chapels were consecrated in Dillingen, Goslar, and Strasbourg. Zoepfl I, pp. 61-76; the legacy of Bishop Ulrich in sainthood, holy places, feast days, and art history is explored in over 600 pages and eighteen articles in *Bischof Ulrich von Augsburg 890-973. Seine Zeit - sein Leben - seine Verehrung*, pp. 143-782.

[44] Documents recording the first royal immunities for the Bishop's city (*Bischofsstadt*) and fortress (*Bischofsburg*) do not survive. However, by the reign of Bishop Ulrich (923-73), the rudiments of episcopal lordship were in place. Under this bishop the cathedral compound also took shape, embracing a network of buildings far more complex than the compound in Constance. In the tenth century the bishop's fortifications surrounded the cathedral, cloister, cemetery, warehouse, the Church of St. John, the episcopal palace, the palace chapel of St. Veit, and three other chapels. By 1002, the wider bishop's precincts (*Bischofsstadt*) embraced the chapel of St. Aegidius and the Collegiate Church of St. Gertrude (after 1071). By the reign of Bishop Ulrich a hospital had been built there as well; Detlev Schröder, *Stadt Augsburg*, pp. 49, 120-121.

renovated the church, bringing it into line with the latest in Gothic style, adding a new east choir and high altar.[45]

Although Bishop Witgar (d. 887) added the sash of the Virgin Mary to the cathedral's collection of holy objects, this church of the bishops could never compete with the venerable and sainted episcopal relics found across town in St. Ulrich and Afra.[46] From the first recorded burial of Wikterp (d. 771) to the reign of Ulrich I (923-973) at least six bishops were buried in the sanctuary first dedicated to St. Afra; five of those early bishops were remembered in part due to their elevation to sainthood.[47] In addition, the Cathedral of St. Mary housed the bones of sixteen medieval bishops, topping St. Ulrich's in number of high and late medieval bishops if not in the sacred reputation of their early medieval counterparts.[48] Most importantly the cloister passageways of the cathedral became a virtual necropolis for canons and episcopal staff as well as for the relatives of the clergy and the lay benefactors of the cathedral.[49] Many clerics buried elsewhere were still honored by elaborate epitaphs and memorial plates inscribed in the passages of the cathedral. Although at first only a few bishops such as Ulrich I and Hartmann of Dillingen (1248-86) interred family in the cathedral, from the fifteenth to the seventeenth century burials and epitaphs become more fashionable.[50]

What the Cathedral of St. Mary lacked in relics and sainted bish-

---

[45] Denis A. Chevalley, *Der Dom zu Augsburg* (Munich: R. Oldenbourg, 1995), pp. 1-4. On the patronage and architectural projects of the bishops of Augsburg during the Middle Ages, see Chevalley, pp. 7-142; Plaucidus Braun, *Die Domkirche zu Augsburg und der hohe und niedere Clerus an derselben* (Augsburg: Schlossers Buch- und Kunsthandlung, 1829), pp. 2-49.

[46] Zoepfl I, p. 53.

[47] Wikterp (d. c. 771), Tozzo (d. c. 778), Sintpert (d. c. 807), Nidker (d. c. 830), and Ulrich (d. 973) were sainted after death. Of the earliest bishops of Augsburg, dating to Liutold (d. 996), the *only* episcopal burial place recorded is St. Ulrich and Afra. In fact, the Augsburg chronicler, Clemens Sender (d. c. 1536), cites the tradition that twenty-four bishops of Augsburg were buried in the sanctuary of St. Afra; Sender, *CDS* 23 (4), p. 16, 7-8.

[48] See Appendix C. The grave plates of ten late medieval bishops of Augsburg survive today as well as thirteen plates of bishops from the late sixteenth century to the present; for a detailed discussion of each grave plate and its location in the cathedral, see Chevalley, *Der Dom zu Augsburg*, pp. 285-302.

[49] Karl Kosel has painstakingly analyzed all 423 surviving markers in the corridors of the cloister, including 331 graves; see *Der Augsburger Domkreuzgang und seine Denkmäler* (Sigmaringen: Jan Thorbecke Verlag, 1991), especially pp. 87-480.

[50] Zoepfl, pp. 68, 183. The earliest surviving grave dates from the thirteenth century. Kosel, *Der Augsburger Domkreuzgang und seine Denkmäler*, p. 6. While Kosel recently cataloged a remarkable number of lay shrines in the east

ops she made up for with the burials and memorials of cathedral canons, episcopal staff, and lay benefactors. The costly carvings and florid script of the grave-plates, epitaphs, and memorials reveal not only an elaborate veneration of the dead but also a desire to place them under the wings of the cathedral, the church of the canons and the bishop.[51] In this way the cathedral could accrue a different kind of holiness, a sanctity shared in the remains of dutiful bishops, conscientious clergy, and pious lay people. The cathedral could be the church of the bishop and the church of the bishop's people.

In both Constance and Augsburg the cathedral was not merely a majestic ornament to the glory of the city or to the artistic taste of a single cleric. Rather, in both cities the cathedral remained the bishop's church, his charismatic center in a city of parishes and monasteries, his defiant architectural edifice in contrast to city hall. The bishop saw to the preservation and promotion of his primary church. Along with the cathedral canons he ensured that a damaged cathedral would be rebuilt and that suitable altars would be endowed and blessed to serve the faithful. Within the sanctuary of this church the bishop would find his final place of rest and would be perpetually venerated by the chants of the worshiping canons. Here, in the middle of a commune increasingly dominated by the laity, rose the bishop's holy city, founded on the relics of saints and the bones of his episcopal predecessors. The cathedral stood as a living reminder of the early Middle Ages when this church ruled not only a clergy obedient to the bishop and the souls of the diocese but also the streets and alleys, markets and squares, assemblies and councils of urban folk—a city once dominated by its episcopal lord. In Augsburg two sanctuaries framed the city, reminding the populace of the bishop's former glory. On the eve of the Reformation these islands of sainted holiness and ancient prerogatives still rose above a sea of lay power. In fact, the ritual of the bishops not only dominated the cult of the cathedral but also extended to the city beyond. All roads led to the

---

and south wings of the cloister, nearly sixty years ago Albert Haemmerle focused on the identity and burial place of the cathedral canons. Haemmerle found eighty-seven epitaphs in honor of cathedral canons from the dawn of the chapter to 1600, including fifty canonical graves; see *Die Canoniker des Hohen Domstifts zu Augsburg bis zur Saecularisation* (Zürich: self-publication, 1935).

[51] Yet a clear distinction was made between episcopal burials and the internment of other clerics. While the cloister or *Domkreuzgang* housed the graves and memorials of the laity and clerics, the bishops of Augsburg were buried in the sanctuary, the most sacred of spaces in the cathedral complex.

cathedral for the bishops of Constance and Augsburg. And on those same roads they would continue to enter the city, tread on avenues presumed to be under lay control, and advertise their ancient claims to a city deemed *free*, *imperial*, and perhaps still *episcopal*.

3. *The 'Adventus' of the Bishop: Entry, Procession, and Installation*

The inherent power of ritual and the locus of episcopal ritual—the cathedral—provides a critical backdrop for the bishop's activity in the civic theater. Now the making of a bishop takes center stage. It is not surprising that a high priest who blesses and who confers divine grace must himself be made holy by consecration just as an ecclesiastical prince must undergo some ceremony approximating royal coronation (the reception of secular *regalia*). But in Constance and Augsburg the making of a bishop was never confined to the precincts of the cathedral or priestly rites at the high altar. Rather, a bishop would make the city his stage, theatrical platform, and place of transformation, the arena for his rite of passage. The bishop-elect initiated his reign with a grand entry, a majestic procession through the gates and down the main streets of his cathedral city. Each stage of this entry might display not only the prestige of the bishop but also the defiance of the city and the disputed claims negotiated between the two.

Civic leaders met a new bishop with caution, for his symbolic behavior was more than posturing, more than empty ceremony proclaiming episcopal powers that had been denied and dissolved centuries before. Every entry of a bishop-elect was an *inclusus*, a fresh negotiation and integration of a domestic and foreign power, a bishop of city and empire. He not only brought the traditions of episcopal rule native to the city but also a web of regional and far-flung alliances. Nearly every bishop had intricate ties with the local and national nobility, nearby monastic houses and the German church hierarchy. His domestic policy could favor one movement of church reform over another, while his foreign policy could complement or severely undermine civic aims. Every bishop arrived with a familial or personal tendency to support either the reigning emperor or pope. The politics of a bishop could jeopardize the standing of a city, leading to imperial siege or papal excommunication. Every bishop had to be integrated into the traditions of the cathedral chap-

ter, the structures of diocesan rule, and the restrictions of lay civic
government. Entries could reveal a great deal. A change in behavior,
a new clause in charters, a slight variation in the bishop's gait—all of
these signs could intimate a bishop's intentions, his willingness to
honor the harmonious relationship of the past or his desire to challenge the status quo, to regain lost political ground at civic expense.
A bishop could raise the stakes and state his protest without actually
declaring war.[52] Likewise, the civic populace could take advantage of
an entry for its own purposes. To the bishop and his noble entourage
citizens could appear defiant and confident, displaying their due respect for the bishop and their desire for peaceful cohabitation while
advertising the strident independence of a free and imperial city.[53]

Between 1200 and 1600 cities came to host and sponsor their own
elaborate entries and spectacles with ever greater passion and preci-
sion. Civic chronicles are exceptional evidence for the proliferation of
spectacles. But these documents also hint at a greater desire to record
and explore the nature of these events.[54] Therefore, at the very time
when a bishop's legal and political standing in the city was in ever
greater jeopardy, his entries were being recorded in ever greater detail.

When a bishop formally entered a cathedral city, he often behaved
like a king. Indeed, contemporary research has focused on the rituals

---

[52] Sheila Lindenbaum has pointed out the duplicitous nature of ritual behavior,
how it declares and conceals motive: "The point is not that the rulers consciously
and cynically exploited less powerful groups within the city, or that they always acted
in perfect unison in relation to these groups, but that rulers and ruled alike became
implicated in a web of habitual social practices through which the oligarchy's power
was exercised and simultaneously disguised;" in "Ceremony and Oligarchy. The
London Midsummer Watch," in *City and Spectacle in Medieval Europe*, p. 176.

[53] Lorraine Attreed has explored how rituals of welcome established peaceful relations between princes and towns while promoting the profile of a city: "Ceremonies bore witness to the prestige of the community, they even expressed the power
relationships of its members, and they permitted a visual reminder of the ordered
and unified structure of all parts of the urban social body;" in "The Politics of Welcome. Ceremonies and Constitutional Development in Later Medieval English
Towns," in *City and Spectacle in Medieval Europe*, p. 209.

[54] As Barbara Hanawalt and Katherine Ryerson point out: although public spectacle was not unique to the later Middle Ages, "... it was the taste for elaborate
description that was new;" see "Introduction," in *City and Spectacle in Medieval Europe*,
p. x. Several studies have explored this greater use of and interest in spectacles in the
later Middle Ages and Renaissance; see two works by Roy Strong: *Art and Power.
Renaissance Festivals 1450-1650* and *Splendor at Court. Renaissance Spectacle and the Theater
of Power*; and for an even broader framework, see the observations of David I.
Kertzer on processions from the Renaissance to Ronald Reagan in *Ritual, Politics, and
Power* (New Haven: Yale University Press, 1988), pp. 77-101.

of royalty, the entries of secular rulers.[55] As *the* carriers of imperial and Christian ritual after the fall of the Roman Empire bishops may well have preserved elements of these spectacles.[56] As Ernst Kantorowicz has shown, kings and bishops received strikingly similar liturgical acclamations throughout the Middle Ages; he proposes that a sharing of symbols in the early Middle Ages explains this similarity:

> "The history of the medieval state is, to a great extent, the history of the interchanges between royal and sacerdotal offices, of the mutual exchange of symbols and claims. To the extent that the idea of kingship became sacerdotal, priesthood became regal."[57]

The provenance of episcopal ritual behavior is not at issue here. However, bishops may well have preserved and adopted royal ceremony in the early Middle Ages. After all in Germany they were imperial princes. In the later Middle Ages most prince-bishops continued to ride into free cities like kings, reclaiming on a ritual level the rights and privileges they once had held as civic lords. The majesty of their entries and the elaborate nature of their celebrations mirrored the ceremonies of their secular counterparts. Moreover, the entry was not first of all about consecration. A bishop came into his city and processed magnificently to his cathedral in order to take up his reign as prince-bishop of his secular lands (*Hochstift*) and as shepherd of his diocese. When he received the episcopal miter and took his place on the bishop's throne, did he consummate his consecration, inauguration, or, most threatening of all to the city, his coronation?[58]

In the symbolic language of royalty and prelates the entries of

---

[55] See the work of Lawrence M. Bryant, especially *The King and the City in the Parisian Royal Entry Ceremony* and "Configurations of the Community in Late Medieval Spectacles. Paris and London during the Dual Monarchy," in *City and Spectacle in Medieval Europe*, pp. 3-33. See the collection of articles on the role of ritual in the relationship between ruler and subjects: *Rites of Power. Symbolism, Ritual, and Politics Since the Middle Ages*, ed. Sean Wilentz (Philadelphia: University of Pennsylvania, 1985).

[56] Lawrence Bryant comments on this general 'ecclesiastical transfer': "The beginnings of medieval spectacles have most commonly been seen in the disappearance of ancient forms of spectacles and the reemergence of their redeemable aspects in Christian rituals;" in "Configurations of the Community in Late Medieval Spectacles," in *City and Spectacle in Medieval Europe*, p. 10.

[57] *Laudes Regiae*, p. 112.

[58] The clergy not only imitated royal coronations but from the early Middle Ages were vital participants in king-making. Janet L. Nelson explores this connection in "Hincmar of Reims on King-making: The Evidence of the *Annals of St. Bertin*," in *Coronations. Medieval and Early Modern Monarchic Ritual*, ed. J. M. Bak (Berkeley: Univer-

rulers echoed the *adventus Christi*. The language of kings and clerics converged and mingled in the two-fold coming of the Son of God.[59] The advent of Christ in Jerusalem on Palm Sunday and his second coming at the end of time came to be symbols for the entry of a righteous king in medieval literature and iconography. One bishop of Constance appears to have understood this metaphor in a third sense: Henry of Hewen (1436-62) entered his episcopal city like a king, not only with the splendor and dignity of the princes of his age but also in imitation of the first *adventus* of the Christian *King of Kings*. For the magistrates of Constance this was yet another piece of the symbolic puzzle which needed to be put in its place.

The Entries of the Bishops of Constance

In December of 1436 nobles and knights, squires and their servants marched on the free and imperial city of Constance. They arrived by the hundreds in martial armor and holy vestments to penetrate the battlements of the city and witness the exaltation of a new high priest of the church of Constance. This Christmas season they came to remember the first coming of Christ and to celebrate the long awaited arrival of Henry of Hewen.[60] The advent of a bishop would

---

sity of California Press, 1990), pp. 15-34. For an excellent general survey of recent studies on medieval coronations in general, see Carlrichard Brühl, "Kronen- und Krönungsbrauch im frühen und hohen Mittelalter," *HZ* 234 (1982), pp. 1-31; and Janos M. Bak, "Coronation Studies—Past, Present, and Future," in *Coronations*, pp. 1-15.

[59] The *adventus* tradition has classical, Byzantine, and western roots; on the classical and Byzantine background, see Kantorowicz, "The 'King's Advent' and the Enigmatic Panels in the Doors of Santa Sabina," in *Selected Studies* (Locust Valley, New York: J. J.Augustin, 1965), pp. 37-75; and Sabine G. MacCormack, *Art and Ceremony in Late Antiquity. The Transformation of the Classical Heritage*, vol. 1 (Berkeley: University of California Press, 1981), pp. 17-92, 222-266. On the *adventus Christi* as a symbol for medieval spectacle and royal power, see Kantorowicz, *The King's Two Bodies*, p. 255, n. 191; and Lawrence Bryant's review of Gordon Kipling's work, in "Configurations of the Community in Late Medieval Spectacles," in *City and Spectacle in Medieval Europe*, p. 11.

[60] Three versions of Henry of Hewen's entry of 1436 survive, more than any other event of its kind in the chronicle literature of Constance: Ruppert, pp. 192-193, 276-277; Schulthaiß-*Chronik*, pp. 58-59; see the account of this entry in Ruppert, pp. 446-447. The summary of his entry provided here will be supported by substantial quotes from the above texts. Claus Schulthaiß (d. 1500) recorded the second text found in Ruppert's collection (pp. 276-277); he held magisterial office in Constance. Claus was the grandfather of the prolific chronicler, Christoph Schulthaiß; Ruppert, p. xvii.

Brief accounts of other consecrations and entries are extant in the chronicle lit-

parallel and even upstage the advent of Christ, a new shepherd of the church would take his place among those shepherds of the holy nativity.

From August to December of 1436 Henry of Hewen made the torturous journey from canonical selection to ecclesiastical and communal installation. On August 4 the cathedral canons of Constance had elected one of their own; Henry was a member of the chapter and at the same time held the position of deacon in the cathedral in Strasbourg.[61] Shortly thereafter Pope Eugenius IV (1431-47) confirmed the election and bestowed the bishopric upon him.[62] During the following months communal representatives beholden to the See of Constance approached the newly elected and confirmed bishop in order to offer homage and secure their traditional rights and privileges.[63] Henry was lord of his secular territory months before he became bishop of the city of Constance.[64] On October 10 the cathedral canons of Constance and the new bishop hammered out a working agreement (*Wahlkapitulation*) for rule of the diocese.[65] Finally, on December 22 all the bells of Constance announced the ritual sanctification of a new bishop. The consecrating bishops (Weihbischöfe) of Strasbourg, Basel, and Constance anointed Henry in the Cathedral of Our Dear Lady in the presence of the local clergy, the abbots of Petershausen and Kreuzlingen, and the full complement of the small

---

erature for the period from the mid-fourteenth to late fifteenth centuries. See the records pertaining to the following bishops: Nicholas II (Schulthaiß-*Chronik*, pp. 49-50), Henry of Brandis (*Heinricus de Dissenhofen und andere Geschichtsquellen Deutschlands im späteren Mittelalter*. Fontes Rerum Germanicarum, vol. 4, ed. J. F. Boehmer, Stuttgart: G. Cotta'schen Buchhandlung, 1868, p. 110, 5-18), Burchard of Hewen (Schulthaiß-*Chronik*, pp. 51-52), Burchard of Randegg (Ruppert, 241-242), Hermann of Landenberg (Ruppert, 255-256, Schulthaiß-*Chronik*, pp. 68-69), and Hugo of Hohenlandenberg (Schulthaiß-*Chronik*, pp. 78-79).

[61] *REC* 4:9791, 9792, 9794, 9796.

[62] The exact date of confirmation varies. However, Pope Eugenius at no time appears to have questioned the election. See *REC* 4:9798, 9804, 9805, 9807.

[63] For example, Lindau (*REC* 4:9808), Markdorf (*REC* 4:9824), Meersburg (*REC* 4:9825), Bischofszell (*REC* 4:9827), Neunkirch (*REC* 4:9829), and Klingau (*REC* 4:9831).

[64] At some point in the years 1436-37 Henry received the prince-bishop's *regalia* from Emperor Sigismund. However, the date and place is not recorded, though Henry received imperial confirmations of his right to wield high justice (*Blutbann*) in July of 1437 (*REC* 4:9961). Emperor Sigismund conferred all the privileges of the Hochstift to the bishop on the same date (*REC* 4:9962).

[65] *REC* 4:9825.

and large city councils.[66] Christoph Schulthaiß recorded a celebration so elaborate that it seemed like "a grand wedding ceremony."[67] After the consecration a princely meal was provided for all the priests and city councilmen of whom twelve attended.[68] Although cathedral canons had elected him and the pope had confirmed him, although he had recognized the privileges of his diocesan subjects and received the holy chrism of consecration in his own cathedral, although he had sat at table with fellow clergy and lay magistrates, Henry of Hewen was not a full-fledged bishop. He had yet to make the ceremonial *adventus* into his venerable episcopal city.

After his consecration Henry departed from Constance for the episcopal castle of Gottlieben, located west of Constance on the south bank of the Rhine. By Christmas Eve a large local and foreign contingent of nobles, knights, and their stewards as well as civic couriers had joined the bishop in Gottlieben.[69] On that day clerics and magistrates were making simultaneous preparations in Constance. A large company gathered in Our Dear Lady, the civic clergy together with cathedral and collegiate canons, parish priests, episcopal staff, and students. They donned celebrative vestments and the headgear of their respective orders and with the relics of their saints in train they prepared to meet the approaching bishop in song.[70] City magistrates formed a small cadre with twenty armed men under their command; they followed behind the clergy of Constance from the cathe-

---

[66] Several details vary from one source to another, pointing to at least two different accounts of the entry instead of one document standing behind all of the versions. The discrepancies are minor and do not detract from a basic narrative observed in all the accounts. For example, Christoph Schulthaiß appears to follow his grandfather Claus on the ringing of bells to welcome the bishop and the presence of the *Weihbischof* of Basel, numerous clerics, and both city councils; Ruppert, p. 276, Schulthaiß-*Chronik*, p. 59. However, the younger Schulthaiß does not simply copy the elder; there is variation of style, vocabulary, and content. All of these details are absent in Dacher's account; Ruppert, pp. 192-193.

[67] "... als an grossen hochziten;" Schulthaiß-*Chronik*, p. 59, 2.

[68] "Diewil hat man ain fürstlich mal zugericht und alle priesterschaft, so zugegen gwesen, darzu geladen, ouch den ganzen rat. Aber es wurdent vom rat nit mer dan zwölf darzu verordnet;" Ruppert, p. 276, 30-32.

[69] "Als nun das ambt und die wyhin beschach, enmornend an dem hailigen aubent, rait er gen Gottlieben und och all, die mit im inritten woltent, vil ritter und knecht, darzu vil stettbotten ..." Ruppert, p. 192, 14-17.

[70] "... samlotent sich in das münster uff das am nachmittag und laitent sich all an in ir habit, die prelaten mit iren ynfeln und corkappen, darzu all örden mit ir zierd, als sy dan pflegent zu gehen an unsers herren fronlychnamstag umb die statt, alle laienpriester und schüler mit irem gesang und mit hailtum;" Ruppert, p. 192, 18-22.

dral to Emishover gate. There they spread out along the route into the city and waited to welcome the bishop.[71]

At about the same time Henry of Hewen departed with his entourage from Gottlieben. Just before arriving at the city his suffragans joined the throng; the bishop-elect dismounted and received a white horse from his marshall; he mounted and rode on to the city, arriving with his massive escort now numbering as many as 1,060 horses.[72] Henry stopped before the gates of the city and dismounted; he stood over against the civic party "as a lord and bishop."[73] The council and mayor of Constance then welcomed the bishop with due respect and commended themselves to him. Henry returned their kind words.[74] With formal contact now completed the bishop mounted his horse while four city magistrates, including the mayor, moved into position; they carried a baldachin over the bishop and guided him through the gate and into the city. As they prepared to enter those previously exiled, *all verbotten lütte*, were allowed to join an

---

[71] "Und noch den selben gaistlichen allen do giengent die räte, nach den räten giengent by zwaintzig gewappneter mit stangen und hubent das volk uff, das sy nit die herren trungent. Also gieng man mit dem hailtumb und procession bis für Emißhover tor hin uff die braiten, langen wyß, do wartet man sie;" Ruppert, p. 192, 22-26. The gate is identified as the "Mentzisthor" by Claus Schulthaiß (Ruppert, p. 276, 37) and the "Müntznis Tor" by Christoph Schulthaiß (Schulthaiß-*Chronik*, p. 59, 16).

[72] "Nun rait er von Gottlieben mit allem sinem volk über die hochstrauß herin und do er kam uff dieselb wyß, do stund er ab und ettliche herren und graven mit im und ward angelait als ain bischof von dem suffragani. Nun saß er uff ainem wyssen roß, das empfing im Ulrich Schilter, der was sin marschalk ..." Ruppert, p. 192, 27-31. The number of horses, *"wol mit 1060 pferden"* is recorded in the other accounts; Ruppert, p. 277, 1; Schulthaiß-*Chronik*, p. 59, 29.

[73] "... Do er abgestanden was und da stund als ain herr und bischoff ..." Schulthaiß-*Chronik*, p. 59, 29-30.

[74] "Do er sich nun het angelait, do kament die rät von Costentz und empfingent in loblich und erlich und empfahlent sich im gnädenclich. Desglichen danket er inen mit vil schönen worten, gegenainander geprucht;" Ruppert, p. 192, 33-35. In contrast to Dacher, Claus Schulthaiß portrays the two sides forming up on either side of a road and there exchanging greetings: "... und stalt sich sin zug zu ainen und die von Costantz zu andern syten, also das ain straß zwischet inen herin gieng. Do empfieng inen Ulrich Schilter, burgermaister;" Ruppert, p. 277, 1-3. There are a number of discrepancies in the various accounts here. The identity of the Marshall and Bürgermeister is varied. Claus Schulthaiß names Ulrich Schilter as Bürgermeister; Ruppert, p. 277, 3. Gebhard Dacher (Ruppert, p. 192, 31, 37) and Christoph Schulthaiß (*Chronik*, p. 59, 25, 34) most likely offer the correct version, identifying Schiltar as the bishop's marshall and Hans of Cappel as Bürgermeister.

There is also some disagreement regarding when the bishop mounted his white horse—either some distance from the city (Ruppert, p. 192, 27-32) or just prior to entering the city and after his exchange with the city council (Ruppert, p. 277, 2-7*)*.

incoming procession of some 500 persons.[75] With his staff in hand and his miter upon his head, Henry entered a city of pealing bells. He was accompanied not only by students and all of his clergy but also by his distinguished colleagues—the consecrating bishop of Constance, the abbots of Reichenau, St Gall, and Einsiedeln, all bedecked in glorious raiment.[76] It was a spectacle of sight and sound. This parade of clerics now made its way to the final destination of this long entry, the Cathedral of Our Dear Lady. Before a large congregation of clergy and laity Henry of Hewen led the evening service.[77]

The following morning, surrounded by his canons, the secular and religious clerics of Constance, the city council and other distinguished laity, Henry sang his first full mass as bishop. Those in attendance honored the new bishop with sumptuous gifts, each according to his rank and station.[78] On Christmas night the new bishop of Constance hosted a grand feast, serving 460 guests, including sixteen counts and ten abbots. Sometime during the festivities of Christmas Day, Henry of Hewen swore to honor all immunities, imperial rights and privileges held by the city.[79]

Only here, in the nave of his cathedral, within the walls of his city,

---

[75] "Und ward also gar erwürdenclich under ainer hymeltzen, die trugent vier der rät, das warent Hans von Cappel, burgmaister, Hainrich Tettikover, Lutfried Montpat und Ulrich Blaurer, der kurz, in die stat gefüert. Indem hettent sich gesamlet all verbotten lüte, wyb und man ... und die verbottnen hubent hindnan die ratsherren und kament also mit dem herren in die statt;" Ruppert, p. 192, 36-193. No account reports that the bishop mounted his horse after greeting the city magistrates. However, he is *led (gefüert)* into the city or rides in a mounted band: "Etliche setzen, syge er mit 500 pferden ingeritten;" Schulthaiß-*Chronik*, pp. 59, 35-36.

[76] "Man lüt mit allen glogen. Also viengen die crütz an und giengent darnach die schüler und die gantz pfaffhait in der statt. Also hüb da under ainem guldinen himeltzen der abt von Ow, der abt zu sant Gallen und der abt zu Ainsiedlen, und der wychbischoff und was der bischoff gar kostlich angelait mit seiner inflen und stab; desglichen die äpt;" Schulthaiß-*Chronik*, p. 60, 2-7.

[77] "Und do er also mit den herren in das münster kam, do vieng er die complet an ..." Ruppert, p. 193, 4-5.

[78] "... enmornend an dem hailigen tag winechten, do sung er das fronampt. Do warent alle prelaten mit ir ynfelen und ward im groß gut geopfret von den prelaten und andern gaistlichen und weltlichen. Die tumherren schanktent im ainen großen silbernen kopf und etwas darinne. Die rät empfingent in des ersten mit fünfzig pfund haller in ainem messin beckin und sy opfrotent dryssig pfund pfennig och in ainem messin beckin und nit mer und das ist ir gewonheit von alter her. Die herre, die caplon zu dem münster, die opfrotent drissig guldin, die von s. Stefan sechs malter habern, die von s. Johanns vier malter habern, der abbt von Richenaw zwen ochsen, der abt von Sant Gallen zwen ochsen und yederman nach sinen statten und state;" Ruppert, p. 193, 4-16.

[79] "Der bischof hat hoch zit mit gantzem pracht, mit prelaten, grauffen, rittern

in the movements of liturgy, among the gifts of his flock, and at the tables of his guests, only in this context did Henry of Hewen complete his initiation into the holy episcopacy of Constance. In 1436 the Holy Night and Christmas Morning of the infant savior gave added significance to this entry as the first coming of Christ coalesced with the *adventus* of a new bishop. Four months later Henry would complete his liturgical entry in high fashion. For the first time in forty years, a bishop would sing the Easter mass in Our Dear Lady.[80]

*   *   *

The elevation of Henry of Hewen to the office of bishop serves to highlight critical issues about the role of ritual and episcopal power. This ritual is all the more significant since Bishop Henry was an insider. As a canon he was already familiar with the streets and alleys of Constance, the sanctuary and choir of the cathedral, and the machinery of diocesan government. In fact, he was not a cleric called from afar and thus due a regal entry on his *first* and exalted 'visit' to Constance. In pomp and prestige the entry certainly upstaged his consecration. The holy days of Christmas were reserved for the entry, while the three consecrating bishops anointed Henry a full two days before this high holiday. A distinguished audience—high clergy, lower clergy, city councilmen—attended this grand consecration. The cathedral provided the backdrop for the ceremony; it was primarily a matter for the church and the clergy.[81] In the case of entry all of Constance was part of the ritual procession and part of the

---

und knechten. Der grauffen waren 16 und würdent über alle mal 460 essen geben. Es ward ouch darby 10 äpt;" Schulthaiß-*Chronik*, p. 60, 25-28. Further details about continued festivities over the next four days can be found in Schulthaiß-*Chronik*, p. 60, 29-36. The exact moment of the exchange of oaths between bishop and magistrates is unclear. But Schulthaiß identifies *"wyhenecht abend,"* Christmas night, and places the event after his description of the feast; Schulthaiß-*Chronik*, p. 60, 39-41; see *REC* 4:9867.

[80] March 31, 1437; *REC* 4:9917.

[81] This consecration does reveal the regional affiliations of the diocese and this bishop. The consecrating bishops of Basel and Strasbourg represented two bordering dioceses and performed the anointing along with the *Weihbischof* of Constance. The two abbots from the neighboring communities of Kreuzlingen and Petershausen participated in the ceremony and cemented their ties to the bishop. Other unnamed abbots and clerics were also present; Ruppert, pp. 192, 12-14; 276, 27-30; Schulthaiß-*Chronik*, p. 59, 4-7.

drama—the clergy, the banished, the city councilmen, the surrounding countryside, the city streets, and the cathedral.

On Christmas Eve Henry began his *adventus*. His point of origin was the castle at Gottlieben west of Constance on the banks of the Rhine, a location firmly in the hands of the bishop. His route did not take him along the river or directly overland to a gate in the middle of the city. Rather, the bishop rode on a long arc overland in order to reach Emishover gate to the south. This route bisected the former *Bischofshöri*, the ancient fields and villages that were granted to the bishop in the seventh century.[82] Via this entry point the bishop would ride the length of the city to the cathedral. A century before Bishop Nicholas II (1334-44) had taken an alternate route, coming by ship from Überlingen and arriving across the Rhine from Constance in Petershausen; he made his way into the city on the far north side, near to the cathedral and the clerical quarter of the *Niederburg*.[83]

In addition to Henry's route his princely entourage of over 1,000 horses, mounted by counts as well as knights and their stewards, displayed his seigniorial claims over countryside and city. This vast company paralleled the periodic entries of emperors who likewise arrived with noble riders in train. Emperor Sigismund had entered Constance shortly before Christmas in 1430 with four dukes, numerous counts, lords, and free knights.[84] In 1442 Emperor Frederick III (1440-93) first paused at the episcopal palace in Gottlieben, greeting the bishop before he rode on to Constance to be received by the city council. Later the bishop welcomed the king a second time and ushered him into the cathedral under a baldachin.[85] With an intended resemblance to the visitation of kings and emperors Bishop Henry rode at the head of a large aristocratic train and entered the city mounted on a white horse—all signs of lordship contesting the self-rule of the city.[86] After greeting the city in his lordly stance the bishop received the shade of a baldachin, carried by four city

---

[82] Helmut Maurer, "*Die Bischofshöri*. Studien zur 'Gründungsausstattug' des Bistums Konstanz," *FDA* 100 (1980), pp. 10-25. Maurer I, pp. 28-30.

[83] There is little evidence about the routes taken by other bishops; on Nicholas II, see Schulthaiß-*Chronik*, pp. 49-50.

[84] Ruppert, p. 170, 24f.

[85] Ruppert, p. 222, 29f.

[86] On the white horse and French royal entries, see Bernard Guenée, *Les entrées royales françaises de 1328 à 1515* (Paris: Centre National de la Recherche Scientifique, 1968), pp. 25, 63, 110, 275.

councilmen.[87] Finally, after his first mass, Henry offered a sumptuous banquet for his 460 clerical, civic, and noble guests, a display of episcopal largess and bounty as well as a final stage of the traditional coronation practiced by kings and popes.[88]

If the bishop's behavior underscored his lordly status, it did not overshadow his role as high cleric of the diocesan church. All the clergy processed from the cathedral through the gate of the city, singing and bearing the sacred treasures of the bishopric—the holy relics—while church bells celebrated his arrival.[89] Henry processed under the city's baldachin but among his own kind, the clergy and distinguished abbots of neighboring cloisters. His entry brought holy amnesty as the exiled were allowed to join his holy procession. His entourage—now swelled with nobility, clergy, and laity—proceeded to the cathedral. Here stood the incarnation of episcopal power in the city, its holy and immune ground still remaining under episcopal lordship; here Henry reconstituted the holy community of Constance, joining the bones of bishops and the remnants of saints to the mighty throng gathered to hear his first mass.

While Henry of Hewen flaunted his princely and episcopal powers, he also committed himself to subtle negotiations with the city council of Constance. In fact, with the election, entry, and death of each bishop, the city was yet again forced to placate, appease, and oppose another threat to civic independence, a dance of ritual and negotiation, which established the nature of the civic-episcopal relationship for the bishop's term of office to come. Although a gap of nearly three months between the election of Henry and his entry at Christmas could indicate careful planning, it is likely that bishop and city took some time to work out many of their differences in frequent negotiations. Episcopal entries could be delayed if an election was contested or if two rival candidates maneuvered politically and mil-

---

[87] Baldachins were used not only to honor a distinguished visitor, but also to shelter or represent relics in procession; see Trexler, *Public Life in Renaissance Florence*, pp. 250, 306, 309; and Kempers, "Icons, Altarpieces, and Civic Ritual in Siena Cathedral, 1100-1530," in *City and Spectacle in Medieval Europe*, p. 107.

[88] See Lawrence M. Bryant, "The Medieval Entry Ceremony at Paris," in *Coronations*, p. 100; and Bernhard Schimmelfennig, "Papal Coronations in Avignon," in *Coronations*, pp. 190-191.

[89] James M. Murray has drawn attention to the importance of the *soundscape* as a complement to landscape in ceremonies of entry; "The Liturgy of the Count's Advent in Bruges, from Galbert to Van Eyck," in *City and Spectacle in Medieval Europe*, p. 143.

itarily for the throne.[90] Moreover, negotiations between bishop and city could stall if one side or the other made new or extraordinary demands.[91] The magistrates of Constance consistently followed two policies throughout the later Middle Ages: first, the city council might deny the bishop's festive entry until its demands were met; clearly the bishop was not lord of the city; second, if differences were resolved, the city council invariably permitted episcopal entry and allowed the bishop to parade into the city with all the pomp of princely power. The bishop could behave as if he were once more a civic lord as long as the fine print (*Verschreibung*) made clear where performance left off and actual jurisdiction began.

But civic participation did not cease with pre-entry discussions. The city council was in attendance at the consecration ceremony and the banquet following. On the day of entry magistrates marched out in the procession to greet the bishop and they, not the clergy, exchanged the first words of welcome immediately outside the city.[92] As in the negotiations before entry the bishop had to deal with the magistrates and recognize their rightful rule before he was allowed to proceed. Perhaps there was honor in the distance the magistrates covered but the extent of civic authority was clearly marked out as well; the bishop acknowledged the city council and its armed escort *before* he rode through the gate. Furthermore, the baldachin likewise carried ambiguous or multiple meanings. Did the bishop enter under an awning worthy of kings, princes, and relics or did he proceed through the streets of Constance under a 'sky' created by the city

---

[90] Disputed elections and delayed entries were not uncommon. Nicholas of Riesenburg (1384-87), the candidate of the Roman pontiff, and Mangold of Brandis (1384-85), the choice of the Avignon pope, jockeyed for office and for the right to reside in Constance. The cathedral canons of Constance held an election that resulted in a divided vote in January of 1384. Although Mangold received more votes than Nicholas, he never set foot in Constance. It was Nicholas who entered Constance in June of 1384 with nearly a six month delay between his contested election and his installation; *REC* 6945, 6950, 6951; Schulthaiß-*Chronik*, pp. 49-50. Otto IV of Sonnenberg (1474-91) waited seven years for his contested election with Lewis of Freiberg (1474-80) to be resolved in his favor. Only then did he receive his consecration and enter Constance; Ruppert, p. 451; Schulthaiß-*Chronik*, p. 72.

[91] See above, pp. 138-139.

[92] Richard Trexler has shown that the distance travelled by the signoria to meet a visitor in fifteenth-century Florence communicated the level of honor bestowed upon the visitor. If the signoria awaited the visitor at city hall, the honor was slight. But if the magistrates processed to the city gates, then the prestige bestowed upon the guest was considerable. While Trexler's attention to distance is most useful here, his interpretation of Florentine ritual may not apply in Constance; see *Public Life in Renaissance Florence*, pp. 308-311.

council?[93] Did the baldachin signify more about the bishop's dignity or the magistrates' jurisdiction? Perhaps the awning implied restriction as well as dignity.

The magistrates did, however, grant the bishop his due honor as the most powerful clergyman in the city, attending the consecration as well as the first mass. In the bishop's own legitimate space in the cathedral the city council bestowed worthy gifts.[94] While this gesture implied respect, Gebhard Dacher comments that, in keeping with the custom of a city council's gifts to bishops, there was nothing special about this offering to Bishop Henry: "this is nothing more than what has customarily been given from the earliest days."[95] The city council gave fifty pounds of *Haller* in a brass kettle and 30 pounds of pfennig in a second brass kettle.[96] This amount may be usefully measured in comparison to royal gifts. When Emperor Frederick III visited Constance in 1442, the gratuity was far more substantial. The city presented two hundred gulden (or gold florins) to the king along with a beautiful cauldron worth 230 gulden.[97] In comparison with the gifts of other clerics in attendance at Henry's first mass the gifts of the city council were respectable. Even though

---

[93] The German word for baldachin is *Himmel*, which has the primary definition of *heaven*.

[94] Trexler has noted how gifts to foreign visitors in Florence functioned in political negotiation: "Gifts had meaning with a ritual of exchange, where their aesthetic value ideally induced sincerity and subjectivity, and thus facilitated diplomatic contacts. Governments spent such money and skill in order to convince the ruler of their love ..." *Public Life in Renaissance Florence*, p. 326. On gift-giving in the context of the nobility and monastic houses, see Constance B. Bouchard, *Sword, Miter, and Cloister. Nobility and the Church in Burgundy, 980-1198* (Ithaca: Cornell University Press, 1987), pp. 171-246.

[95] "... nit mer und das ist ir gewonheit von alter her;" Ruppert, p. 193, 12.

[96] The value of the gift granted to the bishop in surviving records does seem to vary after Henry of Hewen, although the precise denomination of the gift is sometimes left out of the records. Hermann of Breitenlandenberg (1466-74) received 25 pounds pfennig and a cauldron valued at three soldin; Schulthaiß--*Chronik*, p. 68; *REC* 4:13187. The city council not only gave Hugo of Hohenlandenberg (1496-1531, 1531-32) 16 pounds in a copper cauldron after his mass but also ten bins of fine fish, "which were good" (*die gut waren*) and 16 containers of wine; Schulthaiß-*Chronik*, p. 78, 33; pp. 78-79).

[97] Ruppert, p. 223. The value of these coinages varied from place to place and time to time. But the gulden or florin was the standard central European currency in gold. The fifty pounds of Haller and thirty pounds pfennig were the standard penny in this case in copper and silver; these coinages denoted a significant difference in amount and species. For the value of the various coinages, see John H. Munro, "The Coinages of Renaissance Europe, ca. 1500," in *Handbook of European History 1400-1600. Late Middle Ages, Renaissance, and Reformation*, eds. T. A. Brady Jr., H. A. Oberman, and J. D. Tracy (Leiden: E.J. Brill, 1994), vol. I, pp. 671-678; vol. II, pp. 683-690.

the council did not match the chaplains of the cathedral, who gave
the new bishop 30 gulden, they did exceed the canons of St
Stephan's and St. John's who paid in units of oats (*Haber*).[98] In any
case the chroniclers noted the amount given by the city among those
deserving precise rendering. In the fifteenth century the gift remained at roughly the same amount, thus fixing a typical present for
a new bishop. The city council gave far more to a visiting king. The
bishop did not receive a gift worthy of the highest secular lord.

Each stage of the bishop's entry was choreographed. The city
council countered every move made by the bishop and the bishop in
turn used every stage to display episcopal power—the consecration,
procession, proper entry, first mass, and banquets. The bishop took
each step with lordly flare. The city council in turn confined his field
of motion. But the ultimate prize in this clever game was not victory.
Rather, careful maneuvering would lead to equilibrium and cooperation, to the careful definition of rights and privileges, in short, to a
grateful stalemate that would undergird civic and episcopal cohabitation. Sometime before, during, or after the ritual stages of entry the
bishop would draft and swear to a document that detailed the legal
relationship of the two parties—the *Verschreibung*.[99]

Unfortunately surviving records do not allow us to reconstruct the

---

[98] Six malter of oats from the canons of St Stephen's and 4 malter from the
canons of St John. The expensive gifts most likely came from the abbots of
Reichenau and St Gall who each gave the bishop two oxen; Ruppert, p. 193, 14-15.

[99] The oath-taking ceremony is not confined to a specific point in entry festivities.
The reputation of the bishop, the suspicions of the city council, the delay of papal
and imperial approbation, and even the complications of planning a gala event may
all have played a role in scheduling the *Verschreibung*. Since the time of publication of
the decree is not consistent—before, during, or after entry—it appears that each
individual case and circumstance dictated how and when the *Verschreibung* ceremony
occurred. Four of the twelve bishops issued their *Verschreibungen* before formal entry
into the city and first mass: Burkhard of Hewen (*REC* 3:7176), Henry of Hewen,
Otto of Sonnenberg (StAK A II 30; GLA 5: 7206), and Thomas Berlower (Ruppert,
pp. 451-452). But on five occasions bishop and city came to agreement *after* the
bishop had made his formal entry or at least celebrated first mass in the cathedral,
suggesting that the date of the *Verschreibung* could be negotiated and was not always a
precondition of entry. Those bishops were Henry of Brandis (StAK A II 30, 24rf),
Nicholas of Riesenburg (StAK A II 30, 30r-33r), Burkhard of Randegg (StAK A II
30, 54r-58r; GLA 5-7188), Hermann of Breitenlandenberg (StAK A II 30, 59r-62v)
and Hugo of Hohenlandenberg (Schulthaiß-*Chronik*, p. 76; StAK A II 30, 75r-79v,
GLA 5-7210). In three cases, there is no record of entry, but the *Verschreibungen*
survive—Marquard of Randeck (StAK A II 30, 34r-37v; GLA 5: 7189; *REC* 3:7589,
7590; Ruppert, p. 327; Schulthaiß-*Chronik*, p. 53), Albert Blarer (*REC* 3: 8003;
Schulthaiß-*Chronik*, p. 54), and Otto III of Hachberg (StAK A II 30 42r-45v; *REC*
3:8340).

setting of any late-medieval *Verschreibung* in Constance.[100] Where did
the ceremony take place? Who read the document? Where did the
bishop and his staff stand, the city councilmen and public witnesses?
Sometime during his processional entry on December 24, Henry of
Hewen drafted and had his *Verschreibung* read before the city council
and witnesses. We know at least that the bishop did remain in
Constance on the night before his first mass, and almost certainly
resided in his episcopal palace. The *Verschreibung* of Henry of Hewen
indicates that the ceremony took place on "Christmas evening."[101]
Since chronicle sources regarding Henry's entry are careful to note
his exact location at all times—in the cathedral, in Gottlieben, at a
city-gate—it is highly likely that the *Verschreibung* was held in the bishop's palace where he was last seen hosting a banquet.[102] A number
of lines in the document allude to the public nature of the event.
First, Henry is not simply drafting a decree, he is swearing an
oath;[103] he pledges to uphold the interests of the mayor, city
councilmen, the guild-master, citizens of the city of Constance, rich
and poor, the members of his staff, and the residents of his diocese.[104] Second, the surviving document assumes multiple audiences;
it is thus addressed to those publicly present as well as to later readers

---

[100] The emphasis here is on the ritual function of the *Verschreibung*; for an extended discussion of individual articles and their implications for the relationship of
bishop and city in the late medieval Constance, see below, pp. 66-72.

[101] "Geben an dem hailigen weyhtnnacht Aubent ..." GLA 5: 7200, 45; StAK A
II 30, p. 53v, 15-16. It is not entirely clear whether Christmas eve or the night of
Christmas day is meant; the chronology of the accounts suggests the latter.

[102] Both Marquard of Randeck (1398-1406) and Albert Blarer (1407-10) made
their pronouncements in Gottlieben, the bishop's castle south of Constance, giving
further evidence that the *Verschreibung* occurred on episcopal ground; although in the
case of Marquard the city did not respond for several days and eventually stated its
approval in Constance; *REC* 3:7589, 7590, 8003; Ruppert, p. 327, Schulthaiß-
Chronik, p. 54. Moreover, no mention is made of a non-ecclesiastical location, such as
city hall or a market square. Episcopal ground is also likely since these festivities
belonged to the bishop, while the city council sought to assure that certain matters
were crystal clear regarding authority in the city.
The *Verschreibung* has received far less attention than the citizen's oath. For the
overall background to this oath and pacts in general, see Wilhelm Ebel, *Der Bürgereid
als Geltungsgrund und Gestaltungsprinzip des deutschen mittelalterlichen Stadtrechts* (Weimar:
Hermann Böhlaus, 1958), especially pp. 70-142.

[103] "Dise vorgenempten stuck vnd Artickel alle gemainlich vnd yeglichen in sunder haben wir vorgenempter Bischof Hainrich gelobt vnnd verhaißen by vnsern
fürstenlichen truwen in aids wise ze halten vnd daby ze beliben nach Innhalt diß
briefs ane alle geverde;" GLA 5: 7200, 39-40; StAK A II 30, 15-21.

[104] The various recipients are referred to throughout the *Verschreibung* in GLA 5:
7200 and StAK A II 30, pp. 50-53.

and listeners, "...to those who are looking on or who are listening or reading."[105] Thus, Henry of Hewen and the magistrates of Constance participated in a meeting that had grave implications for civic and episcopal liturgy; the charter and written word supplemented the rituals of procession and worship. While the location of the meeting is unknown, this *Verschreibung* closes with a list of six men who served as witnesses, including the brother of Henry of Hewen.[106] This contract sealed the relationship between bishop and city, detailing exactly which rights the bishop would claim and how he would seek to protect the long held privileges of the city of Constance. The following morning Henry of Hewen would come to the cathedral to lead distinguished foreign guests, diocesan clergy, city councilmen, and citizens of Constance in his first mass as bishop of Constance.

Negotiation between bishop and city did not always occur as a simple matter of course.[107] In fact, Thomas Berlower (1491-96) attempted to reclaim episcopal rights in a fashion later attributed to Luther; he posted the first draft of his *Verschreibung* on a door of the cathedral. This copy included the name of the dreaded Henry of Brandis, former Bishop of Constance (1357-83), who to the clergy must have symbolized the assertive reclamation of the bishop's rights and to the laity represented the wanton abuse of episcopal power. The city council was deeply offended by both the gesture and content of Berlower's *Verschreibung* and thus denied Thomas his entry for

---

[105] "... die in ansehent oder hörent lesen." GLA 5: 7200, 2; StAK A II 30, p. 50, 10.

Brigitte Bedos-Rezak gives critical background to this statement in her research on literacy and record-keeping in the cities of northern France. She notes how written and sealed charters functioned "as sacred texts and icons for the rituals of a civic liturgy." In fact, "the act of writing itself was performed as a spectacle in medieval towns;" "Civic Liturgies and Urban Records in Northern France, 1100-1400," in *City and Spectacle in Medieval Europe*, pp. 40, 42 respectively. Bedos-Rezak notes how lay folk participated in a ceremonial cycle when they received a charter: "Townspeople desired the document; purchased its support; enacted ritually the covenant it recorded; witnessed its writing, sealing, or division and distribution into several parts; received it; paid for it; ritually touched it; and brought it back home, there to be kept for possible later use." "Civic Liturgies and Urban Records," p. 43.

[106] The witnesses represent Henry's familial, aristocratic, and clerical connections. In addition to Hans of Hewen, the list includes representatives of the nobility—Count Wilhelm of Tettnang, Hainrich of Stoffeln—and members of the cathedral clergy, Dean Iohannsen Littin and Albrecht Blarer, canon of the Cathedral; GLA 5: 7200, 42-44; StAK A II 30, p. 53, 27-38.

[107] Indeed, the period between Henry's election in August and his entry in December may in part be related to unresolved issues between bishop and city.

fourteen months; finally, in June of 1492 he wrote a *Verschreibung* agreeable to the city and entered with all the usual pomp.[108]

While entry accounts survive for some bishops of Constance, episcopal and civic archivists of Constance were careful to record nearly every *Verschreibung* from 1357 to 1496.[109] In fact, information regarding the consecration, entry, and first mass is missing for a number of late medieval bishops, but their *Verschreibungen* have been carefully preserved. The reviled and envied Henry of Brandis drafted the first *Verschreibung* known to us and all but one of his successors followed suit until the lengthy exile of bishop and clergy in the sixteenth century.

When the bishop proclaimed the *Verschreibung*, the magistrates received confirmation of their rights and privileges. The bishop arrived as a prince of the empire and shepherd of the church, but at some point he had to confront his civic rivals and swear an oath. This document was no oath of homage between a lord and his menial subjects. The bishop had to recognize the legitimacy of lay rule. Cooperation was based not only on the drafting of contracts but also on the stages of entry that allowed the bishop to flaunt all of his prerogatives and powers. During this process the magistrates defended their territory by intervening directly in the entry (meeting the bishop with at the gate), directing episcopal movement (guiding the bishop under a baldachin), and requiring confirmation of civic rights (the *Verschreibung*). Through the rituals of consecration, entry, and installation, the bishop of Constance received the charisma of his office, the sanctuary of his cathedral, and the recognition of the civic populace—clerical and lay. Through the ritual of entry the bishop displayed his princely power, manifest in his regal arrival and his large entourage; this ritual allowed Henry of Hewen to display a form of episcopal lordship now denied by the city. Through ritual and negotiation city and bishop become unwieldy but workable partners in a city of citizens and clerics, a city sacred and secular.

---

[108] Ruppert, pp. 451-452. The *Verschreibung* of Thomas Berlower appears in GLA 5: 7208 and StAK A II 30, 69v-73v.

[109] No record of the *Verschreibung* of Bishop Frederick of Zollern (1434-36) survives; he ruled only two years and may never have submitted a draft. However, records of his first entry do survive; *REC* 3:9605, Schulthaiß-*Chronik*, p. 57.

The Entries of the Bishops of Augsburg

On Saturday, June 17, 1470 Hanns of Stain, chief administrator of
the bishop of Augsburg, made his way to the chamber of the
Augsburg city council. He brought disturbing news. The council had
expected the imminent arrival of the new bishop, John of
Werdenberg (1459-86), but not at the head of a train of 1800 horses
requiring stable and feed.[110] The magistrates stiffened at the news,
then delivered an ultimatum: the bishop could bring only eight hundred horses into Augsburg. The council then set out to secure the
city. All carpenters and craftsmen were called in to spend a half-day
barricading the side streets from one end of the city to the other—
from the far southern gate, the *Rothentor*, to the northern reaches of
the city by the cathedral. The bishop's parade would be confined to
a single avenue.[111]

The following day the bishop's escort formed outside the city. At
noon representatives of the dukes of Bavaria and Swabia rode forward to meet the bishop who had travelled from Zußmerhausen with
a host from Württemberg. Three dukes and twenty-eight counts met
the bishop at a stone house and rode on to the city gate.[112] Mean-
while, the mayor and magistrates, dressed in full costume with silk
banners and arms at their sides, formed their band. They rode out at
the head of a company of 200 horses to a trough outside the city; the
gate closed firmly behind them. There on the border between city
and countryside the civic and episcopal companies met. The mayor
stood to welcome the bishop:

> "Gracious prince and lord, when your grace and the city council are
> joined as planned, this city council and whole commune of rich and

---

[110] "... als man im raut saß, kam der hofmaister, herr hanns vom Stain, und sagt,
sein herr het 1800 pferd, das man im umb herberg besech;" *CDS* 22 [3], p. 228, 12-
13. This entry of John of Werdenberg, provided by Hektor Mühlich, is the most
thorough account of its kind in the Augsburger chronicle literature.

[111] "... des erschrak ain rat, dann darvor hett man gesagt, er precht nur 800
pferd, und was ain rat in sorgen. also beschickt man all zimmerleut und wurden in
dem halben tag all nebengassen verschrankt, das [sie] von Rotenthor bis gen unser
frawen nur in der ainen gassen beleiben mußten;" Mülich, *CDS* 22 [3], p. 228, 14-
18.

[112] "... also am Sontag, do es mittag was, kamen die Bair über Lech, hertzog
Ludwigs zeug, der hertzogen von München zeug, oben herab der swebisch zeug und
neben Zußmerhausen der bischof und des von Wirtenbergs volck, und sammelten
sich bei den ziegelstädeln und waren 3 hertzogen, 1 bischof und 28 grafen;" Mülich,
CDS 22 [3], p. 228, 18-22.

poor folk would receive your grace with the highest honor and with full humility."

Each party swore this agreement to the other. Then the mayor opened the gate, rode with the bishop's entourage into the city, and broke ranks with him near the cloister of St. Margareta.[113]

At this point the bishop's company stopped at St. Ulrich's. Then the large princely company rode three abreast with great pomp and in full costume with their retinue of pages riding impressive horses and bearing large banners. To either side of this procession armed men of the city stood on the saltbarn, the dance house, the guild houses, and the gates—from one end of the city to the other—monitoring the progress of the parade. With holy relics in his train the bishop proceeded to St Leonhard's Chapel where he placed the episcopal miter on his own head. Then John of Werdenberg and his princely escort completed their procession at the cathedral where the bishop took his place at the altar.[114]

Festivities continued into the evening and resumed the following morning. After the service each guest rode to his lodging for the night. But many came to the bishop, including the city magistrates, offering gifts—a golden cauldron valued at 100 gulden with 200 gulden within.[115] The next morning around the eighth hour the storm bell rang out, calling the community to the square before city hall.

---

[113] "... also ritten von hinnen hinaus bis zuo der trenck an die schrancken burgermaister und ratgeben mit 200 pferden, wolgerüst, mit seiden fanen in harnasch; da tät man das Rotthor nach in zuo. Also stuonden bie burgermaister ab und sprachen also: 'gnediger fürst und herr, ain rat und ain gantz gemain, reich und arm, empfacht eur fürstlich gnad mit ganßen trewen und aller diemüetigkeit und, nachdem eur gnad mit ainem rat veraint sind, das dem nachgegangen werd.' das gelopten sie ainander. da hieß der burgermaister das thor auf thuon und rait mit unserm volck am ersten herein und hielten in die gassen vor sant Margarethen über..." Mülich, *CDS* 22 [3], pp. 228: 22—229: 1-8.

[114] "... da rait des bischofs zeug für sich hinauf für sant Ulrich, allweg drei neben ainander vast kostlich, wolgerüst, außerwelt volck, und iegclichs fürsten volck besonder, und allweg die knaben auf grossen rossen mit grossen vannen bei ainander vorher. do was auf dem saltzstadel, auf dem tantzhaus und auf den zunftheusern vil gewaupnets volcks, das sich sehen ließ und all thor besetzt, und ee der letst zum Rotenthor herein was, do was der erst zuo unser frowen. also gieng man mit dem hailtuom da stuond der bischof ab zuo sant Lenhart in der iudengassen und setzt sein infel auf, und die fürsten giengen mit im in thumb, do satzt man in auf den altar;" Mülich, *CDS* 22 [3], p. 229: 8-16.

[115] "... darnach rait iederman an sein herberg. do schanckt man dem bischof Johanns von der stat ain vergulte scheurn, was 100 gulden wert, und darinn 200 gulden ..." Mülich, *CDS* 22 [3], p. 229: 16-18.

With his princely retinue John of Werdenberg rode to the place where the large council had assembled. The bishop and city swore to uphold their mutual rights. After the ceremony Bishop John invited distinguished dignitaries to his chambers for a grand feast, including a *reien* for the foreign guests, a dance which attracted the footfall of the bishop of Eichstätt, several dukes, and the cathedral dean. In addition to the ball there was a tournament in which 165 nobles took part.[116] Finally, while the princely company dispersed, the bishop remained in the city. On June 21 Bishop John sang the mass for the *corpus Christi* feast in Augsburg; he himself carried the body of Christ through the city.[117]

*   *   *

The arrival of Augsburg Bishop John of Werdenberg offers an illuminating comparison to the entries of the bishops of Constance.[118] In many ways the bishop and city of Augsburg conducted themselves like their counterparts to the west. But in Augsburg the confrontation of cleric and city was more severe. Bishop John remained with his princely retinue throughout the entry. The size of his company was sufficient to shock the city council into stringent defensive measures. The nobility arrived in mass with John at Augsburg, escorted him

---

[116] "... darnach des andern tags morgen umb die 8. ur fieng man, die sturm zuo leuten. do rait der bischof auf das rauthaus mit den fürsten, do was der groß rat besamlet, do schwuor ietweder tail dem andern, bei irem alten herkomen zuo beleiben. der bischof legt aber seinhand auf sein brust und sprach: 'sic ego juro,' das was sein aid. do rait der bischof mit den fürsten haim, und die burgermaister und die rät die in empfangen hetten, und fürsten und herren assen mit im, und wurden all herren vom hof gespeist und gefüetert. nach tisch hett man den fremden herrn ain tantz, do gab man unserm bischof ain raien, do tantzten hertzog Albrecht und hertzog Cristoff im vor und der bischof von Eystett und Hertzog Hanns, thuombrobst, nach; und waren 165 edel turnierer;" Mülich, *CDS* 22 [3], pp. 229: 22—230: 1-9.

[117] "... und am aftermäntag rait iederman darvon, also belaib der bischof hie und sang das ampt in *die corporis Cristi* und truog das sacrament in der process;" Mülich, *CDS* 22 [3], p. 230: 10-12.

[118] There are few Augsburg texts comparable to those in Constance and none with the multi-source richness surrounding the entry of Henry of Hewen. This paucity of detailed description makes the account of John of Werdenberg's entry all the more invaluable. Sketchy entry information does survive for the following bishops: Burkhard of Ellerbach (Zoepfl I, p. 327), Eberhard of Kirchberg (Mülich, *CDS* 22 [3], pp. 50-52; Anonymous chronicle, *CDS* 22 [3], p. 465), Peter of Schaumberg (Burkard Zink, *CDS* 5 [2], pp. 369-370; Mülich, 22 [3], p. 67). Wherever entry accounts or notations are recorded, the event is described as a customary rite for bishop and city, not as an exceptional ceremony or episcopal imposition.

through the city, joined him in his first mass, and the next morning led him to city hall. They dined, danced, and to top off the celebration, jousted. The bishop was himself a prince, the Count of Werdenberg, and at this time remained in his princely role.

The magistrates did not contest John's aristocratic pretensions: they greeted him outside the city with deference, with appropriate appellations—*prince*, *lord*, *your grace*—and were suitably submissive. They did not dispute the princely power of the bishop; rather, they harnessed it. The bishop could parade down the major avenue of the city but to either side the streets were barricaded, the houses topped with armed men, the gates of the city guarded. Unlike Constance where the magistrates joined a clerical procession to meet the bishop and sheltered him with a baldachin, the councilors of Augsburg rode with two hundred armed and adorned men, their horses, dress, and demeanor demonstrating who ruled the city and controlled access to its streets.[119] The *Rothentor* was closed during the ceremony of greeting; and the mayor, not the bishop, opened it. As in Constance the magistrates escorted the bishop but only the short distance inside the walls to the cloister of St. Margareta. The long and steady contact of Bishop Henry of Hewen and the magistrates of Constance throughout the procession in the city is absent here; the Augsburgers veered away shortly after entering the city. After his admission to Augsburg Bishop John and his company moved from St Ulrich's to the cathedral without civic approbation; he was *prince*-bishop of Augsburg for two days; he transversed a narrow stretch of pavement; he was under a civic quarantine. If the magistrates attended the bishop's first mass, the chronicler did not record their presence. In this account the city council was only periodically involved in the bishop's ritual of entry. Bishop John could ride through the city as a prince. But the citizens either ignored his parade or observed it from armed barricades and rooftops.

Bishop John and the city council did, however, complete a careful and orderly process of negotiation. The mayor's cordial greeting and

---

[119] In fact, the aggressive tactics of the city parallel later and more militant measures taken by the Strasbourg city council in October of 1507. Bishop Wilhelm of Honstein likewise found his route through the city carefully laid out and he confronted over two thousand armed citizens and peasants as he processed to the cathedral, "... the only place in Strasbourg where the bishop was still master;" Thomas A. Brady, Jr., "Rites of Autonomy, Rites of Dependence," in *Religion and Culture in the Renaissance and Reformation*, p. 17.

the bishop's reply went according to plan. As in Constance the magistrates came to the bishop's palace to offer congratulatory gifts. The Augsburgers were far more generous; their gifts not only signified respect but also demonstrated civic wealth and economic power. Moreover, the bishop had to process to the center of civic space, to city hall and the magistrates turf, in order to render the mutual oaths that hopefully would seal the bishop and city of Augsburg in a binding and peaceful relationship.

As in Constance sound played a role in the entry. The tolling of the storm bell still rung out the ancient claims of the bishop over his city. Sixty-five years earlier Bishop-elect Eberhart of Kirchberg (1404-13) had demanded that the magistrates call the people by ringing the bell; the tone that signaled a civic emergency could also draw the citizens to the side of their bishop. The city council refused, noting the novelty and audacity of the request.[120] In protest Eberhart of Kirchberg mounted his horse and rode back to Dillingen. He now demanded that the magistrates come to his city to swear an oath. Less than two months later Bishop Eberhart was back in Augsburg. This time the magistrates rang the bell. Bishop and city swore to uphold their mutual rights.[121] Over half a century later, at the elevation of John of Werdenberg in 1469, the crowd again heard the peeling bell.

These ritual negotiations between bishop and magistrates occurred in four very different civic spaces. They first met outside the city in neutral territory. There they agreed to cooperate in the present festivities and in the years to follow. Then they crossed the threshold from countryside to city together, unified as they entered the city. Next magistrates marched into episcopal space when they came to the episcopal palace to honor the bishop with gifts. Finally, the bishop returned the favor, parading to the square before city hall to swear his oath. Careful attention to each segment of civic space allowed both bishop and city to recognize each other's prerogatives without losing face and risking open hostility. The bishop received the limited recognition of this city and the charisma of his office through ritual, through official entry, procession to his cathedral, in-

---

[120] "... das wolt ain raut hie nit thun, dann mann hetts vor nie keinem bischof getaun;" Hektor Mülich, *CDS* 22 [3], p. 50: 11-12.
[121] Mülich, *CDS* 22 [3], p. 50: 12- 51:1; see also the *Anonymous Chronicle, CDS* 22 [3], p. 465: 4-10.

stallation, and his first mass. The magistrates added their stages to the process by receiving the bishop outside the walls and by demanding that the bishop parade to city hall.

Amidst all the confrontation and negotiation John of Werdenberg came to Augsburg as a shepherd of his church. The city did not deny him access to his sacred highway, the route from the church of the martyrs and sainted bishops, St. Ulrich's, to the Cathedral of St. Mary. Augsburg was still framed by the spires of St. Ulrich's and St. Mary's and those spires yet stood for the bishops of Augsburg. On his way to the cathedral the bishop put on the miter, placing his episcopal identity above his position as a prince of the empire. Holy relics reinforced the numinous aura of the procession.

Like Henry of Hewen, John of Werdenberg seemed to have a remarkable grasp of liturgical drama. As Henry combined his *advent* with the celebration of Christmas, so John completed his *adventus* with one more procession. The new bishop led the annual *corpus Christi* procession and carried the body of Christ through the city in his own hands. Not only did John take center stage in the most popular celebration of the later Middle Ages, he also made a formal procession through sections of the city denied him in his entry four days earlier.[122] As a priest and bishop John might have drawn on ecclesiastical ritual to overcome civic hostility toward his princely status. For one day the shepherd of Augsburg was in charge, leading a procession both lay and clerical through *his* city. During the *corpus Christi* celebration the magistrates of Augsburg participated in silence. Through this sacramental ritual the new bishop reconfigured his authority and profile in the city; through this ritual the image of the bishop as high priest of the church now displaced the visage of princely intruder.

---

[122] On the dominance of the *corpus Christi* feast and procession in the later Middle Ages, see Miri Rubin, *Corpus Christi. The Eucharist in Late Medieval Culture* (Cambridge: Cambridge University Press, 1991); Charles Zika, "Hosts, Processions and Pilgrimages," *Past and Present* 118 (1988), 25-64; and Mervyn James, "Ritual, Drama and Social Body in the Late Medieval English Town," *Past and Present* 98 (1983), pp. 3-29. Still to be explored is the possibility that episcopal entry ceremonies contributed to or drew upon the popularity and impact of the *corpus Christi* procession. The proximity of John's entry to the *corpus Christi* feast suggests another political dimension of this popular late medieval feast, a dimension heretofore left out of scholarly debate.

Episcopal Entries: Conflict, Cooperation, and Implications

What role did a bishop play when he entered a city? Did he come to receive his coronation, to rule his city as lord? Did he perform an *imitatio Christi*, an *adventus* in which he was the triumphant king of Palm Sunday, the apocalyptic Christ, riding at the head of a godly host to judge the earth? Was he like the bishop of Constance, Henry of Hewen, who associated his entry with the first coming of Christ, arriving on Christmas Eve, receiving magnificent gifts from foreign dignitaries and local folk? Was he a bishop *in utero* coming to the place where bishops were born, to the city and cathedral where his ancestors came to life and now rested, to the city where he would in turn rule and shepherd his diocese?

A bishop took on the roles of prince, lord, priest, shepherd, and apostle of Christ in one long sequence of rituals. This shape-shifting performance allowed him to claim, if only for the moment, rights and privileges long denied him, to flaunt an antiquated episcopal paradigm in the guise of drama and in the frame of a city he once possessed. Ritual made this transfer possible, providing a traditional setting and a sequence of events or behaviors that served to channel the bishop's charisma into yet another conventional episcopal role.

Civic leaders in turn found ways to participate in and limit this performance, to shape the stage on which the bishop could pretend, while making clear exactly where such pretension went too far. They permitted the bishop's entry but only after they conferred with him outside the city. They allowed a sumptuous procession but controlled the route. They might participate in the bishop's consecration, first mass, and sometimes his feast, but they also inserted a rite of their own: the bishop had to swear an oath to the city council before witnesses. In Augsburg the bishop came to city hall, to a place where citizens proclaimed their loyalty. Yet the sounding of the storm bell echoed a time when residents would have fled to the bishop's cathedral-fortress for protection and not to the square before city hall. The citizens of Augsburg conceded to one ritual while the bishop complied with another.

Episcopal entries had several meanings for cities as well as bishops. Civic leaders acknowledged that somehow this place still belonged to the bishop; he deserved his procession; he alone still ruled within his cathedral compound; this drama of entry could only unfold in the frame of his old episcopal city. But the magistrates also advertised

civic rights during entry festivities. They made clear and in detail
how this city no longer belonged to the bishop, how the battlements,
gates, and side-streets were off-limits to princely pretenders. They
included their own ritual behavior, marking out the sections of the
city under their control, simultaneously signifying the pedigree of the
bishop and the political reality of lay civic rule.

Above all, episcopal entries demonstrated points of political conflict as they promoted cooperation and integration.[123] When a
bishop marched or rode majestically through the gate, the ongoing
conflict between commune and city-lord was on full display. Both
sides once again staked out their legal, political, and ritual ground.
The citizens of Augsburg barricaded most of the city, fearful of the
bishop and his princely entourage. Ritual insult played a role. The
city council sometimes denied a candidate formal entry and bishops
refused to come. The magistrates of Augsburg forced the approaching bishop, John of Werdenberg, to reduce his entourage by over
half. Bishop-elect Eberhard of Kirchberg stormed out of Augsburg at
the precise moment of greatest significance to the city council.
Eberhard had completed his procession, first mass, and had received
his gifts. Now, when magistrates refused to ring the storm-bell,
Eberhard departed and ordered the city council to come to
Dillingen, a city in which he was the master, to receive his oath. In
ritual terms the magistrates had been faithful in the entry cycle and

---

[123] Scholars have been debating the role of spectacles and processions. Do they
encourage social cohesion, suppress dissidence, or express hostility? Charles
Phythian-Adams and Mervyn James have argued for late-medieval ceremony as a
balm for fractured, socially divisive communities, a model that echoes Durkheim's
view of religion as a source of social cohesion. They emphasize the cohesive and
unifying function of public ritual; Phythian-Adams, "Ceremony and the Citizen: The
Communal Year at Coventry, 1450-1550," in *The English Medieval Town. A Reader in
English Urban History 1200-1540* (London: Longman, 1990), pp. 238-264; and James,
"Ritual, Drama and Social Body in the Late Medieval English Town," pp. 19-20.

However, Benjamin McRee has shown how guild processions in English towns of
the Middle Ages actually had the opposite effect, putting added pressure on the fault-
lines of civic society. He points out the inherent risk in all ritual and spectacle:
"Ceremony did not have to produce violence to discourage social unity ... Even
when riots did not result, public ceremony could be insidiously divisive, drawing
attention to the lines separating different social groups within the community rather
than working to erase those lines;" See "Unity or Division? The Social Meaning of
Guild Ceremonies in Urban Communities," in *City and Spectacle in Medieval Europe*, p.
189.

For a well-rounded survey of recent anthropology and sociology on ritual and
social cohesion as well as the place of Durkheim and his followers, see Steven Lukes,
Essays in Social Theory (Ipswich: Gregg Revivals, 1977), pp. 52-73.

now found themselves jilted at the altar. In both cases the insult worked and the show continued. John of Werdenberg arrived with a smaller escort. The city council serenaded Bishop Eberhard with a tolling bell and finally received his oath in the proper civic setting.

In many ways episcopal entries functioned subliminally; continuity and change in the scheduled and traditional program proclaimed the subversive agenda of a bishop or city, undermining the previous agreements between the parties.[124] Yet magistrates allowed and indeed participated in the episcopal entries. And bishops were willing to risk insult and undergo negotiation to make a grand entrance and complete installation in the old cathedral.

The episcopal entry was a rite of passage, a liminal period in which city and bishop recreated a religious and political community. In fact, entry was one of the last liminal stages for a new bishop. Unlike cities with their annual rhythm of elections to public office, bishops served for life, if good health, political favor, moral reputation, and doctrinal rectitude permitted. But at the death of a bishop the entire diocese and episcopal administration would be thrown into uncertainty, until clerical factions, papal interests, imperial designs, and the deliberations of the cathedral chapter produced a new bishop. Then papal confirmation, the granting of imperial regalia, the submission of diocesan clergy, and the homage of the bishop's feudal subjects all had to follow. Any one of the parties to an election could seriously jeopardize the process, leaving the church without a bishop or with two rival candidates. If they allowed episcopal entry before an election was resolved, city magistrates risked becoming embroiled in ecclesiastical, regional, or national disputes that were not in the direct political interests of the city.[125]

When a candidate finally had received at least the promise of confirmation from all authorities, the city council usually appeared willing to allow or in part to host the last phase of episcopal elevation. Entry ceremonies not only culminated in ecclesiastical rites—consecration, first mass, episcopal feast—they also served to bring

---

[124] Thomas A. Brady, Jr. offers the title "Rites of autonomy, Rites of dependence" as a way of describing the two dimensions of episcopal entry; in *Religion and Culture in the Renaissance and Reformation*, pp. 9-23.

[125] Bishop Otto of Sonnenberg (1474-91) did not receive consecration or celebrate his first mass in Constance until his disputed election was resolved in 1480 with the death of rival candidate Lewis of Freiberg, however, he did issue his *Verschreibung* for the city of Constance in December of 1475; *REC* 5:14585; Ruppert, p. 451; StAK A II 30, 64r-68r; GLA 5: 7206.

city and bishop into a workable relationship, to display the rights prized and protected by each, to integrate the bishop-elect into the life of the city, and the city into the life of the church.[126] The bishop-elect completed his liminal journey in both the streets of the city and the sanctuary of the cathedral, the civic and the ecclesiastical arena. Through ritual he entered his episcopal city, received his sacred power, and negotiated his standing with the city.

In both Constance and Augsburg bishop and city council negotiated in a liminal space outside the city walls, an ambiguous place where the details of entry could be hammered out.[127] The remaining rites of entry reconstituted the commune anew, a community that had certain freedoms and yet remained in some sense the bishop's city. The familial ties, political alliances, ecclesiastical policies, and civic agenda of the bishop-elect were brought into a carefully defined relationship with a city and city council whose ambitions were likewise variable. The ritual of entry provided a forum in which this relationship could be articulated, defined, and tested. If it functioned according to plan, bishop and city would have a workable and perhaps even fruitful cohabitation. This relationship might then result in

---

[126] Victor Turner has used the idea of liminality in relation to individual phases or rites of passage—girls in ceremonies of puberty and womanhood, clansmen ritually transformed into chieftains. The bishop-elect is indeed such a liminal individual; until the entry and anointing process is complete, he waits in a no-man's land between his noble status or his lower clerical standing and the exalted ranks of apostolic succession. Turner describes this ambiguous state: "Liminal entities are neither here nor there; they are betwixt and between the positions assigned and arrayed by law, custom, convention, and ceremonial;" Victor Turner, *The Ritual Process. Structure and Anti-Structure* (Chicago: Aldine Publishing Company, 1969), p. 95.

Turner also notes the dangers of the liminal state, a condition the church and city feared; a candidate awaiting confirmation of his episcopal office could hold dangerous alliances and promote policies not yet circumscribed by the church and the city. The Great Schism proved devastating on these grounds, leaving dioceses and candidates in a constant state of liminality between legitimate and illegitimate, between heaven and hell. Turner writes: "In this interim of 'liminality', the possibility exists of standing aside not only from one's own social position but from all social positions and of formulating a potentially unlimited series of alternative arrangements. That this danger is recognized in all tolerably orderly societies is made evident by the proliferation of taboos that hedge in and constrain those on whom the normative structure loses its grip during such potent transitions as extended initiation rites in 'tribal' societies ..." *Dramas, Fields, and Metaphors*, pp. 13-14. The city council employed such a taboo when it denied entry to a contested episcopal candidate.

[127] Teofilo Ruiz employs this geographical use of liminality: "Ceremonial entries into the city—royal, ecclesiastical, or noble—always required the bringing out of urban symbols of power or those of the constable's adjoining countryside, to that liminal space ... outside the city's gates;" "Elite and Popular Culture in Late-Fifteenth-Century Castilian Festivals," in *City and Spectacle in Medieval Europe*, p. 304.

public peace, civic prosperity, ecclesiastical harmony, and divine
favor. It would reconstitute the underpinnings of an urban community deemed both free and episcopal. The rituals of entry allowed the
bishop and city to steer a careful course through a potentially haz-
ardous, liminal phase in order to recreate a sacred, ritual community.

4. *The Bishop's Sacred City: Rituals of Life and Death*

The *adventus* of the bishop mirrors the entries of many secular poten-
tates. Like bishops they arrived with great fanfare and spectacle, demanded civic allegiance, and recognized rights and privileges. One
crucial difference separates the bishop from most of his temporal
colleagues. In a symbolic and in some cases a literal sense, the bishop
moved-in. He did not always depart at the end of the festivities. He
might become a permanent resident or an aggressive and meddle-
some neighbor as well as a spontaneous visitor to the city. His clergy
and institutions continued to embody his 'real presence' even when
absent. Ceremonies in the church and in the city continued to demand his attendance. In Constance episcopal ceremony continued to
spill out into the streets long after the last parades and feasts of the
entry-cycle had ceased. As they processed through the city, the bishops of Constance maintained their claim to her urban spaces.
    As ritual served to manifest the bishop's claims, so the varied con-
texts of ritual revealed a great deal about episcopal intent and power.
On the eve of the Protestant Reformation the bishops of Augsburg
were shifting their ceremonial base from Augsburg to Dillingen and
to the diocese at large. However, they did continue to maintain a
lively presence in Augsburg through ritual activity; they too could
claim Augsburg as their own city.
    The Cathedral of our Dear Lady was the center of episcopal ritual
in Constance. Under her vaults the bishop-elect celebrated his first
mass and took his place at the high altar as bishop of the church. But
the significance of the cathedral extended beyond the ceremonies of
consecration, entrance, and installation. This church was an epi-
center of clerical ceremony, and the waves of episcopal expression
reached out to the streets and alleys beyond. When the bishops of
Constance led processions, held diocesan synods, and pronounced
public absolution, the city was again an episcopal stage. When a
bishop died, his funeral parade was remarkably similar to his first

entry. These events continued to display how the bishop remained lord of much, if not all, public and ecclesiastical ritual in the city.[128]

When the clergy and citizenry processed through the streets of Constance, the bishop was at best a part-time participant. But the *corpus Christi* procession of 1379 did pass through all the *spaces* associated with the bishop and his ritual; it began and ended in the cathedral while moving toward Petershausen in the north and through Kreuzlingen immediately south of Constance.[129] By the mid-fifteenth century the guilds of Constance played a critical role in the *corpus Christi* procession. In fact, the city council displayed its reservations about this observance by instituting a civic counter-procession (*der statt crutzgang*) on the Monday after *corpus Christi*.[130] Even for the clergy procession could demonstrate corporate unity or embarrassing division. In 1425 a dispute between Bishop Otto of Hachberg (1410-34) and the cathedral chapter became ominously public. On the feast-day of *corpus Christi* two clerical processions marched into the streets in fierce competition. Bishop Otto and his supporters processed to the church of St. Stephan, while the chapter paraded to the cathedral. Perhaps the thought of two competing ceremonies, each featuring its own piece of the body of Christ, moved the city council to ban lay participation. The Dominicans likewise stayed home. Shortly thereafter magistrates sponsored a procession that included

---

[128] The complete annual ritual cycle—sacred and secular—is yet to be studied comprehensively in Constance and Augsburg. Therefore, it is not possible to measure the precise importance of episcopal ritual over against either the activity of other clerical foundations or the secular calendar of events such as guild processions and government ceremonies (elections, civic oaths). It is clear that the bishop continued to have his own ritual agenda in the city; he incorporated the urban populace as participants or observers of his ceremonial life.

Several works include the main liturgical rites of the cathedral and diocese; they provide an excellent starting point for consideration of ritual in church and city; for Constance see *Die Konstanzer Ritualientexte in ihrer Entwicklung von 1482-1721*, ed. P. A. Dold, (Münster: Aschendorff, 1923), especially pages 95-169; and P. Zinzmaier, "Eine unbekannte Quelle zur Geschichte der mittelalterlichen Liturgie im Konstanzer Münster," *ZGO* 104 (1956), pp. 52-104. For Augsburg see F. A. Hoeynck, *Geschichte der kirchlichen Liturgie des Bisthums Augsburg* (Literatur Institut von Dr. M. Huttler, Michael Seitz, 1889), pp. 153-289, 353-437; on the ritual of the laity in Augsburg, see Immanuel Schairer, *Das Religiöse Volksleben am Ausgang des Mittelalters nach Augsburger Quellen* (Leipzig: B. G.Teubner, 1913), pp. 111-135.

[129] *KC*, p. 323. *Corpus Christi* days and emergency processions of the clergy did not always include the bishop; see Ruppert, pp. 193, 205, 220-221.

[130] Maurer II, pp. 142-143.

the clergy and the laity.[131] In this single record of episcopal participation in the *corpus Christi* procession the city council appears far
more capable of initiating ritual to encourage civic solidarity and
honor the body of Christ. At least for the moment even the bishop's
unflattering ritual had taken the civic stage.

Moreover, processions were part and parcel of the ultimate demonstration of episcopal rule—the diocesan synod. Until the Protestant Reformation the city that hosted the pivotal ecumenical Council
of Constance (1414-18) was also perennially the venue for the bishop's diocesan synods. While most of the festivities and meetings were
held in church sanctuaries—the cathedral and St Stephan's—city
streets still swelled with a wave of clerical visitors. In 1463 over six
hundred came to Constance. On average about 390 priests, monks,
and diocesan officials attended each synod in the fifteenth century.[132]
During a synod the bishop routinely led a short procession from the
cathedral to St Stephen's or moved further into the city by parading
to the church of St Paul.[133] At least eight times during the fifteenth
century a bishop gathered representatives of his diocese inside the
walls of Constance.[134] On those days the clerics were public in their
arrivals and in their processions. The city of Constance was the capital of the diocese and the city of the bishop. Through the ceremonies
of synod the bishop reinforced his oversight of civic churches and
invaded the city's streets with hundreds of clerics marching behind
his shepherd's crozier.

Episcopal rites not only attracted the clergy but also the laity to
Constance. On Maunday Thursday the bishop offered forgiveness to
those in his diocese who had committed sins beyond the capability of
a parish priest to absolve (e.g. murder, arson, incest). After the peni-

---

[131] "Diser zit war grosser zwitracht ze Costantz zwüschent dem bischoff und dem
capittel ... Etliche priester und clöster warend uff des bischoffs siten, die andern, die
adorierten dem capittel. Und uff unseres herren Fronlichmastag, so man solt umb
die stat gon, da waren zwen crutzgang. Der bischoff mit den seinen gieng uff sant
Steffanskirchen uff, und das capittel uff dem münster. Der rat bot, das die burger mit
kainem tail solten gon; gliche gstalt thaten ouch die prediger münch die beliben
ouch dehaimet. Am Montag nach sant Ulrichs tag [July 4], da hat der rath seinen
crützgang, darmit alle gaistliche und weltliche giengent;" Schulthaiß-*Chronik*, pp.
55:31—56:2.
[132] The number is based on records for five synods (1435, 1441, 1463, 1467,
1481); see *KC*, pp. 338, 342, 347; Schulthaiß-*Chronik*, pp. 69-72.
[133] *KC*, pp. 342, 347; Ruppert pp. 185-186, 213, 252; Schulthaiß-*Chronik*, pp. 57,
68, 71-72.
[134] Konstantin Maier, "Die Diözesansynode," *BK* I, pp. 92-94.

tent throng had arrived at the cathedral with burning candles, the bishop led them inside. They knelt in the nave of the church and waited there until the bishop pronounced their absolution.[135] This unholy band could rival the invading masses of an episcopal entry or diocesan synod; in 1427 a crowd of 1,300 sinners made their way to the cathedral, in 1442, 600 men and 632 women. The sudden influx of the penitent seeking the bishop's favor could halt traffic in the city.[136]

Constance served as a gathering point for saints and sinners, emphasizing the bishop's role as leader of synodal reform and as fount of special dispensations. But the bishop also polished his regional and national political profile in the city. In 1444 Bishop Henry of Hewen hosted a four week conference for representatives of the Swiss Confederacy.[137] Imperial visits affirmed the bishop's presence in the city. In December of 1430 Emperor Sigismund (1410-37) arrived in Constance and made his way to his lodgings in the episcopal palace. The bishop's court was the traditional residence of the king when he visited the city.[138] Not only did Emperor Frederick III arrive at the bishop's palace in Gottlieben and receive the city council there in 1442 but also his processional entry into Constance culminated at the bishop's cathedral.[139]

Even as Constance served as the living capital of the diocese, it was a *necropolis* for episcopal remains. Before his burial in the cathedral the deceased bishop had one last opportunity to seize the stage of the city. His departure from earthly life might mirror his first formal entry into the city.[140] Details of communal 'last rites' for three bishops of Constance survive in chronicle sources; two offer significant detail.[141] The case of Nicholas of Frauenfeld offers a surprising

---

[135] Ruppert, p. 154.

[136] Schulthaiß-*Chronik*, pp. 55, 65; Karl Brehm, "Zur Geschichte der Konstanzer Diözesansynoden während des Mittelalters," *DAS* 22 (1904), p. 22, II.

[137] Ruppert, p. 280.

[138] Ruppert, pp. 170-171. Helmut Maurer, "*Palatium Constantiense*," in *Adel und Kirche*, pp. 374-388.

[139] Ruppert, pp. 222-223.

[140] For an excellent discussion of royal funerals, see Ralph E. Giesey, *The Royal Funeral Ceremony in Renaissance France* (Geneva: Librairie E. Droz, 1960); c.f. Gerard Nijsten, "The Duke and His Towns," in *City and Spectacle in Medieval Europe*, pp. 258-260.

[141] For a concise example of an episcopal funeral, see the description of the death and burial of Bishop Burckhard of Hewen (1387-98). His case is intriguing since he died during the uncertain years of the Great Schism (1378-1415). Apparently the

ritual and dramatic cast in which the clergy and nobility were pushed
to the edge of the stage. Bishop Nicholas spent his last years in what
must have seemed true apostolic service. From 1344-47 he saw to the
needs of the poor near his residence of Castel by rooting out corruption in his administration. He canceled all usurious charges and gave
alms to the poor, including fruit and flour desperately needed by his
starving subjects.[142] Even in his last days and hours he responded to
the poverty in his community. He died at 9:00 a.m. on July 25, 1347
just as his servants were handing out alms.[143] When his body was
carried out of the church, the poor thronged around his bier, crying
and shouting "O dear and true father, who will feed us and guide us,
who since you have left us? We will die of hunger, for who will care
for us?"[144] As the procession continued toward Constance rich and
poor pressed in voicing their sentiments and grief without ceasing.
Once in Constance men and women continued to crowd around his
bier; even those who did not admire him in life now mourned him in

cult of episcopal burial was not interrupted, at least in his case; Schulthaiß-*Chronik*, p.
52.

[142] "Das gelt alles hieß er geben umb frucht und mel ... Und darnach und vor
dem zit sines sterbens bedurft er nimmer kain wuchergelt zu überkommend ..."
Ruppert, p. 47, 17-19

[143] These acts of kindness even transcend what was expected at the death of the
wealthy. Georges Duby has eloquently described how the English Earl, William
Marshall (d. 1219), dispersed all of his worldly goods, "whose weight risks dragging
his soul down to hell." When Marshall's body was finally brought to London for
burial, the poor thronged around his procession, similar to the funeral march of
Bishop Nicholas; William made provision for at least one hundred of the poor, who
after his death would be invited to the funeral feast and lavishly wined and dined.

Duby contrasts the funeral of Marshall to that of King Henry II (1154-89) of
England, who died in utter poverty, shorn of mourners and alms for the poor:
"Henry had nothing left but his underclothes and his breeches. A few men of great
loyalty, and William was among them, hurried to him, ashamed of what they saw,
and flung their cloaks over the corpse. Which was buried then, and properly of
course. But the next day the legions of poor men were waiting at the bridge of
Chinon, sure of one thing; they would eat. And there was nothing in the king's
house, not even a crust of bread. The earl asked whether there were any moneys: no
trace of such a thing. And on the bridge they could hear the poor men's anger
swelling, shouting against the scandal, and threatening to destroy everything. The
poor had reason to protest. Shame to the dead king who did not feed his people;"
William Marshall. The Flower of Chivalry (New York: Pantheon Books, 1985 [1984]), pp.
17, 24.

[144] "O lieber und getruwer vatter, wer spiset und füret uns nun fürohin oder wem
verlaußest du uns; nun werden wir hungers verderben füro nit nyemand habend, der
uns uffenthalte?" Ruppert, pp. 47:34-48:2.

death. They followed to the cathedral where he was buried in the same grave as Bishop Henry of Klingenberg (1293-1306).[145]

While the procession of Nicholas of Frauenfeld captured the singular devotion of the common folk, the burial parade of Bishop Frederick of Zollern (1434-36) was clearly in the hands of the clergy and city council. After his death in nearby Gottlieben a prestigious procession—the entire clergy of Constance, students and canons bearing candles, the small and large city council, patricians and burghers dressed in black—met his bier as it arrived at the Giltlinger gate. Four chaplains took up the burden of his body and a civic escort—three patrician and three burgher—walked alongside.[146] The parade of mourners wound its way to St. Stephan's and thereafter to the cathedral: "... there the bishop lay in state for ten or twelve days; it was a grievous sight as all Christian people paid their respects."[147] Magistrates decreed that the small and large council should make their way to all the altars of the church to mourn the dead bishop; they sent five patrician and five burgher women to hold vigil on the mourner's bench (clagsthul). Even as the bishop was finally buried the symmetry of social classes was maintained; five patrician priests and five burgher priests carried his body to the grave.[148] St. Stephan's and Our Dear Lady hosted funeral masses; there the magistrates and the cathedral canons gave alms; citizens and clergy cooperated in Bishop Frederick's honorable burial.[149]

While this study has focused on the rights, privileges, ceremonies, and conflicts that demarcated episcopal and civic power, burial of a bishop could also bind city and country, rich and poor, patrician and burgher, clergy and laity. The funeral cycles of Nicholas of Frauenfeld and Frederick of Zollern attracted the participation of the people of Constance. In the first case the generosity of Nicholas ensured a passionate response from the laity, especially the common folk who had survived on his largess. His procession seems uncontrolled as the crowd presses in and threatens to disrupt an orderly procession.[150]

In the case of Frederick of Zollern the parallels between entry and

---

[145] Ruppert, p. 48.
[146] Schulthaiß-*Chronik*, p. 58.
[147] "er ... lag by zehen oder zwölf tagen und was ain elende gestalt, daran all cristenlut billich sähent;" Ruppert, p. 189:6-7.
[148] Ruppert, pp. 188-189.
[149] "Also ward er mit grossen ehren bestattet;" Schulthaiß-*Chronik*, p. 58: 30.
[150] The scene is reminiscent of early church episcopal elections when the congre-

funeral procession are even more striking.[151] The clergy and city
council met the bishop's entourage at the gate. Though magistrates
did not carry a baldachin, they did flank the bier as it progressed
through the city. Moreover, the city council participated in the funeral ritual, sending a ratio representative of the citizenry to church
altars and vigils. Compared to the entry of bishops their participation
in the funeral was far more prominent. Just as they gave gifts to a
new bishop, so they honored Frederick with their alms. In the case of
Burckhard of Hewen (1387-98) the clergy, city council, and other
distinguished guests enjoyed a sumptuous meal at the bishop's palace
before the burial.[152] As they had dined at his episcopal birth, so they
did again at his death.

The funeral of a bishop reveals a great deal about the power of
ritual and the city of Constance. The burial procession was a grave
public matter; it was not confined to the clergy. The death of a
bishop could stir the passions of all social classes; in these two accounts neither the poor nor the honorable are excluded. This liminal
moment reveals, at least in these cases, the degree to which a bishop
of Constance might actually be prized and cherished by rural folk
and urbanites alike. Furthermore, the bishop once again seized the
stage in Constance—in his funeral procession and his burial. These
ceremonies reveal how the bishop through ritual exercised his authority in the streets and churches of his city. Perhaps they set the
stage for the rituals to come; the entry cycle of a new bishop. The
city council also played a central role at every stage. Here there is
once again cooperation in which magistrates dominated some elements of the ritual and at the same time were absorbed into episcopal rites; they led the procession; they were prominent participants at
the altars, vigils, and burial; but they processed behind and served a
bishop who made claims on civic space even in death. Finally, in
burial the bishop remained a living member of the episcopal cult,
another colleague in the community of dead bishops. In life he ruled

---

gation charismatically chose and then physically seized the new bishop; Augustine of
Hippo (d. 430) was coerced to become bishop in such a fashion; Peter Brown, *Augustine of Hippo* (Berkeley: University of California Press, 1967), pp. 138-139.

[151] Although there is insufficient evidence, it is interesting to ponder if the city
council took the initiative to control the excesses of episcopal funerals and popular
response, particularly after the public and disorderly rites of Nicholas of Frauenfeld.

[152] Schulthaiß-*Chronik*, p. 52.

his diocese from the city of Constance. In death he added his remains to the sacred bones of the cathedral.

*   *   *

The bishops of Augsburg likewise maintained their ritual prowess
after formal entry. In fact, as the town of Dillingen became increasingly central to the episcopal cult, they protected certain rituals that
preserved their tie to the first episcopal city. Augsburg continued to
be the symbolic and sacred capital of the diocese. The churches of
the city sheltered episcopal graves and the relics of prized saints.
While they held tenaciously to the symbolic, sacred, political, and
economic importance of Augsburg, the bishops increasingly shifted
administration and celebration to Dillingen. Two anonymous episcopal sources place a bishop's critical Augsburg entry in the wider context of diocesan politics and operations at Dillingen.[153] Both documents, possibly by the same anonymous clerical author, are a mix-
ture of chronicle and register. Certain events receive prosaic description, while other information is recorded in sixteenth-century spread-
sheets—listings of guests, goods, prices, and schedules. Each source
records a vulnerable and liminal stage in the life of a diocese, the
death and burial of one bishop, the election, consecration, itinerary,
and entry of a new bishop. The first document records the death of
Bishop Frederick II of Zollern (1486-1505) and the succession of
Henry IV of Lichtenau (1505-17). The second chronicles the passing
of Henry and the early days of Christopher of Stadion (1517-43). In
both documents the diocese and Dillingen dominate the horizon, but
all roads still lead to Augsburg for a deceased bishop and a bishop
about to be made.

On March 8, 1505 Bishop Frederick of Zollern received last rites
in Dillingen. He died shortly afterward at eight in the evening. The
episcopal household in Dillingen worked through the night and by
morning Frederick's body was ready for immediate transfer to
Augsburg for a fitting burial. Prior to his departure, the clergy in
Dillingen held a memorial service.[154]

On April 1 the cathedral canons elected Henry of Lichtenau as

---

[153] StaatsA, MBL 221: 42r-73v; MBL 222: 3r-42v.
[154] StaatsA, MBL 221: 42r, 5—42v, 21; Zoepfl II, p. 534.

their new bishop, an Augsburg canon who had been present with bishop Frederick in his final moments.[155] Shortly after his election Henry appears to have made a swift trip to Augsburg. Apparently he skipped the details of a grand formal entry and went directly to the cathedral and episcopal palace for his installation.[156] From this point on Henry would turn his efforts decidedly toward Dillingen and the diocese.

On April 4 Bishop Henry returned to Dillingen in order to complete his episcopal initiation and to take up rule of his church territory. Rites once celebrated only in Augsburg now took place here. Henry received the oaths of his diocesan staff and clergy, including the cathedral canons of Augsburg. Moreover, he was consecrated, not in the Cathedral of St. Mary in Augsburg but rather in the parish church of Dillingen. A sumptuous meal followed. Augsburg had once been the site of the bishop's festive dining. Though early fifteenth century sources are incomplete regarding the site of consecration, beginning with John of Werdenberg (1469-86), bishops regularly received consecration in Dillingen.[157] Now subjects and suffragans, colleagues and canons made the journey to a new episcopal town, a commune completely beholden to the bishop. Furthermore, on July 13, 1506 Bishop Henry held his first diocesan synod in Dillingen.[158] Since the later half of the fifteenth-century Dillingen had provided the usual backdrop for diocesan synods.[159] Here ritual serves as a telling marker of the *Episcopus exclusus* as the bishops of Augsburg

---

[155] "So haben die nachgemelten Thumbherrn auff obgemelten tag vnangesehen gedacht furschrifften vnnd practick mit einhelliger wal zu Bischof erwelt herrn Heinrichen von Lechtnaw;" StaatsA, MBL 221: r, 9-12.

[156] "In dem ain vnd sechtzigisten Iar seins Alters gewest vnnd ist sein gnad...gen Augspurg gezogen was nachdem er auff den Altar gesetzt ward in die pfallutz gefurt vnnd ist Im als einem fursten vnnd Bischoff zum morgenmal gedient worden;" StaatsA, MBL 221: 43r, 15-20. His reception as a prince does not seem to have included his public procession into the city or his meeting with the city council. No other sources shed light on this first trip as bishop to Augsburg. The chronicler records all other stages of his first months, including details about gifts, guests, and menus.

[157] Zoepfl I, pp. 455-456, 489, 542; Zoepfl II, p. 10.

[158] StaatsA 221, pp. 44v-45v; 53v-65r; 69r.

[159] Synods on record were held in Augsburg in 1026, 1135, 1180, 1273, c. 1321, c. 1434-1437, and 1453; in Dillingen in 1469, 1486, 1506, 1517; Zoepfl I, p. 579. It is likely that the more stable venue in Dillingen allowed bishops to call and control synods more regularly than in Augsburg.

shifted major elements of the entry cycle from their old episcopal city to a new venue.

While Henry of Lichtenau stayed only a day or so in his old cathedral city, he spent nearly the entire month of June 1507, touring his *Hochstift* and diocese, an arduous journey for a bishop sixty-one years of age.[160] His itinerary included twenty villages, towns, and cloisters wherein he received homage and hospitality.[161] On June 2 the bishop-elect departed from Dillingen with an escort of twenty-five, including members of his household and the cathedral chapter of Augsburg.[162] In each community, the bishop's behavior echoed a traditional episcopal entry into Augsburg. Upon his arrival Henry was typically guided to the ritual center of the commune or cloister, usually a town hall, parish church, cloister, castle, or dance hall (*Tanzhaus*). At that point the bishop assumed his role as lord; he confirmed imperial rights, and local customs; he negotiated with disgruntled subjects; he received oaths of homage from peasants, servants, episcopal officials, and magistrates. The ceremony was sealed with an exchange of gifts. The bishop usually received some money, a decorated vessel, or an occasional oxen or two, while he acknowl-

---

[160] The sources of Constance and Augsburg provide a distinct contrast. There is no record in such detail in the later Middle Ages regarding the itinerary of the bishop of Constance as he receives homage and oaths throughout his diocese. Perhaps his *Hochstift* was too diffuse to be easily reconnoitered in one month let alone one year. Many of the villages and towns were expected to send representatives to the episcopal court in Constance or some other residence of the bishop (e.g Gottlieben, Meersburg, Markdorf, Bischofszell). On the other hand, the bishop of Augsburg was able to travel his *Hochstift* in one month and demand recognition from communes particularly beholden to him. The records of the itinerary of Henry of Lichtenau and Christopher of Stadion provide a vivid picture of this journey.

Unlike Constance, neither the bishop nor city of Augsburg appears to have maintained a set of the oaths sworn during episcopal entry. It is possible that the documents simply have not survived. But it is likely that this ceremony did not match the *Verschreibung* in Constance in political importance. Unlike the bishops of Augsburg, the bishops of Constance resided in or very near to the city (Gottlieben, Meersburg). When Henry of Lichtenau came to Augsburg for his installation there is no mention of a ceremony at city hall. Perhaps this practice became less and less important after the reign of Bishop John of Werdenberg (1469-86).

[161] StaatsA, MBL 221: 44v, 1—53v, 13. In regard to royal journeys allowing a king to receive homage throughout his realm, Clifford Geertz suggests that, "... royal progresses ... locate the society's center and affirm its connection with transcendent things by stamping a territory with ritual signs of dominance. When kings journey around the countryside, making appearances, attending fêtes, conferring honors, exchanging gifts, or defying rivals, they mark it, like some wolf or tiger spreading his scent through his territory ..." "Centers, Kings, and Charisma," in *Rites of Power*, p. 16.

[162] StaatsA, MBL 221: 46r, 7-8.

edged his dependents with a small monetary gift (*Trinkgeld*). In ten cases Henry's temporary lodging served as a residence; there he received representatives and subjects from surrounding lands.[163]

But the response varied from commune to commune, from elaborate or surprising greetings to open hostility. Both Füssen, the third episcopal residence of the diocese, and Ottobeuron planned to receive their new bishop with a formal procession. The ceremony in Füssen was rained out and festivities were moved to the bishop's castle. In Ottobeuron the abbey displayed a thorough grasp of honorable entry: the abbot of Ottobeuron rode out to meet the bishop; as he drew near to the town, a procession in prayer and song came out to meet him with the bells of the city ringing out a hearty welcome.[164] In Günzburg representatives of the Jewish community offered the bishop a gift but he turned them down.[165] In Buchloe and in Schönegg farmers demanded that their grievances be heard before submitting to the bishop.[166]

For the new bishop of Augsburg the oaths and alliances of the diocese took precedence over the traditional ceremonies of the city of Augsburg. Furthermore, the processions, oaths, and the hostilities of the smaller communes and peasants serve to underscore a certain ritual continuity between the large old episcopal city and the rural diocese.[167] The magistrates and episcopal officials of small communities knew how to use processions and bells to display their enthusiasm for a new bishop. Likewise they could make ritual work in their favor by negotiating before swearing homage or by extending an empty invitation. The mayor of Memmingen came to Ottobeuron to welcome the bishop; he invited the bishop to his city but offered no gift, the chronicler notes.[168] When the bishop completed his arduous trek around the diocese, he did not return to St. Ulrich's or to the Cathedral of St. Mary in Augsburg. Rather, he arrived in his second city of

---

[163] StaatsA, MBL 221: 44v, 1—53r, 13.

[164] StaatsA, MBL 221: 52r, 30—52v, 7.

[165] "Es wolten auch die Iuden daselbs sein gnaden ein selbern becher geschenckt haben den aber sein gnad nit annemen wolt;" StaatsA, MBL 221: 46v, 26-28.

[166] StaatsA, MBL 221: 49r, 27—50r, 5.

[167] Recent research has focused on either the history of cities or the development of the countryside in Early Modern Germany. The contrast between the two has been a hallmark of this research. It will be up to a future generation to knit city and country back together, to show points of contact and interpenetration. Such background would also serve to elucidate the ties between episcopal city and diocese.

[168] StaatsA, MBL 221: 52v, 7-12.

Dillingen. There, with the homage of his *Hochstift* secure, Henry received his consecration. This time the first formal procession of the bishop of Augsburg was oriented around communes in the countryside and diocesan lands. Henry of Lichtenau became a bishop far from the cathedral of his ancestors.

Twelve years later Cathedral Dean (*Dekan*) Christopher of Stadion (1517-43) followed in the footsteps of his predecessor. Even as Bishop Henry's health was failing, Christopher had already been elected as *coadjutor*. On April 12, 1517 Henry of Lichtenau died in Dillingen.[169] About one month later Bishop-elect Christopher of Stadion began his journey through the diocese of Augsburg. He followed a course similar to his predecessor with the same ritual negotiations and confirmations.[170] As before, Füssen welcomed her bishop with a procession as did the abbey of Ottobeuron.[171] After finishing his *pilgrimage* Christopher returned to Dillingen where in July 1517 the Bishop of Eichstätt consecrated him as bishop of Augsburg. In September Christopher opened a diocesan synod once again in Dillingen.[172] Throughout his reign he would make this town the actual capital of his diocese.

Yet Christopher did not ignore the traditional venue in Augsburg. Rather, he continued to appear in his episcopal city under the guise of the empire and in the reverence owed to deceased bishops. In fact, Christopher made his first appearance in July of 1517, one day after his consecration. Surviving sources do not report a formal entry in the tradition of John of Werdenberg.[173] But Christopher did arrive to claim a princely pedigree. Emperor Maximilian himself received the new bishop of Augsburg in the episcopal palace; he conferred upon Christopher the regalia of the empire and the right to enforce high justice (*Blutbann*); he confirmed the rights and privileges of the

---

[169] After a memorial service in the parish church the clergy divided the remains of Bishop Henry; his entrails were kept in Dillingen and were buried in the chapel of the bishop's palace. His corpse was transferred to Augsburg, where it was interred on April 15; Zoepfl I, p. 563. This unusual separation of Henry's remains may well have been a matter of necessity; his aged and wasted condition may have precluded the delivery of a complete corpse to Augsburg. Yet the clergy of Dillingen ensured that their piece of Henry received a worthy resting place, suggesting again the importance attached to the graves of bishops.

[170] StaatsA, MBL 222: 3r, 1—14v, 18; 19v, 10—29v, 22.

[171] StaatsA, MBL 222: 10v, 20—11v, 13; 13r, 3-9.

[172] StaatsA, MBL 222: 30v, 1—32r, 6; Zoepfl II, pp. 1-13.

[173] See below, pp. 140-145.

diocese.[174] In one ceremony Christopher received his princely pedigree and territorial powers without negotiating with or even including the city council of Augsburg; in this free and imperial city Maximilian had bestowed the scepter and sword of imperial lordship.[175]

Thirteen years later the empire would again provide a stage on which Christopher displayed his princely power in his own episcopal city. In 1530 the imperial diet met in Augsburg. By this time the bishop was in the fight of his life with a city council tending increasingly to support Protestant movements. At the diet Philip Melanchthon unveiled the statement of faith that would define Lutheranism over against the medieval church. The *Augsburg Confession* would rival the venerable Bishops of Augsburg.

While the estates of the empire gathered in Augsburg, Christopher of Stadion took advantage of his dual role as prince of the empire and shepherd of the church. He rode into Augsburg on June 9, 1530 without contacting city hall; he was, after all, one among many princes, bishops, abbots, counts, and civic representatives of the empire.[176] On June 15 the emperor arrived. The Archbishop of Mainz began the diet with a speech welcoming the emperor.[177] After further opening exercises the delegates assembled near city hall for a procession to the cathedral. Here Christopher of Stadion took up his role as bishop of Augsburg and as a high priest of the German empire. All the clergy of the city had gathered in the Cathedral of St. Mary; they dressed in their finest vestments, gathered the relics of the city, and marched to the Perlach Tower near city hall. In route they met Christopher, his consecrating bishop, and the abbot of St. Ulrich's. When the clerical procession reached the emperor, he rode

---

[174] StaatsA, MBL 222: 32r, 7—32v, 10; Zoepfl II, p. 11.

[175] "... des zepters vnnd schwerts [die] Regalien;" StaatsA, MBL 222: 32r, 27.

[176] Clemens Sender, CDS 23 [4], p. 260: 9-12. When an emperor entered Augsburg, either on a royal visit or as part of an imperial diet, the bishop of Augsburg often played a public role. In 1418 the contested candidate for the episcopate in Augsburg, Frederick of Grafeneck, led the welcoming party out to greet Emperor Sigismund "als ain Bischof in der process;" Burkard Zink, CDS 5 [2], p. 63: 11-12. In the mid-1430s Bishop Peter of Schaumberg (1424-69) arrived in the city as part of the entourage of Emperor Sigismund; although Peter was also bishop he received the welcome of his own clergy and citizenry as a representative of the empire; Burkard Zink, CDS 5 [2], p. 157: 8-14. Bishop Frederick of Zollern (1486-1505) made a similar entry with Emperor Maximilian in 1504; CDS Sender, 23 [4], pp. 103: 9—104: 4.

[177] Clemens Sender, CDS 23 [4], 262: 24—263: 18.

in the shade of the civic banner, a baldachin carried by six cathedral canons and moved on to the cathedral.[178] The delegates of the diet followed in his train. During the first segment of the service Emperor Charles V (1519-56) took center stage. As he knelt in the middle of the sanctuary with a green branch in his hand, his impressive entourage formed up around and behind him. Then all eyes moved to the front of the cathedral. There stood Christopher of Stadion along with his consecrating bishop and the abbot of St. Ulrich's. After a brief prayer (*versickel*) the bishop of Augsburg sang the mass.[179] Furthermore, on *corpus Christi* day (June 16) Bishop Christopher again led the festive mass in the cathedral and then took his place near the front of this national procession honoring the body of Christ.[180] For a few hours the ancient church of the bishops of Augsburg had become the cathedral of the 'German Nation' and the episcopal city of the diocese was the capital of the empire. Although he resided and ruled for the most part from Dillingen, Christopher used the rituals of empire to process through the streets of the original cathedral city. In 1530 he led emperor and princes, city council and citizenry.[181]

Imperial ritual provided a critical framework for the bishops of Augsburg. They could move through the streets in the shadow of the emperor, immune to civic designs. In worship services and religious processions during an imperial diet, the citizens of Augsburg witnessed a bishop who could shepherd both a city and an empire. In addition to taking advantage of imperial diets the late medieval bishops of Augsburg looked to the grave, the funeral, the processional last rites of a fallen colleague. Beginning in the mid-fifteenth century a new form of episcopal entry appears to have received greater emphasis in Augsburg. Bishops came with the same impressive entourage, but with somber purpose. They did not arrive to negotiate with

---

[178] Sender, CDS 23 [4], p. 274: 5-15.

[179] "an der glingen seitten ... ist gestanden der bischoff von Augsbpurg mit dem weichbischoff und [der] abbt von sant Ulrich, und nach etlichen antiffen hat der bischof etlich versickel und collect gesungen;" Sender, CDS 23 [4], p. 277: 14-17.

[180] Sender, CDS 4 [23], p. 279: 23—280: 1. Ritual also served to divide the delegates and expose loyalties. During this service and procession the Protestant princes refused to participate and held a meeting of their own instead; p. 279: 12-22.

[181] In 1500 Augsburg had also hosted an imperial diet. Once again a bishop of Augsburg was prominent in the liturgical and processional festivities. Frederick of Zollern (1486-1505) sang the mass in front of the delegates on Pentecost and he carried the host in the *corpus Christi* procession; Sender, CDS 4 [23], pp. 82-83.

the city council. They came to mourn and to remember their episcopal dead.

Neither the powers nor the ritual of the bishop remained fixed in
late-medieval Germany. Peter of Schaumberg (1424-69) reshaped
the office of bishop in his living and in his dying. He took on the
episcopal mantle of Augsburg after a schism in the diocese. During
the next fifty-five years Bishop and eventually Cardinal Peter put this
church territory on solid economic and administrative footing. He
fiercely defended episcopal rights in the city of Augsburg while making Dillingen the actual city of bishops. When Peter of Schaumberg
died on April 12, 1469 the clergy of Dillingen sang a funeral mass.
The next day his body was transferred to Augsburg.[182] The civic
clergy, episcopal staff, and servants processed through Augsburg and
brought his body to the cathedral in a casket draped with a black
wool overlay, topped with a white cross and the miter of a cardinal.
After an overnight vigil a consecrating bishop sang the mass and
Peter was buried in the cathedral.[183] Peter of Schaumberg was certainly the most esteemed late-medieval bishop of Augsburg; perhaps
the most revered even since the days of the sainted Bishop Ulrich
(923-73). It appears that his original funeral services in Dillingen and
Augsburg did not satisfy his admirers. Almost two weeks after the
death of Bishop Peter clergy and laity came from all over the diocese,
and embassies arrived from distant corners of Germany. For three
days, April 26-28, mourners grieved and celebrated the life of their
bishop. The memorial cycle began with a long procession to the
cathedral. Monks and mendicants, canons and parish clergy of
Augsburg formed the first massive stage of the train.[184] Then came
the cathedral canons and numerous clergy, abbots, and bishops from
outside Augsburg. The new bishop of Augsburg, John of Werdenberg (1469-86), and the cathedral dean completed this first wave
of clergy. At this point clerics and servants processed, bearing the
symbols of Peter of Schaumberg. In the center was a bier with a
series of velvet overlays; placed on top of the them all was a cardi-

---

[182] Zoepfl I, p. 451.

[183] Hektor Mülich, *CDS* 22 [3], pp. 224: 18—225: 9

[184] "... am ersten giengen die örden mit grossen creutzen, die carmeliten und ir
provincial, darnach parfuosser, darnach prediger, darnach Benedicter, der was vil,
darnach hailigcreutzer und Iörigier und Augustiner, und hätten vier bröbst, darnach
Mauricier, darnach cartheuser und des hailigen gaists orden ..." Hektor Mülich, *CDS*
22 [3], p. 225: 11-15.

nal's miter.[185] The funeral bier, bearing the symbolic presence of Peter, formed the heart of the procession and divided the clergy from the laity. Relatives of the deceased held the place of honor behind the bier. They were followed by emissaries from Bavaria and Brandenburg among others. Finally, the city council and people of Augsburg brought up the rear.[186]

This pilgrimage to the cathedral was only the beginning. Over three days the procession moved south to St. Ulrich's cloister, the first episcopal church in Augsburg, back to the cathedral, then to the Collegiate Church of St. Maurice, the sanctuary in the center of the city, and back once more to the cathedral. In each sanctuary various clerics and monks of the city and diocese held services and received generous gifts and offerings. Finally, a large feast was held in the episcopal palace for all in attendance, including counts, knights, nobles, and their servants.[187]

This series of processions and ceremonies comprised the final entry of Bishop and Cardinal Peter of Schaumberg. The schedule of events paralleled the first entry of a bishop as he moved through the streets to the cathedral. But there are three crucial exceptions. First, this entry criss-crossed Augsburg, as the corpse of a bishop marked out the old borders and pathways of the episcopal city. There were no barricades and no armed rooftops. Second, on these three days clerics from near and far were integrated into sensitive moments of the memorial cycle; this is especially evident when the Abbot of Ottobeuron sang a mass in the Collegiate Church of St. Maurice.[188] Augsburg was clearly the capital of the bishop's wider ecclesiastical territory. Third and most telling, the magistrates and indeed the entire populace of Augsburg had no role in the planning and execution of the processions and ceremonies. They appeared in the rear of a spectacular clerical parade; their voices were silent; they had nothing to negotiate; they processed and most likely watched as Augsburg became a city of priests, and once more the city of Peter of Schaumberg.

The successor to Peter, Bishop John of Werdenberg, made his

---

[185] "... darnach ritter und knecht truogen ain par, die was verdeckt mit ainem schwartzen samat und ob dem ain guldin tuoch, ob den ain plawer samat, auf dem allem lag der rot cardinalhut;" Mülich, *CDS* 22 [3], p. 225: 23-26.

[186] Mülich, *CDS* 22 [3], p. 225: 26-28.

[187] "... und wurden die frembden, iederman, von hof, gespeiset, grafen, ritter edle und knecht;" Mülich, CDS 22 [3], p. 226: 22.

[188] Mülich, *CDS* 22 [3], p. 226: 7-8.

formal entry into Augsburg about two months after the memorial rites of April, 1469.[189] Unless records have vanished or civic and episcopal chroniclers simply lost interest, it is likely that no immediate successor to Bishop John made such a grand formal entry into Augsburg. Frederick of Zollern (1486-1505), Henry of Lichtenau (1505-17), Christopher of Stadion (1517-43) and their administrations have neither preserved accounts of negotiation with the magistrates of Augsburg nor of planning for processions and feasts. The rich lay chronicle literature of Augsburg is likewise silent. But even if the entries did occur, it is revealing that no chronicler thought them worthy of mention or elaboration. The episcopal chronicles for Henry of Lichtenau and Christopher of Stadion give a detailed itinerary of their early months. Bishop Henry made a brief trip to Augsburg for installation and this is recorded. But no formal entry is described or even cited.

However, the bishops of Augsburg did honor the dead with lavish ritual. The special memorial cycle for Peter of Schaumberg became a permanent part of episcopal ritual. Bishop John of Werdenberg died on February 23, 1486; he was buried with all the usual rites shortly thereafter. But on October 8-11, 1486 Augsburg hosted a special memorial cycle in his honor.[190] Frederick of Zollern died on March 8, 1505 and was buried on March 11 in the cathedral; the memorial cycle followed on November 16-18.[191] After a twelve year career, on April 12, 1517 Henry of Lichtenau passed away; two days later he was buried in the Cathedral of St. Mary. From September 21-24, the diocese held a memorial cycle in his honor in Augsburg.[192]

Although the interval between burial and memorial cycle grew between Peer of Schaumberg and the early sixteenth century from two weeks to around seven months, the logistics of this sort of entry remained the same. The string of processions and services lasted three days. Augsburg, not Dillingen, continued to host the memorial cycle. Fortunately, accounts of two cycles survive in the notes of the episcopal chronicles pertaining to Henry of Lichtenau and Christopher of Stadion. Based on these records it is clear that the

---

[189] See pp. 140-145.
[190] Zoepfl I, p. 451.
[191] Zoepfl I, pp. 534-535; StaatsA, MBL 221: 42r, 1—42v, 16.
[192] StaatsA, MBL 222: 33v, 1—42v, 18. Zoepfl I, pp. 563-564.

successors of Peter of Schaumberg preserved the schedule of processions, ceremonies, and hospitality.

The memorial cycle for Frederick of Zollern appears in the itinerary of new bishop Henry of Lichtenau.[193] In this account processions and distinguished guests are emphasized. On November 18, 1505 Bishop Henry arrived in Augsburg. The next day, between 12:00 and 1:00 p.m., the clergy of the city and diocese of Augsburg joined representatives of other communes, lords, and nobles in the bishop's palace. Their procession, glimmering with numerous candles, surrounded the bier of Bishop Frederick, departed from the palace, and paraded through the city to St. Ulrich's. Unlike the first memorial procession for Peter of Schaumberg the citizens of Augsburg do not appear in the account.[194] The cathedral, St. Ulrich's, and St. Maurice's continued to provide the venues for special services. The episcopal chronicler preferred to list guests, goods, gifts, and total cost and to offer only a bare-bones description of activity. But his data reveals how this cycle continued to attract the attendance of diverse and distant clerics and laymen. In addition to the clergy of Augsburg and the episcopal court of Bishop Henry, the tally included eight princely embassies, thirty-one prelates of the diocese, eight civic representatives, sixty-four nobles, and around two hundred diocesan clergy.[195] Moreover, Bishop Henry hosted about 750 guests per meal in the palace and cloister of the cathedral.[196] Even the number of horses, an issue that unnerved the city council when Bishop John of Werdenberg made his entry, is noted here.[197]

In 1517, on the eve of the Reformation, the memorial cycle in Augsburg continued to be remarkably well-attended. In fact, when Christopher of Stadion served as host for the recently deceased Henry of Lichtenau from September 21-24, attendance had in-

---

[193] StaatsA, MBL 221: 65v, 1—68v, 22.

[194] "... am Morgen Samstags zwischen ainem vnnd zwayen ist sein gnad [Bishop Henry] mit der Procession aller gaistlicheit der Stat Augspurg den Prelaten des Bistumbs der Fursten vnnd Stet Botschafften vnnd anndern Herrn vnnd von Adel sampt einer Bar mit vil Kertzen als gewonheit ist aus der Pfaltz zu Sannt Vlrich gegangen;" StaatsA, MBL 221: 65v, 4-10.

[195] This tally does not clearly distinguish in every case between a single attender and an embassy of a given place. Moreover, it appears that only the most distinctive guests are recorded here. The effort to garner the name of every participant would have been next to impossible; StaatsA, MBL 221: 66r: 1—68v: 3.

[196] StaatsA, MBL 221: 68v, 4-22.

[197] A low of 106 and a high of 334 horses to be fed and watered per day is recorded; StaatsA, MBL 221: 68, 18-23.

creased. About 1,100 people per day sat at table in the episcopal palace or cathedral cloister and joined in the round of processions and services. From 214 to 350 horses required feeding.[198] The number of notable guests in attendance was about equal to the cycle for Frederick of Zollern. Among those honoring Henry of Lichtenau were the embassies of eight princes, two bishops, thirty prelates, and eight cities; once again, the diocesan clergy numbered about two hundred.[199] Overall, the summary of events reflects continuity with the past. But in the first lines of the prose description Bishop Christopher of Stadion appears to have a more prominent role than his predecessor Henry of Lichtenau. He took direct responsibility for the implementation of the memorial cycle.[200]

When a bishop formally entered his episcopal city, a series of rituals, sacred and secular, signified his status as a prince of the empire and a shepherd of the church. Even a bishop shorn of his political sovereignty could display both the rights he had lost and the ceremonial powers he preserved through the medium of ritual. However, this *adventus* was not the only forum for a public demonstration of episcopal power. In Constance clerical processions, imperial visits, diocesan synods, absolution ceremonies, and episcopal funeral rites provided ongoing opportunities for a bishop to exert his continuing influence and to claim his old episcopal city as the capital of his diocese. Until the Protestant Reformation the bishops of Constance continued to maintain this city as the primary venue for their episcopal administration and ceremony. Bishops were consecrated in Constance; here they sang first mass and forgave sinners; and here they were buried in the Cathedral of Our Dear Lady. Constance was a free and imperial city; but the bishop still laid claim to the streets through the of medium ritual, reminding magistrates that Constance was yet beholden to the successors of St. Konrad, the patron saint of cathedral and city.

Late-medieval Augsburg had witnessed the steady retreat of episcopal rights and ceremonies. By the end of the fifteenth century Dillingen was the de facto residence of the bishop. Here a bishop

---

[198] StaatsA, MBL 222: 36r, 6-22.
[199] StaatsA, MBL 222: 34r, 7-34v.
[200] "... hat der Hochwurdig Furst mein gnediger herr Bischoff Cristoff zu Augspurg weilennd bishcoff Heinrichs loblicher gedechtnus besingknus *furgenomen*;" StaatsA, MBL 222: 33v, 2-5. In contrast, Henry of Lichtenau is described as "gen Augspurg komen" with no reference to his direction of events; MBL 221: 65v, 3.

could reign as lord of the city. His overarching authority offered a secure and clearly defined stage for his consecration and synods, the homage of his subjects, and the administration of his diocese. Yet the city of Augsburg remained the heart of the diocese. The bishop did continue to exert his authority through ritual long after his political rights and privileges had withered away. New bishops spent most of their early months in Dillingen or travelling in the diocese. From the perspective of a modern historian of the sixteenth century the grand and formal entry of a new bishop appears to have lost its lustre. However, the city of Augsburg continued to answer to episcopal initiatives, especially those appearing in the ceremonial sphere. During imperial visits and diets both the princely and priestly profile of the bishop received added definition.

In death the bishops of Augsburg found life. The Cathedral of St. Mary and the cloister of St. Ulrich's still combined to form the sacred center of the diocese, the cemeteries of saints and bishops. As they down-played, neglected, or perhaps gave up on formal entries, the bishops of Augsburg placed greater emphasis on the cult of the dead. In addition to the first burial service they orchestrated a three day memorial cycle that allowed them to reclaim Augsburg as their own city. They marched in processions without negotiating entry, facing the barricades of the workers, and the opposition of the city council. They hosted distinguished guests who recognized the bishop as noble and prince. While they no longer fought to regain civic lordship, they maintained Augsburg as the symbolic and, even in death, the ritual capital of the diocese—their episcopal, cathedral, and sacred city. The critical dimension of the memorial cycle appears not only in solemn parades and services but also in the potent combination of the living and the dead. For three days a new bishop, most likely making his first formal entry into Augsburg, drew on the resources of his predecessors. As he organized events, processed through the city, and sang the mass, a new bishop tapped into the sacral power of holy clerics whose graves formed the foundations of churches and whose holiness could sanctify a city. When he honored his predecessors in the streets of Augsburg, a new bishop joined with those ancestors who had once ruled the city as mighty lords. The memorial cycle linked his uncertain reign with the consummated rule of his immediate predecessor.[201] Through the mediation of the dead

---

[201] The half-year delay between the burial of a bishop and his festive memorial

the nascent bishop could enter the episcopal city of his ancestors. In a display of ritual, diocesan, and priestly power the bishop reconnoitered the city, advertising all the dimensions of his rule that lay beyond the grasp of the city council. In the liminal place between life and death the new bishop joined the residual charisma of centuries of predecessors in order to proclaim the ties of spiritual lordship. To break this form of priestly power the magistrates would have to assault the last bastion of episcopal power—the sacrosanct ritual of the church.

*   *   *

Although their civic rights and privileges faded during the Middle Ages, through the rituals of priesthood, cathedral, diocese, empire, and episcopacy, the bishops of Constance and Augsburg continued to reclaim their ancient and ancestral cathedral cities. These rituals were not merely the trappings of some hidden or clandestine power. Ritual itself channeled power; access to ritual or the ability to enact ritual was power. Ritual provided the framework within which negotiations between bishop and city were carried out. Ritual permitted the bishop to flaunt his old powers as he entered the gates even while swearing allegiance to the rights of the city. In processions, synods, imperial visitations, funerals, and memorial cycles, the bishop continued to assert ancient claims on civic space. In order to capture this last bastion of episcopal power the city would be forced to abrogate the bishop's ritual. When they expelled a bishop during the Middle Ages, the magistrates might weaken the bishop's political and economic claims. His departure could be a crude mockery of entry; the bishop might leave in humiliation, disarray, or protest. The residents of Utrecht understood this well when they drove their bishop out of town with due reverence on a cart of dung.[202] In order to facilitate his return the bishop might surrender a privilege, cancel a tax, or recognize a lay governing body. Despite often impressive gains magistrates left episcopal ritual in place; this omission inevitably assured the bishop's return to his sacred city. Even if he did not rule in

---

for his predecessor may have provided just enough time to ensure that a new bishop would enter the city in full command of his office. He could lead or participate in the memorial cycle as a bishop who had toured his diocese, received consecration, and held his first synod.

[202] Dauch, *Die Bischofsstadt*, p. 208.

person, the bishop continued to reach through the clergy and rites beholden to him. If he was not lord of the commune, the bishop still ruled through the ministrations of ritual; he held sway over some of the most important rituals of all, those that ensured salvation—last rites and Christian burial.

If the magistrates of Constance and Augsburg wanted to free their cities of all episcopal influence, they had to find a way to claim for themselves the sacred rites that the bishops and his clergy alone could perform. They had to reject the ritual that served as a medium for episcopal power and yet find a way to replace that power; they had to claim authority over the sacred city. If they could institutionalize this charisma, the bishop would no longer be necessary. The Protestant Reformation provided this opportunity, justifying the expulsion of the bishop and the annulment of his sacral power.

CHAPTER FIVE

THE 'LAST RITES' OF A BISHOP: REFORMATION IN CONSTANCE AND AUGSBURG

In the summer of 1516 Henry of Lichtenau (1505-17) submitted a grievance to the German Emperor. The bishop objected to a civic coat of arms that had been placed on a column in the lane between the episcopal palace and the cathedral. In response to this complaint Emperor Maximilian ordered the magistrates of Augsburg to remove the civic icon; episcopal and imperial crests were hung in its place.[1] This minor infringement on the episcopal immunity enjoyed by the cathedral compound anticipated the final, cataclysmic encroachment of city against bishop twenty-one years later. In 1537 the magistrates of Augsburg dissolved all episcopal immunities, expelled the clergy, and eradicated the last vestiges of episcopal power and presence. The crest of Augsburg came to symbolize civic lordship over every square foot enclosed by city walls, including the cathedral and bishop's palace. The city council of Augsburg controlled the city—secular and sacred.

In Constance the bishop's rule had been terminated with equal decisiveness. In fact by 1537 the bishop of Constance and his clergy had been in exile for more than ten years. The magistrates had moved swiftly against the bishop in the early 1520s, protecting dissident preachers as soon as they appeared in the city. By 1528 the bishop and his cathedral canons as well as his clerical courts and episcopal administration had moved out to various towns along Lake Constance.

In both cities the leaders of Protestant movements had first challenged, then altered the content of preaching and finally disputed the mass; in short order they defied the oversight of the bishop in all spiritual matters. In this confrontation the magistrates of Constance and Augsburg breached the final wall of the bishop's defenses; if episcopal legitimacy and competence in ecclesiastical and spiritual matters could be refuted, then the lay city council could drive the

---

[1] Zoepfl I, p. 558.

bishop from the city once and for all, establishing magisterial rule over the sacred city.

The growth and eventual dominance of Protestant movements in Constance and Augsburg is the final chapter of the *Episcopus exclusus*—the banishing of the bishops. During the 1520s and 1530s episcopal exile became permanent; lay magistrates renounced all episcopal claims on civic institutions, ecclesiastical property, clerical personnel; they denied the bishop's competence to oversee the care of souls. Magistrates denied a bishop's access to sacred relics and altars, to the sanctuaries and streets that had served as the stage for episcopal ritual; they also removed objects now considered heretical, claiming clerical properties and sanctuaries for civic coffers and Protestant services. In this way the bishop's 'last rites', his sacramental and spiritual powers, were decreed ineffective and heretical. In this way, reforming magistrates 'pronounced' last rites on the bishop's real presence, his clergy and clerical properties, on *his* sacred city.

Throughout the Middle Ages the bishops of Constance and Augsburg had confronted and contested the loss of episcopal rights and privileges as well as the difficulties of periodic expulsion. They always assumed that residents would eventually restore episcopal access and residency. During the 1530s and 1540s, however, the bishops of Constance and Augsburg faced a lengthy and potentially permanent banishment. We now explore the tactics and survival of the exiled bishops of Constance and Augsburg, a facet long obscured in scholarship. This lacuna is in part due to the emphasis on the City Reformation and to our propensity to study winners over losers. But lack of scholarly attention might be addressed to the paucity of documents as well. Episcopal sources from the first half of the sixteenth century are meager compared to their civic counterparts. We can only fasten on specific events and singular moments when the documents allow us a peek at what appears to be a desperate time for bishop, cathedral chapter, and clergy. This sketch, however, may serve as a first attempt to view the onset of Reformation from a distinctively episcopal perspective, to avoid the temptation to tell the story through civic records.

Before 1500 episcopal fortunes in Augsburg and Constance sometimes paralleled each other and sometimes diverged. But the convergence of these two episcopal traditions during the sixteenth century is even more striking than their medieval similarities. This period of definitive and disastrous exile led to new and desperate contact and cooperation between the bishops of Constance and Augsburg. As a result they joined forces in an effort to survive as 'refugees', driven from their sacred cities. We will first explore how these bishops sought to thwart the growth of Reformation movements in the cities they still claimed to rule as overseers of the church.

1. *Confrontation and Conservation*[2]

Reformation pamphlets and preachers found a sympathetic audience in the city of Constance. In less than twelve years the city council replaced the bishop as shepherd of the church and overseer of the parish clergy. So it is tempting to see the arrival of some treatises of Luther and the expression of Zwinglian sentiments in Constance in 1519 as the first step of a swift and calculated plan of invasion and conversion. When Jakob Windner, a priest in St. Stephan's, was reading Luther in 1519, the plague had disrupted both lay and clerical government. With 4,500 dead, bishop, cathedral chapter, and all but four city councilors had fled the city. While Luther's writings entered Constance during this time of lax civic and episcopal oversight, Bishop Hugo of Hohenlandenberg (1496-1530, 1530-31) even encouraged the first reception of Ulrich Zwingli in Zürich (Diocese of Constance). Concurring with Zwingli the bishop rejected the

---

[2] The triumph of civic Reformation movements is a main theme of many works in German urban historiography of the 1520s and 1530s. This development dominates the history of sixteenth century Constance and Augsburg as well. Wolfgang Dobras carefully presents the scholarship of the last twenty years in "Konstanz zur Zeit der Reformation," in *Konstanz in der frühen Neuzeit. Reformation. Verlust der Reichsfreiheit. Österreichische Zeit* (Konstanz: Verlag Stadler, 1991), pp. 11-146; his work builds on and updates the thorough archival study of Hans-Christoph Rublack, *Die Einführung der Reformation in Konstanz* (Gütersloh: Gerd Mohn, 1971) and the general review of events found in Hermann Buck and Ekkehart Fabian, *Konstanzer Reformationsgeschichte in ihren Grundzügen* (Tübingen: Osiandersche Buchhandlung, 1965).

The magisterial work on the Reformation in Augsburg, though badly in need of updating, is Friedrich Roth's four volume *Augsburgs Reformationsgeschichte* 1517-1555, 4 vols. (München: Theodore Ackermann, 1901-1911); Lyndal Roper has given a new profile to gender history in sixteenth century Augsburg in *The Holy Household. Women and Morals in Reformation Augsburg* (Oxford: Clarendon Press, 1989); Herbert Immenkötter provides the best collation of recent research in "Kirche zwischen Reformation und Parität," in *GSA*, pp. 391-412.

preaching of Roman indulgences for St. Peter's in his diocese and lent his legitimation to the Swiss preacher and his message.[3]

By May 1522, however, Bishop Hugo expressed growing concern about the cadre of evangelical preachers in his cathedral city and the dissemination of Reformation movements in his diocese. Dispatching an "Earnest Admonition for Peace and Christian Unity" to prelates, deans, provosts, courts, preachers, pastors, counts, free knights, nobles, mayors, city councils, and commoners, the bishop especially addressed the situation in Zwingli's Zürich.[4] Since the city now lay completely outside the empire and Habsburg domain, the bishop could not count on military force to make episcopal reasoning more persuasive. Hugo appealed for maintenance of public peace and an end to slanders against the church:

> "Under the clergy and the secular authorities of our diocese we wish to spread the calm of peace, ignite the flames of love, cultivate unity, and preserve enjoyment of concord. Instead we see the Christian church, the gathering of those who honor Christ, operating as a wicked opponent of a peace we all really desire."[5]

Although he did not mention Zwingli or his views on fasting, the mass, and the clergy, Bishop Hugo framed this careful appeal for restraint and brotherly love with the preacher of Zürich in mind. At the same time he was concerned about Constance as well. Preachers in the cathedral and St. Stephan's expounded on the biblical text without reference to the treasury of papal, conciliar, and episcopal wisdom.[6]

By the end of 1522 it was clear that the bishop's conciliatory approach had borne little fruit. In January 1523 Hugo sent an episco-

---

[3] Rublack, *Die Einführung der Reformation in Konstanz*, pp. 16-17, 205-208; Dobras, "Konstanz zur Zeit der Reformation" in *Konstanz in der frühen Neuzeit*, p. 40.

[4] "Ernstlich ermanung des fridens vnd Christlicher einigkeit des durchlüchtigien Fürsten vnnd genaedigen herren, Hugonis von Landenberg Bischoff tzuo Constanz, zu Frieden und christlicher Einigkeit, mit schöner Auslegung und Erklärung;" in *Flugschriften aus den ersten Jahren der Reformation*, vol. 4, ed. O. Clemen (Nieuwkoop: B. De Graaf, 1967), pp. 285-291.

[5] "... damit vnder geystlichen vnd weltlichen vnsers Bistumbs die ruow des fridens zuoneme, inbrinstigkeit der lieb entzunt, einigkeit gepflantzt werd vnd verglychung der gemuot beharre. Wir wissen auch, das zanck vnd ergernuß den zuogang boeser werck bereytent, zwitracht vnd nyd erweckend vnd vngebuerlichem wesen vursach geben. So wir nun sehen die Christenlich kilch, versamlung der Christgloebigen begriffend, vß boeslicher fuerderung des benider fridens;" "Ernstliche Ermanung," p. 287, 16-24.

[6] Dobras, "Konstanz zur Zeit der Reformation," in *Konstanz in der frühen Neuzeit*, pp. 39-43.

pal commission headed by Johannes Fabri, the Vicar General of the
diocese, to Zürich to participate in a theological disputation. Fabri
argued vigorously for an authorized ecclesiastical council as the only
legitimate body for judging matters of doctrine and practice.[7]
Against this position Zwingli proposed the civic assembly in Zürich
as a holy synod. By the end of the disputation episcopal officials
realized that debate held under civic authority was not much more
effective than fatherly admonition to preserve ecclesiastical harmony.
Although the proceedings of the disputation did not culminate in a
complete rejection of episcopal oversight, the biblical text alone—*sola
scriptura*—was henceforth to be cited as the final court of appeal in all
contested issues in Zürich.[8]

After his failure to reassert episcopal authority in Zürich Bishop
Hugo attempted a new strategy in Constance. In February 1523 he
opted for direct intervention, inviting the well-known Tübingen professor and supporter of the traditional church, Dr. Martin Plantsch,
to preach in the cathedral in Constance.[9] Plantsch arrived at the
cathedral on his scheduled day, but before he moved forward to

---

[7] See *DKP*, 15 January 1523, 7510, pp. 267-268.

[8] For a general account of this civic disputation in Zürich, see Gottfried W.
Locher, *Die Zwinglische Reformation im Rahmen der europäischen Kirchengeschichte* (Göttingen:
Vandenhoeck und Ruprecht, 1979), pp. 110-115. Locher notes that the outcome of
the disputation infringed on episcopal authority, but did not initiate a complete rejection of the bishop's church: "Die Literatur spricht freilich durchgehend von der
Gründung der Zürcherischen Landeskirche. Dazu ist zu sagen, daß den politisch
versierten Ratsherren durchaus bewußt gewesen sein muß, daß sie hier de facto die
Kompetenzen des Bischofs zuhanden nahmen und sich damit als christliche
Obrigkeit engagierten. Aber es wurde mit der Verpflichtung auf das Evangelium
durachaus keine Trennung beschlossen und keine neue Kirche gegründet. Viel mehr
drängt die Bewegung nach einer Erneuerung des kirchlichen wie des staatlichen
Lebens, wobei durchaus mittelalterlich die Einheit beider Bereiche vorausgesetzt und
postuliert wird;" p. 115.
On the episcopal visitation in Zürich and developments during the years 1522-
1523, see Heiko A. Oberman, *Masters of the Reformation. The Emergence of a New Intellectual Climate in Europe* (Cambridge: Cambridge University Press, 1981 [1977]), pp.
210-239.

[9] "Der hochwurdig furst m. g. h. von Costantz hat vngevarlich diß maynung
furgehalten, wie yetzo der predicant des thumstifts ain zyt lang nit anhaimsch geweßt
vnd aber herr doct. Martin Plansch von Tuwinger ain berumpter hochgelerter mann
yetzo ain zytlang hie sich enthalten, hab ir f. gnad inn ankomen, vff das fest puri-
ficationis Marie, vff welches gemelts predicanten zukunft nit verhofft worden, in
thumstift zepredigen, damit das dannocht das lob gottes vnnd Marie gefurdert, auch
nachred vnnd annders, so durch vnderlassung sollicher sermon daruß enstan möchten, verhut wurden, des sich nun gemelter herr doctor Martin vndertänigclich begeben und sich ainer sermon verfaßt hab;" 3 February 1523; *DKP* 6, 7536, p. 271, 3-
12.

preach, cathedral preacher John Wanner had taken charge of the service and occupied the pulpit. Wanner went on to preach his own evangelical sermon.[10] The cathedral chapter promptly called Wanner to its chambers for disciplinary action. He refused to appear and turned instead to the city council for protection.[11] This confrontation was typical of civic and episcopal relations over the next four years. The magistrates of Constance shielded those clerics who preached exclusively from the biblical text, protecting them from ecclesiastical discipline. When Bishop Hugo reprimanded the council, the magistrates argued that disciplinary action would result in widespread public unrest. Finally, after guarding evangelical expositors from episcopal punishment for a full year, on 9 February 1524 the city council issued a "Preaching Mandate," requiring preachers to expound the scriptures alone. The city council was now disputing the bishop's oversight of clergy, pulpit, and doctrinal truth.[12]

The German Peasants' Revolt provided a further and decisive opportunity for civic encroachment on the church. After the "Preaching Mandate" of 1524 the magistrates of Constance had become cautious, giving in to episcopal opposition to their plan to hold a public disputation and ordering evangelical clerics to delay their wedding vows. However, during the spring and summer of 1525, episcopal lands were ravaged by peasant armies, compelling Bishop Hugo to plead with the magistrates of Constance for assistance.[13] The city council agreed on one condition. Since Constance too was vulnerable to marauding armies, the clergy must swear an oath of obedience and loyalty to the city and submit to taxation. Only the bishop, his household, the consecrating bishop, and cathedral canons

---

[10] "Darnach habe es sich begeben vber vnd wider ettlicher herren vom capitel, so vnder dem ampte an gedachtem fest versamelt gewesen syen vnnd im auch bevolhen, doct. Martin vff dißmal statt zegeben, bevelch vnnd maynung, do berurter doct. Martin vff die kantzel wollen stygen, hab gemelter predicant yn furkomen vnnd sich vor imm hinuff gelißen, das dann demselben herren doctor zu großer schmach, auch ir f. g. vnnd ainem wurdiegen thumcapitel zu verrachtung raiche;" 23 February 1523; *DKP* 6, 7536, p. 271, 24-30.

[11] See the report of the cathedral chapter on 6 February 1523; *DKP* 6, 7544, pp. 274-275.

[12] Dobras, "Konstanz zur Zeit der Reformation," in *Konstanz in der frühen Neuzeit*, pp. 46-49.

[13] The bishop sought assistance particularly for his vulnerable city of Meersburg on the other side of Lake Constance. See Rublack, *Die Einführung der Reformation*, pp. 42-45. Tom Scott and Bob Scribner describe the course of the war in the diocese in their introduction to *The German Peasants' War: A History in Documents* (London: Humanities Press International, 1991), pp. 19-28.

would be exempted. After fervent objections Bishop Hugo and the cathedral chapter reluctantly agreed, perceiving this arrangement as a short term, emergency measure.[14]

The revolt and its aftermath were decisive for city and bishop. After the peasant armies had been vanquished the magistrates of Constance refused to revoke the clergy's oath of civic obedience and Bishop Hugo chose not to dispute the ruling.[15] A few months later the city council made additional demands, requiring the clergy to contribute workers or funds for the expansion of civic fortifications; this time only the bishop was exempt from a general tax.[16]

During the late summer months of 1526 the episcopal household began to transfer operations to Meersburg. In October after envoys of the Swabian nobility failed to convince magistrates in Constance to eliminate civic demands on the clergy, Bishop Hugo gave the order to evacuate, following the example of episcopal predecessors who had forsaken Constance as an act of self-preservation or protest.[17] Between the last months of 1526 and the summer of 1527 the clergy withdrew to destinations around Lake Constance: the cathedral chapter and secular clergy to Überlingen, the episcopal court to Radolfzell, the canons of St. Stephan to Bischofszell in Switzerland, and the Bishop of Constance across the lake to Meersburg.[18] The

---

[14] "Als nun die uffrürige puren je lenger je mer gesterck wurden, ouch die vorstat Petershusen uffforderten, hat der rath für ain notturft angesehen, und uff 20 apprell beschlossen, das alle priester, ouch alle münch, und deren aller knecht, darzu der tumbherren knecht, dem rath und statt, den gewonlichen knechts- oder hindersässen ayd schweren sollen ... Das habend sy gethon, dessen hat sich aber der bischoff höchlich beschwerdt, und ouch das tumbcapittel, und habend sich derhalben hin und her vil handlungen verloffen ... Uff 25 aprell sind alle capitula der priester, desglichen der ordensluten und alle ander berüft worden und inen der ayd fürgehalten, und von inene geschowren worden;" Schulthaiß-*Chronik*, p. 85, 10-22.

In June of 1525 the magistrates found yet another way to penetrate the episcopal immunity. They demanded access to the cathedral tower in order to maintain surveillance of the countryside north of the city, claiming that the tower of the bishop's church blocked the view from St. Stephan's, their usual viewing point; 26 May 1525; *DKP* 6, 8400, p. 386; 2 June 1525; *DKP* 6, 8407, p. 387.

[15] "Nach dem Bericht der zum B. verordneten Dhh. hält es der B. nicht für rätlich, jetzt mit der Stadt über die Eidesleistung zu verhandeln..." 8 March 1526, *DKP* 6, 8800, p. 431, 2-3.

[16] Schulthaiß-*Chronik*, pp. 85-86.

[17] For example, Bishop Otto of Hachberg (1410-34) withdrew from Constance in protest in 1429 and again in 1431; *REC* 3:8430, 9286.

[18] Schulthaiß-*Chronik*, p. 84, 88; Rublack, *Die Einführung der Reformation*, pp. 46-48, 73.

Bishop Hugo was distracted by events elsewhere in his diocese, preeminently in his Swiss homeland. While he negotiated with Constance from 1522-27 he continued

pattern of withdrawal and expulsion continued. In 1529 Bishop Hugo admitted a distinguished band of clerical refugees, the exiled bishop and cathedral canons of Basel, to Freiburg im Breisgau, a diocesan city.

As the clergy departed from Constance city officials manned the gates and confiscated liturgical vessels and vestments, demanding that clerics settle debts before leaving and refusing to allow the transfer of the cathedral treasury to another city. The relics of the sainted Bishop Konrad (934-75), treasured throughout the diocese, were apparently burned by iconoclasts who cast the ashes into the Rhine.[19] In 1415 the bishops of the church catholic had committed the heretic John Hus to the flames at the Council of Constance and deposited his ashes in the same river. A century later heretics had defiled and destroyed the bones of *the* episcopal saint, scattering the sainted relics of the sacred city. A long and seemingly permanent exile of the bishops of Constance had begun.

*   *   *

In July, 1517 Christopher of Stadion (1517-43), after serving as a cathedral canon and Coadjutor of the diocese, was elected bishop of

---

to confront Reformation movements south of the border. Hugo initiated an episcopal campaign to check Zwingli and the Reformation movement in Zürich to prevent further breaking of the fast, marriage of the clergy, dissolution of the mass, and confiscation of priestly incomes. Six publications were issued from the episcopal chancery to defend orthodoxy and maintain order in the diocese. Episcopal emissaries attended twelve assemblies of the confederacy and three disputations, attempting to counter Zürich and to shore up support among the other cantons. In early April 1524, Bishop Hugo proclaimed a common front with the bishops of Basel and Lausanne in a joint declaration upholding orthodoxy and episcopal rights.

Almost without exception the bishop of Constance failed. The Reformation movement continued to gather momentum in Zürich as church revenues were confiscated and the bishop's oversight denied. After Bern embraced the Reformation in 1527 the extreme southern reaches of the diocese broke free from the bishop of Constance. But undoubtedly the greatest blow had already come from cantons faithful to the old church. In 1523 a Swiss Assembly dominated by Roman Catholic cantons formulated a startling policy: errant clergy would be punished without consulting the bishop in most cases. Episcopal jurisdiction was further curtailed when seven Roman Catholic cantons met in January, 1525 and formulated a doctrinal mandate of some forty-seven articles. In Switzerland the bishop of Constance was no longer head shepherd either in matters of faith or practice; August Willburger, *Die Konstanzer Bischöfe Hugo von Landenberg, Balthasar Merklin, Johann von Lupfen (1496-1537) und die Glaubensspaltung* (Münster: Aschendorff, 1917), pp. 32-76.

[19] Franz Hundsnurscher, "Die Kathedrale des Bistums," in *Glanz der Kathedrale. 900 Jahre Konstanzer Münster* (Konstanz: Städtische Museen Konstanz, 1989), p. 38.

Augsburg. His ascendancy was due in part to the financial backing of the wealthy Augsburger, Jakob Fugger, and in part to the support of nearby humanists and theologians. John Eck dedicated his edition of Dionysius Areopagite to Christopher; Johannes Altenstaig followed suit, pledging his *Vocabularius thelogiae* to the new bishop.[20] Although Christopher began his reign with local funding and scholarly praise, he did not devote his episcopal career to ecclesiastical administration or theological study. From the beginning of his reign Christopher of Stadion was occupied with the spread of Reformation movements in his diocese and cathedral city.[21] In fact, it was in Augsburg, in the Carmelite cloister of St. Anne, that Cardinal Cajetan interrogated Martin Luther in October of 1518. At the time Luther noted the conspicuous absence of Christopher of Stadion, explaining to his friend Spalatin with some relief that "the bishop is not in the city."[22] After three days Luther's supporters grew increasingly concerned for his safety. Finally, Christoph Langenmantel, a cathedral canon in Augsburg, helped Luther to flee through a small gate in the northern wall, ensuring his escape on an old horse.[23]

Reformation movements in Augsburg would prove as elusive to Bishop Christopher as Luther seemed to his adversaries when he slipped out of the city in 1518. Unlike his counterpart Hugo of Hohenlandenberg in Constance, however, Christopher of Stadion had some time to formulate and revise episcopal policy. While the magistrates of Constance instituted a new church order in less than a decade, the city council of Augsburg took nearly twenty years to deliberate over these issues. Supporters of Luther and Zwingli in Augsburg came initially from clerics who read the Reformers' works and printers who profited from their popularity.[24] The bishop's first

---

[20] Friedrich Zoepfl, *Das Bistum Augsburg und seine Bischöfe im Reformationsjahrhundert.* Geschichte des Bistums und seine Bischöfe, vol. II. (München: Schnell and Steiner, 1969), pp. 6-10; henceforth cited as Zoepfl II.

[21] Friedrich Zoepfl has carefully traced the career of Christopher of Stadion; Zoepfl II, pp. 1-172.

[22] "Episcopus Augustensis abest ab urbe," *WABr* 1.209, 20f, Luther to Spalatin, 10 October 1518.

[23] Herbert Immenkötter, "Kirche zwischen Reformation und Parität," in *GSA*, pp. 392-393.

[24] In addition to Carmelite prior Johann Frosch and the Benedictine Veit Bild, Luther found initial support among the cathedral canons, including Christoph Langenmantel, Bernhard and Konrad Adelmann of Adelmannsfelden, Johann Oecolampadius, and Urbanus Rhegius. Immenkötter, "Kirche zwischen Reformation und Parität," in *GSA*, pp. 392-393."

decisive step against Luther was a victory over the printers of Augsburg who refused to copy *Exsurge Domini,* the papal Bull condemning Luther. John Eck saw to its printing in Ingolstadt and it was read from the cathedral pulpit in Augsburg in late December, 1520. The episcopal position also received critical support when the magistrates of Augsburg posted the imperial ban against Luther (Worms, 1521) on the door of city hall.[25]

During the decade of the 1520s bishop and city clashed over ecclesiastical jurisdiction. As in Constance evangelical clerics eventually sought the protection of the city council against the bishop and his clerical court in Augsburg and Dillingen.[26] By the time of the Augsburg Diet of 1530 episcopal oversight was still recognized in many churches of the city.[27] The city council had kept the demands of Lutherans, Zwinglians, and Anabaptists in check, conducting mass arrests of the Anabaptists in 1527 and 1528. Civic concessions were made, as in Constance, to the evangelical preachers who took over monastic and mendicant parish churches as the monks and friars converted or departed; by 1526 magistrates recognized Lutheranism as a legitimate expression of Christian faith in the city.[28]

After the Augsburg Reichstag in 1530 limited episcopal rule was still recognized in the city. In fact, the presence of the emperor and imperial estates in Augsburg had prompted the evangelical preachers to leave the city. The magistrates did not embrace the *Confessio*

---

[25] *CDS* 25 (5), p. 166, 211.

[26] Urbanus Rhegius, a dedicated supporter of Luther, was compelled to give up his post as cathedral preacher in 1521. Matthias Kretz, a cleric faithful to the old church, replaced Rhegius. However, Bishop Christopher and the chapter found it difficult to discipline and expel clerics from the city. For two years bishop and chapter attempted to arrest Johann Frosch, the Prior in the Carmelite cloister of St. Anne's; Johannes Speiser, a preacher in the Collegiate Church of St. Maurice, was also targeted. Both appealed to the city council for protection in October of 1523. Although Frosch eventually resigned from his order, he continued as preacher in St. Anne's. He was the first cleric in Augsburg to marry. In fact, preachers in St. Anne's (Frosch, Rhegius, Stephan Agricola) and the Franciscan cloister (Urbanus Rhegius, Michael Keller, Johannes Schillingen) were among the earliest to disseminate evangelical doctrine and to remain beyond the reach of the bishop; Zoepfl II, pp. 34-36; 52-53.

[27] Similar to Hugo of Hohenlandenberg, Bishop Christopher had to concentrate on Reformation movements throughout the diocese. From 1522-25 Christopher aggressively pursued evangelical clerics in Dillingen, Ellwangen, Lauingen, Leipheim, Memmingen, Mindelheim, Nördlingen, and Schwabniederhofen; Zoepfl II, pp. 34-50.

[28] For examples of early evangelical preaching in Augsburg, see *CDS* 25 (5), pp. 199-201, 204-209.

Augustana presented during the imperial diet, continuing to defer questions of faith to a forthcoming church council. Priests still celebrated mass in the city and offered religious instruction.[29]

Finally, in 1533 the magistrates of Augsburg moved against the old church.[30] The city council sent envoys to the bishop in Dillingen with a letter proclaiming the Bible as the only standard of doctrinal truth; they also listed non-biblical doctrines firmly rejected by the evangelical preachers in Augsburg, including fasting, oral confession, prayers to saints, use of incense and consecrated candles in worship, the refusal to offer the cup in communion, and the binding character of monastic vows.[31] The bishop's reply centered on two basic alternatives. He maintained the need for a public disputation but only if a judge agreeable to both parties could be found.[32] Christopher also took the line that had been successful for over a decade, advising them to wait for a church council or a definitive imperial diet to settle the issue.[33] Surprisingly, the magistrates of Augsburg agreed to

---

[29] Herbert Immenkötter, "Wahrhafte Verantwortung. Zur 'Abthuung der papistischen Abgötterey' in Augsburg 1537," *JVAB* 21 (1987), 83-84; Zoepfl II, p. 107.

[30] The most thorough study of the Reformation in Augsburg during the mid-1530s remains Karl Wolfart's *Die Augsburger Reformation in den Jahren 1533/34* (Aalen: Scientia, 1972 [1901]).

A number of factors influenced the emergence of a more assertive civic policy in matters of church and Reformation. First, the city council had slowly come to embrace a Zwinglian interpretation of the Lord's Supper over against the Lutherans. Second, Augsburg had made a commitment to join the Schmalkaldic League in 1531. Third, Charles V had recognized this confederation at the Reichstag of Nuremberg in 1532 in order to gain Protestant military support against Ottoman invasion; this confirmation eased the delicate strategic position of Augsburg as the Wittelsbach and Habsburg remained clearly in the camp of the old church; see Immenkötter, "Wahrhafte Verantwortung," in *JVAB* 21 (1987), 83-85.

[31] The civic letter is preserved in Sender, *CDS* 23 (4) pp. 346-351.

[32] "... wir tragen auch nochmalen kain scheuchen, die itzunt mit guottem grund biblicher schrifft und dem wort gottes zuo verandtwurten, wa wir uns zuovor ains richters, der uns nach der verhöre und disputacion, welcher seiner sach fuog und das wort gottes recht verstend und interpretierte, entschiden solte, vergleichen wurden. dann one das wurde unser disputacion nit allein frucht, sunder mer widerwillen, grösere weitterung oder zweiung geböchen, wie das die erfarung nach etlichen dergelichen beschechen disputacion offenbarlich zuo erkennen gibt;" Sender, *CDS* 23 [4], p. 351: 21-28.

[33] "Und ob wir gleich unsers klainen verstands halben dise artickel zuo verandtwurten nit wisten, als wir doch mit der gnad gottes wol thon möchten, noch dann wurde uns nit gepüren, die aus aigner vermesshait abzuostellen, weil die hievor durch gemeine cristenliche concilia appropbiert, bestet, als recht und cristenlich erkündt worden, auch noch auff disen tag alle cristenliche nation, die gelerter, geschickter, messiger und verstendiger dann wir geacht werden, die also auserhalb ains tails hochteutschs lands halten; diewell auch ro. kai. mt. und gemeine stende des

Christopher's first demand regarding a disputation. They suggested that Christopher himself serve as judge, although the city maintained the right of appeal if his ruling was not acceptable.[34] However, this plan was fiercely contested and thwarted by an unsolicited imperial missive, insisting that both sides wait for a general ecclesiastical or imperial settlement.[35]

The demise of medieval episcopal rule in Augsburg occurred in two stages. Less than a month after the imperial admonition against disputations the city council forbade 'papal preaching' in the city. In this ruling episcopal immunities and jurisdiction still played a role; celebration of the mass continued in churches directly under the bishop's oversight: the Cathedral of St. Mary, St. Maurice, St. Ulrich, St. Peter, St. George, Holy Cross, St. Stephan, and St. Ursula.[36] Next after hesitating for an additional two and a half years the magistrates finally took full control of ecclesiastical matters in the city. On 17 January 1537 they ordered all clergy either to submit to civic authority and swear the citizen's oath or to depart from the city.[37] Twelve churches and chapels were closed or turned over to evangelical preachers. The cathedral chapter and other clerics left Augsburg. The bishop's own venerable cathedral was invaded, pillaged, and converted into a Protestant church.[38] For the first time in over nine hundred years the bishop of Augsburg neither resided, nor ruled, nor held right of access to this city shaped by bishops. In Constance Hugo contested the advance of reformation initiatives and then withdrew in protest. In Augsburg Christopher attempted to conserve episcopal presence and space; his clergy was eventually expelled.

---

reichs das alles in irem abschid also erkendt und zuo halten gepotten, und zuoletzt kai. mt. ain offen mandat, daß es der religion und glaubens halben, und das daran hangt, wie es damalen gestanden ist..." Sender, *CDS* 23 [4], pp. 351:29-352:8.

[34] Sender, *CDS* 23 [4], pp. 379-382.

[35] Immenkötter, "Wahrhafte Verantwortung," pp. 87-88.

[36] Sender *CDS* 23 [4], 389-391; Immenkötter, "Wahrhafte Verantwortung," p. 87.

[37] The original hand-written copy of this decree can be found in StadtA, Litt., January 17, 1537.

[38] Shortly after the decree images were removed from church sanctuaries. Altars and paintings were taken away or destroyed on the spot; sculptures and epitaphs were smashed; *CDS* 29 [6], pp. 76-82; Immenkötter, "Kirche zwischen Reformation und Parität," in *GSA*, pp. 391-392.

2. Surviving the 'Episcopus exclusus' in Exile

Despite lost revenue and destruction of church property in Augsburg the episcopal regime of Bishop Christopher quickly mobilized to deal with this new level of civic encroachment. Since the reign of Peter of Schaumberg (1424-69) Dillingen on the Danube had been the actual capital of the diocese of Augsburg. Under the direction of the episcopal administration in Dillingen the churches and cloisters of the bishopric capably absorbed the refugee clergy from Augsburg.[39] In addition to shoring up his clergy and institutions elsewhere in the bishopric of Augsburg, Bishop Christopher spent the last seven years of his reign guarding the interests of the Roman Church on the regional and national level. His successor, Cardinal Otto, Truchseß of Waldburg (1543-73), continued a vigorous pursuit of episcopal claims in the city of Augsburg.[40] Bishop Otto also turned Dillingen into a critical nucleus for the resurgent Catholic Reformation, founding a university in the city in 1559 and setting up a Roman Catholic press to spearhead literary efforts against the Protestants.[41]

Christopher of Stadion had already set this aggressive episcopal agenda shortly after the expulsion of his clergy in January of 1537. One month later Bishop Christopher sent out a thirty-seven page printed appeal to the estates of the German Empire, condemning Augsburg's abject treatment of the clergy, confiscation of church property, and severe violation of clerical rights.[42] Thirteen surviving letters show how a number of secular rulers and clerics responded to the gravamina of the Augsburg bishop.[43] Most remarkable is a letter

---

[39] The cathedral canons, the collegiate canons of Holy Cross, and the Dominican sisters of St. Ursula transferred to Dillingen; most of the Benedictine monks of St. Ulrich moved to Unterwittelsbach; the canons of St. Maurice transferred to Landesberg, the canons of St. George to the castle Guggenberg, and the canons of St. Stephan to Höchstädt; Immenkötter, "Kirche zwischen Reformation und Parität," in GSA, p. 400.

[40] Zoepfl II, pp. 173-463.

[41] Friedrich Zoepfl, *Geschichte der Stadt Dillingen an der Donau*, pp. 31-34.

[42] Bishop Christopher published this decree in conjunction with the exiled cathedral chapter; the original copy received by the magistrates of Augsburg survives: "Wahrhafte Verantwortung ... ," StadtA, Litt., 26-2-37; Herbert Immenkötter has provided a critical edition of the decree in "Wahrhafte Verantwortung. Zur 'Abthuung der papistischen Abgötterey,' in Augsburg 1537," *JVAB* 21 (1987), pp. 90-111. For the response of the Swabian and Bavarian Nobility to these events, see StadtA, Litt., 22-4-37.

[43] The letters of sympathy represent a cross-section of the estates, including the clerical offices of the archbishop of Trent, the bishops of Bamberg and Freising, the

from the cathedral chapter of Constance, written from their residence in exile in the city of Überlingen:

> "Only today did we receive your letter ... With deep and sincere sympathy we learned exactly how the citizens of Augsburg treated the clergy. How much it reminded us of our own situation. Ten years ago we left the city of Constance. But continually even to this day we have encountered the same severe violence and disgrace."[44]

This letter of consolation opens a rare window on the experiences of the clergy of Constance in exile. The pace of episcopal succession during this period confirms the dire report of the canons. The minutes of the chapter end cryptically in 1526, the year of clerical withdrawal from Constance.[45] Sources for this period are rare and scattered, reflecting the failure to establish elsewhere a stable episcopal archive. Episcopal leadership was generally unsteady. While two remarkably capable bishops tended to the refugee clergy of Augsburg, the bishop's ring changed hands six times in the diocese of Constance during two decades of exile—more than any other diocese in the empire. Contested elections and reluctant candidates most likely left the episcopal administration divided and paralyzed. Hugo of Hohenlandenberg gladly resigned after three decades (1497-1528). His successor, Balthasar Merklin, had been heavily promoted by the Habsburg regime.[46] Merklin was also Vice-Chancellor of the empire and his itinerary was dominated by imperial matters. This position did give him the opportunity to confront his episcopal adversaries face to face. At the Diet of Augsburg (1530) Merklin, the elected bishop of Constance, personally received the Protestant *Confessio*

Stift of Ellwangen, the abbots of Fulda and Reichenau, and the secular representatives of the Habsburg administration in Innsbruck and the imperial chancellery, the Margrave of Brandenburg, the ruler of Ducal Saxony, the Pfalzgraf of the Rhine and Duke of Bavaria. Most notable is a letter of consolation from Otto, Erbtruchseß of Waldburg, cathedral canon in Speyer and Augsburg; in six years he would be elected as the new bishop of Augsburg; StaatsA, MB Lit., 151.

[44] "... Uff heut datum haben von E.F.G. E.r. und gunst wir ain Schreiben sampt ettlichen beyligenden buchlin empfangen und darauß mitt underthanigen hertzlichen mittleiden vernomen wolcher gestalt gegen E.F.G. E.r. und gunst sampt derselben Clerisy die von Augsburg gehandelt ... Und wievol uns von denen von Costentz vor zehen gantzen Jarren und noch fur und fur bis uff des heutigen tag nit minder frävel ... gwalt und schmach begegnet;" 23 April, 1537; StaatsA, MB Litt, 151.

[45] The minutes of the Augsburg cathedral canons are also interrupted between 1531 and 1541; see StaatsA, Neuburger Abgabe, Akten 5482-5499.

[46] See Rudolf Reinhardt, "Balthasar Merklin, 1530-1531," in *HS* I, 2.1, pp. 385-389."

Tetrapolitana from representatives of four cities, including Constance. Merklin's ubiquitous presence at the Diet of Augsburg prompted an envoy from Protestant Ulm to report home: "the Bishop of Constance now rules the Empire."[47] However, Merklin was never to be installed in his episcopal seat, dying in Trier (28 May 1531) only 17 months after the resignation of Bishop Hugo.[48]

Four bishops followed Balthasar Merklin in quick succession. Hugo of Hohenlandenberg was pressed back into service in 1531, but died a half year later. Cathedral Canon John of Lupfen was then elected and ruled for five years, resigning in 1537.[49] John of Weeze (1538-48), who had a long and distinguished career with the Roman curia and empire, fulfilled much of the promise of Merklin.[50] Ironically, the new bishop, still excluded from his cathedral city of Constance, was already the exiled archbishop of Lund and refugee bishop of Roskilde in Denmark. John of Weeze immediately addressed the financial crisis in the diocese, demanding the cancellation of papal fees for new bishops and aggressively seeking a critical contribution to the *Hochstift*, an annual income of 3,000 florin promised by Emperor Charles V.[51] Bishop John lived long enough to celebrate the subjugation of the city of Constance to Habsburg forces in 1548.

With the episcopal crozier changing hands six times, conditions in the diocese continued to deteriorate. By 1531 cities such as Biberach and Geislingen had to contend with reform movements; Esslingen, Reutlingen, and Ulm, now Protestant, no longer recognized any form of episcopal authority.[52] In the northern expanse of the diocese Habsburg sovereignty had discouraged religious dissent and undergirded episcopal rule.[53] By June 1534 Duke Ulrich of Württemberg had driven back Habsburg forces, regained control of his duchy, and began to institute reform measures hostile to episcopal jurisdiction.[54]

---

[47] Cited in Willburger, *Die Konstanzer Bischöfe*, p. 155.

[48] Willburger, *Die Konstanzer Bischöfe*, p. 167.

[49] Rudolf Reinhardt, "Johannes von Lupfen, 1532-1537," in *HS* I, 2.1, pp. 389-392.

[50] Rudolf Reinhardt, "Johannes von Weeze, kaiserlicher Generalorator, Erzbischof von Lund, Bischof von Roskilde und Konstanz," *RJKG* 3 (1984), 99-111.

[51] Rudolf Reinhardt, "Johannes von Weeze, 1538-1548," *HS* I, 2.1, pp. 392-398; Reinhardt, "Johannes von Weeze," *BK* I pp. 107-109.

[52] Willburger, *Die Konstanzer Bischöfe*, pp. 193-206.

[53] G. Bossert. "Die Jurisdiktion des Bischofs von Konstanz im heutigen Württemberg 1520-1529," *Württembergische Viertaljahrsheft fürLandesgeschichte*, N.F. 2 (1893), 260-281.

[54] Willburger, *Die Konstanzer Bischöfe*, pp. 152-166.

For the most part the bishops followed a course first established in relation to Reformation movements in Constance and Zürich. Despite civic and princely resistance the bishops of Constance continued to summon, reprimand, and excommunicate errant clergy, declaring their jurisdiction even as it was diminishing. Moreover, the Swabian League and the Imperial Diets provided forums for the airing of episcopal grievances which were seldom addressed, yet alone rectified.[55]

Episcopal policy did prove to be effective in regard to some financial matters. Throughout their exile the bishops applied steady pressure on their former 'capital city'. Although incomes and rents within the city had been confiscated, the fate of rural revenues were unclear. Did they belong to the place to which the benefice adhered, namely Constance, or to the recipient, in this case, the clergy in exile. Episcopal representatives won several important victories, culminating in an assembly in the Thurgau region in 1532; rents and incomes would adhere to the clerical persons.[56] Moreover, from 1535 to 1540, John of Lupfen and John of Weeze successfully pursued a source of revenue which would stabilize the episcopal treasury—the wealthy cloister Reichenau. By imperial decree this venerable island community was added to the *Hochstift* of Constance, the lands directly possessed by bishop and cathedral chapter.[57]

Without their old cathedral city or the support of other communes now turned Protestant or a second residence similar to Dillingen, the bishops of Constance lacked a significant base from which to rule and reconstitute regional authority. This lack of political support became especially obvious when subjects refused to fill episcopal coffers in response to an imperial tax. From 1542 to 1544 the episcopal chancellery received apologies or explanations from clergy, lower nobility, and secular officials from nearly every part of the diocese re-

---

[55] Bishop Hugo tried to investigate the clergy in the cities of Esslingen, Reutlingen, Biberach, Isny, and Lindau at the Bundestag in Donauwörth, 1527; *Deutsche Reichstagsakten*, Jüngere Reihe, Bd. 7, I. Halbband, p. 119, 1007, 1030; he also presented his case at the Bundestage in Augsburg 1528 (pp. 244-245) and Ulm (p. 1108). Note as well the Speyer Reichstag of 1529 (pp. 492-493) and the report of Conrad Zwick on issues pertaining to city and bishop (pp. 770-771, 1265-66).

[56] Dobras, "Konstanz zur Zeit der Reformation," in *Konstanz in der frühen Neuzeit*, pp. 59-61; Willburger, *Die Konstanzer Bischöfe*, pp. 183-184.

[57] The magistrates of Constance continued vigorously to oppose the transfer of Reichenau to the bishops of Constance; Dobras, "Konstanz zur Zeit der Reformation," in *Konstanz in der frühen Neuzeit*, pp. 116-119.

garding the payment of the *Türkenhilf*, the tax raised to defend Germany from Ottoman invasion.[58] Although neither episcopal letters of enquiry nor the reports of tax collectors survive, it is clear that overlapping civic and rural judicatories were yet again undercutting the bishop's authority as a cleric and especially as a Prince-bishop of the Empire. Almost all the letters of explanation, citing the imperial mandates of Speyer (1542) and Nuremberg (1543), explain why the imperial tax could not be paid to the bishop and why some secular officials could raise funds directly from the clergy. This justification for secular taxation of the clergy was often cited:

> "... each of our subjects, including both the clergy and the laity, must be taxed only in the place where he resides. So I have taxed the clergy who live under my Lord as Judicial Lord and their goods and in this place where my office can be found ..."[59]

But the nature of lordship over the clergy remained unclear; was the bishop or the local secular authority 'lord' of those sacred persons and places?

The Benedictine cloister of Mehrerau, east of Lake Constance, came under particular scrutiny from May to November of 1542; apparently the cloister had not paid its expected *Türkenhilf* to the bishop of Constance. Four letters reveal what appears to be an increasingly complicated investigation of imperial and regional tax law.[60] In the first Abbot Ulrich of Mehrerau explains how he had proceeded carefully, writing to his secular lord for clarification, given that the Emperor is "... my regional lord and defender and at the same time the bishop (your grace) is my spiritual overlord ..."[61] In a second letter Abbot Ulrich refers to the answer of the regional governor and regent from Innsbruck who explains the rights and privileges

---

[58] GLA 82a, 698.

[59] "... ain yder syndt (dabey dann bede stendt Gaistlich vnnd weltlich zuversteurn syndt) allain an dem ort do er gesessenn soll gesteurt werden. Vnnd mir deßhalben zuvor durch wolgemelten meinen gn Herren als gerichtsherren vnnd an dem ort meiner amptsverwaltung nach die gaistlichenn personen vnnd guter seinen Hershafften zuversteuren ..." GLA 82a/698, Document IV. Vogt of Brandenburg to the bishop of Constance, 23 May 1542.

[60] GLA 82a, 698, Letter 1—Ulrich, Abbot of Mehrerau to Bishop Johann of Constance: May 29, 1542; Letter 2—same correspondent and recipient: June 6, 1542; Letter 3—Statthalter Amptverwalter and Regent of the "oberösterreichischer Lande" to Bishop Johann of Constance: June 2, 1542. Letter 4—same correspondent and recipient: 16 November 1542.

[61] GLA 82a, 698, Letter 1: "... der R Ko M als meinen Castvogt vnd schirmhern dergleichen E F G als meinen gaisslichen oberern ..."

of his office, including taxation of all subjects, and particularly of cloister Mehrerau. In the end the governor himself did write; he did not deny the rights of episcopal taxation, but pointed out that Mehrerau was an exception.

Apparently Bishop John of Weeze continued to press his case, for six months later the Habsburg governor replied in a lengthy and fiery letter to him and stressed two main points: first, this secular administration in no way seeks to deny "your venerable jurisdiction and justice" (*Irer alten Hergebrachten Iurisdiction und gerechtigkait*). Second, "your efforts against the Abbot and other clergy who are under the House of Austria and its authority... have no legitimacy here."[62] The governor's frequent references to Hapsburg supremacy, not found in the first official explanation, make clear that he contended that the Bishop of Constance had overstepped his bounds as shepherd of the church and prince of the Empire.

Episcopal records from the 1540s are fragmentary at best and particularly unhelpful in regard to matters of taxation. Did Bishop John of Weeze pursue some new means of increasing episcopal revenue? Or did local and regional secular authorities find another way to extend their own jurisdiction, again at the expense of the battered diocese of Constance? A partial explanation can be found in the Swabian Circle (*Kreis*).

In April 1531 the first assembly of the Swabian Circle was held in Esslingen; it was one among ten circles, a new imperial system born of the imperial reforms of 1500-1512 and activated when the empire needed armies and funds to defend against Ottoman invasion. Unlike the estates of the empire the circles were geographical entities. The Swabian Circle covered much of southwestern Germany from the Rhine to the eastern extremities of the Diocese of Augsburg. Among its most powerful members were the Duke of Württemberg, the Margrave of Baden, the bishops of Augsburg and Constance, and the larger imperial cities such as Augsburg, Constance, Esslingen, and Ulm.[63]

The deliberations of the Swabian Circle assembly in Ulm (1542) reveal more information about the case of John of Weeze. Efforts to

---

[62] GLA 82a, 698, Letter 4: "Irer begerens an den obgemelten Abbt vnnd annder gaistlich so vnnder dem Hauß Osterreich vnd desselben oberkaiten vnd gebieten gesesser sein mit nichten befuegt ist ..."

[63] Adolf Laufs, *Der schwäbische Kreis. Studien über Einungswesen und Reichsverfassung im deutschen Südwesten zu Beginn der Neuzeit* (Aalen: Scientia, 1971), pp. 156-162.

raise soldiers and funds had been hampered by a fundamental over-lapping in the imperial taxation system. The imperial administration required both the circles and the estates to collect revenues, leading to confusion over jurisdiction and duplicate taxation on individuals and communities. This may explain the sudden influx of letters to the episcopal chancellery; those beholden to the bishop of Constance had paid their dues to a secular official. The decision of the Ulm assembly is particularly revealing. The office holders of the circle decided to investigate the case of Kaißhaim, a cloister that since 1531 had been listed as a member of the Swabian Circle. In 1542 the abbot of Kaißhaim reported that he would now raise a contingent of soldiers required by Otto Henry, Elector Palatine, a member of the Bavarian Circle. The Swabian Circle disputed Otto Henry's claims, making a final appeal to the Imperial Diet. Presenting the case was John of Weeze, Bishop of Constance, whose leadership was not accidental,[64] since he had been appointed the clerical representative of the Swabian Circle in the same year.[65] The Swabian Circle provided the bishop with a platform for regional leadership more stable than his diocesan authority and more promising than the recovery of his former cathedral city. Since the circles offered a new context in which the bishop's territorial claims could be adjudicated, he and his colleagues no longer had to rely on the resources of the old episcopal city of Constance. Instead the bishops of Constance could now pursue their claims to jurisdiction under the banner of Swabian Circle and *Türkenhilf*.

Already in the 1530s the circle system had served the interests of exiled bishops. Early in 1535 Bishop Christopher of Stadion received an urgent letter from Franz of Waldeck, Bishop of Münster, appealing to Christopher to use his influence in the Swabian Circle in order to mobilize its forces to march on Münster and help retake the bishop's city.[66] Thirty-two subsequent letters attest to the efforts of Bishop Christopher on behalf of his Westphalian colleague. Once again this correspondence provides valuable insight into conditions in the diocese of Constance. In response to Christopher of Stadion's request for financial support for the bishop of Münster, John of

---

[64] Laufs, *Der schwäbische Kreis*, pp. 199-205.
[65] Bernd Wunder, "Der Bischof im schwäbischen Kreis," *BK* I, p. 189.
[66] StaatsA, MB Lit. 1104 (Reichstagsakten), 18 January 1535, Bishop Franz of Münster to Bishop Christopher of Augsburg.

Lupfen, Bishop of Constance, reported on the empty coffers of the diocese, coffers too depleted to support a crusade against the Anabaptists:

> "The small, remaining part of our clergy has been led into such poverty by those sects (the Zwinglians and Lutherans) that they (the clergy) have nothing to offer us. Likewise our episcopal institutions (*Gestiffte*) are not able to provide lordship as others do over land and people. We cannot even begin to rectify the decline of our jurisdiction and our episcopal justice."[67]

The correspondence of the Swabian Circle reveals two characteristics of episcopal exile. One, during the heyday of the Protestant imperial cities and the Schmalkaldic League, the bishops of Constance were able to state their grievances and attempt to regain lost revenues through the workings of this constitutional body, originally as a member in the 1540s and then held leading roles in the clerical membership. Two, the circle system served as an episcopal network, allowing the exiled bishops of Constance and Münster to seek the assistance and influence of other bishops—in this case the bishop of Augsburg. In fact, until the sixteenth century the bishop of Constance had found his episcopal allies to the west and south in Lausanne, Basel, and Strasbourg; the bishop of Augsburg drew his support in the east from Freising and Eichstätt. Increasingly the bishops of Constance and Augsburg would turn to one another for mutual support.[68] Now the circle system had substituted for a point of reference that bishops had deemed indispensable—the episcopal city.

*   *   *

During the 1520s and 1530s the bishops of Constance and Augsburg could no longer claim the status of a mere resident alien in their episcopal cities. The magisterial acceptance and implementation of a

---

[67] "... Deßgleichen der vberig clainfueg gehorsam tail vnser Clerisey erzelter Secten halb in so große Armueth gefurt das er vnns nichtzit furtragen kan. Auch dargegen gedachter vnser Gestiffte nit wie Anndre weder mit solchen herschafften Land noch Leuten versehen. Daraus wir den Abgang vnnser Iürisdiction vnd anndrer Bischoflichen Gerechtigkaiten zum wenigsten nit ersetzen kunden;" Ibid. 7 June 1535, StaatsA, MB Lit., 1104.

[68] This connection between the bishops was most likely already made in the Swabian League; Hugo of Hohenlandenberg, Christopher of Stadion, and Bishop Wilhelm III of Honstein of Strasbourg met in Tübingen in early May, 1523 to discuss reform in their dioceses; Willburger, *Die Konstanzer Bischöfe*, pp. 108-110.

Protestant church government marked the culmination of the *Episcopus exclusus*. During the previous four centuries civic leaders had repeatedly expelled bishops or denied them entry, while some bishops fled in terror or in protest. Both civic and clerical leaders could always assume that the exile would be temporary. Although his legal, political, or economic standing might be diminished, the bishop had legitimate claims to property and institutions in the city. Wherever he resided in exile the bishop remained the chief overseer of the clergy and the shepherd of all souls in his diocese. By the late 1520s in Constance and the late 1530s in Augsburg lay magistrates ruled cities that did not need and did not acknowledge episcopal rights in any sphere of urban life. This exile was not merely a temporary absence from the city. The new structures of civic and ecclesiastical government no longer included or tolerated the office of medieval bishop.

Since Dillingen was already firmly established as a secondary episcopal capital outside the old cathedral city, it is tempting to surmise that the bishop of Augsburg fared far better than his western colleague in Constance who had no such recourse. Yet signs of the *Episcopus exclusus* can also be identified in Dillingen as well. While Bishop Otto, Truchseß of Waldburg, was absent from Dillingen in July of 1546, the residents of the city were compelled to swear allegiance to the Protestant Schmalkaldic League, forcing the cathedral canons of Augsburg to flee the city. Three months later imperial soldiers restored the regime of Bishop Otto in Dillingen. The Bishop fled a second time in March, 1552.[69] Moreover, this second episcopal city would never completely replace Augsburg as a venue for the ritual of the bishops. Christopher of Stadion and Truchseß Otto grasped the importance of the old city in death and life.

In late March, 1543 a feeble Christopher confessed his doubts and fears to a papal nuncio in Nuremberg. Despite his ecclesiastical expertise and his grasp of the Lutheran threat, Bishop Christopher was certain that the upcoming ecumenical assembly would begin without him; his health would certainly fail him if he attempted the long journey to the Council of Trent.[70] Besides, the frail bishop could not

---

[69] Zoepfl, *Geschichte der Stadt Dillingen an der Donau*, pp. 31-34.

[70] Bishop Christopher's reservations about papacy and empire reveal a great deal about episcopal morale on the eve of Trent and the Schmalkaldic war. Christopher was in regular attendance at imperial diets, including the congress of 1530 in Augsburg and was present for the Reichstag in Nuremberg in 1543. But in 1537,

afford to divert his attention from Lutheran agitators who might further ravage the church of Augsburg in his absence. In his view neither the pope nor the emperor could capably protect his diocese.
Two weeks later Christopher had a premonition. On Saturday, April
14, 1543 he took his evening meal in the Aegidius Cloister in Nuremberg. Admitting his weariness and weakness to his table guest he
said that his journey to Trent was an impossibility and he wondered
if he would see his episcopal city of Dillingen once more. Shortly
after dinner Bishop Christopher suffered a stroke. He died at seven
the next morning with only the Dean of the Augsburg Collegiate
Church of St. Maurice at his side.[71]

The exiled Christopher had not spent his final days at home in his
ancient episcopal capital, Augsburg, or in his second episcopal city,
Dillingen; he was not surrounded by his usual company of servants,
canons, and old friends. Instead he died in the Imperial and Protestant city of Nuremberg, in the service of a pope and a king whom he
did not trust to shield his battered church.[72] The indignity of a sec-
ond-rate funeral followed his lonely death. Christopher did not receive the honors bestowed on his esteemed episcopal ancestors—
burial in a chapel of the hallowed Augsburg cathedral and a lavish
three day memorial celebration in remembrance of his sanctity and

---

when his clergy had been expelled, the empire did not come to his aid with martial
support. Perhaps Bishop Christopher had his doubts about conciliar reform as well.
He was in attendance when the Fifth Lateran Council opened in May of 1512. As a
cleric with Erasmian loyalties he may well have agreed with Erasmus' satire of Pope
Julius II (see below, pp. 11-13). He most likely had his own concerns based on direct
and previous experience of ecumenical councils; see Zoepfl II, p. 5, 66-87.

[71] Zoepfl II, pp. 136-137.

[72] Nuremberg provides an intriguing counterpart to the south German cities of
Constance and Augsburg. Similar to Augsburg, Nuremberg played a critical role in
national politics, especially as a host to imperial diets and as a favorite of itinerant
emperors. Like the Swabian city of Ulm, Nuremberg was not an episcopal city.
Nuremberg was located on the fringe of the diocese of Bamberg, similar to the
burghers of Ulm who lived barely within the diocese of Constance. Although Nuremberg was not an episcopal city, the citizens did manage to break the lordship of
the Hohenzollern Burgrave in the later Middle Ages. The latter did not have the
formidable ritual resources of a prince-bishop. Ironically, after 1537, Christopher of
Stadion almost certainly found an easier entrance and short term residence in Nuremberg as opposed to his old episcopal city of Augsburg, revealing that the policies
of south German cities toward the clergy cannot be so easily predicted or catego-
rized. On the growth of Reformation movements here, see Günther Vogler, "Imperial City Nuremberg, 1524-1525," in *The German People and the Reformation*, pp. 33-49.
For a broader picture of civic life and political developments, see Gerald Strauss,
Nuremberg in the Sixteenth Century (Bloomington: Indiana University Press, 1976 [1966]),
especially pp. 154-186.

service.[73] Instead Christopher of Stadion was buried before the high altar in the parish church of Dillingen—an exile from Augsburg in life and death.[74]

In early May 1543 the cathedral chapter of Augsburg awaited the arrival of the newly elected bishop, Cardinal Otto, Truchseß of Waldburg (1543-73). As Christopher had ended his life and career without a proper episcopal burial, so Bishop Otto would enter his office without making the traditional procession around the sacred venues of Augsburg's avenues and churches. Indeed, Otto was installed as the bishop of Augsburg in Dillingen without entering Augsburg during his first year. In less than one month the city council of Augsburg had abrogated three hallowed episcopal rituals, the honor and esteem trumpeted at entry and installation at the beginning of an episcopal reign and both the funeral rites and memorial processions which were the celebration of a distinguished and faithful career at its end—the expected last rites of a faithful bishop.

In this time of physical and ritual exile the cathedral canons of Augsburg presented a grave reckoning to their incoming bishop. Not surprisingly they recounted the shameful story of their banishment: six years before the city council had driven the clergy of Augsburg from their homes and their source of financial support (*heusslichen wonungen*). "Against every law and justification" (*wider Recht unnd alle billichait*), the clergy had been cut off from the ancient sanctuaries of the city and diocese, the "Mother Churches" (*Muetterkirchen*) of Augsburg.[75] In short, expulsion was not simply a matter of economic hardship or illegal seizure of property. The clergy of Augsburg had

---

[73] In contrast, Christopher's predecessor, Henry of Lichtenau (1505-17), had been entombed in the Gertrude Chapel of the Augsburg cathedral; John Eck had been invited to preach; StaatsA, MBL 222: 16r, 1—18v, 10; Zoepfl I, p. 563.

[74] See StaatsA, MBL 585: 2v, 1-7. Christopher himself chose this burial site; Zoepfl II, p. 137. Although he was the first bishop buried in Dillingen, four of five of his episcopal successors chose to be interred there despite access to the cathedral in Augsburg. Bishop Otto (d. 1575) was originally buried in Rome but his remains were later transferred to Dillingen in 1614. Bishops Marquard of Berg (d. 1591), Johann Otto of Gemmingen (d. 1598), and Henry of Knoeringen (d. 1646) were all buried in Dillingen. In the later sixteenth century only John Egolph of Knoeringen (d. 1575) was interred in the Augsburg cathedral. Burial in the first church of the Augsburg bishops was not resumed until Bishop John Christoph of Freiburg (d. 1690); Plaucidus Braun, *Die Domkirche in Augsburg*, pp. 133-139.

[75] "Dieweil ain Erwurdig Thumbcapitul unnd andere gaistlichen von ainem Rath der Stat Augspurg wider Recht unnd alle billichait von Irer Muetterkirchen vnnd heußlichen wonungen schmehlich vertriben worden;" StaatsA, MBL 261: 5r, 4-7.

been torn from the maternal heart of their church territory, the old episcopal city and its sacred churches and cloisters.

Christopher and Otto, the two bishops who weathered the Protestant Reformation, were cut off from two churches in particular—the 'mother churches' of Augsburg, the sanctuary of the Benedictine cloister, St. Ulrich's, the first bishop's church in Augsburg, and the Cathedral of St. Mary, the sanctuary wherein bishops were laid to rest. At its heart *the Episcopus exclusus* signified far more than physical dislocation. Expelled bishops were driven off stage, refused access to the theater which gave meaning to their ritual and denied the ritual which granted them charismatic and sacred power in the city.

CONCLUSION: THE SACRED CITY AFTER EXILE

During the 1520s in Constance and the 1530s in Augsburg magistrates took full responsibility for the material and spiritual well-being of their citizens; they drafted church orders (*Kirchenordnungen*), decreed new and more severe standards for public morality (*Polizeiordnungen*), and 'civilized' their clergy. Through the oath of citizenship pastors submitted to the civic regime and became integrated members of the body politic. The ritual of the clergy revolved around parish churches and city hall. In Constance and Augsburg lay magistrates and Protestant pastors replaced the bishop and his clergy.

This period of autonomous and lay ecclesiastical leadership would be short-lived in Constance and would be curtailed in Augsburg. As the events of the third and fourth decades of the sixteenth century made the ultimate expulsion of the bishop possible, so the defeat of the Schmalkaldic League and the enforcement of the Augsburg Interim in the late 1540s opened civic gates to the bishops in exile.

Less than three months after the imperial victory over Protestant forces at Mühlberg (April 24, 1547) the estates of Germany were anticipating a crucial imperial diet to be held in Augsburg. The chief superintendent of the empire arrived two months before the opening of the convocation. This imperial official did not reach Augsburg at such an early date merely to prepare for the coming diet. The chief superintendent was Otto, Truchseß of Waldburg and Cardinal Bishop of Augsburg (1543-73). Upon his arrival Otto immediately took up residence in the episcopal palace. On July 23 he entered the city again, this time in the company of the emperor and a large military force. On August 2 Emperor Charles V ordered the city council to hand over the keys to the bishop's church. Three days later Bishop Otto consecrated the Cathedral of St. Mary anew and led the first Roman Catholic services to be held there in a decade. Otto had lived to see his exile end; the empire had restored his right of entry into Augsburg. With rites of cleansing and the singing of his first mass completed, always a critical stage in the formal entry of a new bishop, Otto consummated his return to the city.[1]

While the citizens of Augsburg opened their gates to emperor and

---

[1] Zoepfl II, pp. 218-219.

bishop, the magistrates of Constance chose to resist imperial decrees regarding civic submission and proper religion. In August of 1548 Spanish soldiers besieged and captured the city. In response to their disloyalty and disobedience the emperor's brother, King Ferdinand, delivered the conditions of surrender and subjugation in person; he repealed the imperial status of the city and installed a Habsburg overseer who would direct the city government and answer to political interests in Innsbruck. Constance now belonged to Austria.[2]

In May of 1551, three years after the submission of the city, Bishop Christopher Metzler (1548-61) finally made his formal entry into Constance.[3] In many ways his arrival echoed the entries of previous bishops. He left Meersburg, crossed Lake Constance, and proceeded toward the northern edge of the city. The magistrates of Constance met Christopher at a city gate and gave a formal welcome; the ringing of bells heralded his coming. The bishop thanked the members of the council for their kinds words of greeting. But throughout this exchange the magistrates never once referred to the *Verschreibung*, the charter that had framed relations between bishop and city since the late fourteenth century. Now city councilors were unable to negotiate on their own behalf. The Habsburg overseer possessed the right to deal with high church dignitaries and foreign powers. The magistrates introduced themselves as the docile servants of the house of Austria (*gehorsame underthonen*). After this public meeting Christopher proceeded to the Cathedral of Our Dear Lady; for the first time in Constance he sang the mass as the bishop of diocese and cathedral city.[4]

The eventual return of Bishops Otto and Christoph to the old capitals of their dioceses may suggest that the Protestant Reformation was merely another example of the typical ebb and flow of episcopal exile and return in the Middle Ages. After all Protestant leaders were no more successful than their medieval counterparts when attempting to exile a bishop on a permanent basis. Indeed, some have argued that in the long run Reformation movements were particularly ineffective in episcopal territories and cities.[5]

Even if the magistrates did not achieve a complete and lasting

---

[2] Dobras, "Konstanz zur Zeit der Reformation," in *Konstanz in der frühen Neuzeit*, pp. 141-146.

[3] See Rudolf Reinhardt, "Christoph Metzler, 1548-1561," *HS* I, 2.1, pp. 398-401.

[4] *Schulthaiß-Chronik*, pp. 91-92.

[5] Bob Scribner argues that the impact of the Protestant Reformation is exagger-

victory over episcopal power and even if it appears that bishops capably endured and survived exile until they could reclaim their holy places in the city, the Protestant Reformation still proved to be a watershed in civic-episcopal relations in Constance and in Augsburg. The bishops of Constance never again regained even partial control of their cathedral city. In fact, after 1548 neither the citizens nor the bishop restored their full authority in the city; the Habsburg governor made clear that Constance would be ruled from Innsbruck and Vienna. The rigorous and remarkably effective program of 'recatholicization' would be subservient to Habsburg aims and would include the assistance of the Jesuits; by the first quarter of the seventeenth century there were few remnants left of the Protestant majority that had expelled its bishop and had defied the emperor in the first half of the sixteenth century.[6] As Protestantism receded in Constance the bishops withdrew as well and came to reside permanently in Meersburg. Cardinal Bishop Mark Sittich (1561-89) turned this sleepy village into a princely residence. Meersburg, not Constance, hosted diocesan synods; here Mark Sittich built a seminary for the training of his clergy.[7] After 1527 Constance was no longer a bishop's city; after 1548 it was an increasingly hostile place for Protestants.

In contrast, Augsburg became a bi-confessional city, tolerating Protestantism and Roman Catholicism.[8] Bishop Otto and his successors continued to protect their immunities in the city and pursue

---

ated in these areas: "... it was largely within the boundaries of prince-bishops, those powerful territories that so aroused the ire of the reforming critics, that the movements were inhibited and checked in the long-term. The Reformation was never able, through massive dissent and disobedience, to capture a major bishopric or, more than temporarily, a major residential episcopal city." Scribner, "Germany," in *The Reformation in National Context*, eds. B. Scribner, R. Porter, and M. Teich (Cambridge: Cambridge University Press, 1994), pp. 8-9.

[6] See Wolfgang Zimmermann, *Rekatholisierung, Konfessionalisierung, und Ratsregiment. Der Prozeß des politischen und religiösen Wandels in der österreichischen Stadt Konstanz 1548-1637* (Sigmaringen: Jan Thorbecke, 1994); and Zimmermann, "Konstanz in den Jahren von 1548-1733," in *Konstanz in der frühen Neuzeit*," pp. 147-312.

[7] See Rudolf Reinhardt, "Mark Sittich von Hohenems, 1561-1589," in *HS* I, 2.1, pp. 401-412; Alfred A. Strnad, "Mark Sittich von Hohenems und Andreas von Österreich," in *BK* I, pp. 396-402.

[8] For the social and political implications of the Reformation and the resulting bi-confessional community, see Katarina Sieh-Burens, *Oligarchie, Konfession und Politik im 16. Jahrhundert. Zur sozialen Verflechtung der Augsburger Bürgermeister und Stadtpfleger 1518-1618* (München: Ernst Vögel, 1986).

episcopal policies on the civic stage. The Protestants did not relinquish all the autonomy they had gained when they expelled the bishop. Although they continued to clash with their old episcopal nemesis from time to time, these citizens of Augsburg had their own parishes and church government; they divided and shared the sacred city with the bishop. Protestants could also count on frequent episcopal absence from Augsburg. The bishops of Augsburg continued to develop Dillingen not only as their own preferred residence but also as a university town (as of 1554) and as a base for the Catholic Reformation. The bishops of Augsburg appear never to have considered an immediate transfer of their episcopal administration back to their first cathedral city.

This final arrangement in Augsburg—the cohabitation of two churches and the acceptance of the bishop's continuing role—points to a larger issue in the encounter of bishops and cities. During the Middle Ages residents not only rose up periodically to expel a bishop but for long periods they also accepted and relied on his ministrations in the city. Although much is made of the 'landed' or aristocratic background of the high clergy, bishops became city-dwellers as well; the episcopal city was the bishop's regional capital, the location of his cathedral, the site of his holy relics and graves—his sacred city. Despite expulsion and exile a bishop or his successor eventually found his way back into the episcopal city. When they were unable to take a city by force, bishops continued to rule through their office in the church. Even in exile they had powers that extended back over the walls, enabling them to disrupt trade and endanger souls. Eventually magistrates had to submit to the bishop's spiritual sovereignty and allow his return.

During the Protestant Reformation, however, lay rulers and city councils claimed the last arsenal of episcopal rule—the bishop's oversight of the church. With these powers in hand magistrates could drive out the bishop, banish his clergy, confiscate church property, and 're-form' the sacred topography of the city. During this exile the bishops of Constance adopted policies similar to those already in practice in Dillingen. They began to expand the village of Meersburg, turning this small lake-side town into a diocesan capital; there, not in Constance, they built a new episcopal palace and a seminary. The city of Constance would continue to serve as a source of revenue; the cathedral would remain standing as a sign of the bishop's former power in the city and as a justification for his peri-

odic visitation and residence. Yet from 1537 onwards both the bishops of Constance and Augsburg would rule their territories from new
cities of their own making.

*   *   *

In his episcopal city and this volume the bishop has taken center
stage. The nature and practice of episcopal power is laid bare, including his roles as city-lord, prince-bishop, and shepherd of the
church. Moreover, the bishop is no longer subsumed under the
grand stories of civic emancipation and City Reformation. By focusing on the *Episcopus exclusus* we acknowledge the importance of the
urban context while at the same time uncovering a remarkable series
of bench-marks for the narrative of episcopal history. During the
Middle Ages the bishops of Constance and Augsburg lost many economic, legal, political, and ecclesiastical rights and privileges. The
nature and degree of these losses appear not only in charters but also
in fierce confrontation and violence, whenever bishops were driven
from their cities, denied entry, or withdrew into temporary exile.
These documents and conflicts, however, attest to the tenacity, resiliency, and survival of the urban bishop. After every expulsion in the
Middle Ages the bishop regained access to the city and continued his
rule through negotiation (the *Verschreibung* in Constance), seignorial
remnants, and episcopal ritual.

Just as this book has lifted up the expulsions of bishops from the
footnotes of medieval history and fleshed out the exile and endurance
of the German bishop, so too we have turned from the treatises of
the Reformers and the gravamina of the cities to see the Protestant
Reformation from a decidedly episcopal point of view. During the
first half of the sixteenth century banishment and survival again serve
to describe the plight and the resourceful response of the German
episcopacy. Indeed, the Protestant Reformation marks the culmination of the *Episcopus exclusus*, when every last vestige of episcopal influence and authority was eradicated from Constance and Augsburg.
Despite this complete expulsion and exile, bishops managed to find
new alliances and resources that ensured their survival while refugees
on the land. After 1548 a new era of urban and episcopal history is
shaped by the decrees of Trent, the ministrations of the Jesuits, the
strategies and policies we now describe as Confessionalization, and
the creation of legal, multi-confessional civic populations. By turning

away from the grand Reformation narratives and the story of the City Reformation we see how the bishops of Constance and Augsburg turned to each other and to an imperial institution (the Swabian Circle) for consolation and support.

The paradigm of the *Episcopus exclusus* allows us to see both the continuing symbolic importance of the original cathedral city and the essential functions of the new episcopal residences on the land. To survive the tumult of the medieval and early modern periods the bishops of Constance and Augsburg found refuge in new episcopal cities and made them primary residences for centuries to come. Yet the bones of their predecessors and the sanctuaries of their 'mother churches' ensured their fierce loyalty to the ancient sees and communities of Constance and Augsburg, and to Konrad and Ulrich— sainted Lords of the Sacred City.

APPENDIX A   ECCLESIASTICAL TERRITORIES

The following list, reflecting territorial structures in the sixteenth century, includes bishoprics that were either part of the imperial church (*Reichskirche*) at some time in the Middle Ages or were in some way related to the imperial church and empire.[1] Archbishoprics and bishoprics were connected to the German church in various ways including princely status, imperial grants and fiefs, and military service to the crown.[2] Archbishops are listed twice when the archbishopric not only has jurisdiction over a German bishopric, but also was part of the German church.

AB=*See of Archbishop*   B=*See of Bishop*   *=*Status of Imperial Prince*

Aquileja	*Besançon*	*Bremen*
Aquileja (Patriarch)*	Besançon (AB)*	Bremen (AB)*
Laibach (B)	Basel (B)*	Hamburg (AB)*
Trent (B)*	Lausanne (B)*	Lübeck (B)*
		Ratzeburg (B)*
		Schwerin (B)*

---

[1] This list is based on the sequence of bishoprics and archbishoprics provided by Georg May; *Die deutschen Bischöfe angesichts der Glaubensspaltung des 16. Jahrhunderts*, pp. vii-xi.

[2] In addition to a single Patriarch, seven Archbishops, and thirty-nine bishops in the imperial church, twenty-nine imperial abbots also held princely rank: Benedikt-beuren, Disssentis, Ebersberg, Einsiedeln, Ellwangen, Epternach, Fulda, Hersfeld, Inden, Kempten, Korvey, Lorsch, Lüders, Luxeuil, Murbach, Ottobeuren, Pfäfers, Prüm, Reichenau, Rheinau, St. Emmeram, St. Gallen, St. Gislen, St. Oyen, Selz, Stablo, Tergernsee, Weissenburg, Werden; sixteen women's abbeys were likewise represented in the imperial church: Andlau, Buchau, Elten, Essen, Gandersheim, Gernrode, Herford, Hohenburg, Lindau, Niedermünster, Nivelle, Obermünster, Quedlinburg, Remiremont, Säckingen, and Zürich; Albert Werminghoff, *Geschichte der Kirchenverfassung Deutschlands im Mittelalter*, pp. 209-210.

Leo Santifaller has traced the sovereign rights (*Hoheitsrechte*) of the individual German archbishops and bishops under the Ottonian and Salian emperors; for example forty-two archiepiscopal and episcopal territories received imperial immunities; thirty-six held specific jurisdictional immunities (*Bannimmunitäten*); *Zur Geschichte des Ottonish-Salishen Reichskirchensystems*, pp. 78-101. Joachim Stieber identifies seven archbishops and thirty-nine bishops as "major ecclesiastical princes" in the fifteenth century on the basis of their contributions to imperial armies or their holding of imperial fiefs; *Pope Eugenius IV the Council of Basel and the Secular and Ecclesiastical Authorities in the Empire*, p. 435.

Cologne
Cologne (AB)*
Liège (B)*
Minden (B)*
Münster (B)*
Osnabrück (B)*
Utrecht (B)*

Mainz
Mainz (AB)
Augsburg (B)*
Constance (B)*
Chur (B)*
Eichstätt (B)*
Halberstadt (B)*
Hildesheim (B)*
Paderborn (B)*
Speyer (B)*
Strasbourg (B)*
Verden (B)*
Worms (B)*
Würzburg (B)*

Salzburg
Salzburg (AB)*
Brixen (B)*
Chiemsee (B)
Freising (B)*
Gurk (B)
Lavant (B)
Passau (B)*
Regesnburg (B)*
Seckau (B)
Vienna (B)
Wiener Neustadt (B)

Gnesen
Breslau (B)
Lebus (B)

Lund
Reval (B)
Schleswig (B)

Prague
Prague (AB)
Olmütz (B)

Reims
Cambrai*

Trier
Trier (AB)*
Metz (B)*
Toul (B)*
Verdun (B)*

Vienne
Geneva (B)*

Magdeburg
Magdeburg (AB)*
Brandenburg (B)*
Havelberg (B)*
Merseburg (B)*
Naumburg (B)*

Riga
Riga (AB)
Dorpat (B)
Ermland (B)
Kulm (B)
Kurland (B)
Ösel (B)
Pomesanien (B)
Samland (B)

Exempt Bishoprics[3]
Bamberg (B)*
Kammin (B)
Meissen (B)*
Sion (B)*

---

[3] Bamberg was a member of the archdiocese of Mainz until achieving exemption in the late thirteenth century; J. Kist, "Bamberg," *LTK* 1, p. 1216. Kammin was declared exempt beginning in 1188, sixteen years after the founding of the diocese; B. Stasiewski, "Kammin," *LTK* 5, p. 1272. Meissen received exempt status in 1399; P. F. Saft, "Meißen," *LTK* 7, 244. After periods as suffragen bishops to the archbishops of Vienne and Tarantaise, Sion was granted exemption in 1513; E. Tscherrig, "Sitten," *LTK* 9, p. 800.

APPENDIX B   THE BISHOPS OF CONSTANCE

The names of twenty-five bishops exist from the period prior to Salomo III (d. 838). Early Medieval bishops are listed here if they either appear in the chapters above or if burial information survives. (C) denotes buried in the Cathedral of Our Dear Lady (*Das Münster unserer lieben Frau*) in Constance. After Diethelm of Krenkingen (d. 1206), all bishops are listed to the mid-sixteenth century. Sixtus Werner (1626-27) was the first bishop to be interred in the Cathedral of Our Dear Lady after the Reformation; five bishops would follow his example.

BISHOP	REIGN	BURIAL SITE
John	760-82	Reichenau
Salomo I	838-71	
Salomo III	890-919	Constance (C)
Noting	919-34	Constance (C)
Konrad I	934-75	Constance (C)
Gebhard II of Bregenz	979-95	Petershausen
Theodorich	1047-51	Constance (St. Stephen's)
Rumold	1051-69	Constance (C)
Gebhard of Zähringen	1084-1110	Reichenbach
Ulrich I of Dillingen	1111-27	Constance (C)
Hermann I of Arbon	1138-65	Constance (C)
Hermann II of Fridingen	1183-89	Constance (C)
Diethelm of Krenkingen	1189-1206	Constance (C)
Werner of Stauffen	1206-09	Constance (C)
Konrad II of Tegerfelden	1209-33	Constance (C)
Henry I of Tanne	1233-48	Constance (C)
Eberhard II of Waldburg	1248-74	Constance (C)
Rudolf II of Habsburg	1274-93	Constance (C)
Frederick I of Zollern	1293	
Henry II of Klingenberg	1293-1306	Constance (C)

BISHOP	REIGN	BURIAL SITE
Double Election		
Rudolf of Hewen	1306-07	
Lewis of Strasbourg	1306-07	Basel
Gebhard IV of Bevar	1307-18	Constance
Double Election		
Konrad of Klingenberg	1318-19	
Henry of Werdenberg	1318-19	
Rudolf II of Montfort	1322-34	Arbon (unholy burial)
Double Election		
Albrecht of Hohenberg	1334-35	
	1344-45	
Nicholas of Frauenfeld	1334-44	Constance (C)
Ulrich III Pfefferhart	1345-51	Constance (C)
John III Windlock	1352-56	Constance (C)
Double Election		
Albert of Hohenberg	1356-57	
Ulrich of Friedingen	1356-57	
Henry III of Brandis	1357-83	Constance (C)
Avignon Bishops		
Mangold of Brandis	1384-85	Reichenau
Henry Bayler	1387-88	
Roman Bishops		
Nicholas of Riesenburg	1384-87	Olmütz
Burkard I of Hewen	1387-98	Constance (C)
Frederick II of Nellenburg	1398	
Marquard of Randegg	1398-1406	Constance (C)
Albert Blarer	1407-10	Constance (C)
Otto III of Hachberg	1410-34	Constance (C)
Frederick III of Zollern	1434-36	Constance (C)
Henry IV of Hewen	1436-62	Constance (C)
Burkhard II of Randegg	1462-66	Constance (C)
Hermann III of Breitenlandenberg	1466-74	Constance (C)

BISHOP	REIGN	BURIAL SITE
Double Election		
Lewis of Freiberg	1474-80	
Otto IV of Sonnenberg	1474-91	Constance (C)
Thomas Berlower	1491-96	Constance (C)
Hugo of Hohenlandenberg	1496-1530	
Balthasar Merklin	1530-31	Trier
Hugo of Hohenlandenberg	1531-32	Meersburg
John II of Lupfen	1532-37	Engen
John III of Weeze	1538-48	Reichenau
Christopher Metzler	1548-61	Meersburg
Mark Sittich of Hohenems	1561-89	Trastavere

APPENDIX C   THE BISHOPS OF AUGSBURG

The names of ten bishops survive from the period prior to Wikterp. But historical veracity and the approximate dates of their reigns cannot be determined with any certainty. Marcianus (534-74) is the exception. The earliest name, Zosimus or Dionysius, is traced back to the fourth century. Bishops were traditionally buried in two sanctuaries in Augsburg: [St. Ulrich and] St. Afra, the first episcopal church of the diocese and, from the late tenth century, the Cathedral of St. Mary. John Egolph of Knoeringen (d. 1575) was the first bishop to be buried in the Cathedral of St. Mary after the Reformation. John Christopher of Freiburg (d. 1690), however, was the next bishop to be interred in the cathedral.

BISHOP	REIGN	BURIAL SITE
Wikterp	d. 771	St. Afra [later St. Ulrich and Afra]
Tozzo	772-c778	St. Afra
Sintpert	778-c.807	St. Afra
Hanto	807-c.815	
Nidker	816-c.830	St. Afra
Udalmann	830-c.832	
Lanto	832-c.860	
Witgar	c.861-87	
Adalpero	887-909	St. Afra
Hiltine	909-23	
Ulrich I of Dillingen	923-73	St. Afra
Henry I	973-82	
Eticho	982-88	
Liutold	989-96	Cathedral of St. Mary
Gebhard	996-1001	Cathedral of St. Mary
Siegfried I	1001-06	
Bruno of Bavaria	1006-29	St. Maurice (Augsburg)
Eberhard I	1029-47	

BISHOP	REIGN	BURIAL SITE
Henry II	1047-63	Cathedral of St. Mary
Embriko	1063-77	Cathedral of St. Mary
Double Election		
Siegfried II	1077-96	
Wigolt	1077-88	
Hermann	1096-1133	
Walther I of Dillingen	1133-52	Seligenstadt
Konrad of Hirscheck	1152-67	St. Ulrich and Afra
Hartwig I of Lierheim	1167-84	Cathedral of St. Mary
Udalschalk	1184-1202	Cathedral of St. Mary
Hartwig II	1202-08	Cathedral of St. Mary
Siegfried III of Rechberg	1208-27	
Siboto of Seefeld	1227-47	Kaisheim
Hartmann of Dillingen	1248-86	Cathedral of St. Mary
Siegfried IV of Algishausen	1286-88	Cathedral of St. Mary
Wolfhard of Roth	1288-1302	Cathedral of St. Mary
Degenhard of Hellenstein	1303-07	
Frederick I Spät of Faimingen	1309-31	Cathedral of St. Mary
Ulrich II of Schönegg	1331-37	Cathedral of St. Mary
Henry III of Schönegg	1337-48	Schwäbisch Gmünd
Markward of Randegg	1348-65	Aquileia ·
Walter II of Hochschlitz	1365-69	Cathedral of St. Mary
John I Schandland	1371-72	Koblenz
Burkhard of Ellerbach	1373-1404	Cathedral of St. Mary
Eberhard II, Count of Kirchberg	1404-13	Wiblingen
Double Election		
Frederick of Grafeneck	1413-14	
Anselm of Nenningen	1414-23	Blaubeuron
Peter I of Schaumberg	1424-69	Cathedral of St. Mary
John II Count of Werdenberg	1469-86	Cathedral of St. Mary

BISHOP	REIGN	BURIAL SITE
Frederick II, Count of Zollern	1486-1505	Cathedral of St. Mary
Henry IV of Lichtenau	1505-17	Cathedral of St. Mary
Christopher of Stadion	1517-43	Dillingen
Otto, Truchsess of of Waldburg	1543-73	Rome

APPENDIX D   RESIDENCY PATTERNS—THE BISHOPS OF CONSTANCE (1322-1480)

The following tables reveal residency patterns based on the register of sur-viving sources in the *Regesta Episcoporum Constantiensium*. Only a fraction of the documents indicate a location for episcopal activity. Yet wherever a bishop promulgates a decree, drafts a letter, or blesses an altar, there he has established his court or has made an especial journey in episcopal service. Residency patterns are not completely accurate; episcopal activity was not always recorded and documentary evidence did not always survive. How-ever, evidence from nearly a century and one-half should indicate if bishops were entirely absent from Constance or when they chose to reside in certain locations in a given year. The data is organized according to year of reign, location, and number of documents indicating episcopal presence in the said place. The sequence of years and data for each bishop begins with the first year in which he is in noted in residence as bishop. The preference and aristocratic pedigree of individual bishops has required a varied list of possi-ble locations for each individual bishop.

Rudolf of Montfort, whose residency patterns are covered first, became bishop in the year of King Lewis the Bavarian's decisive victory at Mühldorf (1322); the reign of Lewis had a divisive impact on the relations between bishop and city in Constance for three decades and served as a prelude to the controversial and aggressive reign of Henry of Brandis (1357-83).

Rudolf III of Montfort 1322-34

Year	Constance	Gottlieben	Arbon	Other
1322	-	-	-	1
1323	9	1	-	1
1324	17	1	-	-
1325	18	-	1	-
1326	18	-	1	-
1327	17	-	1	-
1328	9	-	1	2
1329	9	-	-	1

Rudolf II of Montfort 1322-34 (continued)

Year	Constance	Gottlieben	Arbon	Other
1330	6	-	-	10
1331	7	1	-	1
1332	11	-	2	2
1333	4	-	-	2

Nicholas I of Frauenfeld 1334-44

Year	Constance	Castel	Winterthur	Other
1334	3	1	-	7
1335	-	-	8	2
1336	1	-	5	8
1337	5	-	1	1
1338	4	-	-	5
1339	4	1	-	-
1340	6	2	-	1
1341	5	-	-	-
1342	7	-	-	-
1343	5	-	-	2
1344	2	-	2	-

Ulrich Pfefferhart 1345-51

Year	Constance	Castel	Klingnau
1345	-	-	-
1346	9	1	-
1347	11	-	-

Ulrich Pfefferhart 1345-51 (continued)

Year	Constance	Castel	Klingnau
1348	18	-	2
1349	18	-	-
1350	34	-	-
1351	2	-	-

John III Windlock 1352-56

Year	Constance	Gottlieben
1352	-	-
1353	-	-
1354	4	4
1355	5	3
1356	1	-

Henry III of Brandis 1357-83

Year	Constance	Klingnau	Gottlieben	Zürich	Other
1357	16	1	-	-	1
1358	34	3	3	-	1
1359	43	9	1	-	1
1360	20	3	2	-	3
1361	17	1	5	-	-
1362	47	1	-	-	-
1363	21	-	8	-	-
1364	20	-	4	-	-
1365	16	1	-	2	6

Henry III of Brandis 1357-83 (continued)

Year	Constance	Klingnau	Gottlieben	Zürich	Other
1366	2	2	-	-	4
1367	16	-	2	2	5
1368	3	1	-	5	4
1369	-	-	-	-	-
1370	-	1	-	1	2
1371	-	3	-	-	3
1372	10	11	1	-	1
1373	20	-	1	-	1
1374	27	-	1	-	1
1375	12	1	4	-	-
1376	14	7	4	-	1
1377	9	14	-	-	2
1378	10	14	-	1	3
1379	8	17	3	-	-
1380	10	5	1	-	1
1381	8	9	3	-	2
1382	13	3	8	-	1
1383	4	16	1	-	-

Mangold of Brandis 1384-85 (Avignon)

Year	Marbach	Schaffhausen	Kaiserstuhl	Reichenau
1384	4	1	2	2
1385	-	-	-	-

Henry Baylor 1387-1409 (Avignon)

Henry served as bishop from 1387-1388 and then to 1409 as Administrator of the bishopric of Constance; information regarding his residency is sketchy at best; his dominant location for each year is listed.

Year	Place
1387	Avignon
1388	-
1389	-
1390	Avignon
1391	Avignon
1392	Avignon
1393-1396	-
1397	Avignon
1398-1399	-
1400	Alet
1401	-
1402	Alet
1403-1405	-
1406	Genoa
1407	Paris, Marseilles
1408	-
1409	Alet

Nicholas of Riesenburg 1384-87 (1388) (Rome)

Year	Constance	Gottlieben	Ulm	Zürich	Other
1384	1	-	-	-	-

Nicholas of Riesenburg 1384-87 (1388) (Rome) (continued)

Year	Constance	Gottlieben	Ulm	Zürich	Other
1385	7	-	2	4	3
1386	15	5	-	-	-
1387	8	-	-	-	1
1388	-	-	-	-	2

Burkhard of Hewen 1388-98 (Rome)

Year	Constance	Gottlieben	Engen	Other
1388	7	2	-	3
1389	8	-	2	-
1390	29	1	-	-
1391	5	-	2	-
1392	5	-	1	-
1393	13	2	-	-
1394	6	1	-	-
1395	13	-	-	-
1396	7	-	-	-
1397	16	-	-	-
1398	13	-	-	-

Frederick of Nellenburg 1398 (Rome)
(resigns nine days after election)

Marquard of Randeck 1398-1406 (Rome)

Year	Constance	Gottlieben	Other
1399	10	12	-
1400	8	8	3
1401	6	3	3
1402	11	1	7
1403	11	7	2
1404	15	1	4
1405	28	-	3
1406	13	-	5

Albert Blarer 1407-10 (Rome)

Year	Constance	Other
1407	17	5
1408	19	5
1409	22	4
1410	16	1

Otto III of Hachberg 1410-34

Year	Constance	Gottlieben	Klingau	Meersburg	Other
1411	3	-	1	-	10
1412	-	4	6	-	-
1413	8	-	-	-	2
1414	4	-	-	-	-
1415	7	-	-	-	-
1416	2	-	-	3	-

Otto III of Hachberg 1410-34

Year	Constance	Gottlieben	Klingau	Meersburg	Other
1417	12	-	-	-	2
1418	9	-	-	-	8
1419	14	-	1	-	1
1420	15	-	-	-	-
1421	18	-	-	-	-
1422	13	-	-	-	-
1423	8	-	-	-	-
1424	9	-	-	-	-
1425	7	-	-	-	-
1426	5	-	-	-	-
1427	4	-	-	-	-
1428	9	-	-	-	6
1429	13	-	-	-	3

Otto III of Hachberg 1410-34 (continued)

Year	Constance	Schaffhausen	Other
1430	1	13	1
1431	10	-	-
1432	3	7	-
1433	4	3	-
1434	1	2	-

Frederick II Count of Zollern 1434-36

Year	Constance	Gottlieben	Other
1434	-	-	-
1435	5	6	7
1436	2	3	4

Henry IV of Hewen 1436-62

Year	Constance	Gottlieben	Meersburg	Other
1436	15	-	-	3
1437	30	2	2	9
1438	10	-	2	6
1439	2	2	1	4
1440	1	7	-	4
1441	11	4	1	2
1442	14	3	-	-
1443	8	1	-	3
1444	14	-	-	1
1445	21	-	-	1
1446	14	-	-	2
1447	7	-	-	9
1448	9	-	-	-
1449	4	-	-	3
1450	4	-	-	2
1451	6	2	-	2
1452	18	-	-	2

Henry IV of Hewen 1436-62 (continued)

Year	Constance	Gottlieben	Meersburg	Other
1453	3	-	-	-
1454	9	-	-	1
1455	13	-	-	4
1456	21	-	-	-
1457	11	-	-	3
1458	10	-	-	1
1459	11	-	-	-
1460	6	-	-	2
1461	8	-	-	-
1462	6	-	-	2

Burkhard of Randegg 1462-66

Year	Constance	Other
1463	32	6
1464	33	-
1465	12	1
1466	6	1

Hermann of Breitenlandenberg 1466-74

Year	Constance	Other
1466	6	1
1467	23	-
1468	41	1
1469	30	-

Hermann of Breitenlandenberg 1466-74 (continued)

Year	Constance	Other
1470	31	-
1471	20	-
1472	17	-
1473	15	-
1474	13	-

Lewis of Freiberg 1474-80

Year	Constance	Radolfzell	Other
1474	1	2	-
1475	-	20	-
1476	-	27	-
1477	-	1	-
1478	-	1	2
1479	-	7	2
1480	-	-	1

Otto IV of Sonnenberg 1474-91

Year	Constance	Other
1475	19	1
1476	29	2
1477	1	-
1478	5	-
1479	4	-
1480	5	-

BIBLIOGRAPHY

I. *Abbreviations*

ARG	*Archiv für Reformationsgeschichte*
BK I	*Die Bischöfe von Konstanz.* Vol. I
BK II	*Die Bischöfe von Konstanz.* Vol. II
CDS	*Die Chroniken der deutschen Städte*
CH	*Church History*
DAS	*Diözesanarchiv von Schwaben*
DKP	*Die Protokolle des Konstanzer Domkapitels*
EO	*Erasmi Opuscula*
FDA	*Freiburger Diözesan-Archiv*
GLA	Badisches Generallandesarchiv, Karlsruhe
GSA	*Geschichte der Stadt Augsburg von der Römerzeit bis zur Gegenwart*
HJ	*Historisches Jahrbuch*
HRG	*Handwörterbuch zur deutschen Rechtsgeschichte*
HS	*Helvetia Sacra*
HZ	*Historische Zeitschrift*
JEH	*Journal of Ecclesiastical History*
JHVD	*Jahrbuch des historischen Vereins Dillingen an der Donau*
JVAB	*Jahrbuch des Vereins für Augsburger Bistumsgeschichte*
KC	"Konstanzer Chronik von 307-1466"
LTK	*Lexikon für Theologie und Kirche*
Maurer I	*Konstanz im Mittelalter*, Volume I
Maurer II	*Konstanz im Mittelalter*, Volume II
MB	*Monumenta Boica*

REC	*Regesta Episcoporum Constantiensium*
RJKG	*Rottenburger Jahrbuch für Kirchengeschichte*
RQ	*Renaissance Quarterly*
Ruppert	*Die Chroniken der Stadt Konstanz*
Schulthaiß-*Chronik*	*Constanzer Bisthums-Chronik*
Schulthaiß-*Collect.*	*Collectaneen*
StaatsA	Staatsarchiv Augsburg
StadtA	Stadtarchiv Augsburg
StAK	Stadtarchiv Konstanz
StAM	Stadtarchiv Meersburg
TDNT	*Theological Dictionary of the New Testament*
TRE	*Theologische Realenenzyklopädie*
UBA	*Urkundenbuch der Stadt Augsburg*
UHA	*Die Urkunden des Hochstifts Augsburg*
WABr	*D. Martin Luthers Werke: Briefwechsel*
ZGO	*Zeitschrift für die Geschichte des Oberrheins*
Zoepfl I	*Das Bistum Augsburg und seine Bischöfe im Mittelalter*
Zoepfl II	*Das Bistum Augsburg und seine Bischöfe im Reformationsjahrhundert*
ZSR	*Zeitschrift der Savigny-Stiftung für Rechtsgeschichte*

II. *Manuscript sources*

Augsburg, Staatsarchiv (StaatsA)
    Münchener Bestand, Litteralien: 151, 221, 222, 255I, 255J, 261, 585, 1104
    Neuburger Abgabe, Akten: 5482-5499.

Augsburg, Stadtarchiv (StadtA)
    Litteralien (Litt)
        January 17, 1537
        April 22, 1537

Karlsruhe, Badisches Generallandesarchiv (GLA)
    D: 317
    5: 7206, 7207, 7208, 7210, 7211, 7212
    65: 288, 291
    67: 499

82a: 698
209: 353

Konstanz, Stadtarchiv (StAK)
    A I: 8
    A II: 15, 24, 28, 29, 30

Meersburg, Stadtarchiv (StAM)
    U: 2, 19, 30, 146, 173, 186, 205.

Württembergische Landesbibliothek
    HB, V. Beatus Widmer. *Cosmographia*.

III. *Printed Sources*

Chroniken der deutschen Städte vom 14. bis ins 16. Jahrhundert. Vols. 4, 5, 18, 22, 23, 25,
    29, 34. Göttingen: Vandenhoeck und Ruprecht, 1965/1966f. [1865f].
Die Chroniken der Stadt Konstanz. Ed. P. Ruppert. Konstanz: Leop. Mayr, 1891.
Collected Works of Erasmus. Vols. 5, 6. Trans. M. J. Heath. Toronto: University of
    Toronto Press, 1986.
Decrees of the Ecumenical Councils. Vol. 1. Ed. N. P. Tanner. Washington, D.C.:
    Georgetown University Press, 1990 [1972].
Deutsche Reichstagsakten. Jüngere Reihe. Vol 7. I. Göttingen: Vandenhoeck und
    Ruprecht, 1963.
Eliot, T. S. *Murder in the Cathedral*. New York: Harcourt, Brace, and Jovanovich, 1963
    [1935].
Erasmus, Desiderius. *Erasmi Opuscula. A Supplement to the Opera Omnia*. Ed. W. K.
    Ferguson. The Hague: Martinus Nijhof, 1933.
Heinricus de Dissenhofen und andere Geschichtsquellen Deutschlands im späteren Mittelalter. Fon-
    tes Rerum Germanicarum. Vol. 4. Ed. J. F. Boehmer. Stuttgart: G. Cotta'schen
    Buchhandlung, 1868.
Hugo of Hohenlandenberg. "Ernstliche Ermahnung Hugo von Landenbergs
    Bischofs zu Konstanz, zu Frieden und christlicher Einigkeit, mit schöner
    Auslegung und Erklärung." In *Flugschriften aus den ersten Jahren der Reformation*. Vol.
    4. Ed. O. Clemen. Nieuwkoop: B. De Graaf, 1967, pp. 285-337.
The Julius exclusus' of Erasmus. Trans. P. Pascal. Bloomington: Indiana University
    Press, 1968.
"Konstanzer Chronik von 307-1466." Ed. F. Mone. *Quellensamlung der badischen
    Landesgeschichte*. Vol. 1. Karlsruhe: G. Macklot, 1848, pp. 309-349.
Die Konstanzer Ritualientexte in ihrer Entwicklung von 1482-1721. Ed. P. A. Dold.
    Liturgiegeschichtliche Quellen. Vols. 5, 6. Münster: Aschendorff, 1923.
D. Martin Luthers Werke: Kritische Gesamtausgabe, Briefwechsel. Vol. 1. Weimar: H.
    Böhlau, 1930.
Monumenta Boica. Ed. Academia scientiarum Boica. Vols. 29.1, 33.1, 33.2, 34.1, 34.2.
    München: Typis Academicis, 1814f.
"Die Protokolle des Konstanzer Domkapitels." Ed. M. Krebs. *ZGO* 61 (1952); 62
    (1953); 63 (1954), Beiheft; 64 (1955), Beiheft; 65 (1956), Beiheft; 67 (1958),
    Beiheft; 68 (1959), Beiheft.
"Reformation Sigmund." In *Monumenta Germaniae Historica: Staatschriften des späteren
    Mittelalters*. Vol 4. Ed. H. Koller. Stuttgart: Anton Hiersemann, 1964.
*Regesta Episcoporum Constantiensium. Regesten zur Geschichte der Bischöfe von Constanz von
    Bubulcus bis Thomas Berlower 517-1496*. Ed. Badische Historische Commission. 4
    Vols. Innsbruck: Universitäts-Verlag, 1905-1941.
Das Rote Buch. Vol. I. Ed. O. Fegger. Intro. K. Beyerle. Konstanzer Stadt-
    rechtsquellen 1. Konstanz: Merk, 1949.

Schulthaiß, Christoph. "Constanzer Bisthums-Chronik von Christoph Schulthaiß." Ed. J. Marmor. *FDA* 8 (1874), 1-101.

Die Statutensammlung des Stadtschreibers Jörg Vögeli. Ed. O. Fegger. Konstanzer Stadtrechtsquellen 4. Konstanz: Merk, 1951.

Die Urkunden des Hochstifts Augsburg 769-1420. Ed. W. Vock. Schwäbische Forschungsgemeinschaft bei der Kommission für Bayerische Landesgeschichte, Reihe 2a, Vol. 7. Augsburg: Verlag der Schwäbischen Forschungsgemeinschaft, 1959.

Urkundenbuch der Stadt Augsburg. Ed. C. Meyer. Vol. I: 1104-1356. Augsburg: A. F. Butsch, 1874.

"Vertrag zwischen Bischof Hugo und der Stadt vom 20. October 1511." In Jörg Vögeli. *Schriften zur Reformation in Konstanz, 1519-1538.* II.I. Beilage 4. Ed. A. Vögeli, pp. 632-639.

Vögeli, Jörg. *Schriften zur Reformation in Konstanz. 1519-1538.* Ed. A. Vögeli. Tübingen: Osiandersche Buchhandlung, 1973.

"Wahrhafte Verantwortung. Zur "Abthuung der papistischen Abgötterey' in Augsburg 1537." Ed. H. Immenkötter. *JVAB* 21 (1987), 90-111.

Zinsmaier, P. "Eine unbekannte Quelle zur Geschichte der mittelalterlichen Liturgie im Konstanzer Münster." *ZGO* 104 (1956), 52-104.

IV. *Secondary Literature*

Ahrens, Karl-Heinz. "Die verfassungsrechtliche Stellung und politische Bedeutung der märkischen Bistümer im späten Mittelalter." In *Mitteldeutsche Bistümer im Spätmittelalter.* Ed. R. Schmidt. Lüneburg: Nordostdeutsches Kulturwerk, 1988.

Alter, Willi. "Von der Konradischen Rachtung bis zum letzten Reichstag in Speyer (1420/22-1570)." In *Geschichte der Stadt Speyer.* Vol. 1. Ed. W. Eger. Stuttgart: Kohlhammer, 1982.

Anglo, Sydney. *Spectacle, Pageantry, and Early Tudor Policy.* Oxford-Warburg Studies. Oxford: Clarendon Press, 1969.

Anticlericalism in Late Medieval and Early Modern Europe. Eds. P. A. Dykema and H. A. Oberman. SMRT 51. Leiden: E. J. Brill, 1993.

Arnold, Benjamin. "German Bishops and their Military Retinues in the Medieval Empire." *German History* 7 (1989), 161-183.

Arnold, Benjamin. *Count and Bishop in Medieval Germany. A Study in Regional Power 1100-1350.* Philadelphia: University of Pennsylvania Press, 1991.

Arnold, Benjamin. *Princes and Territories in Medieval Germany.* Cambridge: Cambridge University Press, 1991.

Attreed, Lorraine. "The Politics of Welcome: Ceremonies and Constitutional Development in Later Medieval English Towns." In *City and Spectacle in Medieval Europe,* pp. 208-231.

Augsburger Stadtlexikon. Geschichte, Gesellschaft, Kultur, Recht, Wirtschaft. Eds. W. Baer, J. Bellot et al. Augsburg: Perlach Verlag, 1985.

Axton, Marie. *The Queen's Two Bodies. Drama and the Elizabethan Succession.* Royal Historical Society Studies in History. London: Royal Historical Society, 1977

Baer, Wolfram. "Die entwicklung der Stadtverfassung 1276-1368." In *GSA*, pp. 146-150.

Baer, Wolfram. "Das Stadtrectht von Jahre 1156." In *GSA*, pp. 132-138.

Baer, Wolfram. "Der Weg zur königlichen Bürgerstadt (1156-1275)." In *GSA*, pp. 135-140.

Baer, Wolfram. "Zum Verhältnis von geistlicher und weltlicher Gewalt in der ehemaligen Reichsstadt Augsburg." In *Aus Archiven und Bibliotheken. Festschrift für Raymond Kottje zum 65. Geburtstag.* Ed. H. Mordek. Frankfurt: Peter Lang, 1992, pp. 429-441.

Bak, Janos M. "Coronation Studies—Past, Present, and Future." In *Coronations. Medieval and Early Modern Monarchic Literature*. Ed. J. M. Bak, pp. 1-15.

Bakthin, M. M. *The World of Rabelais*. Trans. Helene Iswolsky. Cambridge: Massachuttes Institute of Technology Press, 1968.

Barlow, Frank. *Thomas Becket*. Berkeley: University of California Press, 1986.

Battenberg, Friedrich. "Gerichtsbarkeit und Recht im spätmittelalterlichen und frühneuzeitlichen Worms." In *Residenzen des Rechts*, pp. 37-76.

Bauer, Markus. *Der Münsterbezirk von Konstanz. Domherrenhöfe und Pfründhäuser im Mittelalter*. Konstanzer Geschichts- und Rechtsquellen. N.F. 35. Sigmaringen: Jan Thorbecke, 1995.

Baumgartner, Frederick J. *Change and Continuity in the French Episcopate: The Bishops and the Wars of Religion 1547-1610*. Durham: Duke University Press, 1986.

Baxendale, Susannah Foster. "Exile in Practice: the Alberti Family in and out of Florence 1401-1428." *RQ* 44 (1991), 720-756.

Becher, Matthias. "Mittelalter." In *BK* I, pp. 15-24.

Bechtold, Klaus D. *Zunftbürgerschaft und Patriziat. Studien zur Sozialgeschichte der Stadt Konstanz im 14. und 15. Jahrhundert*. Konstanzer Geschichts- und Rechtsquellen N. F. 26. Sigmaringen: Jan Thorbecke, 1981.

Bedos-Rezak, Brigitte. "Civic Liturgies and Urban Records in Northern France, 1100- 1400." In *City and Spectacle in Medieval Europe*, pp. 34-54.

Das Benediktiner-Reichsstift Sankt Ulrich und Afra in Augsburg (1012-1802). Ed. M. Hartig. Germania Sacra, Serie B. Augsburg: Dr. Benno Filser, 1923.

Benson, Robert L. *The Bishop-Elect. A Study in Medieval Ecclesiastical Office*. Princeton: Princeton University Press, 1968.

Bergeron, David M. *English Civic Pageantry 1558-1642*. London: Edward Arnold, 1971.

Berner, Hans. *"die gute correspondenz." Die Politik der Stadt Basel gegenüber dem Fürstbistum Basel in den Jahren 1525-1585*. Basler Beiträge zur Geschichtswissenschaft 158. Basel and Frankfurt am Main: Helbing und Lichtenhahn, 1989.

Bischof, Franz Xaver. "Die Kanonisation Bischof Ulrichs auf der Lateransynode des Jahres 993." In *Bischof Ulrich von Augsburg 890-973*, pp. 197-218.

Bischof Ulrich von Augsburg 890-973. Seine Zeit - sein Leben - seine Verehrung. Festschrift aus Anlaß des tausendjährigen Jubiläums seiner Kanonisation im Jahre 993. Ed. M.Weitlauff. Weißenhorn: Anton H. Konrad, 1993.

Bischof, Xaver. "Das Ende des Hochstifts und Bistums." In BK I, pp. 45-55.

Die Bischöfe von Konstanz. Geschichte und Kultur. Vols. I, II. Eds. E. L. Kuhn, E. Moser, R. Reinhardt, and P. Sachs. Friedrichshafen: Robert Gessler, 1988.

Bischofs- und Kathedralstädte des Mittelalters und der frühen Neuzeit. Ed. F. Petri. Städteforschung A. 1. Köln: Böhlau, 1976.

Bisson, Thomas N. "Celebration and Persuasion: Reflections on the Cultural Evolution of Medieval Consultation." *Legislative Studies Quarterly* 7 (1982), 181-204.

Bloch, Marc. *The Royal Touch. Monarchy and Miracles in France and England*. New York: Dorset, 1989 [1961].

Blumenthal, Uta-Renate. *The Investiture Controversy. Church and Monarchy from the Ninth to the Twelfth Century*. Trans. U. Blumenthal. Philadelphia: University of Pennsylvania Press, 1988 [1982].

Bossert, G. "Die Jurisdiktion des Bischofs von Konstanz im heutigen Württemberg 1520-1529." *Württembergische Vierteljahrschrift für Landesgeschichte*, N.F. 2 (1893), 260-281.

Bouchard, Constance Brittain. *Sword, Miter, and Cloister. Nobility and the Church in Burgundy, 980-1198*. Ithaca: Cornell University Press, 1987.

Bouwsma, William J. "The Peculiarity of the Reformation in Geneva." In *Religion and Culture in the Renaissance and Reformation*, pp. 65-77.

Brady, Thomas A., Jr. *Turning Swiss. Cities and Empire, 1450-1550*. Cambridge: Cambridge University Press, 1985.

Brady, Thomas A., Jr. "Rites of Autonomy, Rites of Dependence: South German Civic Culture in the Age of Renaissance and Reformation." In *Religion and Culture in the Renaissance and Reformation*, pp. 9-23.

Brand, Hans Jürgen. "Fürstbischof und Weihbischof im Spätmittelalter. Zur Darstellung der sacri ministerii summa des reichskirchlichen Episkopats." In *Ecclesia Militans. Studien zur Konzilien- und Reformationsgeschichte, Remigius Bäumer zum 70. Geburtstag gewidmet.* Vol. 2. Eds. W. Brandmüller, H. Immenkötter, and E. Iserloh. Paderborn: Ferdinand Schöningh, 1988, pp. 1-16.

Braun, Placidus. *Die Domkirche in Augsburg und der hohe und niedere Clerus an derselben.* Augsburg: Schlossers Buch- und Kunsthandlung, 1829.

Brehm, Karl. "Zur Geschichte der Konstanzer Diözesansynoden während des Mittelalters." *DAS* 22 (1904), 17-26, 44-48, 93-96, 141-144.

Brown, Peter. *Augustine of Hippo.* Berkeley: University of California Press, 1967.

Brück, Anton P. *Mainz vom Verlust der Stadtfreiheit bis zum Ende des Dreissigjährigen Krieges (1462-1648).* Geschichte der Stadt Mainz, Vol. 5. Düsseldorf: Walter Rau, 1972.

Brühl, Carlrichard. "Kronen- und Krönungsbrauch im frühen und hohen Mittelalter." *HZ* 234 (1982), 1-31.

Bryant, Lawrence M. *The King and the City in the Parisian Royal Entry Ceremony: Politics, Ritual, and Art in the Renaissance.* Travaux d'Humanisme et Renaissance 216. Geneva: Librairie Droz, 1986.

Bryant, Lawrence M. "The Medieval Entry Ceremony at Paris." In *Coronations*, pp. 88-118.

Bryant, Lawrence M. "Configurations of the Community in Late Medieval Spectacles: Paris and London during the Dual Monarchy." In *City and Spectacle in Medieval Europe*, pp. 3-33.

Bück, Hermann, and Ekkehart Fabian. *Konstanzer Reformationsgeschichte in ihren Grundzüge.* Tübingen: Osiandersche Buchhandlung, 1965.

Cameron, Euan. *The European Reformation.* Oxford: Clarendon Press, 1991.

Chevalley, Denis A. *Der Dom zu Augsburg.* Die Kunstdekmäler von Bayern N.F.1, Munich: R. Oldenbourg, 1995.

Chrisman, Miriam Usher. *Strasbourg and the Reform. A Study in the Process of Change.* New Haven: Yale University Press, 1967.

Chronic, Halka. *Roadside Geology of Arizona.* Missoula, Montana: Mountain Press Publishing, 1983.

City and Spectacle in Medieval Europe. Eds. B. A. Hanawalt and K. L. Reyerson. Medieval Studies at Minnesota, Vol. 6. Minneapolis: University of Minnesota Press, 1994.

Coronations. Medieval and Early Modern Monarchic Ritual. Ed. J. M. Bak. Berkeley: University of California Press, 1990.

Dameron, George W. *Episcopal Power and Florentine Society, 1000-1320.* Cambridge: Harvard University Press, 1991.

Dann, Walther. "Die Besetzung des Bistums Konstanz vom Wormser Konkordat zur Reformation." *ZGO* 51 (1952), 3-96.

Dauch, Bruno. *Die Bischofsstadt als Residenz der geistlichen Fürsten.* Historische Studien 109. Vaduz: Kraus, 1965 [1913].

Davis, Natalie Zemon. *Society and Culture in Early Modern France.* Stanford: Stanford University Press, 1975.

Demandt, Dieter. *Stadtherrschaft und Stadtfreiheit im Spannungsfeld von Geistlichkeit und Bürgerschaft in Mainz (11.—15. Jahrhundert).* Wiesbaden: Franz Steiner Verlag, 1977.

Der Dom zu Augsburg. Schnell Kunstführer 64. München: Schnell und Steiner, 1985 [1934].

Dictionary of the Middle Ages. Vol. 3. Ed. J. R. Strayer. New York: Charles Scribner's Sons, 1983.

Dobras, Wolfgang. "Konstanz zur Zeit der Reformation." In *Konstanz in der frühen*

Neuzeit. Reformation. Verlust der Reichsfreiheit. Österreichische Zeit. Geschichte der Stadt Konstanz 3. Konstanz: Stadler, 1991, pp. 11-46.

Du Boulay, F. R. H. "The German Town Chroniclers." In *The Writing of History in the Middle Ages. Essays Presented to Richard William Southern.* Eds. R. H. C. Davis and J. M. Wallace-Hadrill. Oxford: Clarendon Press, 1981, pp. 445-469.

Du Boulay, F. R. H. *Germany in the Later Middle Ages.* London: Athelone Press, 1983.

Duby, Georges. *William Marshal. The Flower of Chivalry.* New York: Pantheon Books, 1985 [1984].

Duggan, Lawrence G. *Bishop and Chapter: The Governance of the Bishopric of Speyer to 1552.* New Brunswick: Rutgers University Press, 1978.

Ebel, Wilhelm. *Der Bürgereid als Geltungsgrund und Gestaltungsprinzip des deutschen mittelalterlichen Stadtrechts.* Weimar: Hermann Böhlaus, 1958.

Eberhard, Winfried. "Klerus- und Kirchenkritik in der spätmittelalterlichen deutschen Stadtchronistik." *HJ* 114 (1994), 349-380.

Egli, Emil. "Hugo von Landenberg Bischof von Konstanz." *Zwingliana* 1 (1901), 184-191.

Elm, Kaspar. "Antiklerikalismus im deutschen Mittelalter." In *Anticlericalism in Late Medieval and Early Modern Europe,* pp. 3-18.

Eltis, D. A. "Tensions between Clergy and Laity in some Western German Cities in the Later Middle Ages." *JEH* 43 (1992), 231-248.

Enderle, Wilfried. *Konfessionsbildung und Ratsregiment in der katholischen Reichsstadt Überlingen (1500-1618) im Kontext der Reformationsgeschichte der oberschwäbischen Reichsstädte.* Veröffentlichungen der Kommission für geschichtliche Landeskunde in Baden-Württemberg, Reihe B 118. Stuttgart: Kohlhammer, 1990.

Ennen, Edith. *The Medieval Town.* Europe in the Middle Ages, Vol. 15. Amsterdam: North-Holland, 1979 [1972].

Ettelt, Rudibert. *Geschichte der Stadt Füssen.* Füssen: Verlag der Stadt, 1971.

European Towns. Their Archaeology and Early History. Ed. M. W. Barley. London: Academic Press, 1977.

Feine, Hans Erich. *Kirchliche Rechtsgeschichte.* Vol. 1: Die Katholische Kirche. Weimar: Hermann Böhlaus, 1955.

Fichtenau, Heinrich. *Living in the Tenth Century. Mentalities and Social Orders.* Trans. P. J. Geary. Chicago: University of Chicago Press, 1991 [1984].

Fischer, Steven R. *Meersburg im Mittelalter. Aus der Geschichte einer Bodenseestadt und ihrer nächsten Umgebung.* Meersburg: List und Franck, 1988.

Flint, Valerie J. *The Rise of Magic in Early Modern Europe.* Princeton: Princeton University Press, 1991.

Ford, Franklin. *Political Murder. From Tyranicide to Terrorism.* Cambridge: Harvard University Press, 1985.

Franzen, August. *Bischof und Reformation. Erzbischof Hermann von Wied in Köln vor der Entscheidung zwischen Reform und Reformation.* Katholisches Leben und Kirchenreform im Zeitalter der Glaubensspaltung 31. Münster: Aschendorff, 1971.

Fried, Pankraz. "Augsburg in nachstaufischer Zeit (1276-1368)." In *GSA,* pp. 146-159.

Fried, Pankraz. "Augsburg unter den Staufern (1132-1268)." In *GSA,* pp. 127-131.

Gebauer, J. *Geschichte der Stadt Hildesheim.* Vol 1. Hildesheim: August Lax, 1922.

Geertz, Clifford. "Centers, Kings, and Charisma: Reflections on the Symbolics of Power." In *Rites of Power. Symbolism, Ritual, and Politics Since the Middle Ages,* pp. 13-38.

The German Peasants' War in Documents. Eds. T. Scott and B. Scribner. London: Humanities Press International, 1991.

The German People and the Reformation. Ed. R. Po-Chia Hsia. Ithaca: Cornell University Press, 1988.

Geschichte der Stadt Augsburg von der Römerzeit bis zur Gegenwart. Ed. G. Gottlieb. Stuttgart: Konrad Theiss, 1984.

Giesey, Ralph E. *The Royal Funeral Ceremony in Renaissance France*. Travaux D'Humanisme et Renaissance 37. Geneva: Librairie E. Droz, 1960.

Gilbert, William. "Sebastian Brandt, Conservative Humanist." *ARG* 46 (1955), 145-167.

Gisler, Johannes. *Die Stellung der Acht Orte zum Konstanzer Bistumsstreit 1474-1489*. Zeitschrift für Kirchengeschichte, Beiheft 18. Freiburg: Universitäts Verlag, 1956.

Glatz, C. J. "Zur Geschichte Hugos von Landenbergs, Bischof zu Konstanz." *FDA* 9 (1875), 101-140.

Gottlieb, Theodor. *Das abendländische Chorepiskopat*. Kanonistische Studien und Texte 1. Bonn: Kurt Schroeder, 1928.

Götz, Franz. "Meersburg, Stadt des Bischofs von Konstanz und bischöfliche Residenzstadt." In *Südwestdeutsche Bischofsresidenzen außerhalb der Kathedralstädte*, pp. 27-33.

Guenée, B. and F. Lehoux. *Les entrée royales françaises de 1328 à 1515*. Sources d'Histoire Médiévale 5. Paris: Centre National de la Recherche Scientifique, 1968.

Guggisberg, Hans R. *Basel in the Sixteenth Century. Aspects of the City Republic before, during, and after the Reformation*. St. Louis: Center for Reformation Research, 1982.

Haemmerle, Albert. *Die Canoniker des Hohen Domstifts zu Augsburg bis zur Saecularisation*. Zürich: self-publication, 1935.

Handwörterbuch zur deutschen Rechtsgeschichte. 4 Vols. Eds. A. Erler and E. Kaufmann. Berlin: E. Schmidt, 1971-98.

Hartfelder, Karl. "Der humanistische Freundeskreis des Desiderius Erasmus in Konstanz." *ZGO* 47 (1983), 1-33.

Hausberger, Karl. *Geschichte des Bistums Regensburg*. Vol. 1: Mittelalter und frühe Neuzeit. Regensburg: Friedrich Pustet, 1989.

Hauschild, Wolf-Dieter. *Kirchengeschichte Lübecks. Christentum und Bürgertum in neun Jahrhunderten*. Lübeck: Max Schmidt Römhild, 1981.

Haußmann, Peter. "Die Politik der Grafen von Württemberg in Konstanzer Schisma der Jahre 1474-1480." In *Mittel und Wege früher Verfassungspolitik*. Spätmittelalter und frühe Neuzeit 9. Stuttgart: Klett-Cotta, 1979.

Heal, Felicity. *Of Prelates and Princes: A Study of the Economic and Social Position of the Tudor Episcopate*. London: Cambridge University Press, 1980.

Hecker, Norbert. *Bettelorden und Bürgertum. Konflikt und Kooperation in deutschen Städten des Spätmittelalters*. Europäisches Hochschulschriften: Theologie 146. Frankfurt am Main: Peter D. Lang, 1981.

Hecker, Norbert. *Stellung und Wirksamkeit der Bettelorden in der städtischen Gesellschaft*. Berliner Historische Studien 3, Ordensstudien 2. Berlin: Duncker und Humboldt, 1981.

von Hefele, Joseph. *Conciliengeschichte*. Vol. 6. Freiburg: Herder, 1890.

Hefele, Klaus. *Studien zum Hochmittelalterlichen Stadttypus der Bischofsstadt in Oberdeutschland (Augsburg, Freising, Konstanz, Regensburg)*. Augsburg: Werner Blasaditsch, 1970.

Heinig, Paul-Joachim. *Reichsstädte, Freie Städte und Königtum 1389-1450. Ein Beitrag zur deutschen Verfassungsgeschichte*. Veröffentlichungen des Institutus für europäische Geschichte Mainz, Abteilung Universalgeschichte 108. Stuttgart: Franz Steiner, 1983.

Helvetia Sacra. Abteilung I, 2. 1, 2.2. Das Bistum Konstanz, Das Erzbistum Mainz, Das Bistum St. Gallen. Ed. F. X. Bischof, et al. Basel, Frankfurt am Main: Helbing und Lichtenhahn, 1993.

Hergemöller, Bernd-Ulrich. *'Pfaffenkriege' im spätmittelalterlichen Hanseraum. Quellen und Studien zu Braunschweig, Osnabrück, Lüneburg und Rostock*. 2 Vols. Städteforschung C. Köln: Hermann Böhlau, 1988.

van den Heuvel, Christina. "Städtisch-bürgerliche Freiheit und fürstlicher Absolutismus. Verfassung und Verwaltung der Stadt Osnabrück in der frühen Neuzeit."

In *Recht, Verfassung und Verwaltung in der frühneuzeitlichen Stadt*. Ed. M. Stolleis. Köln: Hermann Böhlau, 1991, pp. 159-171.

Hinschuis, Paul. *Das Kirchenrecht der Katholiken und Protestanten in Deutschland*. Vol. 2: System des katholischen Kirchenrechts mit besonderer Rücksicht auf Deutschland. Graz: Akademische Druck- und Verlagsanstalt, 1959 [1878].

History of the Church. Eds. H. Jedin and J. Dolan. New York: Crossroad, 1980.

Hoeynck, F. A. *Geschichte der kirchlichen Liturgie des Bisthums Augsburg*. Augsburg: Literatur Institut von Dr. M. Huttler (Michael Seitz), 1889.

Hofmeister, Philipp *Mitra und Stab der wirklichen Prälaten ohne bischöflichen Charakter*. Abhandlungen 104. Stuttgart: Ferdinand Enke, 1928.

Hofmeister, Philipp. *Bischof und Domkapitel nach altem und nach neuem Recht*. Berlin: Graphisches Institut Paul Funk, 1931.

Honselmann, Klemens. *Das Rationale der Bischöfe*. Paderborn: Verein für Geschichte und Altertumskunde Westfalens, 1975.

Hsia. R. Po-Chia. "Münster and the Anabaptists." In *The German People and the Reformation*, pp. 50-69.

Hundsnurscher, Franz. "Die Kathedrale des Bistums." In *Glanz der Kathedrale. 900 Jahre Konstanzer Münster*. Konstanz: Städtische Museen Konstanz, 1989, pp. 35-43.

Immenkötter, Herbert. "Kirche zwischen Reformation und Parität." In *GSA*, pp. 391-412.

Immenkötter, Herbert. "Wahrhafte Verantwortung. Zur 'Abthuung der papistischen Abgötterey' in Augsburg 1537." *JVAB* 21 (1987), 72-111.

Isenmann, Eberhard. *Die deutsche Stadt im Spätmittelalter. Stadtgestalt, Recht, Stadtregiment, Kirche, Gesellschaft, Wirtschaft*. Stuttgart: Eugen Ulmer, 1988.

Jahn, Joachim. "Die Augsburger Sozialstruktur im 15. Jahrhundert." In *GSA*, pp. 187-192.

Jahn, Joachim. *Augsburg Land*. Historischer Atlas von Bayern: Schwaben 11. München: Kommission für bayerische Landesgeschichte, 1984.

James, Mervyn. "Ritual, Drama, and Social Body in the Late Medieval English Town." *Past and Present* 98 (1983), 3-29.

Janson, U. "Otto von Hachberg (1410-1434), Bischof von Konstanz und sein Traktat, 'De conceptione beatae virginis.'" *FDA* 88 (1968), 205-358.

Johnson, Donald S. *Phantom Islands of the Atlantic. The Legends of Seven Lands that Never Were*. New York: Walker and Company, 1994.

Kaiser, Reinhold. "'Mord im Dom.' Von der Vertreibung zur Ermordung des Bischofs im frühen und hohen Mittelalter." *ZSR KA* 110 (1993), 95-134.

Kantorowicz, Ernst H. *Laudes Regiae. A Study in Liturgical Acclamations and Medieval Ruler Worship*. Berekely: University of California Press, 1946

Kantorowicz, Ernst H. *The King's Two Bodies. A Study in Medieval Political Theology*. Princeton: Princeton University Press, 1957.

Kantorowicz, Ernst H. "The 'King's Advent' and the Enigmatic Panels in the Doors of Santa Sabina." In *Selected Studies*. Locust Valley, New York: J. J. Augustin, 1965, pp. 37-75.

Karg, August. "Bischof Johann IV. von Konstanz (1351-1356)." *FDA* 3 (1868), 103-121.

Katalog Alte Meister bis 1800. Staatliche Kunsthalle, Karlsruhe. Ed. J. Lauts. Karlsruhe, 1966, pp. 21-23, 54.

Keller, Franz. "Die Verschuldung des Hochstifts Konstanz im 14. und 15. Jahrhundert." *FDA* 30 (1902), 1-104.

Keller, H. L. *Reclams Lexikon der Heiligen und der biblischen Gestalten. Legende und Darstellung in der bildenden Kunst*. Stuttgart: Reclam, 1991 [1968].

Kempers, Bram. "Icons, Altarpieces, and Civic Ritual in Siena Cathedral, 1100-1530," in *City and Spectacle in Medieval Europe*, pp. 89-136.

Kertzer, David. *Ritual, Politics, and Power*. New Haven: Yale University Press, 1988.

Kießling, Rolf. *Bürgerliche Gesellschaft und Kirche in Augsburg im 14. und 15. Jahrhundert. Ein Beitrag zur Strukturanalyse der spätmittelalterlichen Stadt.* Abhandlung zur Geschichte der Stadt Augsburg 19. Augsburg: Hieronymus Mühlberger, 1971.

Kießling, Rolf. "Augsburgs Wirtschaft im 14. und 15. Jahrhundert." In *GSA*, pp. 171-181.

Kießling, Rolf. "Augsburg zwischen Mittelalter und Neuzeit." In *GSA*, pp. 241-251.

Kießling, Rolf. "Bürgertum und Kirche im Spätmittelalter." In *GSA*, pp. 108-213.

Koch, Klaus H. "Bemerkungen zum Anteil der Ministerialität an der städtischen Führungsschicht in Konstanz." In *Stadt und Ministerialität.* Eds. E. Maschke and J. Sydow. Veröffentlichungen der Kommission für Geschichtliche Landeskunde in Baden Württemberg, Reihe B, 76. Stuttgart: W. Kohlhammer, 1973, pp. 92-97.

Konrad, Bernd. "Die Malerei im Umkreis von Hugo von Hohenlandenberg." In *BK* II, pp. 134-142.

Kosel, Karl. *Der Augsburger Domkreuzgang und seine Denkmäler.* Sigmaringen: Jan Thorbecke, 1991.

Koziol, Geoffrey. *Begging Pardon and Favor. Ritual and Political Order in Early Medieval France.* Ithaca: Cornell University Press, 1992.

Kramml, Peter. *Kaiser Friedrich III. und die Reichsstadt Konstanz (1440-1493). Die Bodenseemetropole am Ausgang des Mittelalters.* Konstanzer Geschichts- und Rechtsquellen 29. Sigmaringen: Jan Thorbecke, 1985.

Kramml, Peter. "Heinrich von Hewen." In *BK* I, pp. 384-392.

Kramml, Peter. "Konstanz: Das Verhältnis zwischen Bischof und Stadt." In *BK* I, pp. 288-299.

Kreuzer, Georg. "Augsburg als Bischofsstadt unter den Saliern und Lothar III." In *GSA*, pp. 124-126.

Kreuzer, Georg. "Augsburg in fränkischer und ottonisher Zeit (ca. 550-1024)." In *GSA*, pp. 115-121.

Kreuzer, Georg. "Das Verhältnis von Stadt und Bischof in Augsburg und Konstanz im 12. und 13. Jahrhundert." In *Stadt und Bischof*, pp. 43-64.

Laufs, Adolf. *Der Schwäbische Kreis. Studien über Einungswesen und Reichsverfassung im deutschen Südwesten zu Beginn der Neuzeit.* Untersuchungen zur deutschen Staats- und Rechtsgeschichte, N.F. 16. Aalen: Scientia, 1971.

Layer, Adolf. "Dillingen als zweiter Bischofssitz und Dillingens Pfarrkriche als zweite Kathedralkirche im Bistum Augsburg." *JHVD* 82 (1980), 66-76.

Lengle, Peter. "Handel und Gewerbe bis zum Ende des 13. Jahrhunderts." In *GSA*, pp. 166-170.

Leudemann, Norbert. *Deutsche Bischofsstädte im Mittelalter. Zur topographischen Entwicklung der deutschen Bischofsstadt im Heiligen Römischen Reich.* München: Holler, 1980.

Leuschner, Joachim. *Germany in the Late Middle Ages.* Trans S. MacCormick. Europe in the Middle Ages. Selected Studies 17. Amsterdam: North-Holland Publishing Company, 1980.

Lexikon für Theologie und Kirche. Eds. J. Hofer and K. Rahner. 2nd Edition. Freiburg: Herder, 1957-1965.

Liebhart, Wilhelm. "Stifte, Klöster und Konvente in Augsburg." In *GSA*, pp. 193-201.

Lindenbaum, Sheila. "Ceremony and Oligarchy: The Midsummer Watch." In *City and Spectacle in Medieval Europe*, pp. 171-188.

Locher, Gottfried W. *Die Zwinglische Reformation im Rahmen der europäischen Kirchengeschichte.* Göttingen: Vandenhoeck und Ruprecht, 1979.

Lukes, Steven. *Essays in Social Theory.* Ipswich: Gregg Revivals, 1977.

McConica, James K. "Erasmus and the 'Julius': A Humanist Reflects on the Church." In *The Pursuit of Holiness in Late Medieval and Renaissance Religion.* Eds. C. Trinkaus and H. A. Oberman. SMRT 10. Leiden: E. J. Brill, 1974, pp. 444-471.

MacCormack, Sabine G. *Art and Ceremony in Late Antiquity. The Transformation of the Classical Heritage.* Vol. 1. Berkeley: University of California Press, 1981.

McRee, Benjamin. "Unity or Division? The Social Meaning of Guild Ceremonies in Urban Communities." In *City and Spectacle in Medieval Europe*, pp. 189-207.

Maier, Konstantin. "Die Diözesansynode." In *BK* I, pp. 92-94

Maier, Konstantin. "Zum Amt des Weihbischofs." In *BK.* II, pp. 76-83.

Maier, Konstantin. *Das Domkapitel von Konstanz und seine Wahlkapitulation. Ein Beitrag zur Geschichte von Hochstift und Diözese in der Neuzeit.* Beiträge zur Geschichte der Reichskirche in der Neuzeit 11. Stuttgart: Franz Steiner, 1990.

Maillard-Zechlin, C. "Die Meersburger Münze des Fürstbischofs Hugo von Hohen-landenberg." *FDA* 72 (1952), 213-219.

Martin, G. H. "New Beginnings in North-Western Europe." In *European Towns. Their Archaeology and Early History*, pp. 405-415.

Maurer, Helmut. "*Palatium Constantiense.* Bischofspfalz und Königspfalz im hoch-mittelalterlichen Konstanz." In *Adel und Kirche. Gerd Tellenbach zum 65. Geburtstag dargebracht von Freunden und Schülern.* Eds. J. Fleckenstein and K. Schmid. Freiburg: Herder, 1968, pp. 374-388.

Maurer, Helmut. "Stadterweiterung und Vorstadtbild im mittelalterlichen Konstanz. Zur Problem der Einbeziehung ländlicher Siedlungen in den Bereich einer mittelalterlichen Stadt." In *Stadterweiterung und Vorstadt.* Ed. E Maschke and J. Sydow. Veröffentlichungen der Kommission für Geschichtliche Landeskunde in Baden-Württemberg. Reihe B, 51. Stuttgart: W. Kohlhammer, 1969, pp. 21- 38.

Maurer, Helmut. "Die Ratskapelle. Beobachtungen am Beispiel von St. Lorenz in Konstanz." In *Festscrhift für Hermann Heimpel zum 70. Geburtstag.* Veröffentlichungen des Max-Planck-Instituts für Geschichte 36/II. Göttingen: Vandenhoeck und Ruprecht, 1972, pp. 225-236.

Maurer, Helmut. "*Die Bischofshöri.* Studien zur 'Gründungsausstattung' des Bistums Konstanz." *FDA* 100 (1980), 9-25.

Maurer, Helmut. *Das Stift St. Stephan in Konstanz.* Das Bistum Konstanz 1. Germania Sacra. N.F. 15. Berlin: Walter de Gruyter, 1981.

Maurer, Helmut. "Die Anfänge." In *BK* I, pp. 7-12.

Maurer, Helmut. "Der Heilige Konrad." In *BK* I, pp. 366-372.

Maurer, Helmut. *Konstanz im Mittelalter.* Vol I. Von den Anfängen bis zum Konzil. Geschichte der Stadt Konstanz. Konstanz: Stadler, 1989.

Maurer, Helmut. *Konstanz im Mittelalter.* Vol II. Vom Konzil bis zum Beginn des 16. Jahrhunderts. Geschichte der Stadt Konstanz. Konstanz: Stadler, 1989.

May, Georg. *Die deutschen Bischöfe angesichts der Glaubensspaltung des 16. Jahrhunderts.* Wien: Mediatrix-Verlag, 1983.

Meier, Frank. *Konstanz Stadterweiterungen im Mittelalter. Grundstücksbezogene Untersuchungen zur Erschließungsgeschichte und Sozialtopographie.* Konstanz: Hartung-Gorre, 1989.

Meisel, Peter. *Die Verfassung und Verwaltung der Stadt Konstanz im 16. Jahrhundert.* Konstanzer Geschichts- und Rechtsquellen 8. Konstanz: Jan Thorbecke, 1957.

Merzbacher, Friedrich. *Die Bischofsstadt.* Arbeitsgemeinschaft für Forschung des Landes Nordrhein-Westfallen 93. Köln: Westdeutscher Verlag, 1961.

Minnich, Nelson H. *The Fifth Lateran Council (1512-17): Studies on its Membership, Diplomacy, and Proposals for Reform.* Brookfield, Vermont: Variorum, 1993.

Minnich, Nelson H. "The Participants at the Fifth Lateran Council." In *The Fifth Lateran Council (1512-17)*, pp. 157-206.

Minnich, Nelson H. "The Proposals for an Episcopal College at Lateran V." In *The Fifth Lateran Council (1512-17)*, pp. 214-232.

Moeller, Bernd. *Imperial Cities and the Reformation. Three Essays.* Ed. and Trans. H. C. E. Midelfort and M. U. Edwards, Jr. Durham: Labyrinth Press, 1982 [1962].

Moeller, Bernd. *Reichsstadt und Reformation. Bearbeite Neuausgabe.* Berlin: Evangelische Verlagsanstalt, 1987 [1962].

Möncke, Gisela. *Bischofsstadt und Reichsstadt. Ein Beitrag zur mittelalterlichen Stadtverfasssung von Augsburg, Konstanz, und Basel.* Berlin: Freie Universität, 1971.

Muir, Edward. *Civic Ritual in Renaissance Venice.* Princeton: Princeton University Press,

1981.

Müller, Ewald. *Das Konzil von Vienne 1311-1312. Seine Quellen und seine Geschichte.* Vorreformationsgeschichtliche Forschungen 12. Münster: Aschendorff, 1934.

Munro, John H. "The Coinages of Renaissance Europe, ca. 1500." In *Handbook of European History 1400-1600. Late Middle Ages, Renaissance, and Reformation.* Eds. T. A. Brady Jr., H. A. Oberman, and J. D. Tracy. Leiden: E. J. Brill, 1994, Vol. I, pp. 571-678; Vol. II, pp. 683-690.

Murray, James M. "The Liturgy of the Count's Advent in Bruges, from Galbert to Van Eyck." In *City and Spectacle in Medieval Europe*, pp. 137-152.

Nelson, Janet L. *Politics and Ritual in Early Medieval Europe.* London: Hambledon Press, 1986.

Nelson, Janet L. "National Synods, Kingship as Office, and Royal Anointing: an Early Medieval Syndrome." In *Politics and Ritual in Early Medieval Europe*, pp. 239-258.

Nelson, Janet L. "Symbols in Context: Rulers' Inauguration Rituals in Byzantium and the West in the Early Middle Ages." In *Politics and Ritual in Early Medieval Europe*, pp. 259-282.

Nelson, Janet L. "The Lord's Anointed and the People's Choice: Carolingian Royal Ritual." In *Rituals of Royalty. Power and Ceremonial in Traditional Societies.* Eds. D. Cannadine and S. Price. Cambridge: Cambridge University Press, 1987, pp. 137-180.

Nelson, Janet L. "Hincmar of Reims on King-making: The Evidence of the *Annals of St. Bertin.*" In *Coronations*, pp. 16-34.

The New Catholic Encyclopedia. New York: McGraw-Hill, 1967.

The New International Dictionary of the New Testament. 2 vols. Ed. C. Brown. Grand Rapids: Zondervan, 1967.

Nicholas, David. "In the Pit of the Burgundian Theater State. Urban Traditions and Princely Ambitions in Ghent, 1360-1420. In *City and Spectacle in Medieval Europe*, pp. 271-295.

Nicholas, David. *The Growth of the Medieval City. From Late Antiquity to the Early Fourteenth Century.* A History of Urban Society in Europe. London and New York: Longman, 1997.

Nicholas, David. *The Later Medieval City 1300-1500.* A History of Urban Society in Europe. London and New York: Longman, 1997.

Nijsten, Gerard. "The Duke and his Towns. The Power of Ceremonies, Feasts, and Public Amusement in the Duchy of Guelders (East Netherlands) in the Fourteenth and Fifteenth Centuries." In *City and Spectacle in Medieval Europe*, pp. 235-270.

Nischan, Bodo. *Prince, People, and Confession. The Second Reformation in Brandenburg.* Philadelphia: University of Pennsylvania Press, 1994.

Oberman, Heiko A. *Masters of the Reformation. The Emergence of a New Intellectual Climate in Europe.* Cambridge: Cambridge University Press, 1981 [1977].

1000 Jahre Petershausen. Beiträge zu Kunst und Geschichte der Benediktinerabtei Petershausen in Konstanz. Konstanz: Stadler, 1983.

Osber, Karl. "Der Hohenlandenbergeralter in der Kunsthalle zu Karlsruhe." *ZGO* 75 (1921), 192-201.

Ottnad, Bernd. "Die Archive der Bischöfe von Konstanz." *FDA* 94 (1974), 270-516.

Partner, Peter. *Renaissance Rome 1500-1559: A Portrait of a Society.* Berkeley: University of California Press, 1976.

Pavlac, Brian A. "Excommunication and Territorial Politics in High Medieval Trier." *CH* 60 (1991), 20-36.

Pazzaglini, Peter. *The Criminal Ban of the Siena Commune 1225-1310.* Quarderni di 'Studi Senesi' 45. Milan: Dott. A. Giuffré Editore, 1979.

Phythian-Adams, Charles. "Ceremony and the Citizen: the Communal Year at Coventry, 1450-1550." In *The English Medieval Town. A Reader in English Urban History 1200-1540.* London: Longman, 1990.

Planitz, Hans. *Die deutsche Stadt im Mittelalter. Von der Römerzeit bis zu den Zunftkämpfen.* Wien: Hermann Böhlaus, 1975.

Pötzl, Walter. *Bischof Ulrich und seine Zeit (890-973).* Augsburg: Winfried Werk, 1973.

Press, Volker. "Bischöfe, Bischofsstädte und Bischofsresidenzen. Zur Einleitung." In *Südwestdeutsche Bischofsresidenzen ausserhalb der Kathedralstädte,* pp. 9-26.

Press, Volker. "Bischof und Stadt in der Neuzeit." In *Stadt und Bischof,* pp. 137-160.

Rapp, Francis. *Réformes et Réformation A Strasbourg. Église et Société dans le Diocése de Strasbourg (1450-1525).* Collection de l'Institut des Hautes Études Alsaciennes 23. Paris: Editions Ophrys, 1974.

Rapp, Francis. "Straßburg, Hochstift und freie Reichsstadt." In *Die Territorien des Reichs,* Vol. 5, pp. 72-95.

Reiners, Heribert. *Das Münster unserer Lieben Frau zu Konstanz.* Die Kunstdenkmäler Südbadens: Vol. I. Konstanz: Jan Thorbecke, 1955.

Reinhardt, Rudolf. "Hugo von Hohenlandenberg." In *BK* I, pp. 392-395.

Reinhard, Wolfgang. "Johannes von Weeze, kaiserlicher Generalorator, Erzbischof von Lund, Bischof von Roskilde und Konstanz." *RJKG* 3 (1984), 99-111.

Religion and Culture in the Renaissance and Reformation. Ed. S. Ozment. SCES 11. Kirksville, Missouri: Sixteenth Century Journal Publishers, 1989.

Repgen, Konrad. "Antimanifest und Kriegsmanifest. Die Benutzung der neuen Drucktechnik bei der Mainzer stiftsfehde 1461/63 durch Erzbischöfe Adolf von Nassau und Diether von Isenburg." In *Studien zum 15. Jahrhundert,* pp. 781- 804.

Residenzen des Rechts. Eds. B. Kirchgässner and H. P. Becht. Veröffentlichungen des Südwestdeutschen Arbeitskreises für Stadtgeschichtsforschung 19. Sigmaringen: Jan Thorbecke, 1993.

Reynolds, Susan. *Kingdoms and Communities in Western Europe, 900-1300.* Oxford: Clarendon Press, 1984.

Rieder, Karl. "Beitrag zu den wirtschaftlichen und kirchlichen Zuständen in der Diöcese Konstanz in der zweiten Hälfte des 14. Jahrhunderts. *FDA* 29 (1901), 245-254.

Rites of Power. Symbolism, Ritual, and Politics since the Middle Ages. Ed. S. Wilentz. Philadelphia: University of Pennsylvania Press, 1985.

Rittenbach, Willi and Siegfried Seifert. *Geschichte der Bischöfe von Meissen, 968- 1581.* Studien zur katholischen Bistums- und Klostergeschichte 8. Leipzig: St. Benno-Verlag, 1965.

Roper, Lyndal. *The Holy Household. Women and Morals in Reformation Augsburg.* Oxford: Clarendon Press, 1989.

Rörig, Fritz. *The Medieval Town.* Berkeley: University of California Press, 1967 [1955].

Roth, Friedrich. *Augsburgs Reformationsgeschichte.* 4 Vols. München: Theodore Ackermann, 1901-1911.

Rubin, Miri. *Corpus Christi. The Eucharist in Late Medieval Culture.* Cambridge: Cambridge University Press, 1991.

Rublack, Hans-Christoph. *Die Einführung der Reformation in Konstanz von den Anfängen bis zum Abschluß 1531.* Quellen und Forschungen zur Reformationsgeschichte 40. Gütersloh: Gerd Mohn, 1971.

Rublack, Hans-Christoph. *Gescheiterte Reformation. Frühreformatorische und protestantische Bewegungen in südwestdeutschen geistlichen Residenzen.* Spätmittelalter und Frühe Neuzeit 4. Stuttgart: Klett-Cotta, 1976.

Rublack, Hans-Christoph. "Die Stadt Würzburg in Bauernkreig." *ARG* 67 (1976), 76-100.

Ruiz, Teofilo. "Elite and Popular Culture in Late-Fifteenth-Century Castilian Festivals." In *City and Spectacle in Medieval Europe,* pp. 296-318.

Rütimeyer, E. *Stadtherr und Stadtbürgerschaft in den rheinischen Bischofsstädten. Ihr Kampf um die Hoheitsrechte im Hochmittelalter.* Beihefte zur Vierteljahrschrift für Sozial-und Wirtschaftsgeschichte 13. Stuttgart: W. Kohlhammer, 1928.

Sabisch, Alfred. *Die Bischöfe von Breslau und die Reformation in Schlesien.* Katholisches Leben und Kirchenreform im Zeitalter der Glaubensspaltung 35. Münster: Aschendorff, 1975.

Sage, Walter. "Frühes Christentum und Kirchen aus der Zeit des Übergangs." In *GSA*, pp. 100-112.

Salmon, Pierre. *Mitra und Stab. Die Pontifikalsignien im römischen Ritus.* Mainz: Matthias-Grünewald, 1960.

Santifaller, Leo. *Zur Geschichte des ottonische-salischen Reichskirchensystems.* Österreichische Akademie der Wissenschaften 229.1. Wien: Hermann Böhlaus, 1964.

Schairer, Immanuel. *Das Religiöse Volksleben am Ausgang des Mittelalters nach Augsburger Quellen.* Leipzig: B. G. Teubner, 1913.

Schell, Rüdiger. "Die Regierung des Konstanzer Bischofs Heinrich III. von Brandis (1357-1383) unter besonderer Berücksichtigung seiner Beziehungen zur Stadt Konstanz." *FDA* 88 (1968), 102-204.

Schilling, Heinz. *Die Stadt in der frühen Neuzeit.* Enzyklopädie deutscher Geschichte 24. München: R. Oldenbourg, 1993.

Schimmelpfennig, B. "Papal Coronations in Avignon." In *Coronations*, pp. 179-196.

Schlemmer, Karl. *Gottesdienst und Frömmigkeit in der Reichsstadt Nürnberg am Vorabend der Reformation.* Forschung zur fränkischen Kirchen- und Theologiegeschichte. Würzburg: Echter Verlag, 1980.

Schmidt, Georg. *Der Städtetag in der Reichsverfassung. Eine Untersuchung zur korporativen Politik der freien und Reichsstädte in der ersten Hälfte des 16. Jahrhunderts.* Veröffentlichungen des Instituts für europäische Geschichte Mainz. Abteilung Universalgeschichte 113. Stuttgart: Franz Steiner, 1984.

Schmidt, Rolf. "Das Stadtbuch von 1276." In *GSA*, pp. 140-144.

Schneider, Philipp. *Die bischöflichen Domkapitel, ihre Entwicklung und rechtliche Stellung.* Mainz: Franz Kirchheim, 1892.

Schnith, Karl. "Die Reichsstadt Augsburg im Spätmittelalter (1368-1493)." In *GSA*, pp. 153-165.

Schoppmeyer, Heinrich. *Der Bischof von Paderborn und seine Städte. Zugleich ein Beitrag zum Problem Landesherr und Stadt.* Studien und Quellen zur Westfalischen Geschichte 9. Paderborn: Verein für Geschichte und Altertumskunde Westfalens, 1968.

Schrader, Franz. "Kardinal Albrecht von Brandenburg, Erzbischof von Magdeburg, im Spannungsfeld zwischen alter und neuer Kirche." In *Von Konstanz nach Trient. Beiträge zur Geschichte der Kirche von den Reformkonzilien bis zum Tridentinum.* Ed. R. Bäumer. München: Ferdinand Schöningh, 1972, pp. 419-445.

Schrader, Franz. *Ringen, Untergang, und Überleben der katholischen Klöster in den Hochstiften Magdeburg und Halberstadt von der Reformation bis zum Westfälischen Frieden.* Katholisches Leben und Kirchenreform im Zeitalter der Glaubensspaltung 37. Münster and Leipzig: Aschendorff, 1977.

Schrader, Franz. *Die Visitationen der katholischen Klöster im Erzbistum Magdeburg durch die evangelischen Landesherren 1561-1651.* Studien zur katholischen Bistums- und Klostergeschichte 18. Leipzig: St. Benno Verlag, 1978.

von Schreckenstein, Roth. "Die Ermordung des Bischofs Johann III. von Konstanz." *ZGO* 25 (1873), 1-24.

Schröder, Detlev. *Stadt Augsburg.* Historischer Atlas von Bayern: Schwaben 10. München: Kommission für bayerische Landesgeschichte, 1975.

Schubiger, P. "Über die angebliche Mitschuld der Gebrüder von Brandis am Morde des Bischofs Johannes Windlock von Constanz." *FDA* 10 (1876), 3-48.

Schuler, Manfred. "Die Bischöfe und Musik." In *BK* II, pp. 239-247.

Schuler, Peter-Johann. "Bischof und Stadt vor Beginn der Reformation in Konstanz." In *Kontinuität und Umbruch. Theologie und Frömmigkeit in Flugschriften und Kleinliteratur an der Wende vom 15. zum 16. Jahrhundert.* Ed. J. Nolte. Spätmittelalter und Frühe Neuzeit 2. Stuttgart: Klett-Cotta, 1978, pp. 300-315.

Schulte, Aloys. *Der Adel und die deutsche Kirche im Mittelalter. Studien zur Sozial-, Rechts-, und Kirchengeschichte.* Kirchenrechtliche Abhandlungen 63, 64. Amsterdam: P. Schippers, 1966 [1910].

Schultz, Knut. "Die Ministerialität in Rheinischen Bischofsstädten." In *Stadt und Ministerialität.* Ed. E. Maschke and J. Sydow. Veröffentlichungen der Kommission für geschichtliche Landeskunde in Baden-Württemberg, Reihe B, 76. Stuttgart: W. Kohlhammer, 1973, pp. 16-42.

Schürle, Wolfgang W. *Das Hospital zum Heiligen Geist in Konstanz. Ein Beitrag zur Rechtsgeschichte des Hospitals im Mittelalter.* Konstanzer Geschichts- und Rechtsquellen 17. Konstanz: Jan Thorbecke, 1970.

Schwarzwalder, Herbert. *Geschichte der freien Hansestadt Bremen von den Anfängen bis zur Franzosenzeit (1819).* Bremen: Friedrich Röver, 1975.

Scribner, Robert W. *Popular Culture and Popular Movements in Reformation Germany.* London: Hambledon Press, 1987.

Scribner, Robert W. "Civic Unity and the Reformation in Erfurt." In *Popular Culture and Popular Movements*, pp. 185-216.

Scribner, Robert W. "Reformation, Carnival and the World Turned Up-Side Down." In *Popular Culture and Popular Movements*, pp. 71-102.

Scribner, Robert W. "Why was there no Reformation in Cologne?" In *Popular Culture and Popular Movements*, pp. 217-242.

Scribner, Robert W. "Anticlericalism in the Cities." In *Anticlericalism in Late Medieval and Early Modern Europe*, pp. 147-166.

Scribner, Bob. "Germany." In *The Reformation in National Context.* Eds. B. Scribner, R. Porter, and M. Teich. Cambridge: Cambridge University Press, 1994, pp. 4-29.

Sennett, Richard. *Flesh and Stone. The Body and the City in Western Civilization.* New York: W. W. Norton and Company, 1994.

Siegler-Schmidt, Jörn. *Territorialstaat und Kirchenregiment. Studien zur Rechtsdogmatik des Kirchenpatronatsrechts im 15. und 16. Jahrhundert.* Köln: Böhlau, 1987.

Sieh-Burns, Katrina. *Oligarchie, Konfession und Politik im 16. Jahrhundert. Zur sozialen Verflechtung der Augsburger Bürgermeister und Stadtpfleger 1518- 1618.* München: Ernst Vögel, 1986.

Smolinsky, Heribert. "Die Kirche am Oberrhein im Spannungsverhältnis von humanistischer Reform und Reformation." *FDA* 110 (1990), 23-38.

Spahr, P. Gebhard. "Zur Geschichte der Benediktinerabtei Petershausen 983-1802." In *1000 Jahre Petershausen*, pp. 9-40.

Stadt und Bischof. Eds. B. Kirchgässner and W. Baer. Veröffentlichungen des Südwestdeutschen Arbeitskreises für Stadtgeschichtsforschung 14. Sigmaringen: Jan Thorbecke, 1988.

Stadt und Stadtherr im 14. Jahrhundert. Entwicklungen und Funktionen. Ed. W. Rausch. Beiträge zur Geschichte der Städte Mitteleuropas 2. Linz/Donau: Österreichischer Arbeitskreises für Stadtgeschichtsforschung, 1972.

Starn, Randolf. *Contrary Commonwealth. The Theme of Exile in Medieval and Renaissance Italy.* Berkeley: University of California Press, 1982.

Stieber, Joachim W. *Pope Eugenius IV the Council of Basel and the Secular and Ecclesiastical Authorities in the Empire. The Conflict over Supreme Authority and Power in the Church.* SHCT 12. Leiden: E. J. Brill, 1978.

Strätz, Hans-Wolfgang. "Der Bodensee als Rechtsobjekt in Gegenwart und Geschichte. Einige vorläufige Anmerkungen." In *Der Bodensee. Landschaft, Geschichte, Kultur.* Ed. H. Maurer. Sigmaringen: Jan Thorbecke, 1982, pp. 598-618.

Strauss, Gerald. *Nuremberg in the Sixteenth Century.* New Dimensions in History. Bloomington: Indiana University Press, 1976 [1966].

Strnad, Alfred A. "Mark Sittich von Hohenems und Andreas von Österreich." In *BK.* I, pp. 396-403.

Strong, Roy. *Splendor at Court. Renaissance Spectacle and the Theater of Power.* Boston: Houghton Mifflin, 1973.

Strong, Roy. *Art and Power. Renaissance Festivals, 1450-1650*. Suffolk: Boydell Press, 1984.
Studien zum 15. Jahrhundert. Festschrift für Erich Meuthen. 2 Vols. Eds. J. Helmrath and H. Müller. München: R. Oldenbourg, 1994.
Südwestdeutsche Bischofsresidenzen ausserhalb der Kathedralstädte. Ed. V. Press. Veröffentlichungen der Kommission für Geschichtliche Landeskunde in Baden-Württemberg, Reihe B, Vol. 116. Stuttgart: W. Kohlhammer, 1992.
Die Territorien des Reichs im Zeitalter der Reformation und Konfessionalisierung. Land und Konfession 1500-1600. Vol 5: Der Südwesten. Eds. A. Schindling and W. Ziegler. Katholisches Leben und Kirchenreform im Zeitalter der Glaubensspaltung 53. Münster: Aschendorff, 1993.
Theological Dictionary of the New Testament. Eds. G. Kittel and G. Friedrich. Trans. G. W. Bromiley. Grand Rapids: William B. Eerdmans, 1964-1976.
Theologische Realenenzyklopädie. Eds. G. Krause and G. Müller. Berlin: Walter de Gruyter, 1977-1988.
Trexler, Richard C. *The Spiritual Power: Republican Florence under Interdict*. SMRT 9. Leiden: E. J. Brill, 1974.
Trexler, Richard C. *Public Life in Renaissance Florence*. Studies in Social Discontinuity. New York: Academic Press, 1980.
Turner, Victor. *The Ritual Process. Structure and Anti-Structure*. Chicago: Aldine Publishing Company, 1969.
Turner, Victor. *Dramas, Fields, and Metaphors. Symbolic Action in Human Society*. Ithaca: Cornell University Press, 1974.
Turner, Victor. *From Ritual to Theater. The Human Seriousness of Play*. Performance Series, Vol. 1. New York: Performing Arts Journal Publications, 1982.
Uhl, Anton. *Peter von Schaumberg. Kardinal und Bischof von Augsburg 1424-1469*. München: Ludwig-Maximilians-Universität, 1940.
Vasalla, Oskar. "Die Ursachen der Reformation in der deutschen Schweiz." *Zeitschrift für schweizerische Geschichte* 27 (1947), 404-424.
Vögeli, Alfred. "Bischof Hugo von Hohenlandenberg: Von den Anfängen bis zum Beginn der Reformation (1460-1518)." In Jörg Vögeli. *Schriften zur Reformation in Konstanz 1519-1538*. Beilage II. I. Ed. A. Vögeli. Tübingen: Osiandersche Buchhandlung, 1973, pp. 589-625.
Vogler, Günther. "Imperial City Nuremberg, 1524-1525: The Reform Movement in Transition." In *The German People and the Reformation*, pp. 33-49.
Warriors and Churchmen in the High Middle Ages. Essays Presented to Karl Leyser. Ed. T. Reuter. London: Hambledon Press, 1992.
Weber, Dieter. *Geschichtsschreibung in Augsburg. Hektor Mülich und die reichsstädtische Chronistik des Spätmittelalters*. Abhandlungen zur Geschichte der Stadt Augsburg 30. Augsburg: Hieronymous Mühlberger, 1984.
Weber, Max. *Wirtschaft und Gesellschaft. Grundriß der verstehenden Soziologie*. Vol. 1. Tübingen: Mohr-Seebeck, 1985 [1922].
Weiss, Ursula-Renate. *Die Konstanzer Bischöfe im 12. Jahrhundert. Ein Beitrag zur Untersuchung der reichsbischöflichen Stellung im Kräftefeld kaiserlicher, päpstlicher und regionaldiözesaner Politik*. Konstanzer Geschichts- und Rechtsquellen 20. Sigmaringen: Jan Thorbecke, 1975.
Weitlauff, Manfred. "Bischof Ulrich von Augsburg (923-973). Leben und Wirken eines Reichsbischof der ottonischen Zeit." In *Bischof Ulrich von Augsburg 890-973*, pp. 69-112.
Wentz, Gottfried. *Das Bistum Havelberg*. Germania Sacra I.2: Die Bistümer der Kirchenprovinz Magdeburg. Berlin: Walter de Gruyter, 1933.
Werminghoff, Albert. *Geschichte der Kirchenverfassung Deutschlands im Mittelalter*. Vol. 1. Darmstadt: Wissenschaftliche Buchgesellschaft, 1969.
Wightman, Edith M. "The Towns of Gaul with Special Reference to the North-East." In *European Towns. Their Archaeology and Early History*, pp. 303-311.

Willburger, August. *Die Konstanzer Bischöfe Hugo von Landenberg, Balthasar Merklin, Johann von Lupfen (1496-1537) und die Glaubensspaltung.* Reformationsgeschichtliche Studien und Texte 34-35. Münster: Aschendorff, 1917.

Wolfhart, Karl. *Die Augsburger Reformation in den Jahren 1533/34.* Studien zur Geschichte der Theologie und Kirche, 7-2. Aalen: Scientia, 1972 [1901].

Wunder, Bernd. "Der Bischof im schwäbischen Kreis." In *BK* I, pp. 189-198.

Zika, Charles. "Hosts, Processions and Pilgrimages: Controlling the Sacred in Fifteenth-Century Germany. *Past and Present* 118 (1988), 25-64.

Zeydel, Karl H. *Sebastian Brandt.* New York: Twayne, 1967.

Zimmermann, Wolfgang. "Konstanz in den Jahren von 1548-1733." In *Konstanz in der frühen Neuzeit. Reformation. Verlust der Reichsfreiheit. Österreichische Zeit.* Geschichte der Stadt Konstanz 3. Konstanz: Stadler, 1991, pp. 147-312.

Zimmermann, Wolfgang. *Rekatholisierung, Konfessionalisierung und Ratsregiment. Der Prozeß des politischen und religiösen Wandels der österreichischen Stadt Konstanz 1548-1637.* Konstanzer Geschichts- und Rechtsquellen N.F. 34. Sigmaringen: Jan Thorbecke, 1994.

Zimpel, Detlev. *Die Bischöfe von Konstanz im 13. Jahrhundert (1206-74).* Freiburger Beiträge zur mittelalterlichen Geschichte 1. Frankfurt am Main: Peter Lang, 1990.

Zinzmaier, P. "Eine unbekannte Quelle zur Geschichte der mittelalterlichen Liturgie im Konstanzer Münster," *ZGO* 104 (1956), 52-104

Zoepfl, Friedrich. *Das Bistum Augsburg und seine Bischöfe im Mittelalter.* Geschichte des Bistums Augsburg und seine Bischöfe, Vol. I. München: Schnell and Steiner, 1955.

Zoepfl, Friedrich. *Geschichte der Stadt Dillingen an der Donau.* München: R. Oldenbourg, 1964.

Zoepfl, Friedrich. *Das Bistum Augsburg und seine Bischöfe im Reformationsjahrhundert.* Geschichte des Bistums und seine Bischöfe. Vol. II. München: Schnell and Steiner, 1969.

Zorn, Wolfgang. *Augsburg. Geschichte einer deutschen Stadt.* München: Hermann Rinn, 1955.

INDEX OF SUBJECTS

anticlericalism: and clerical privilege, 28; in episcopal cities and during the later Middle Ages, 28n53; and evangelical preachers, 36; toward the bishop of Constance, 74-75; as denial of entry and destruction of church property, 85, 92-93, 179

Appenzell War, 55n50

Augsburg, bishops of, 208-210,
aristocratic background of, 90-1; benefices of, 90; burials and memorial cycles of, 7, 121, 122, 157-170, 193-194, 208-210; as cardinal, 97-99, 194, 196; consecration of, 95-96, 100-101, 158, 160, 161; education of, 90n40, 97; entries of, 140-145, 196-197; expulsion of, entry of denied, 79, 82, 84-85, 88, 95, 183, 192; as 'founders' of city, 78-79, 82n15; influence in Augsburg through clergy and churches, 79, 81, 99, 101-102, 169; and interdict decree, 95-96; and Jews, 160, 160n165;
judicial officers of,
Burggrafen, 83, 97; *Vogt*, 83, 84, 86, 87; as lords of Augsburg, 79-84, 98-99; and lordship in decline, 82n15, 85-87, 97, 103; in military service and action, 78-79, 82, 82n15, 85, 91-93, 97; palace of, 80; reception of *regalia*, 161-162; reigns of, length, 89-90; relation to bishops of Constance, 7, 50, 77-78, 90n38, 90n39, 90-91, 93, 184-185, 196-201; relation to empire, 78, 79-89, 91, 95-96, 97-99, 162-163, 193, 196-197; relation to Habsburg, Welf, and Wittelsbach, 81, 82, 87, 91, 92, 96, 165; relation to papacy, 85, 95-96, 97-98, 193; papal confirmation of, 95; residence of, 7, 88, 88n34; transfer of, 100-101;
rights and privileges of, 80,
immunities of, 80n9, 85, 89, 91, 103; financial, 83, 97; minting of coins and oversight of markets, 81n13, 92, 97, 100, 100n78; *Stadtrecht*, 83-84, 88, 89; taxes and tolls, 83, 85n24, 86, 97;
See also bishop; Constance, bishop of

Augsburg, cathedral chapter of, 80, 85n24, 86-87, 90, 97, 100, 157, 180, 183,
and prohibition of citizens as canons, 101-102
See also cathedral chapter; Constance, cathedral chapter of

Augsburg, churches of, 50n35, 101, 194-195,
Cathedral of St. Mary (*Dom zu Augsburg, Mariens Heimsuchung*), 7, 80, 103, 115, 119-122, 141-145, 160, 162, 165, 166, 167, 183, 196; compound and citadel of, 80, 81, 85, 95, 120n44, 208-210; cloister of, 121; episcopal burials in, 122, 208-210; patron saint of, 119; relics of, 121;
See also cathedral
Monastic and mendicant churches and cloisters, 81, 141, 183,
St. George, 183, 184n39; St. Gertrude, 81; St. Leonhard, 141; St. Maurice, 81, 165, 167, 183, 193, 208; St. Peter, 81, 183; St. Stephan, 79, 81, 183; St. Ulrich and Afra, 79, 82n15, 84, 103, 119-122, 141, 143, 160, 162-163, 165, 167, 183; episcopal burials in, 120, 208-209

Augsburg, city of,
as bi-confessional, 198-199; chronicle literature of, 106-107; civic defense of, 82, 88; clerical population of, 28n52; development of civic institutions of, 85-86; as episcopal capital, 81-82; as host of imperial diets, 7-8, 162-163, 196; as imperial city, 82-84, 87, 99, 105; invasion of, 78-79, 82; lay initiative in, 83-84, 88; lay oversight of churches of, 101; oaths of, clerical swearing of, 92; origins and growth of, 78-81, 82; population of, 99n76; relationship of bishop and city, 6-7; taxation of clergy in, 91-92; *Stadtbuch* of (1276), 86, 87; *Stadtrecht* of (1156), 83-84, 88, 89
See also imperial city

Augsburg Confession (1530), 7-8, 162, 181-182;

Augsburg, diocese of, 50, 77, 80, 80n9, episcopal courts of (*das Kuriengericht*),

81; in relation to Constance, 7, 50, 77-78; in relation to neighboring dioceses, 99; size and geography of, 81; synods of, 100-101, 158, 158n159, 161
See also diocese; Constance, diocese of
Augsburg, *Hochstift* of, 83, 91,
  Dillingen as part of, 87; pawning of properties, 87; and submission to bishop, 159-161
Augsburg Interim (1548), 196
auxiliary bishop, *See* consecrating bishop

Bann (Verbannung), and exile, 2n5, 29n54
See also Episcopus exclusus
Bischofsburg, 29n55
Bishop, administration of, 26-27, 30; ancient virtues of, 1, 11-12; aristocratic background of, 22, 40, 123; as city lord *(Stadtherr)*, 1-2, 19-20, 23-24, 39; charismatic power of, 104, 105, 113; civic presence of, 45, 199-200; consecration of, 32n60; and consecrating or auxiliary bishop, 27; death of, 15, 15n12, 16, 16n13, 164-170; desacralization of, 16; extent and nature of authority and power, 21-22, 30; as founder and patron of cities, 22n32; and fortifications of, civic, 24n40; humanist model of, 40-42; immunities of, 28-29, 29n54; and imperial *regalia*, 24n37, 26n47; as imperial prince, 24-25, 123; as impetus for lay government, 24; and Jews, 160, 160n165; lay advocates of, 36n68; magic of, 1n3; in military service, 19-20, 25n44, 29n55, 78-79, 85, 91-93, 97; and minting of coins, 24; murder and martyrdom of, 15-16, 19n24, 48, 53; in the New Testament, 26n46; origins of episcopal office, 26n46; as overseer of markets, mints, and tolls, 24, 24n39; as prince of the empire, 24-25; and 'real presence' in city, 19-30, 104, 105; residence of, 18-19, 103-104, 211-221; rituals of, 104, 108-109, 113, 152-153; as sacramental mediator, 4-5, 103, 152, 153; as saints, 1, 1n2, 77-78, 79; as Shepherd of the Church *(Oberhirt)*, 26-28, 103, 145; and taxation and tolls, collection of, 24; vestments and iconography of, 26
See also Augsburg, bishops of; Constance, bishops of
burial rites and sites, 7, 108, 118-119, 120, 122, 150-151, 153-170, 205-210

cathedra, 113
cathedral *(ecclesia cathedralis)*, 22n32, 113-123; as center of clerical immunities, 29, 103, 114, 133, 146-147; as center of ritual performance, 103-104, 111-113, 146-147, 150-151; as *necropolis*, 7, 153-154, 156-157, 193-194, 205-210; in relation to episcopal rule, 4-5; as sacred city, 4-5
See also Augsburg, churches of; Constance, churches of
cathedral chapter, 61,
  administration of *Hochstift*, 25, 26-27; origins of, 25; role in resistance to reformation, 32, 32n60;
See also Augsburg, cathedral chapter of; Constance, cathedral chapter of
cathedral city *(Kathedralstadt)*, *See* episcopal city
cathedral compound or precinct *(Dombezirk)*, 18, 29, 59, 61-62, 72, 114, and *Domburg* or *Bischofsburg*, 29n55, 114, 114n21, 146; relation to transfer of residence, 18-19
chronicle literature, civic, 105-107; and episcopal entries, 124
city leagues and associations, 91n43, 91-93
Confessio Tetrapolitana, 185-186
consecrating or auxiliary bishop *(Weihbischof, Hilfsbischof)*, 27
Constance, bishops of, 205-207, and absolution of sinners, 152-153; archival sources for, 8 n.8, 185; aristocratic background of, 40, 47, 50; and attempts to restore episcopal rights, 46-47, 72-76; benefices of, 40n3, 50-51; burial of, 7, 118-119, 153-157, 205-207; as citizens, 54, 54n49; civic background of, 48, 49-50; confirmation of civic rights, 66-72; consecration of, 56n53, 127; and contracts and negotiations *(Verschreibungen)* with city, 66-72, 75-76, 187; and decree of interdict, 48, 53, 58; double elections of, 48n26, 205-207; during Great Schism, 54; education of, 40, 51n37, 186; ecclesiastical careers of, 50-51, 186; entries of, 67, 126-139, 197-198; expulsion and withdrawal of, 52-56, 178-179; imperial support of, 46-47, 60-61, 75-76; 116-117, 132; imperial hostility towards, 47-48, 53; installation of, 66-72, 126-139, 197-198; as lord of city *(Stadtherr)*, 46-47, 49n27, 60-62;

and loss of lordship, 103; *mensa episcopalis* of, 58; murder of, 48, 53, 54n49; as patrons of arts and humanism, 40-43; and oaths to city magistrates, 54, 54n49, 66-72, 177-178; palace of, 117; reigns of, length, 49-50, 186; relation to Habsburg lands and foreign policy, 44, 75, 175 188-189; relation to papacy, 40n3, 49n27; relation to the Swabian Circle, 189-191; relation to Swiss Confederacy, 7 39, 72-73 175-177, 178n18, 197-198; residency patterns of, 7, 45, 54n46, 56-59, 211-221;

rights, privileges, and civic officers of, 60n64,

immunities, 103, 116; *Ammann*, 62, 62n72, 65, 66, 68-69, 71, 74, 76; *Vogt*, 62, 63-64, 65; market rights, 62; mint and currency of, 61, 69, 74; clerical sale of wine, 74n112, 76; ritual power of, 105, 108, 168; rule of through ritual, 104; secular careers of, 51

Constance, cathedral chapter of, 40n2, 50-51, 53, 55, 55n52, 61, 75, 127, 131, 176-178

See also cathedral chapter; Augsburg, cathedral chapter of

Constance, churches and cloisters of, Cathedral of Our Dear Lady (*Das Münster unserer Lieben Frau*) and precinct, 43n9, 45, 61-62, 77, 115-119, 146-147, 153, 155, 156-157, 168, 176-177, 197, 205-207; altars of, 118; burial of bishops in, 118, 205-207; and episcopal entries, 126-139; episcopal patronage of, 115-116; immunities of, 116; St. Maurice Rotunda of, 117-118; patron saints of, 116; relics of, 77, 103, 117-119; Petershausen, 73 St. John, 53, 136 St. Laurentius (*Ratskapelle*), 64 St. Lawrence, 77 St. Paul, 77 St. Stephan, 53, 62n73, 64, 74, 77, 136, 152, 155, 174, 175, 178, 205

Constance, city of, chronicle literature of, 106-107; clerical sale of wine in, 74, 74n112; defeat of and submission of, 197-198; as episcopal capital, 39, 45, 152; as imperial city: 39, 47, 59-60, 63-65; civic charity of (*Heiliggeistsspital, Raiten, Siechenhaus*), 64; civic control of churches of, 64-65, 172-179; civic (lay) government of, 3-64, 63n77, 63n79; contracts and negotiations (*Verschreibungen*) with bishop,

66-73, 75-76, 136-139, 172-179, 197; economic development of, 62-63; legal institutions of, 65; as modelled on Rome, 77; origins and growth of, 39, 60-63; patron saints of, 77; population of, 39, 99n76; and protest against *falsche Carolina*, 46-47, 60n65, 67; relationship to Swiss Confederacy, 73, 73n108; resistance to bishop, 52-53; territorial expansion of, 66

Constance, Council of (1414-18), 7, 54-55, 55n50, 66, 72, 93-94, 116-117, 119

Constance, diocese of, 71, 77, administration and offices of, 43n10; Archdeacon (*Archidiakon*), consecrating bishop (*Weihbischof*), Deans (*Dekane*), Official (*Offizial*), rural chapters (*Dekanate*), 27, 27n49; clergy of, 43; cloisters of, 43; *geistliches Gericht* (clerical court) of, 54, 56, 58, 68, 178; and German Peasants' Revolt, 177-178; origins of, 61-62; patron saints of, 103, 117-119; parishes of, 43; in relation to Augsburg, 7, 77-78; secular competition to, 43-44, 188-191; size of, 43; synods of, 41, 74, 152, 198

Constance, *Hochstift* of, 67-68, 73-74, 127, 186-191,

and *Bischofshöri*, 61, 66, 132; financial condition of, 44-45, 186-191; and German Peasants' Revolt, 177-178; size of, 44

corpus Christi feast, 142, 145, 151-152, 163

Diocese (*Bistum*), 1, 25n45, 27n49, and cathedral, 114; of empire, 203-204; rule of, 26-27; offices of, 27, 27n49; and secularization of, 2, 2n5; synods of, 27

See also Augsburg, diocese of, Constance, diocese of

Doge (Venice), 114

entry (*adventus*), episcopal, 108, 112-113, 197, 123-150, aristocratic participants, 126, 128-129, 132, 140, 142-143; as *adventus Christi*, 126; as coronation, 124-126; baldachin in, 129, 132-133, 134-135, 163; civic greeting at, 129, 140-141, 197; civic hostility toward, 140, 141, 142, 143, 143n119, 144; and impact on exiled, 129-130, 133; feasting at, 130, 133, 141, 142; first mass during,

130, 133; gifts offered, 130, 135-136; in imperial procession, 162-163; as *inclusus*, 123; in memorial processions, 164-170; lay participation in, 128-131, 133-139, 140-145, 146-147; political negotiation before and during, 133-134, 140, 143-145, 146, 148; oaths sworn at, 130, 136-139, 142; and palm sunday, 112; after Reformation, 196-198; and relics, 128, 141, 145; as a rite of passage, 148-149; as ritual insult, 147-148; size of, 129-130, 132, 140; soundscape of, 133n89, 141, 144, 146, 197

entry of kings and emperors, 124-126, 132, 162-163

episcopal city (*Bischofsstadt*), 203-204, as centers of trade, 24; as diocesan capital, 152-154, 168; as episcopal creation, 6; and immunities, 28-29; importance of for bishop, 4, 45, 103; lordship over, 3-4, 23-24; as original source of civic identity, 22; origins of, 22n32; as ritual theater, 111-112, 123; as sacred city, 1-2, 4, 103, 105, 108, 197-200, 201; and sacred space, 4; significance of loss, 36;
See also Antilla: the isle of seven cities; Constance, bishop of; Augsburg, bishop of

episcopal conquest of free city, 19-20
episcopal historiography, 5-6
episcopus exclusus, 9, 158-159, 172-173, 178-179, 183, 191-201,
in conciliar decree, 13-15; cycles of expulsion, 37; culmination of, 5, 7, 31-38 178, 183; definition of, 2-3; economic impact of, 185-186, 190-191; as erosion, exfoliation of rights and privileges, 3; as exfoliation, 3n6; and investiture controversy, 16-17; in Italy, 2n5, 13-15; and loss of ritual and civic theater, 194-195; mockery of expulsion, 20; as murder and martyrdom, 15-16, 48; and pattern of exile in Holy Roman Empire, 17-18, 30-36; and rule while in exile, 14-15 See also Augsburg, bishops of; Constance, bishops of

eucharist, as metaphor for episcopal presence, 21
excommunication, 3, 11, 28, 108-109 See also interdict

falsche Carolina, 46-47, 60n65, 67

fortifications, civic, 24, 24n40
free city (*freie Stadt*), 30-31, 31n57, 103, infringing on episcopal ritual, 114-115; origin of lay institutions, 22n32, 24

funerals and memorial cycles, episcopal, 7, 15n12, 193-194,
aristocratic guests at, 164-165, 167, 167-168; and the poor, 154n143, 154-155, 156; episcopal leadership of, 168; feasting at, 156, 167, 168; lay and magisterial participation in, 154-155, 155, 156; processions in, 164-170; routes taken, 165, 167

German Peasants' Revolt, 31n59, 177-178
Great Schism (1378-1415), 47-48, 53, 93

Habsburg, foreign policy and territories of, 36, 44, 65n87, 87, 91, 94n56, 175, 182n30, 186, 188n60, 188-189, 197-198

Hochstift, 1, 25, 26, 125,
mensa capitularis, 25; *mensa episcopalis*, 25; submission to bishop, 159-161 See also *Hochstift*, Augsburg; and *Hochstift*, Constance

Holy Roman Empire, 48, 82-85,
bishops as officers of and princes of, 6, 24n37, 24-25, 26n47, 97, 185-186; and conflict with Swiss Confederacy, 39-40; diets of, 17n19, 97, 181, 182, 185-187, 188; and episcopal ritual at diets, 162-164; ecclesiastical territories of, 203-204; and election of bishops, 123-124; and episcopal cities, 6; and Fifth Lateran Council, 12n5; *Hofgericht* of, 97; *Reichskammergericht*, 98; rituals of, 109n8, 110
See also Augsburg, bishop of; Constance, bishop of

Humanism,
and bishops of Constance, 41-43; and Desiderius Erasmus, 12n7, 41n6; and Sebastian Brant, 40-43

immunities, episcopal and clerical, 28-29, 61-62, 72, 104,
privilegium fori, 28; *privilegium immunitatis*, 28

imperial city (*Reichsstadt*), 30n56, 30-31, 31n57, 44, 63-64, 86,
clerical population of, 28n52
interdict, 3, 28, 47, 47n21, 48, 53, 95-96

See also excommunication
Investiture Controversy, 15-17, 26n47, 52-53, 63, 82, 82n15

"Julius Excluded From Heaven (*Julius Exclusus*)", 11-13

Lateran Council, Fifth (1512-17), 12n5, 13
Lateran Synod (993), 78
lay advocates, 36n68
liminality, 149-150, 170
lordship,
civic (*Stadtherrschaft*), 19-20, 22-24, 60-62, 65n87; territorial, 25, 34n63, 36, 38n73, 91-93, 187-191; and ritual, 139, 143, 168, 169-170

mendicants,
civic immunities vs. bishop, 38; in Augsburg, 81, 81n12; in Constance, 53
ministerials, episcopal, 28

Order of the Lion, 92

papacy, 11-13, 26, 40n3, 47-48, 52-53, 54, 55n50, 87, 94, 94n54, 95, 96, 97, 114, 123, 192n70,
of Avignon, 47, 54n49, 87-88; General Consistory of, 97; and Great Schism, 54, 72; *servitium commune* in payment to, 90n42, 186
Peace of Augsburg (1555), 8
prince-bishop, *see* bishop

'Reformatio Sigismundi', 25n44
Reformation, 30n56,
and Anabaptists, 181; and confiscation of church property, 173, 179, 183; clerical oaths of loyalty during, 177-178, 196; contact and cooperation between bishops of Constance and Augsburg, 173-174, 184-185, 190-191, 191n68; episcopal discipline and reprimand of, 174-183; episcopal perspective on, 173; episcopal protest against, 184-195; as form of *Episcopus exclusus*, 5, 7, 30-38, 172-173; failure of due to episcopal rule, 35; and German Peasants' Revolt, 31n59, 177-178; and oversight of clergy and preachers, 172-173, 176-177, 181; and taxation of clergy, 177-178; in Zürich, 174-176
residence, episcopal, 20-21, 103-104, 108, 150,

outside of episcopal city, 18-19; transfer of, 17-19, 87, 88n34, 99-100, 157-164, 172-173, 179
Ritual, 4, 105, 110-111, 123, 168, 169-171,
of absolution, 152-153; and 'arena', 112; burial of dead, 95-96, 150-171, 193-194; and charisma, 104, 105, 110, 112-113, 146, 170, 171; and civic solidarity or disunity, 115n23, 147n123; and civic stage, 103-104; *corpus Christi* feast, 142, 145, 151-152, 163; of consecration, 95-96; definition of, 104; episcopal rule via, 108-109, 146-150, 171; as 'frame', 111; historiography of, 109-113; imperial, 109n8, 110; as 'institutionalization of charisma', 104, 105; as insult, 147-148; and official writing as civic spectacle, 138n105; as paradigm, 112; as polysemic, 112n15; at imperial diets, 162-163; and synods, 152; and communal prestige, 124
See also sacred space; entry, episcopal
ritual community, 133, 136, 139, 148-150

sacred space, 4, 133,
cathedral as, 45; and episcopal immunities, 28-29; and episcopal memorial processions, 169-170
See also Augsburg, churches of, cathedral; Constance, churches of, cathedral; entry, episcopal; ritual
Schmalkaldic League, 182n30, 191
synods, episcopal, 27, 113-114, 152
Swabian Circle (*Kreis*), 7, 189-191, 201
Swabian City League, 92
Swabian League, 73, 187, 187n55, 191n68
Swabian War (1498-99), 39, 76
Swiss Confederacy, 7, 39, 40, 44, 71, 72-73, 99, 153, 172-178, 178n18

Türkenhilf, 188-190

Vienne, Council of (1311-12), 13-15

Welf, house of, 81, 82, 82n15
Wittelsbach, house of, 36, 81, 82n15, 87-88, 91, 92, 94n56, 140, 182n30, 189-190
Worms, Concordat of (1122), 26n47
Worms, Diet of (1521), 17n19, 181
Württemberg, Duchy of, 44, 94n56, 140, 186, 189

INDEX OF PERSONS AND PLACES

Adalpero, Bishop of Augsburg (887-909), 208
Adolf of Nassau, Archbishop of Mainz (1461-75), 19-20
St. Afra (d. c. 304), 78, 80
Albert I, Emperor of Germany (1298-1308), 65n87
Albert V, Emperor of Germany (1438-39), 97
Albert of Brandenburg, Archbishop of Mainz (1514-45), Archbishop of Magdeburg (1513-45), Bishop of Halberstadt (1513-45), 34-35
Albert of Hohenberg, bishop elect of Constance (1334-35, 1344-45, 1356-57), 206
Alet, 215
Alexander III, Pope (1159-81), 114
Andlau, 203
Anglo, Sydney, 109
Anselm of Nenningen, Bishop of Augsburg (1414-23), 209,
    education of, 90n40; consecration of, 96; conflict with Augsburg, papacy, and empire, 94-97
Antilla, the isle of seven cities, 1n4
Aquileia, 82n15, 203, 209
Arbon, 74, 206, 211, 212
Arnold of Heiligenberg, Bishop of Constance (imperial appointment) (1092-1112), 52-53
Arnold of Selenhofen, Archbishop of Mainz (d. 1160), 19n24
Arnold, Benjamin, 24n42,
    on military functions of a bishop, 25n44; on Bistum and Hochstift, 25n45; on territorial rule in Eichstätt and the role of advocates, 36n68
Aschaffenburg, 20
Athanasius, Bishop of Alexandria (d. 373), 1, 15
Attreed, Lorraine,
    on rituals of welcome and civic/royal relations, 124n53
Augustine, Bishop of Hippo (354-430), 1, 155n150
Avignon, 215

Baden, Margrave of, 189
Bamberg, 18, 90n38, 99, 184n43, 204

Basel, 18, 33, 40n3, 50, 50n35, 51n37, 127, 128n66, 179, 191, 203, 206
Bauer, Markus,
    on the development of the cathedral precinct and immunity in Constance, 61n70, 114n21
Baumgartner, Frederick J.,
    on the French episcopacy, 30n56
Baylor, Henry (1387-1409), appointed Bishop and Administrator of Constance (Avignon), 54n48, 57n55, 215
Becket, Thomas, Archbishop of Canterbury (d. 1170), 1, 16n13
Bedos-Rezak, Brigitte,
    on official acts of writing as civic spectacle, 138n105
Benediktbeuron, 203
Benno, Bishop of Metz (10th century), 15n12
Benson, Robert L.,
    on episcopal election, 21n30
Berlower, Thomas, Bishop of Constance (1491-96), 40n2, 207,
    conflict with Constance, 45-46, 99; origins, education, and imperial service of, 50, 51, 51n37, 51n38; and Verschreibung with Constance, 67, 70-72, 138, 139n108
Besançon, 203
Biberach, 186
Bild, Veit, Benedictine monk, Augsburg (1481-1529), 180n24
Bischofszell, 74, 178
Bisson, Thomas,
    on medieval royal assemblies as forms of persuasion, 110-111
Blarer, Albert, Bishop of Constance (1407-10), 206, 217,
    reign of, 49; career and education of, 51n36, 51n37
Blaubeuron, 209
Bloch, Marc,
    on the healing power of monarchs, 1n3
Bohemia, 50n32
Bologna, 51n37, 90n40
Bonn, 50n32
Botzheim, Johann of, Cathedral Canon of Constance (c. 1480-1535), 41n6
Brady, Thomas A., Jr.,

on episcopal entry into Strasbourg, 21n29, 143n119, 148n124; on Swiss appeals to Constance, 73n108

Brandenburg, 33, 34n63, 184n43, 204

Brant, Sebastian (1458-1521), 40-42

Bremen, 18, 31, 203

Breslau, 31, 50n32, 204

Brixen, 18, 204

Bruno of Bavaria, Bishop of Augsburg (1006-29), 208

Bryant, Lawrence, 109,
on the survival of classical spectacles in Christian ritual, 110n10, 125n56

Buchau, 203

Buchloe, 160

Burkhard of Ellerbach, Bishop of Augsburg (1373-1404), 209,
career of, 90n39; conflict with Augsburg, 91-93, 97; entry of, 142n118

Burkhard I of Hewen, Bishop of Constance (1387-98), 206, 216,
aristocratic background of, 50n31; career and education of, 51n36, 51n37; and swearing of civic oath, 54, 54n49; civic funeral for, 153n141, 156

Burkhard II of Randegg, Bishop of Constance (1462-66), 206,
aristocratic background of, 50n31; residency of, 58, 220

Cajetan, Thomas (1469-1534), 180

Cambrai, 15n11, 15n12, 16n15, 17n19, 18, 204

Castel, 154, 212, 213

Charles IV, Emperor of Germany (1347-78), 46, 48, 51, 60, 91

Charles V, Emperor of Germany (1519-56), 163, 182n30, 196

Chiemsee, 204

Christopher of Stadion, Bishop of Augsburg (1517-43), 210,
installation and ceremonies of, 157, 161-63, 166-167; and Reformation in Augsburg, 179-185; correspondence with bishops of Münster and Constance, 190-191; meeting with bishops of Constance and Strasbourg, 191n68; last days and death of, 192-194

Chur, 18, 40n3, 50, 50n35, 56, 82n15, 204

Clement VII, Pope, Avignon (1378-94), 54n48

Cologne, 15n11, 35, 50n35, 204

Constance, Lake of (Bodensee), 39, 74, 118, 178

St. Constantius,
as relic of the Cathedral of Our Dear Lady, Constance, 117

Cremona, 15n11

Croatia, 50n33

Dacher, Gebhart (15th century), 106, 106n3

Dagobert I, King of the Franks (623-39), 61

Dameron, George W., 28n50

Dauch, Bruno,
on episcopal residency and expulsion, 17-18; on relics and episcopal power in Augsburg, 100n81

David of Augsburg, Franciscan preacher and author (d. 1272), 81n12

Degenhard of Hellenstein, Bishop of Augsburg (1303-07), 209

Degler-Spengler, Brigitte,
on the impact of papal/imperial intrigue in Constance, 47n21

Demandt, Dieter,
on failure of civic freedom in Mainz, 19n24

Diessenhofen, 75

Diethelm of Krenkingen, Bishop of Constance (1189-1206), 205

Diethelm of Steinegg, Cathedral Dean and General Vicar of Constance (d. 1358), 48n24

Dillingen on the Danube, 7, 79, 87, 88n34, 94, 99-100, 103, 150, 157-59, 161, 163, 164, 166, 168, 169, 184, 192-94, 210,
Church of St. Peter of, 100, 158, 194

Dinkelsbühl, 81

Dissentis, 203

Dobras, Wolfgang, 174n2

Döffingen, 93

Dorpat, 204

Du Boulay, F. R. H.,
on city leagues in Germany, 91n43; on chronicle literature, 105n2

Duby, Georges,
on the deaths and rituals of William Marshall and King Henry II of England, 154n143

Eberhard I, Bishop of Augsburg (1029-47), 208

Eberhard II of Kirchberg, Bishop of Augsburg (1404-13), 90n38, 142n118, 144, 147, 209

Eberhard II of Waldburg, Bishop of

Constance (1248-74), 205
Eberhard, Winfried,
on chroniclers' views of ecclesiastical corruption and reform, 107n5
Ebersberg, 203
Eck, John (1486-1543), 180, 181
Ehingen on the Danube, 40n3
Eichstätt, 18, 36n68, 50n35, 99, 142, 161, 191, 204
Einsiedeln, 50, 130, 203
Ellwangen, 181n27, 184n43, 203
Elm, Kaspar, 28n53
Elten, 203
Eltis, D. A.,
on anticlericalism in episcopal cities, 28n53
Embriko, Bishop of Augsburg (1063-77), 209
Engen, 207, 216
Epternach, 203
Erasmus, Desiderius (1466?-1536), and 'Julius Excluded', 11-12, 12n7; 41n6
Erfurt, 34, 40n3, 50n35, 90n40
Ermland, 36, 204
Essen, 203
Esslingen, 31n58, 186, 189
Eticho, Bishop of Augsburg (982-88), 208
Eugenius IV, Pope (1431-47), 97, 127

Fabri, Johannes, General Vicar of Constance (d. 1541), 41n6, 176
Ferdinand I (1503-64), Archduke of Austria, King of Bohemia and Hungary, Emperor of Germany (1556-64), 197
Fichtenau, Heinrich, on the public dying of bishops, 15n12
Finland, 61
Flint, Valerie J.,
on magic and the clergy, 1n3
Florence, 97, 109, 114n22, 133n87, 134n94, 135n94
Franz of Waldeck, Bishop of Münster (1532-53), 190-191
Frederick I, Emperor of Germany (1152-90), 83, 84, 116
Frederick I of Zollern, Bishop of Constance (1293), 205
Frederick I Spät of Famingen, Bishop of Augsburg (1309-31), 87, 100, 209
Frederick II, Emperor of Germany (1215-50), 85
Frederick II of Zollern, Bishop of Augsburg (1486-1505), 90n38, 210; memorial cycle for, 166-167
Frederick II of Zollern, Bishop of Con-

stance (1434-36), 50n35, 139n109, 206; funeral rites for, 155-156; residency pattern of, 57n57, 219
Frederick III, Emperor of Germany (1440-93), 51, 66, 97, 132, 153, 157
Frederick of Grafeneck, elected Bishop of Augsburg (1413-14), 90, 94-95, 209
Frederick of Nellenburg, Bishop of Constance (1398), 206, 216,
and his reaction to financial difficulties in the diocese, 44n12; 50n31
Freiburg im Breisgau, 33n62, 90n40, 179
Freising, 17-18,
as example of enduring episcopal lordship over a city, 23n36; 35, 90n39, 99, 184n43, 191, 204
Friesach, 40n3
Frosch, Johann, Carmelite Prior in Augsburg (sixteenth century), 180n24, 181n26
Fugger, Jakob (1463-1525), 180
Fulda, 184n43, 203
Füssen, 94, 160, 161

Gandersheim, 203
Gebhard, Bishop of Augsburg (996-1001), 208
St. Gebhard II, Bishop of Constance (979-995), 118, 205
Gebhard III of Zähringen, Bishop of Constance (1084-1110), 53, 205
Gebhard IV of Bevar, Bishop of Constance (1307-18), 206
Geertz, Clifford,
on the 'charismatic center', 112-113
Geislingen, 186
Geneva, 33, 204
Genoa, 215
Gerhard of Groesbeeck, Bishop of Liège (1564-80), 32n60
Gernrode, 203
Gnesen, 204
Gottlieben, 58, 74, 128, 132, 153, 155, 211, 212, 213, 214, 215, 216, 217, 218, 219
Gregory VII, Pope (1073-85), 52
Guelders, 110
Günzburg, 160
Gunzenlee, 85
Gurk, 204

Halberstadt, 33, 204
Hallum, Robert, Bishop of Salisbury (d. 1417), 119
Hamburg, 203

Hanawalt, Barbara,
on the elaborate description of spectacle in the later Middle Ages, 124n54
Hanto, Bishop of Augsburg (807-c.815), 208
Hartmann of Dillingen, Bishop of Augsburg (1248-86), 209,
dissolution of lordship of and denial of entry, 37n70, 85-87; burial of relatives in cathedral, 121
Hartwig I of Lierheim, Bishop of Augsburg (1167-84), 209
Hartwig II, Bishop of Augsburg (1202-08), 209
Hausberger, Karl,
on episcopal rule in Regensburg, 32n60
Havelberg, 33, 204
Heal, Felicity, 30n56
Hefele, Klaus, 23n35, 23n36, 60n64, 61n71, 62n47, 62n72,
on the regalia of the bishop, 24n37; on economic growth of episcopal cities, 24n39; on the cathedral precinct in Constance as a *Fluchtburg*, 61n70; on the creation of a lay market space in Constance, 63n76; on episcopal immunities in Augsburg, 80n9
Heidelberg, 51n37, 90n40
Heinig, Paul-Joachim,
on imperial and free cities, 31n57
Henry of Werdenberg, Bishop of Constance (1318-19), 206
Henry I, Bishop of Augsburg (973-82), 208
Henry I of Tanne, Bishop of Constance (1233-48), 205
Henry II, Bishop of Augsburg (1047-63), 80, 82n15, 209
Henry II, King of England (1154-89), 16n13, 154n143
Henry III of Brandis, Abbot of Einsiedeln, Bishop of Constance (1357-83), 206,
conflict with city of Constance, 46-54, 60, 63, 65, 66, 91, 93, 99, 138; residency of, 57n56, 57n58, 58-59, 213-214
Henry III of Schönegg, Bishop of Augsburg (1337-48), 88, 209
Henry IV of Lichtenau, Bishop of Augsburg (1486-1505), 210,
career of, 90n39; election and installation of, 157-161; memorial cycle of, 166-168, 172

Henry IV, King and Emperor of Germany (1056-1106), 16, 52, 80, 82, 157
Henry IV of Hewen, Bishop of Constance (1436-62), 206,
reign of, 49; aristocratic background of, 50n31; career and education of, 50n35, 51n37; residency of, 56, 58n60, 219-230; *Verschreibung* of, 70n103; entry of, 126-139, 142n118, 146, 153
Henry of Hewen, Bishop of Chur (1491-1505), 33n62
Henry of Klingenberg, Bishop of Constance (1293-1306), 48n22, 64n81, 155, 205
Herford, 203
Hergemöller, Bernd-Ulrich,
on 'war' between clergy and laity in Hanseatic cities, 28n53
Hermann, Bishop of Augsburg (1096-1133), 82n15, 209
Hermann I of Arbon, Bishop of Constance (1138-65), 205
Hermann II of Fridingen, Bishop of Constance (1183-89), 205
Hermann III of Breitenlandenberg, Bishop of Constance (1466-74), 50n31, 51n36, 51n37, 58, 206, 220-221
Hermann of Wied, Archbishop of Cologne (1515-47), 35, 42n8
Hersfeld, 203
Hilary of Poitiers (d. 367/368), 15
Hildesheim, 18, 33, 204
Hiltine, Bishop of Augsburg (909-23), 208
Hinwil, 40n3
Hohenburg, 203
Hsia, R. Po-Chia, 31n59
Hugo of Hohenlandenberg, Bishop of Constance (1496-1530, 1530-31), 207, 185, 186,
view of Constance, 22n33; episcopal ideals and agenda of, 39-46, 52; aristocratic background of, 50, 50n35; career and education of, 51n36, 51n37; conflict and negotiations with Constance, 72-76; in comparison to Augsburg, 99, 180; residence of, 103; and Protestant Reformation, 174-178, 187n55; meeting with bishops of Strasbourg and Augsburg, 191n68; withdrawal from Constance, 178-179
Hus, John, 66, 179

Immenkötter, Herbert, 174n2
Inden, 203
Ingolstadt, 181
Innocent IV, Pope (1243-54), 85
Innsbruck, 198
Irenaeus, Bishop of Lyons (d. 200), 15
Isenmann, Eberhard,
    on clerical population in cities, 28n52

James, Mervyn, on late-medieval cer-
    emony as a source of communal soli-
    darity, 147n123
Johannes of Mecklenburg, Bishop (d.
    1066), 15n.12
John, Bishop of Constance (760-782),
    205
John XV, Pope (985-96), 120
John XXII (1316-34), Pope, 47, 53, 87
John XXIII (1410-15), Pope, 90, 94-95
John I of Schandland, Bishop of Augs-
    burg (1371-72), 209
John II of Lupfen, Bishop of Constance
    (1532-37), 186-187, 190-191, 207
John III of Weeze, Bishop of Constance
    (1538-48), Archbishop of Lund,
    Bishop of Roskilde, 186-190, 207
John II of Werdenberg, Bishop of Augs-
    burg (1469-86), 209,
    career of, 90n39; entry of, 140-145,
    147; memorial cycle for Peter of
    Schaumberg, 164-166; funeral and
    memorial cycle for, 166
Julius II, Pope (1503-13), 11-13

Kaiser, Reinhold,
    on the murder of bishops, 15-16,
    18n22
Kaiserstuhl, 214
Kaißhaim, 190, 209
Kammin, 33, 204
Kantorowicz, Ernst, 109, 125,
    corporeal imagery in, 21n30; on the
    roots of the *adventus* tradition, 126n59
Karlmann, Bishop-designate of Con-
    stance (1069-71), 52
Kempers, Bram,
    on lay initiatives in sacred and civic
    spheres, 115n23
Kempten, 203
Kießling, Rolf,
    on territorial hostility toward Augs-
    burg during the later Middle Ages,
    94n56; 81n12, 83n17, 84n22, 86n24,
    101n85
Klingau, 53, 57n56, 212, 213, 214, 217,

218
Koblenz, 209
Konrad von Hirscheck, Bishop of Augs-
    burg (1152-67), 209
St. Konrad I, Bishop of Constance (934-
    975), 205,
    as saint and relation to St. Ulrich of
    Augsburg, 77-79, 168, 179, 201; im-
    pact on Constance and cathedral, 103,
    117-118; 168, 179.
Konrad II of Tegerfelden, Bishop of
    Constance (1209-33), 205
Konrad of Klingenberg, Bishop-elect of
    Constance (1318-19), 206
Korvey, 203
Kosel, Karl,
    on the cathedral cloister, graves, and
    grave plates in Augsburg, 121n49,
    121n50
Koziol, Geoffrey, 109,
    on ritual as *polysemic*, 112n15
Kramml, Peter,
    on the cathedral compound in Con-
    stance, 61n70,
    on market rights in Constance, 63n76
Kreuzlingen, 73, 74, 127
Kulm, 36, 204
Kurland, 204

Laibach, 36, 203
Langenmantel, Christoph, Cathedral
    Canon, Augsburg (early sixteenth cen-
    tury), 180, 180n24
Lanto, Bishop of Augsburg (832-c.860),
    208
Lauingen, 181n27
Lausanne, 33, 191, 203
Lavant, 204
Le Mans, 15n11
Lebus, 33, 204
Leipheim, 181n27
Leudemann, Norbert,
    on the growth of the cathedral com-
    pound and the need for larger episco-
    pal residences, 18-19; on bishops and
    civic fortifications, 24n40; on episco-
    pal immunities, 29n55; on episcopal
    cities of the eighth and tenth centuries,
    61n69; on the *Domburg*, 114n21
Lewis of Bavaria, King and Emperor of
    Germany (1324-47), 47, 48, 53,
    65n87, 87
Lewis of Freiberg, provisional Bishop of
    Constance (1474-80), 51n38, 56,
    57n55, 207, 221

Lewis of Strasbourg, Bishop of Constance (1306-1307), 206
Liège, 17n19, 18, 31, 204
Lindau, 70, 96, 203
Lindenbaum, Sheila,
    on how ritual declares and conceals motive, 124n52
Liutold, Bishop of Augsburg (989-96), 208
Locher, Gottfried W.,
    on Zwingli and reformation in Zürich, 176n8
Lorsch, 203
Lothar III, King of Germany (1125-37), 82n15
Lübeck, 33, 203
Lüders, 203
Lund, 204
Luther, Martin (1483-46), 34, 174, 180, 181
Luxeuil, 203

McRee, Benjamin,
    on civic processions as socially divisive, 147n123
Magdeburg, 18, 33, 50n32, 204
Mainz, 15n11, 16n15, 18, 19-21, 50n35, 90n38, 99, 162, 204
Mangold of Brandis, Abbot and *Kellermeister* of Reichenau, Bishop of Constance (1384-85), 46-47, 50, 54n48, 57n55, 66, 206, 214
Marbach, 214
Markdorf on Lake Constance, 74
Marquard of Randeck, Bishop of Constance (1398-1406), 50n31, 51n37, 58n60, 70, 217
Markward of Randegg, Bishop of Augsburg (1348-65), 209
Marseilles, 215
Marshall, William (d. 1219), 154n143
Martin V, Pope (1417-31), 95, 96, 97
Maurer, Helmut,
    on the borders of the diocese of Constance, 43n10; on the selection of Constance for the ecumenical council, 55n50; on the expansion of the city of Constance, 59n63; on the history of Constance, 60n64; on the role of St. Stephan's in Constance, 62n73; on the episcopal palace in Constance, 117n29;
Maximilian, Emperor of Germany (1483-1519), 73, 75, 161, 172
May, Georg,

German bishops and the Reformation, 30n56
Meersburg, 48, 53, 57n56, 58, 58n59, 65n87, 74, 177n13, 178, 197-199, 207, 217, 218, 219, 220
Mehrerau, Benedictine cloister, 188-189
Meissen, 33, 204
Melanchthon, Philip (1497-1560), 162
Memmingen, 160, 181n27
Mergenthau, 85
Merklin, Balthasar, Bishop of Constance (1530-31), 185-186, 207
Merseburg, 33, 204
Metz, 15n12, 17n19, 18, 204
Metzler, Christoph, Bishop of Constance (1548-61), 197, 207
Milan, 14n10, 15n11, 16n15
Mindelheim, 181n27
Minden, 18, 33, 50n35, 204
Minnich, Nelson H.,
    on the Fifth Lateran Council, 12n5
Moeller, Bernd, 35n64
Molitoris, Ulrich, 74n112
Möncke, Gisela, 23n35, 60n64, 61n69,
    on the shift of Constance from *Bischofsstadt* to *Reichsstadt*, 64n80
Mühlberg (1547), 196
Muir, Edward,
    on religion, politics, and ritual in Venice, 109; on the Doge in Venice, 114n22
Mülich, Hektor (15th century), 107, 107n4
Münster, 31, 190-191, 204
Murbach, 203
Murray, James M.,
    on the soundscape in medieval entries, 133n89

Naumburg, 33, 204
Nelson, Janet,
    on how religious ritual shaped royal and imperial coronation ceremonies, 109-110; on the role of clergy in king-making, 125n58
Neuburg on the Danube, 81
Nicholas, David, 16n15,
    on the survival and growth of bishop's cities, 22n32; on city-lords, 24n41; on the ceremonial calendar in Flanders, 108n7
Nicholas V, Pope (1447-55), 97
Nicholas II of Frauenfeld, Bishop of Constance (1334-44), 205, 212,
    and conflict of with empire, 48, 53,

57n56 87-88; entry of, 132; funeral of, 48n22, 153-155, 156n151
Nicholas of Riesenburg, Bishop of Constance (1384-87), 206, 215-16, career of, 50, 50n32, 51; and swearing of civic oath, 54, 54n49; and *Verschreibung*, 66, 70, 71, 93
Nidker, Bishop of Augsburg (816-c.830), 208
Niedermünster, 203
Nijsten, Gerard, on ritual and social solidarity, 110, 110n11
Nivelle, 203
Nördlingen, 181n27
Noting, Bishop of Constance (919-34), 205
Nuremberg, 89, 188, 193, 193n72

Oberman, Heiko A., on the episcopal visitation in Zürich, 176n8
Obermünster, 203
Oecolampadius, Johann (d. 1531), 180n24
Olmütz, 50, 204, 206
Ösel, 33, 204
Osnabrück, 31, 204
Otto I, Bishop of Constance (1071-85), 52
Otto I, Emperor of Germany (936-73), 78, 117
Otto III of Hachberg, Bishop of Constance (1410-34), 206, 217-18, aristocratic background of, 50n31; career and education of, 50n35, 51n37; and Council of Constance, 54; conflict with Constance, 55; residency patters of, 57n56; and *Verschreibung*, 70, 71; coronation of Bishop Anselm of Augsburg, 96; conflict with cathedral chapter, 151-152
Otto IV of Sonnenberg, Bishop of Constance (1471-91), 40n2, 50n31, 51n36, 51n37, 55, 56n53, 58, 65n87, 207, 221
Otto, Cardinal, Bishop of Augsburg, Truchseß of Waldburg (1543-73), 184, 192, 194-195, 196-198, 210
Otto Henry, Elector Palatine (1556-59), 190
Ottobeuron, 160, 161, 165, 203

Paderborn, 18, 31, 204
Padua, 51n37

Pankraz of Sinzenhofen (1538-48), Bishop of Regesnburg, 32n60
Paris, 215
Passau, 18, 50n35, 99, 204
Pavia, 51n37
Pavlac, Brian A., on episcopal excommunication, 28n50
Pelagius, patron saint of the Cathedral of Our Dear Lady in Constance, 117
Peter, Apostle, 11-12, 15
Peter I of Schaumberg, Cardinal, Bishop of Augsburg (1424-69), 209, reputation of, 89; career and conflict with Augsburg, 97-102; transfer of residence, 103, 184; funeral and memorial cycle of, 164-165
Petershausen, 73, 118, 127, 132, 151, 205
Pfäfers, 203
Pfefferhart, Ulrich, Bishop of Constance (1345-51), 48, 49, 53, 206, 212-213
Phythian-Adams, Charles, on late-medieval ceremony as a source of communal solidarity, 147n123
Plantsch, Martin, 176-177
Poland, 61
Pomesanien, 33, 50n32, 204
Prague, 51n37, 90n40, 204
Press, Volker, 20n26, 21n28, 30n56, 31n59, on the role of territorial lordship and episcopal rule, 36
Prüm, 203
Prussia, West, 50

Quedlinburg, 203

Radolfszell, 58, 178, 221
Rapp, Francis, 20n27, 32n60
Ratzeburg, 33, 203
Ravensburg, 70
Regensburg, 18, 31, 204
Reichenau, 47, 50, 64n81, 73, 74, 91, 117, 130, 184n43, 187, 203, 205, 206, 207, 214
Reichenberg, 40n3
Reims, 204
Reiners, Heribert, on the maintenance and expansion of the cathedral in Constance, 119n38
Remiremont, 203
Reutlingen, 31n58, 186
Reval, 31, 204
Reynolds, Susan, 18n22
Rhegius, Urbanus (d. 1541), 41n6,

180n24, 180n26
Riga, 31, 204
Rome, 12n5, 40n3, 77, 94, 96, 98, 102, 114, 210
Rublack, Hans-Christoph, 31n59,
 on the failure of Reformation movements in episcopal cities, 35; 174n2
Rudolf I, Emperor of Germany (1273-91), 86
Rudolf II of Montfort, Bishop of Constance (1322-34), 206, 211-212
Rudolf I of Habsburg, Bishop of Constance (1274-93), 205
Rudolf of Hewen, Bishop of Constance (1306-07), 206
Rudolf of Swabia (d. 1080), 52
Ruiz, Teofilo,
 on liminality between city and countryside, 149n127
Rumold, Bishop of Constance (1051-69), 205
Ryerson, Katherine,
 on the elaborate description of spectacle in the later Middle Ages, 124n54

Säckingen, 203
St. Emmeram, 203
St. Gall, 70, 117, 130, 203
St. Oyen, 203
Salomo I, Bishop of Constance (838-71), 205
Salomo III, Bishop of Constance (890-919), 61, 63, 77, 117, 118, 205
Salzburg, 18, 31, 50n35, 99, 204
Samland, 33, 204
Santifaller, Leo,
 on the aristocratic identity of the german episcopate, 22n31
Schaffhausen, 55, 58, 59n62, 214, 218
Schleswig, 33, 204
Schmidt, Georg,
 on free cities and imperial cities, 31n57
Schönegg, 160
Schroeder, Detlov,
 on the cathedral compound in Augsburg, 120n44
Schulte, Aloys, 22n31
Schulthaiß, Christoph (d. 1584), 106, 106n3
Schulthaiß, Claus (d. 1500), 126n60
Schwabniederhofen, 181n27
Schwäbisch Gmund, 81, 209
Schwerin, 33, 203
Scribner, Robert,

on anticlericalism, 28n53; on Erfurt, 34n63; on Cologne, 35n65; on the Peasants' Revolt, 177n13; on Reformation movements in prince-bishoprics, 197n5
Seckau, 204
Seligenstadt, 209
Selz, 203
Sender, Clemens (d. c. 1537), 106, 107n4
Sennett, Richard,
 on images of the human body, the city, and the cathedral, 113n19
Siboto of Seefeld, Bishop of Augsburg (1227-47), 209
Siegfried I, Bishop of Augsburg (1001-06), 208
Siegfried II, Bishop of Augsburg (1077-96), 82n15, 209
Siegfried III of Rechberg, Bishop of Augsburg (1208-27), 209
Siegfried IV of Algishausen, Bishop of Augsburg (1286-88), 209
Sieglerschmidt, Jörn,
 on lay procurement of ecclesiastical patronage rights, 38n73
Siena, 114-115
Sigismund, Emperor of Germany (1410-37), 66, 95, 96, 97, 117, 132, 153
Sintpert, Bishop of Augsburg (778-c. 807), 119, 208
Sion, 204
Sittich, Mark, Cardinal, Bishop of Constance (1561-89), 198, 207
Sixtus IV, Pope (1471-84), 40n3.
Speyer, 18, 31, 50n35, 80, 188, 204
Stablo, 203
Steiermark, 50n32
Strasbourg, 18, 31, 50, 50n35, 90n38, 127, 143n119, 191, 204
Stucki, Felix, Cathedral Dean of Constance (d. 1363), 49n27
Stuttgart, 31n58
Szerâd, 90

Tergernsee, 203
Theoderich, Bishop of Constance (1047-51), 205
Thurgau, 43, 66, 71, 72, 75, 187
Toul, 17n19, 18, 204
Tozzo, Bishop of Augsburg (772-c.778), 208
Trastavere, 207
Trent, 40n3, 82n15, 184n43, 203
Trent, Council of (1545-63), 192-193, 201

Trexler, Richard C.,
on religion, politics, and ritual in Florence, 109; 114n22; on civic ritual and the ceremonial calendar in Florence, 114n22; on the functions of the baldachin, 133n87; on rituals of greeting, 134n92, 135n94
Trier, 15n11, 18, 35, 204, 207
Tübingen, 191n68
Turner, Victor,
on arenas, paradigms, metaphors, symbols, and social dramas, 112; on liminality, 149n126

Überlingen, 35n65, 53n42, 70, 132, 178
Udalmann, Bishop of Augsburg (830-c.832), 208
Udalschalk, Bishop of Augsburg (1184-1202), 209
Ulm, 31n58, 92, 186, 189, 190, 215, 216
St. Ulrich I of Dillingen, Bishop of Augsburg (923-73), 208,
saintly profile of, 77, 89, 103, 120, 164, 201; relation to Konrad of Constance, 77-78; defense and expansion of Augsburg, 78-79, 120, 121
Ulrich I of Dillingen, Bishop of Constance (1111-27), 205
Ulrich II of Schönegg, Bishop of Augsburg (1331-37), 209
Ulrich of Friedingen, Bishop-elect of Constance (1356-57), 206
Ulrich, Duke of Württemberg (1487-1550; r. 1498-1519, 1534-50), 186
Utrecht, 18, 32, 170, 204

Venice, 109, 114
Verden, 18, 32, 204
Verdun, 17n19, 18, 204
Vicenza, 14n10
Vienne, 13-15, 204
Vienna, 50, 51n37, 198, 204
Vorderösterreich (Upper Austria), 44

Walther I of Dillingen, Bishop of Augsburg (1133-52), 209
Walter II of Hochschlitz, Bishop of Augsburg (1365-69), 209

Wanner, John, cathedral preacher of Constance (1520s), 177
Weber, Max: on institutionalization of charisma, 104n1
Weissenburg, 203
Welf IV (11th c.), 82
Werden, 203
Wiblingen, 209
Wiener Neustadt, 204
Wigolt (1077-88) counter-bishop of Augsburg, 82, 209
Wikterp, Bishop of Augsburg (d. 771), 119, 208
Wilhelm of Honstein, Bishop of Strasbourg (1506-41), 20, 21n29, 191n68
Willburger, August,
on the Reformation in Switzerland and the episcopal response, 178n18; on the cooperation of the bishops of Constance, Augsburg, and Strasbourg, 191n68
William of Holland, King of Germany (1247-1256), 63-64
Willoweit, D.,
on episcopal immunities, 29n54
Windlock, John III, Bishop of Constance (1351-56), 48, 49, 53, 54n46, 206, 213
Windner, Jakob, priest of St. John's church in Constance (1520s), 174
Winterthur, 212
Witgar, Bishop of Augsburg (c.861-87), 208
Wolfhard of Roth, Bishop of Augsburg (1288-1302), 209
Worms, 15n11, 32, 204
Württemberg, 44, 140, 186, 189
Würzburg, 18, 31, 99, 204

Zink, Burkard (d. 1474/75), 107, 107n4
Zoepfl, Friedrich, 79n8,
on benefices and education of bishops of Augsburg, 90n38, 90n39, 90n40
Zwingli, Ulrich (1484-1531), 174, 175, 180
Zürich, 31n58, 40n3, 50n35, 54, 58, 59n62, 174-176, 187, 203, 213, 214, 215, 216

STUDIES IN MEDIEVAL
AND REFORMATION THOUGHT

EDITED BY HEIKO A. OBERMAN

1. DOUGLASS, E. J. D. *Justification in Late Medieval Preaching.* 2nd ed. 1989
2. WILLIS, E. D. *Calvin's Catholic Christology.* 1966 *out of print*
3. POST, R. R. *The Modern Devotion.* 1968 *out of print*
4. STEINMETZ, D. C. *Misericordia Dei.* The Theology of Johannes von Staupitz. 1968 *out of print*
5. O'MALLEY, J. W. *Giles of Viterbo on Church and Reform.* 1968 *out of print*
6. OZMENT, S. E. *Homo Spiritualis.* The Anthropology of Tauler, Gerson and Luther. 1969
7. PASCOE, L. B. *Jean Gerson: Principles of Church Reform.* 1973 *out of print*
8. HENDRIX, S. H. *Ecclesia in Via.* Medieval Psalms Exegesis and the *Dictata super Psalterium* (1513-1515) of Martin Luther. 1974
9. TREXLER, R. C. *The Spiritual Power.* Republican Florence under Interdict. 1974
10. TRINKAUS, Ch. with OBERMAN, H. A. (eds.). *The Pursuit of Holiness.* 1974 *out of print*
11. SIDER, R. J. *Andreas Bodenstein von Karlstadt.* 1974
12. HAGEN, K. *A Theology of Testament in the Young Luther.* 1974
13. MOORE, Jr., W. L. *Annotatiunculae D. Iohanne Eckio Praelectore.* 1976
14. OBERMAN, H. A. with BRADY, Jr., Th. A. (eds.). *Itinerarium Italicum.* Dedicated to Paul Oskar Kristeller. 1975
15. KEMPFF, D. *A Bibliography of Calviniana.* 1959-1974. 1975 *out of print*
16. WINDHORST, C. *Täuferisches Taufverständnis.* 1976
17. KITTELSON, J. M. *Wolfgang Capito.* 1975
18. DONNELLY, J. P. *Calvinism and Scholasticism in Vermigli's Doctrine of Man and Grace.* 1976
19. LAMPING, A. J. *Ulrichus Velenus (Oldřich Velenský) and his Treatise against the Papacy.* 1976
20. BAYLOR, M. G. *Action and Person.* Conscience in Late Scholasticism and the Young Luther. 1977
21. COURTENAY, W. J. *Adam Wodeham.* 1978
22. BRADY, Jr., Th. A. *Ruling Class, Regime and Reformation at Strasbourg, 1520-1555.* 1978
23. KLAASSEN, W. *Michael Gaismair.* 1978
24. BERNSTEIN, A. E. *Pierre d'Ailly and the Blanchard Affair.* 1978
25. BUCER, Martin. *Correspondance.* Tome I (Jusqu'en 1524). Publié par J. Rott. 1979
26. POSTHUMUS MEYJES, G. H. M. *Jean Gerson et l'Assemblée de Vincennes (1329).* 1978
27. VIVES, Juan Luis. *In Pseudodialecticos.* Ed. by Ch. Fantazzi. 1979
28. BORNERT, R. *La Réforme Protestante du Culte à Strasbourg au XVIᵉ siècle (1523-1598).* 1981
29. SEBASTIAN CASTELLIO. *De Arte Dubitandi.* Ed. by E. Feist Hirsch. 1981
30. BUCER, Martin. *Opera Latina.* Vol I. Publié par C. Augustijn, P. Fraenkel, M. Lienhard. 1982
31. BÜSSER, F. *Wurzeln der Reformation in Zürich.* 1985 *out of print*
32. FARGE, J. K. *Orthodoxy and Reform in Early Reformation France.* 1985
33, 34. BUCER, Martin. *Etudes sur les relations de Bucer avec les Pays-Bas.* I. Etudes; II. Documents. Par J. V. Pollet. 1985
35. HELLER, H. *The Conquest of Poverty.* The Calvinist Revolt in Sixteenth Century France. 1986

36. MEERHOFF, K. *Rhétorique et poétique au XVIe siècle en France.* 1986
37. GERRITS, G. H. *Inter timorem et spem.* Gerard Zerbolt of Zutphen. 1986
38. ANGELO POLIZIANO. *Lamia.* Ed. by A. Wesseling. 1986
39. BRAW, C. *Bücher im Staube.* Die Theologie Johann Arndts in ihrem Verhältnis zur Mystik. 1986
40. BUCER, Martin. *Opera Latina.* Vol. II. Enarratio in Evangelion Iohannis (1528, 1530, 1536). Publié par I. Backus. 1988
41. BUCER, Martin. *Opera Latina.* Vol. III. Martin Bucer and Matthew Parker: Florilegium Patristicum. Edition critique. Publié par P. Fraenkel. 1988
42. BUCER, Martin. *Opera Latina.* Vol. IV. Consilium Theologicum Privatim Conscriptum. Publié par P. Fraenkel. 1988
43. BUCER, Martin. *Correspondance.* Tome II (1524-1526). Publié par J. Rott. 1989
44. RASMUSSEN, T. *Inimici Ecclesiae.* Das ekklesiologische Feindbild in Luthers "Dictata super Psalterium" (1513-1515) im Horizont der theologischen Tradition. 1989
45. POLLET, J. *Julius Pflug et la crise religieuse dans l'Allemagne du XVIe siècle.* Essai de synthèse biographique et théologique. 1990
46. BUBENHEIMER, U. *Thomas Müntzer.* Herkunft und Bildung. 1989
47. BAUMAN, C. *The Spiritual Legacy of Hans Denck.* Interpretation and Translation of Key Texts. 1991
48. OBERMAN, H. A. and JAMES, F. A., III (eds.). in cooperation with SAAK, E. L. *Via Augustini.* Augustine in the Later Middle Ages, Renaissance and Reformation: Essays in Honor of Damasus Trapp. 1991 *out of print*
49. SEIDEL MENCHI, S. *Erasmus als Ketzer.* Reformation und Inquisition im Italien des 16. Jahrhunderts. 1993
50. SCHILLING, H. *Religion, Political Culture, and the Emergence of Early Modern Society.* Essays in German and Dutch History. 1992
51. DYKEMA, P. A. and OBERMAN, H. A. (eds.). *Anticlericalism in Late Medieval and Early Modern Europe.* 2nd ed. 1994
52, 53. KRIEGER, Chr. and LIENHARD, M. (eds.). *Martin Bucer and Sixteenth Century Europe.* Actes du colloque de Strasbourg (28-31 août 1991). 1993
54. SCREECH, M. A. *Clément Marot: A Renaissance Poet discovers the World.* Lutheranism, Fabrism and Calvinism in the Royal Courts of France and of Navarre and in the Ducal Court of Ferrara. 1994
55. GOW, A. C. *The Red Jews: Antisemitism in an Apocalyptic Age, 1200-1600.* 1995
56. BUCER, Martin. *Correspondance.* Tome III (1527-1529). Publié par Chr. Krieger et J. Rott. 1989
57. SPIJKER, W. VAN 'T. *The Ecclesiastical Offices in the Thought of Martin Bucer.* Translated by J. Vriend (text) and L.D. Bierma (notes). 1996
58. GRAHAM, M.F. *The Uses of Reform.* 'Godly Discipline' and Popular Behavior in Scotland and Beyond, 1560-1610. 1996
59. AUGUSTIJN, C. *Erasmus. Der Humanist als Theologe und Kirchenreformer.* 1996
60. McCOOG S J, T. M. *The Society of Jesus in Ireland, Scotland, and England 1541-1588.* 'Our Way of Proceeding?' 1996
61. FISCHER, N. und KOBELT-GROCH, M. (Hrsg.). *Außenseiter zwischen Mittelalter und Neuzeit.* Festschrift für Hans-Jürgen Goertz zum 60. Geburtstag. 1997
62. NIEDEN, M. *Organum Deitatis.* Die Christologie des Thomas de Vio Cajetan. 1997
63. BAST, R.J. *Honor Your Fathers.* Catechisms and the Emergence of a Patriarchal Ideology in Germany, 1400-1600. 1997
64. ROBBINS, K.C. *City on the Ocean Sea: La Rochelle, 1530-1650.* Urban Society, Religion, and Politics on the French Atlantic Frontier. 1997
65. BLICKLE, P. *From the Communal Reformation to the Revolution of the Common Man.* 1998
66. FELMBERG, B. A. R. *Die Ablaßtheorie Kardinal Cajetans (1469-1534).* 1998

67. CUNEO, P. F. *Art and Politics in Early Modern Germany.* Jörg Breu the Elder and the Fashioning of Political Identity, ca. 1475-1536. 1998

68. BRADY, Jr., Th. A. *Communities, Politics, and Reformation in Early Modern Europe.* 1998

69. McKEE, E. A. *Katharina Schütz Zell.* 1. The Life and Thought of a Sixteenth-Century Reformer. 2. The Writings. A Critical Edition. 1999

70. BOSTICK, C. V. *The Antichrist and the Lollards.* Apocalyticism in Late Medieval and Reformation England. 1998

71. BOYLE, M. O'ROURKE. *Senses of Touch.* Human Dignity and Deformity from Michelangelo to Calvin. 1998

72. TYLER, J.J. *Lord of the Sacred City.* The *Episcopus Exclusus* in Late Medieval and Early Modern Germany. 1999

Prospectus available on request

BRILL — P.O.B. 9000 — 2300 PA LEIDEN — THE NETHERLANDS